THE

WORDS OF THE LORD JESUS.

BY

RUDOLF STIER,

DOCTOR OF THEOLOGY, CHIEF PASTOR AND SUPERINTENDENT OF SCHKEUDITZ.

VOLUME FIRST.

TRANSLATED FROM THE SECOND REVISED AND ENLARGED GERMAN EDITION.

BY THE

REV. WILLIAM B. POPE,

LONDON.

NEW EDITION.

PHILADELPHIA:
SMITH, ENGLISH, AND CO.
NEW YORK: SHELDON & CO. BOSTON: GOULD & LINCOLN.

MDCCCLIX.

TRANSLATOR'S PREFACE.

The work which is now introduced to the English reader has been for fifteen years in high esteem among the divines of Germany, as well as of several other countries. The respect which occasional extracts have received, and the ample references to it among recent expositors, warrant the expectation that it will be no less cordially welcomed among the British churches.

No one will read it, as such a book should be read, without feeling that he is under the guidance of one who is profoundly imbued with the mind of Christ. The author's aim is the loftiest which mortal man can set before himself—to unfold the meaning and harmony of all the recorded words which fell from the lips of the Word made flesh. That the Lord's own sanction is manifestly given to the attempt, is the highest tribute we can pay to it.

The *form* of the work may possibly be in some respects repulsive to the reader unaccustomed to German theology. The minute subtilty of its analysis, its keen inquisition into the secret thread of every discourse, with some occasional novelties of theory or exposition, will not disparage it to the student who keeps the original text always before his eye, and understands the rare value of criticism which combines deep thought with deeper devotion. The very frequent vindication of the true meaning against fanciful or infidel interpretations sometimes interrupts the current of the exposition; but it must be remembered that the work is throughout an unwearied protest against Rationalist opinions. These bring its own distinguishing excellencies into relief; and every work of orthodox German Theology has, as such, a strong preliminary claim to our favour.

Finally, as the Translator is not necessarily responsible for all the opinions of the original; so neither ought the original to be absolutely judged of by the translation, which but faintly reproduces its peculiar qualities of style.

LONDON, April 1855.

CONTENTS OF THE FIRST PART.

THE FIRST WORDS.

THE GOSPEL OF ST MATTHEW.

HARMONY.

THE

DISCOURSES OF THE LORD JESUS,

ESPECIALLY

ACCORDING TO ST MATTHEW.

EXPOUNDED BY

RUDOLF STIER,

DOCTOR OF THEOLOGY, SUPERINTENDENT AND CHIEF PASTOR OF SCHKEUDITZ.

SECOND EDITION, REVISED AND ENLARGED.

FIRST PART,

CONTAINING THE FIRST WORDS OF OUR LORD ACCORDING TO ALL THE EVANGELISTS: EMBRACING ST MATTHEW, CHS. IV.—XI.

Isa. lii. 6:

כִּי־אֲנִי־הוּא הַמְדַבֵּר הִנֵּנִי׃

I am He that doth speak : behold it is I.

PREFACE.

Discourse—the revelation of the inner man by utterance to others—admits of a wide variety of gradation and method; and one kind of revelation may be more direct and distinctively such than another. As this is true of man, so is it also of God the Lord. He had spoken *πολυμερῶς καὶ πολυτρόπως* in past time, before as yet the Eternal Word Himself was made flesh; but now the human exegesis of the *λόγια τοῦ θεοῦ* has received its ultimate and highest task. It can propose to itself now no loftier aim than to repose with John, the eagle of the Church of the last times, upon the full assurance:—*Θεὸν οὐδεὶς ἑώρακε πώποτε· ὁ μονογενὴς υἱὸς, ὁ ὢν εἰς τὸν κόλπον τοῦ πατρὸς ἐκεῖνος ἐξηγήσατο.*

Hearing Him, and the Spirit who takes of His in the Apostles, we find the only sound principle for the interpretation of the ancient Scriptures which bare witness of Him, and pointed to Him. No historical and psychological *ἐπίλυσις* of ours, may ever avail to empty or invalidate for us one single כֹּה אָמַר יְהוָה or נְאֻם יְהוָה; but, on the other hand, whatever is recorded in the inviolable *γραφή*, though without this preface, is regarded by us who discern the power of God in such Scripture, as *ῥηθὲν ἡμῖν ὑπὸ τοῦ θεοῦ*, Matt. xxii. 31. But then we also at the same time perceive the distinction which still subsists between all the former revelations of God, and the last by his Son: a distinction which is indicated in the Prophetic Scripture itself. In the very centre and heart of the revelations of God by Isaiah, which are yet waiting for their true interpretation, that, namely, which shall accord with the word of Christ and His apostles, the God of Israel promises (Isa. lii. 6), that when His people's true and everlasting redemption shall come, *He himself, who spake, would be there,* and evidence His presence by a new, then first openly proclaimed הִנֵּנִי (comp. ver. 7 with ch. xl. 9). But the perfect Theophany thus promised was to be accomplished, according to the uninterrupted testimony of Isaiah—a testimony which grows in clearness from that first עִמָּנוּ אֵל and אֵל גִּבּוֹר shining out of the darkness, like a faint star of hope, to the very end of his closely-connected and ever soaring predictions—by Him who is at once the Servant of the Lord and the Lord Himself. The twelfth and thirteenth verses of ch. lii. are inseparably united, but the אֲנִי הוּא הַמְדַבֵּר of ver. 6 refers back to ch. xl. 5, and also to ch. xlviii. 16. From this latter point—the transitional termination of a second main division of the entire Isaiah-prophecy—the Messianic vision emerges clear and distinct from the type out of which it grew, and becomes absolutely independent of it. Whatever system of interpretation wilfully returns back into the type again, must necessarily lose the full and entire sense of the letter itself; in which beneath Israel's deliverance from Babylon the true and everlasting redemption is pretypified, and in Cyrus the builder of the Temple is indicated That one עֶבֶד יְהוָה to come. Then cries the prophet, as the type and in the name of That coming one; *from the time that it was, there am I; and now the Lord God and His Spirit hath sent me!* Here, for the first time, the Eternal Sent of the Eternal, came forward in the first person to announce Himself: an announcement which grows progressively more distinct in the third great division, from ch. xlix. onwards. The emphatic suffix in מֵעֵת הֱיוֹתָהּ refers back to the creation of heaven and earth, ver. 13 (comp. ch. xlv. 18—19), and the proper antithesis of מֵעֵת is the anticipatory עַתָּה and הִנֵּנִי of the Revelation in the flesh. I, the self-same אֲנִי הוּא, ver. 12, who was present at the beginning of the existence of all things, at that first יְהִי וַיְהִי, when the Eternal Word was with God (Prov. viii. 27 has also שָׁם אָנִי), come now as *Sent,* and also as יְהוָה גֹּאַלְךָ, ver. 17. Thus He is truly הַמְדַבֵּר, the Eternal Word, *He that speaketh,* not merely here by the prophets, but in the most absolute sense from the beginning and from eternity. To both these places in Isaiah,[1] the Lord refers in Jno. xviii. 20 and viii. 25. The sublime and mysterious answer, in the latter passage particularly, to the *Σὺ τίς εἶ;* of the Jews, is only rightly understood when we regard the Lord as asserting Himself in the absolute *ἐγώ εἰμι*, אֲנִי הוּא to be the *λαλῶν*, and as referring to His *words*, which all must *hear*.

Oh that all those, who, like these Jews, are still for ever putting questions, could understand and *hear* this answer, and all that the Truth sent from the Truth had to say and to judge concerning them and the world. Had it not been too bold, I would fain have prefixed this title to my book,—*The words of the Word.* If, as one of the Fathers says, every act in the history of the Eternal Word incarnate, is itself Word and Doctrine—how great is the claim upon our attention, when we hear it said of Him :—*He opened His mouth and spake!* There is deeper significance in any one word of the Lord Jesus, which He Himself said, (Acts xx. 35), than in all the sayings of the Apostles and Prophets. His *λόγοι* are the most express outbeamings of the *λόγος*.

But have we these words, just as He spoke them? This is the question of modern criticism, which refuses to take for granted what should, however, be taken for granted by all who believe in a Revelation of the Son of God;—namely, that His words cannot have fallen to the ground, cannot have dropped and been lost through the sieve of erring human composition.[2] Yes, we possess that which He spake! Not indeed in the letter of the *verba ipsissima*, but through the mediating witness of the Evangelists, elevated in the Spirit. Yet are they truly and essentially the *ipsissima*, as His teaching for the world and the Church. Thou shalt know them to be such, if the same Spirit under whose influence the Gospels are written, shall explain to thee and illustrate their letter. John, the fourth Evangelist, who adheres with the least tenacity of all to the literal, original expression, gives us nevertheless, as is manifest to every one, the words of the WORD in their most spiritual and living reality. Each Evangelist

[1] For the exposition of which, I may appeal to my "Isaiah, not Pseudo-Isaiah" (Barmen 1850.)

[2] That, to borrow Hase's expression, a "supernatural preservation of these archives" must be classed among "those unknown propitious circumstances" which established the authority of the Gospels.

has his peculiar gift from the Lord, his own peculiar plan and aim in his Spirit-moved spirit; but through the combination of all the *Holy Ghost* has so wrought out one wonderful scheme, that the whole of what these four Evangelists present to us as the utterance of the Son of God incarnate, carries with it its own evidence in its perfect harmony. Alas, that it should be said of us, sed nos non habemus aures, sicut Deus habet linguam—oh, that we could but *read* and *hear!*

We must assuredly read as men, what the Lord has humanly spoken, and consigned to human record. But to every man who reads *as of the truth* (John xviii. 37), it is given to *hear* and to *see* the glory of the incarnate word: for in these Gospels His manifestation, His life, His teaching, are truly transfigured into an ever-living and life-giving *Spirit-word.* It was of necessity that the word should first be made flesh, but equally so that the flesh should become spirit again: and it is as such that the Word now speaks to the world. This is the essential principle of life; from which—as an incorruptible seed—the Faith and the Church derive their being. Could we imagine—I speak as a fool—the Church of Christ utterly vanquished, and expelled from the face of the earth; yet, if one of these four gospels—and let that one be even St Mark's—were to fall into the hands of conscientious and sincere readers, out of this that Church must of necessity, and assuredly would, spring up anew.

The theological investigation and exposition even of the orthodox has to this very day been far too much occupied with inquisition into the tradition-threads which bind together the human and the divine, with the harmonizing of the histories and so forth; leaving far too much in abeyance the task of penetrating to the substance—the *words of the Lord Jesus.* We are too much disposed, if not to ravel that which God has woven into its thread again, at least to pry too curiously into warp and woof, into its minutest fabric and texture. But just as this answers no good purpose, generally speaking, in the κτίσις, so will it not avail in the γραφή which itself is a καινὴ κτίσις. It is because this is not sufficiently remembered, that while we have commentaries enough upon the Gospel of Matthew, Mark, &c., we have very few indeed upon the words of the Lord which they contain.

The latest, most extravagant criticism of the Gospels,—which to the many thousands of those who hang upon the lips of their Master, and live from day to day upon His words of eternal life, is nothing less than sheer madness ;—this frenzied infidelity is utterly unable now to hear, by reason of the raging of its fever-fantasies. Could these victims of delusion but begin to give heed to *what He says to them*, from his first *Μετανοεῖτε* to all that He signified in that great cry *Ἐγώ εἰμι*—then would the history itself in this light soon become clear and self-convincing. All right understanding of the origin of the Gospels, as far as we may understand it, must rest upon the living, believing, apprehension of their contents, which are unlike aught else in the world's history. Without the most profound exegesis of the words of our Lord, all the labour of the harmonists must be exposed to perpetual error. We find, for example, in the latest and best of them, that of Ebrard, an occasional separation of things essentially united, or sometimes an incorrect identification of discourses uttered at various times.[1]

1 Once more, and more earnestly than ever, must we in the second edition protest against Rauh's method of defence against Baur (Deutsche Zeitschrift für Christl. Wiss. u. s. w.), which with its homœopathy is little likely to cure this criticism run mad. It is itself merely the same sophistry, though practised on the other side; the same perverse method of dealing with the word—first rending it asunder, then patching it together again. Poor Synoptics! how must they suffer for the honour of John! "The confused and fortuitous synoptical narration—evidencing but faint traces of any connexion—broken threads!" Such is the style in which they are spoken of. "In helpless, perplexing nakedness" this thing or that appears in their account. A "perfectly misleading answer of the Lord, following some external sound, has wandered away" to the place where it now stands, and the Johannæan connexion is absolutely necessary in order to our "understanding, in any degree, the Synoptical narrative." "Things somewhat similar are easily enough joined together," and so many things are "drawn one to another, which have no internal connexion." We are told of "reminiscences, which have passed out of buried controversies into the traditional form of gnomic sentences, or rather, these Sayings have been collected together out of traditions, true in particular cases, but widely dispersed." The "traces of connexion" which are allowed to exist, are *just enough* to bind together the whole into one mechanical conglomerate. Let me be laughed at or not, let men shrug their shoulders or not, I *rebuke* in the name of the Spirit of Truth that *license* of our youngest Licentiates which leads them so far astray as to censure and sit in judgment upon the Recorders on whose word the whole Church rests. Does not all ecclesiastical experience down to

To my believing brethren, therefore, I would fain administer a useful hint:—Look well at what now lies under your shears; take heed lest sometimes, if not often, you be tempted incautiously to clip it even as others do. And as to these others? Unhappy men, they will be likely enough to say concerning me and my book, if it happens to meet their eyes:—Here is one coming out of his dark corner again with all hardihood, who seems to know nothing of what we have long since made plain, who is bold enough and simple enough to put faith in the so-called discourses of our Lord—that marvellous medley which has been compounded under the inscriptions κατὰ Ματθαῖον, Μάρκον, &c. (we know this and can explain it all, as if we had been there!) Yes, dear Sirs, you may indeed *say* this; but what conflict it would cost your conscience to read for yourselves, let your conscience answer. Permit me, on the other hand, to tell you in all friendliness—There are those who have given patient and industrious attention to every thing that has sprung from the lofty wisdom of your unbelief, but whose faith in the testimony of God's Spirit in Holy Writ, has not seldom found its most effectual invigoration and its most convincing argument in the self-contradictory folly of your books—the darkness of which has only served to make their own light the brighter and more precious.

It will now be once more made evident that I, for my own insignificant part, belong to the number of those who, enjoying

this very day demonstrate that precisely this mechanical conglomerate, these broken threads, these helpless, perplexed and naked relations and sayings which in themselves are so inexplicable, do most mightily take hold of the living and simple believer, and so inexhaustibly instruct him, that he needs no help of any of the theologians? Therefore, we hold it better to say, that wherever there is any actual deviation from specific historical truth, any transposition, dislocation, &c. (of which instances do occur, but far, far less frequently than is now-a-days generally supposed; always occurring, moreover, in non-essentials, and never involving the slightest falsification)—*the Holy Ghost*, the true and only *traditor* of this tradition, has intentionally and significantly so ordered it, with that *Wisdom* which we, the learned, should be willing to learn from, since it is continually and most undoubtedly justified of those simple ones, its children. I may presume, that *some little* theoretical and scientific justification of it, also, for the learned, may be derived from my books, if their suggestions and views are admitted by unprejudiced minds.

themselves the kernel, and inviting others to its enjoyment, will not allow themselves to be involved in the contests which are everywhere raging about the mere shell; who would rather sit as convivæ than as investigating and over-curious coqui, at the Lord's well-spread table; who rather take the medicine than chemically analyze it. Let others inspect the swaddling-clothes of Immanuel with even greater anxiety than the wise men of the East, my regard is fixed upon Himself, who is folded within them. But in saying this, I cannot forget that both swaddling-clothes and manger, though woven and built by sinful hands, were consecrated for Him and through Him. That I, in like manner, hold fast the rigid *inspiration* of the Word in which we find and possess the Christ, yet not in the mechanical fashion of that orthodoxy which seems sometimes to gaze in blank amazement at Him who was born of woman, as if He had fallen from heaven in his swaddling-clothes;—this I must finally and most earnestly beg every one to observe, *on account of the persevering injustice with which I have been treated on this particular.*[1]

To construct a detailed historical harmony of the Gospels I regard as a thing impossible, inasmuch as the testimony of the Spirit leaves behind and transcends the mere common and subordinate historical truth; and has something far better to teach us than merely when and where, and with what relations one to another, this and that was spoken or done. Who ever asks with such fond pertinacity about the date of any saying of Plato or Goethe? But to acknowledge this, and in consequence to concede willingly to sound criticism more than they at any cost are willing to do, is certainly a better defence against that pseudo-criticism which now rushes in to the assault, laboriously seeking out untruthfulnesses, in that which as to all essentials is pure truth itself, and contains not a single iota of that which is actually false. Ingeniously and diligently to investigate *that* historical element of which we have no record, may, in profane literature, be a blameless pastime of learned curiosity; but to neglect and perplex that which is given us in Holy Writ through such bye-

[1] That unjust treatment still continues—eight years after this was first written. Probably I may be able to exhibit, after a while, more clearly, in what way my *rigid* and yet not *mechanical* view of Inspiration is on either hand distinguished from the old and the new doctrine.

play of inquisitiveness, must ever be a perverted πάρεργον where man ought earnestly to seek what he has *to do*. So also while adjusting and arranging the minute specialities which *are* before us, to sacrifice the contemplation and ever-growing knowledge of those great momentous matters which are plainly revealed, and thus with the best intention through too much labour upon the shell, to neglect to taste, or to be diverted from enjoying the kernel, is scarcely less a perversion than that. There is for thoughtful criticism an uncontroverted and real remainder in which we have ample scope; so ample, that our very reason requires, and much more our Faith, that we should not adventure upon further subtle investigations until that which we have —I do not say is fixed upon its sure external foundations, for it is given to us for a higher purpose than that but—has passed into our whole perception and life. Seek we, in this matter also, the kingdom of God and His righteousness, so shall the needful critical knowledge be added unto us; and our position with relation to the Great Fact of Redemption in Christ be more like that of the Apostles.

That Jesus of Nazareth, as the Son of God come in the flesh, did, in His generation, so live, so teach, so suffer, so die, so rise again, as the four Evangelists with all their differences unite perfectly in relating, is a truth, attested to be the most certain of all certain truths by the whole history of the world before Him and since, by Israel's permanence among the nations, as well as that of Christianity itself. The entire mystery of all history finds in this its centre and only solution. Similarly the longing, and questioning, and seeking of every man's inner spirit, finds here its simple fulfilment and answer,—here, where all the lines so wonderfully converge, and every thing significantly tells us that the Revelation of the Divine penetrates all human individuality. Simply to accept this is no false simplicity but the highest wisdom, which reverently hearkening in the obedience of faith, to the Eternal Wisdom, is rewarded by the right perception of the Truth which is unto salvation.

From this point of view it appears to be in most cases altogether a matter of indifference, whether this or that was spoken and done here or elsewhere. Wherever it *is* matter of importance, the Providence of God has ordered that it shall be authentically plain before us, and be easily found by that modest and earnestly-seeking investigation, for which in His condescension scope has been left. But, otherwise, we should thankfully receive what through God's grace is written for us, remembering that the true meaning, which the Eternal Wisdom calls us to seek, lies rather in the how it is written than in the how it took place.

The spirit and design of this exposition is purely and properly *exegetical*; and all who, like myself, adhere firmly to this, may be justified in making it their glory. To be inveighed against by enemies, and blamed by friends, for reading and understanding the Old Testament as Christ and His Apostles read and understood it, is an honour for which one may meekly thank his God. When Theology shall direct its aim to that point where "Prophecy and Fulfilment" meet together and are united in their interpretation (more entirely and firmly than in *Hofmann's* book, which does *not* fulfil the sounding prophecy of its title); then will it find no more reason to blame any simple apostolical ἵνα πληρωθῇ, or any such reading of the ancient Scripture, as those of the Epistle to the Hebrews. But to be rebuked and set aside, as if acting upon one's own caprice and imposing the meaning instead of expounding it, when one only aims to let the King of Truth speak, as He is pleased to speak with evidence which breaks through all obscurity and concealment: to be rebuked for this, that one would rather take to his ears and to his heart the wonderful words of the Eternal Word in all their immediate power as they are uttered and beam forth from Himself, instead of their so much prized translation into the poor and narrow language of man, with all the concomitant perversions, and endless disputations (through which process of so-called exposition the very essence of the text is ofttimes lost):—to be blamed for this would be indeed a most grievous affliction, and yet one must be prepared for it.

That discussions and treatises concerning the recognition of the one object of Exegesis should be exceedingly in vogue among those to whom that all-holy object as exhibited in the Gospels is not yet established as such, is as natural as it is useful. Let every man labour according to his call. It is quite necessary, indeed, that the settlement of the object of Faith—

"here speaks the Son of God, who preserves and illustrates to us through His Spirit, all that He spoke in the flesh"—should precede the exposition of those sayings as His. Then only when this *criticism* has reached its positive goal, does *Exegesis* properly begin. But we find naturally enough among those who take the other position with respect to the Word, a system of compromise with doubt, through which even orthodox men sometimes are led to deny the Faith in particulars which they acknowledge on the whole, and to mix matters with their exposition, which have no more relation to it than philosophical prolegomena on the being and attributes of God would have to the Lord's Prayer; and then to speak *upon* the Word and *round about* the Word, in a spirit of confused and undecided half rejection and half acceptance of its contents. But it is natural enough, on the other hand, that we should decline to term this Exegesis, which speaks *out* of the Word which is given to us.

Our exegetical stand-point is not that of seeking and finding, still less that of missing here and rejecting there: but that of *having*. The great הִנֵּנִי of the revelation of God in the flesh, of the spirit in the letter, has become to us of all certainties the most certain. Let us be permitted on our part, while so much license is being given, to speak as we believe and because we believe; out of the Word, not round about it; according to its own peculiar system, not according to the system of any Science, Theology, or Philosophy, nor of any dogmatic or confession; not translating it into any heterogeneous form of speech or of thought, and not raising again upon every point the discussion of the possession of our sure and certain foundation. Nor let it be thought unbecoming, that in order to *such* hearing and acceptance, we offer with all solemnity what should be heard and received by the *entire man*. All sound exposition of the Divine word of salvation must, at least, have a hortatory element, for that Word itself is hortatory throughout: in these pages there is not the smallest paragraph which simply ministers food to our critical curiosity. Nothing seems to us more unnatural than a certain *dead, dry* handling of the Word of life—never speaking from the heart to the heart—which is called the "purely scientific." But just in this manner does our falsely-boasted Science in its latest fashions —which, after all, are more or less scanty and pitiful, with their "πίστις" and their "Jahve"—run along its course side by side with the living Confession of the Lord in the Faith of His church. The Bible has never failed, since it was given, to speak *for itself* without the assistance of the learned; and it produces in its believers a believing apprehension of itself, without which it would long ago have gone the way of all waste paper. In its *application to preaching use* in the Church, it has ever preserved its living power, and ever will:—there is the Exegesis of the Spirit *at home*. If the mere Professor (who *sits* so comfortably upon his master's chair, whereas he ought to feel himself obliged to *stand* in the pulpit before "the *Established* Church" [sic.] of the only Master and Lord) cannot use his wisdom in preaching, nor minister therewith to those who do preach, then is that very fact the most decisive testimony against such wisdom.[1] For the Bible is not, once and for all, a mere old document for the learned, but a text for the preacher to the Church and the world, ever and inexhaustibly new. Here do those *emanationes scripturæ*, which Bacon referred to, flow freely forth; not in the wranglings of commentaries, whose Mischna and Gemara confound and obscure the student with the text itself, so that the word, before it can be read, is utterly prevented from speaking by its own exposition.

I have not, as already said, neglected commentaries, whether faithful or heterodox; but I have, with still more diligence, for now about thirty years, sought out, collected, and put to the most living use in my own heart and ministry, the immediate emanations of the living Word. I avow publicly before God and the world that all the theology and criticism of the age, whether infidel, or one-fourth, one-half, three-parts orthodox, has since then only served to strengthen and confirm me in my joyful boast:—I know in whom I believe. I *know* that what I read and possess in the Word will remain when the world passes away; and that its slightest sentence will prove a better dying pillow

1 "A minister who for many long years has drawn edification from the Word of God for his people, may well have sometimes a stray thought, of which a Professor of Theology need not be ashamed"—so says *Theremin* in his Evening-hours, with significant irony. I will be more bold and severe, and maintain, that the Professor of Exegesis often puts forth notions at which the preacher instructed in the living use of Scripture may blush.

than all else that man could conceive or possess. I know that to interpret to the world the words of the Lord Jesus is the loftiest task of human teaching or writing. The Lord is my witness that I approached it, in the publication of this book, with solemn diffidence, being deeply conscious that here and there error might too probably have intruded. Much even now may have escaped my most conscientious revision, which found (I must confess) little to retract; but these "Discourses of the Lord Jesus" have, as a whole, since then received the legitimation of a large circle of the faithful, whose acknowledgments in many ways rendered, of the grace and truth which they contain, I can thankfully lay at the Lord's feet.

In his name, then, let this book once more go forth, and let all men everywhere, who cannot accord with what they deem my too rigid adherence to the written Word, hear once more a testimony, which, thank God, is still unchanged:—I read the canonical text of the Bible as written through the Holy Ghost; but I so read it, not because I have framed for myself beforehand any inspiration dogma, or have devoted myself as a bond-slave to the old dogmatic; but because this Word approves itself with ever-increasing force as inspired to my reason, which, though not indeed sound, is through the virtue of that Word daily recovering soundness. It is because this living Word in a thousand ways has directed and is ever directing my inner being, with all its intelligence, thought, and will, that I have subjected to it the freedom of my whole existence.

The great and fundamental deficiency of *nearly* all learned exegesis, with which mine must for ever differ, is its misapprehension of the *depth and fulness of meaning* which, in accordance with its higher nature, necessarily belongs to every word of the Spirit. Though believed to be the Word of God, it is treated superficially and on principles of partial and one-sided deduction, just as if it were the word of man. In the endeavour to understand it that depth is not explored where, from the one root of the "sensus simplex," the richest fulness of references spring up and ramify in such a manner, that what upon the ground and territory of its immediate historical connexion, presents one definitely apprehended truth as the kernel of its meaning, does nevertheless expand itself into an inexhaustible variety of senses for the teaching of the world in all ages, and especially in the Church, where the Holy Spirit Himself continues to unfold His germinal word even to the end of the days. While this applies to every word of the Spirit in its several measure, to the *Words of the Word,* it applies without measure, to an extent which eternity only will disclose! Many of Christ's utterances make upon the most obtuse mind the overpowering impression of a mysterious, superabounding amplitude of meaning. If others, even the most part of them, appear in their slight drapery of proverbial, rabbinical, parabolical forms of language so humanly simple; yet approach them closely, contemplate them in their ever new applications to various times, and they will be so transfigured before you, that you will cease to deem it incomprehensible that the Church, through the process of centuries of reading and preaching, has never grown weary of them, or that this Word, in its unchangeable might, has triumphantly lived down all the fleeting words of men. If all that enlightened preachers have found for their preaching, or believing readers have found for their edification, in any one parable or any one single ecclesiastical Pericope, could be collected and comprised in fit words—that would be the *entire* Exegesis—so far as this might be possible before the words in futurity shall unfold perfectly its own yet more perfect meaning.

In the words of Christ all the scattered and intersecting rays of truth extant in humanity are collected and blended into the full and perfect light of day. *Ἐγὼ τὴν ἀλήθειαν λέγω, ἐγώ εἰμι ἡ ἀλήθεια*—He cries, standing in the midst of Israel, and in the centre, therefore, of all nations. The preparatory, prophetic Word, finds its end and goal in the Word of Christ: the apostolical word rests upon Him as its foundation, and is in Him already in its rudiments performed. To grasp and illustrate in all their significance the entire relations of His perfect Revelation,—to Judaism, such as it was when the Lord came, compounded of the truth of God and man's inventions;—and to the elements of truth scattered in Heathenism which He confirmed, as well as to all the errors of the Gentiles which He condemned,—is the right Province of sound Theological Science, True Philosophy, that is, the self-consciousness of humanity and its history, can only reach its perfection through a profound understanding of these. For Christianity, or to speak more correctly Christ, is not indeed that Deus ex machinâ which inspires the false speculation of historical inquiry with so much affected horror: but that which old Hippocrates with all his art was after all constrained to do homage to (at the close of his περὶ ἱερῆς νόσου), as the point to which all the eminent in Science come back, though without at first understanding what he meant,—that πάντα θεῖα καὶ ἀνθρώπινα πάντα, finds its full realization only in Him, who is the Godman; whose מוֹצָאוֹת (Mic. v. 1) according to His humanity mount upwards to Adam, as according to His divinity they go up to the bosom of the Father. The Son of God enters into history as the Son of man; and all history has been made by the Finger of God to prepare for Him, and to aspire towards Him. But to embrace this wider field in our comprehension, which indeed before the fulfilment of the mystery of God and the second revelation of all the secrets of that which we too readily dignify with the name of "history," can only approximately be done, is not the more immediate design of exegesis in its stricter sense; although this alone will ultimately set the seal of completeness upon the interpretation of the entire manifestation of Christ, and more especially of His Word. In the mean time true exposition suffers the light which is concentrated in the sun of personal truth to shine immediately upon it, and understands Matt. iv. 17 without the help of any rabbinical מַלְכוּת הַשָּׁמַיִם, as also Matt. xxviii. 19. Jno. xvi. 13 to 15, without the אֲרִיךְ אָדָם קַדְמוֹן and זְעֵיר אַנְפִּין (זְעִיר אַנְפִּין) of the Cabala, and without the Platonic Trias. Hearkening with open ears, it immediately attests that only which Christ testifies: every man can then, according to his ability, go forth from Christ to understand the world and history, and returning back again find rest in him. Let this be understood as spoken in explanation to those, who find wanting in our book the usual *derivations* into Christianity from its connexion with the teachings of the age. We deny not that connexion, but we much prefer to regard the derivation as proceeding *in the opposite direction*, not from the age, but into it.

Let the word of Christ explain itself. This is and must ever be a matter of fundamental importance, and we would fain hope at least to assist many a reader to gain this central point for its understanding. But that for sinful man with his infirm reason, there is now no other *understanding* of divine things than *that of Faith*, in the sense of the scholastic Fides præcedit intellectum, and of the Pauline *αἰχμαλωτίζειν πᾶν νόημα εἰς τὴν ὑπακοὴν τοῦ Χριστοῦ*, so that the private judgment must submit itself to the heart's experience through faith—let him dispute either with God or the devil who is inclined to do so; let him contend against it in his Edom-wisdom who has a mind to be dashed to pieces by this stone of stumbling. To show that on the other hand faith also has an ever-increasing *understanding* of its own, and need not be abashed before any pseudo-reason whatever, (which, indeed, it alone can help out of its *πρῶτον ψεῦδος* into the *γινώσκειν τὴν ἀλήθειαν*), is the proud design of this little contribution of ours—a design which, in the name of the Most Lowly, known to heaven and earth, and in opposition to all the proud, we dare openly to avow. But as to those who believe in the Lord, and yet through a pernicious pseudo-science, either cannot or will not bow to that miracle of the Holy Ghost—the sure transmission of His life and words in the Gospels, which are the central word of the whole invisible Scripture, may the Spirit of Truth bear more and more convincingly His own witness to His own testimony, which tolerates no correction of man.

They are but *hints*, after all, which are now offered—with all their diffuseness they are nothing more. For the author is deeply conscious that upon no one single word has he done more than very partially draw out that fulness of meaning, which is vaster than the ocean and deeper than the abyss. Yet it may be hoped that the reader will find many things that will abide with him, and bear to be further worked out. The apology which in the first edition stood here for the imperfect form and presentation of the work on account of little and fragmentary leisure, may be repeated, as far at least as concerns the first part; for this second edition goes forth amid the duties of a very unpropitious official situation. Yet have I, as it will be seen, done my best to review, revise, and to supplement the whole, with especial reference to what has appeared since or was overlooked at first, as far as this could be done without too much altering or enlarging the book.

To those of my dear readers who call the Lord Jesus their Lord in faith, I give my brotherly greeting. All others may the Lord Himself greet at the outset with His own most solemn words, words which blend His loving-kindness with their severity :—*'Εὰν γὰρ μὴ πιστεύσητε, ὅτι ἐγώ εἰμι, ἀποθανεῖσθε ἐν ταῖς ἁμαρτίαις ὑμῶν.* Do they still ask, *Σὺ τίς εἶ*; there is both answer and advice in his reply :—*Τὴν ἀρχὴν ὅ, τι καὶ λαλῶ ὑμῖν.* Hear these His words to you, so shall you apprehend who He is, and what you are, and further learn to cry—Lord to whom shall we go? Thou hast the words of eternal life, and we believe and are sure that thou art Christ, the Son of the living God; that thou art indeed Christ, the Saviour of the world.

THE FIRST WORDS.

NOT, indeed, absolutely the first. The words of that most marvellous, most holy childhood, in which the Divinity, gradually beaming already through the veil of the purest, most lovely humanity, comes forth from its profoundest mystery into manifestation, an ever-continuous birth of the Eternal Spirit into the Human Spirit, the human soul;—who could comprehend, and retain, and record? Joseph stood at reverent distance, Mary felt and anticipated all that the purest, most simple faith was capable of—and yet but little. The angels more remotely learned the wisdom of God, while they worshipped before the *swaddling-clothes* in which *the Lord*, who should bruise the serpent's head, first moves. Satan began to question and make the experiment whether he has nothing in this One too, and could not understand this new thing. The Mighty One grew up secretly into the consciousness and possession of His inherited dignity—secretly even, at first, to Himself. Just as Christ first fully understood the development of his youth, when He looked back upon it from His manhood, after he had come to the full knowledge of Himself; in like manner will it be vouchsafed to His Church, arrived at maturity, to understand the first earthly history of her Lord, which is reserved for her heavenly study. For nothing befel Him, which was not to be fully and perfectly known. Then will Mary remember and relate all. But for the time that now is, we have the mature Christ in His word, fulfiling His office among us. One word of the Child we have recorded for us, as a note and witness of the hidden portion of His growth and development:—that one word of great moment, in which his relf-recognition first distinctively breaks forth from the depths of His childhood's unconsciousness. Thus it is the *last* peculiar word of His childhood, but at the same time, the *First*, which the *Son of the Father* speaks. In this we find much, here below, to meditate and observe upon—both as to what preceded and what followed it—as far, that is, as we may now understand it. It was entrusted by Mary's lips for record to St Luke, whose gospel in its two first chapters already goes beyond St Matthew and St Mark, reaching forth towards St John's introduction concerning the Word made flesh.

THE FIRST WORDS TO HIS PARENTS CONCERNING HIS FATHER.

(Luke ii. 49.)

Solitary floweret out of the wonderful enclosed garden of the thirty years, plucked precisely there, where the swollen bud, at a *distinctive crisis,* bursts into flower. To mark that, is assuredly the design and the meaning of this record. The *child* Jesus sought to know Himself, and His whole life of childhood was this seeking: here He begins to find out His own mystery, and it is not merely a *first word* to His parents and to us, but also a first word of the Eternal Spirit in the human spirit of the person of the God man. This is attested in ver. 50, which signifies that this was the first "My Father" which had fallen from the lips of the child.

The history connected with this word must be referred to, in order to its being rightly understood. It is pre-eminently objective, simply traces the occurrences as they transpire, and thus says in the best manner, and exhibits most lucidly, what on this occasion was to be said and exhibited. It is not even mentioned at all at the outset that His parents took the *boy* Jesus with them to Jerusalem; yet there is a latent proof in the "twelve years," as indeed in the whole narrative, that this was the *first time.* Scripture is very sparing of words, where the right reader already catches the right meaning. We learn from other sources, that the youth of Israel in that period were reputed בְּנֵי הַתּוֹרָה. All things from his circumcision onwards proceed in the ordinary course with this extraordinary child.

St Luke simply relates that the child Jesus remained behind, without imputing blame to the parents or vindicating Him: the sequel sufficiently explains all. They were justified in leaving the youth to his own discretion in Jerusalem, as they had often done elsewhere; and *supposed* quite innocently, that He would be found in his own place in the company:—their error lay not in this. But that the youth wholly absorbed by the Temple and all that was to be seen and heard there, would give his thoughts to nothing else, that He now would belong *to it*, they considered not before, nor even when it should have been obvious to them, upon their *seeking* Him. Hence we may again collect that it was both for Him and for them the first time.

The mistaken idea that Jesus *taught*, contrary to the becoming order of human life *generally*, and much more of his lowly life, is refuted by ver. 46. He *sat* as a learner, *hearing* those who taught and *asking* them questions.[1]

Strictly, indeed, and properly, asking, as one who as yet knew not, but whose progress and learning went on into ever-increasing wisdom, vers. 40—52. His questions were the pure light-questions of innocence and truth, which keenly and deeply penetrated into the confused errors of the Rabbinical teaching. Rightly to question is the highest wisdom which the learner, as such, can possess. For one genuine question of him who seeks in the right direction already contains more realized truth than a thousand disjointed answers of the false wisdom of books and words. Thus does the galilæan youth in His Divine-human simplicity *confound* the Masters in Israel sitting in the loftiest chairs of the erudition of the age, and the seat of the learner predicts the future throne of the teacher.[2] His light shines forth upon the world now at the first with such simple convincingness, that many of those who were susceptible were astonished at the *understanding* displayed in His questions, and in the *answers* which He gave when, as would naturally enough follow, He was ques-

[1] Not as Sepp, (Life of Christ) supposes that a chair of instruction had been instantly given Him in the midst of the Teachers, in order to resolve questions and to propose them.

[2] " To answer children is indeed an examen rigorosum," says Hamann. But there is herein foreshadowed the future wisdom of Jesus, as Hamann says again: " He who will stop the mouths of scribes and sophists, must—know how to put questions" (Edition of Roth ii. 424.)

tioned in return. At least all who *gave heed to Him*—which many who were scandalised by Him might not as yet, strictly speaking, be disposed to do.

Jesus brings with him a knowledge and understanding of the written Word of God derived from the school of home : He finds this to some extent reproduced in Jerusalem, but only as falsified and overlaid by the errors of human teaching. This contradiction, which at the very first so glaringly manifests itself, stirs mightily his truth-seeking spirit. He had innocently expected to receive from the Masters in the house of God the full and much desired for answer to his accumulated questions, and nothing but truth and wisdom; but he finds it otherwise, and detects the disparity by that sense of truth which from the beginning recoiled from every error. He *could* already have taught, but it enters not His mind that He could, He rather *asks questions.* And what questions, did we but know them! Many a preintimation we may suppose, of his after manner of asking—How is it written, then, in this or in that Scripture? Thus by Holy Writ he presses hard upon the precepts of man, even as babes and sucklings[1] have done by his Spirit in all ages since; and thus without designing it, or being even conscious of doing so, He opens out the meaning of Scripture. The main subject of their communications is the Messiah and His kingdom: this theme arouses most fully the ready presentiment with which He came there, and in the course of this questioning, which is but the asking after Himself, he finds that great answer which the Spirit alone could give Him, He makes the discovery of Himself, in the first consciousness, not yet mature but now truly commencing—*I am He!* This He conceals, in deep and pure humility, from the astonished ones around Him ; but this first reproof of His parents, now least expected, extorts from its profoundest sanctuary, this great utterance.

It was the *first* reproof which He received. They had all along addressed Him as "child" with many a direction and admonition, but had never found anything to reprove. The foster-father

[1] Hence the Rabbins themselves know, that the Word of God out of the mouth of childhood is to be received as from the mouth of the Sanhedrim, of Moses, yea of the Blessed God Himself. Bammidbar rabba, 14.

even now remains standing, as ever, at reverent distance; the mother alone ventures with a mother's right to speak, yet at the same time in the father's name. She only, indeed, ventures upon a question appealing to His tested integrity as a child, as if she would say :—What thou hast now done, I understand not for the first time! Done *to us*,—this gave an unanswerable pathos to her question; for He had never given them pain before. Thy father—thus had Joseph till now been spoken of. Never, indeed, had Mary's lips as yet been bold to say to the "Son of the Highest" (Lu. i. 32) concerning the Most High :—Thy Father! Yet are her words—not *we, thy parents*, but, *Thy father and I* —a most exquisitely delicate expression of that sacred secret which had almost faded away in her soul, but the consciousness of which is already prepared to anticipate the great Word which her son is about to utter.

And He said unto them: *How is it that ye sought me! Wist ye not that I must be about my Father's business?* Instead of acknowledging any error or uttering any regret for their sorrow and anxiety, He gives them a kind and earnest lesson, though without appearing to do so, concerning their whole parental relation, especially in time past. There are two counter-questions in answer to the two questions of His mother. First of all, He puts another *wherefore* against hers, as He becomes conscious of the feeling with which they had *sought Him*. It had been so natural to Him to be and to abide where He was, that He had not thought of their seeking Him at all; and shows that He regards it as quite needless, at least to seek Him *sorrowing* in grief and anxiety, as if it were possible for Him to be in wrong or in danger. The reproof is thus given back, and in such a way, that the blame (as is too often the case, alas, in the human education of children of sin) is reflected upon the parents.[1] But He speaks without any design to shame or correct them; He innocently *asks the question* of His parents, as He had done before of the doctors; and all the shame lay in the circumstance itself.

1 Joseph and Mary had scarcely been quite free from such blame in the bringing up of the holy child. "They often treated him as only *their* child, and probably afflicted Him many times by an inappropriate exercise of their parental authority." Roos, Hist. of the Life of Jesus Christ. New edition.

Incomparably and inconceivably *artless*, as elevated as it is childlike, is that *Wist ye not?* That which He here now, while He utters it, begins for the first time to conceive and understand clearly, becomes at the same time so natural to Him, that it is as if He had ever known it, as if it could not be otherwise than it was, as if it must be equally self-explained to every one else.

Mary and Joseph assuredly *knew* who the child of their charge was. But so naturally had the human side of His development proceeded before their eyes, and so accustomed had they been to this alone, as time passed on, that they may well have sometimes nearly lost sight of that which was Higher and Peculiar in Him. Even now, when they were reminded of it by this impressive circumstance, they do not rise above their mere human ideas. And *this* was their fault: not that they for a while trusted Him, uncared for, out of their own hands, and not that they at first supposed that He would re-appear in His right place, but that afterwards, when they found it otherwise, they could sorrowing *seek* Him in any other than that which was *His* right place.

The opposition between His own "*My Father*" and Mary's "thy father," referring to Joseph, is very distinct. In this designedly spoken and deeply pondered expression, lies the deep significance of this whole Word. No human lips had ever hitherto pronounced it, for those approximations to it in the Old Testament and in the Apocrypha[1] are clearly to be distinguished from this *My Father*. Here already, as ever afterwards, only *My* Father —never conjoined with us, *Our* Father! This *My* deepens into a most exclusive, personal appropriation, when the Son of the Highest thus responds to His parents:—Ye—sought *Me!* Wist *ye* not that *I*—? The great truth rises before Him out of Joseph's name of father, that His own true *Father* is He, whom no one in Israel had ever addressed by that name, and Himself never till now: He, in whose house and Temple He now stands.[2]

[1] Isa. lxiii.; Mal. ii. 10; Wisd. xiv. 3; Ecclus. xxiii. 1, not so much in the sense of a personal relation, as in that which is indicated by Deut. xxxii. 6; viii. 5; Ps. ciii. 13.

[2] With this *first* word, which was spoken, withal, in the presence of the Doctors of Israel, König (Incarnation p. 305) combines that last one also spoken to them, Matt. xxii. 42. From beginning to end Jesus thus sets aside the paternity of Joseph, and testifies His own consciousness of a supernatural Origin.

Yet He does not simply say, in my Father's *house*, but according to the more extensive and undefined ἐν τοῖς of the Greek, *in my Father's matters.* The Spirit in the Youth speaks already in the after manner of the Man,—with profound meaning in concise expression. The first and most obvious meaning refers certainly to the place, the *House*, namely, where they should at once have sought Him, or supposed Him to be, rather, without seeking Him at all; but when we thoughtfully penetrate through the surface to the heart of the expression, we find much more than this included in it. And the next sense is that of a conclusive justification of His remaining behind in the temple without reference to His parents' knowledge and permission:—in my Father's *will*, by His guidance and inward direction. When hitherto any specific objection in His mind, conceived rather as a presentiment, might have come into collision with the parental will or the ordinary subordination of childhood, He had subjected and denied Himself; but now, His full age commencing, this also must begin to cease, and from this time forward they must, as He now shows it by a virtual injunction to be His will, leave Him without any further guidance of theirs, knowing by this token that he is about His Father's business. But this emancipation from His earthly parents takes place only as springing from a most firm adherence to His heavenly Father. *To be in any thing* (sein in etwas), as a proverbial expression among men, denotes the occupation of the whole life in it, the being wholly given up to it. Viewed thus, it gives a yet further answer, *how* it came to pass that He remained behind, and is a disclosure of the most secret self-justifying reason of the circumstance:—*I thought of nothing else*, it was my meat, the instinctive aim and impulse of my being, that higher law within me, by obeying which I was not disobedient to you,—I *must!* Here already is the germ of that sacred *must*, which the Lord so often utters in the subsequent way of His obedience. The contrary among other children might have been more or less marked:—dissipating attention to the wonders of the great city, visitations among friends and acquaintances, thoughts about the journey and the return. But both the thoughts and the actions of the Holy Child were entirely absorbed and wrapped up in this one thing. Thus, as von Gerlach observes, this first utterance is even thus early "a word of *self-renunciation*, of self-sacrificing surrender to God, in holy zeal for Him and His House."

Again, if we yet deeper penetrate into the meaning of this Word in relation to the occurrence to which it refers, the question arises, what drew and impelled Him as the youth, for such as yet He was, to the Father? They found Him occupied in *learning* and *asking questions* in the place where *God's word* was to be learned. Then He tells them once more, why He remained, and must have remained there:—I am in my Father's *school* for my own instruction. Inasmuch as He does not say, among the doctors, masters, and wise men, but instead of them names only the Father; His word may be regarded as containing that great and weighty disclosure of His own previous and subsequent inner *education*, for the sake of which principally this record is given to us. Just now, when He begins to be a "son of the law," He first calls God His Father—His master, teacher, educator.[1] Jesus was most inwardly taught of the Father, although not without external and human instrumentality. Life, instruction, holy writ, awakened what was within Him; He seeks His God in the temple, in order to find Him as His Father; among the masters in Israel He asks questions, in order that through them He may receive from on high the true answers; and the Father's inner guidance even connects itself with the custom to take the youth of twelve years' old first up to the feast to present them before the Lord. Thus it was the Father alone who taught Him when his mother early recited or read to Him out of Scripture; and not otherwise was it with the youth, the young man, and the man in the Synagogue at Nazareth. And *what* was it that He learned, upon what were His questionings and investigations set, in that secret education wherein He "heard of the Father" concerning all things, but especially concerning the Old Testament Scriptures and dispensations? That one word was the rudimental object of His study, which at the close of His life's developement was unfolded to Him by the Spirit in all its clearness and power:—*Thou art my Son!*

[1] As *Henry Alford* says very excellently in his English comment. on the New Test. (London 1849)—he has so repeatedly mentioned my Reden Jesu, that I am bound in gratitude to make similar reference to him.

He enquired concerning Himself with vehement desire to know the mystery of His own being and the problem of His life, and concerning the will of Him who had sent Him to finish His work. Jno. iv. 34. In the "labour of His childish spirit, to admit into itself and rightly adjust all things," Divine things according to the word of God in the Old Testament were of chief concern to Him. "Therein lived the childish consciousness of Jesus, in all the profundity of His secret presentiments."[1] As He himself had ever, from the beginning, possessed a consciousness of the object of His life, only as yet concealed in His childish capacity;[2] and as this first clear disclosure (to be followed itself by many such, in advancing clearness and assurance) seems to Him at once as natural as if it had never been otherwise than clear to Him; so in like manner does He in childish confidence ask His parents—*Wist ye* not then every thing concerning me long since? And assuredly, however much such a saying must have astonished them, there was so much in it that was right and true, that they could not but take shame to themselves that they had been troubled about the Son of the Highest, as if any evil could befall Him before the accomplishment of the mission of His life; that they should have thought it needful to guard Him, as if, when out of their immediate care, He could possibly stray beyond His Father's *hand*, and *guidance*, and *protection*. With this last meaning His enquiring word comes round again to the obvious *reply* which the occasion demanded, and gives the reason of His first question: How is it that ye could seek me sorrowing? *Considered ye not* that I am always in my Father's hands and care? But yet once again was this altogether forgotten, under the cross, by the deeply-stricken mother:—I am not alone, for the Father is with me (Jno. xvi. 32).

Let the whole fulness of this significance be once more gathered into this question, which sublimely presupposes the profoundest mystery as manifest:—*knew* ye not all this long ago

[1] So Braune, in his admirable exposition of the Gospels, which we shall now be glad often to compare and cite.

[2] The divine-human self-consciousness under the form of youthful presentiment, present from the beginning, not in any wise superadded later. See Liebner Christology i. 311.

concerning me? And His word contains an impressive reference to the Past, in order to point the view to the Future; an explanation concerning the whole life of the child, and its development into the youth, the young man, the man.[1] Not as if the mind of the child had specifically conceived all which we deduce from His word, but He speaks prophetically of Himself. The Spirit of Christ in Himself spreads its wings, and that word which spontaneously gushed from the deepest source of His life in the Father, becomes to the Son a holy text, which He, too, may search into yet more diligently (1 Pet. i. 11). Yet is it a pure and genuine child-word, the immediate and unstudied utterance, on the border of childhood, of child-like simplicity; and thus it discloses the first independent acting of Him who, passing the limit of childhood, abides still in His Father's business.

And they *understood it not:*—This is recorded concerning the first Word of the Word, and of those who, as being nearest to Himself, had every advantage for understanding it! They pondered the sacred mystery, and thought not that in catching its most obvious sense, they understood it in its fulness. Even Mary herself, like the rest, appears not yet to understand, before the day of Pentecost, the mystery of the person of Jesus—and who is there below that fully *understands* it? Thou, vain expositor, hast not the heart of Mary, probably nothing of the Pentecostal spirit; and yet art thou so ready to cry out—I understand the words which He has spoken?

St Luke's supplement in vers. 51, 52 was necessary, in order to obviate misunderstanding. As soon as that word of holy Righteousness was uttered—The Son of the Father is free! it was again in a sense annulled or suspended, in order to His fulfilment of all righteousness in obedience. The Father's teaching was ever a discipline of obedience (Heb. v. 8) as the Father had inwardly said to Him—Tarry here! so now He says, Go down with them, and be subject to them! So that He is not from this time forth placed in another relation even to Joseph, for the last time referred to in the little saying "to them," who is

[1] Just for this reason we cannot agree with Braune that any "calling to *Activity* in the kingdom of God" is here signified—this would overstep the limits of childhood.

not "His Father," and yet for the sake of His mother and of His true Father, was to be still honoured as such. The mystery folds itself up again in the self-denial of eighteen years, till the time when a new Word brings out its other, mighty significance: —Thus it behoveth us to fulfil all righteousness! till the time when, on the open assumption of His Messiahship, the mother has become "Woman," having no longer any authority, and His "My Father" publicly resounds in His House, and before His people, no more to cease till that *last* Word, which coincides with this first:—Father, into thine hands!

And Jesus *increased*—so that His self-consciousness was not yet strictly speaking perfected and fully developed. As in age, so also He increased through the teaching of the Father, in *wisdom*, in His obedience through the grace of God which descended upon His humanity before it came, through Him, upon us all. The bud now burst unfolds itself from within; in the heart of this child there is no foolishness bound up (Prov. xxii. 15); no folly in Israel or Nazareth has power to affect Him; he advances into all that belongs to manhood, but contracts from it none of its iniquity or sin; all things are constrained to serve Him and minister to His wisdom. The displeasure of God has never rested upon His Holy one, but the complacency of God, His *favour* goes on ever increasing with His increase in wisdom, until it is consummated at His Baptism. Even His favour with *men* increases likewise, for He forbears entirely as yet from testifying against their folly and their sin; and therefore the world as yet hateth Him not. (Jno. vii. 7.) "Let us go on in friendship together," said they in Nazareth. O, what gracious words may have issued from His lips during those eighteen years, which are not recorded! But the words which, by the Father's ordination, He was to testify to the world, are sealed up till His hour was come. Then one after another bursts forth, each, as it were, a deeper stream from the long pent-up Fountain of Eternal Wisdom and Truth.

THE FIRST WORD OF CONSECRATION TO HIS OFFICE.

(Matt. iii. 15.)

The history of our Lord's Baptism, like that of His Cross, is contained in all the four Evangelists; but the *Word* which He then uttered is preserved by St Matthew alone, as being strictly a Word of *Fulfilment*, and therefore belonging especially to the fundamental idea of the first Gospel.

John knew the Lord and yet knew Him not. He knew him not, according to his own testimony (Jno. i. 31), as the Messias and the Son of God; but he knew Him as One, whose whole life from the beginning had silently cried, Which of you convinceth me of sin? Since he had been in the deserts, he had probably seen Him but little, yet often enough, as his life could not have been altogether recluse, to have awakened within him the presentiment which now deepens into conviction. His saying in v. 14 proceeded from the Spirit, who then descended upon him, and is not to be explained on the ordinary principles of human thought. It is a word which marks the transition at that moment taking place within him from presentiment to inward assurance. The question at the same time breaks out in it which had long lain deep in the heart of the humble Baptist,—But who will baptize *me*, who am also myself a sinner? Certainly, according to the ordinance of God, his office and function extended over all, whether they were worse or better than himself, for his mission was to baptize with water; and therefore he baptized without hesitation every Simeon or Nathanael as he came. But here was One greater than Nathanael! John *knew* this not, indeed, until He saw the Spirit descend, according to the sign which had been given him; yet his spirit goes out towards Him with that anticipatory and presentient feeling, which had moved him in his mother's womb towards the mother of his Lord. Jesus comes in all the spiritual grace of gentleness and humility with sinners to the baptism of repentance; as John beholds Him, he sees shining through this deep humility the high Majesty of the

Holy one; and that he has an inward token thereof, constitutes His own dignity. He has baptized many, has seen and in some sense seen through men of all kinds, but no one like this had as yet come before him. They have all bowed down before him: —but before this man, bows down in the irrepressible emotion of his own most profound contrition, the sinful man in the greatest Prophet. It might well have prompted him to cry: Art thou then a sinner, a man? To that point his question ventures not to go, it remains suspended between the thought of the man, and the superadded presentiment of the Spirit.[1] Enough, however, is clear to be uttered thus: Who am I in thy presence, that I in the office and ministry of Baptism should be placed over Thee?

Then answers the Lord with equal grace and majesty, with as much simplicity as fulness of meaning,[2] by another of His distinctive first words,—the first *official word*, with which He prepares Himself for His anointing, and consecration to His office. He first of all gently sets aside the prohibition and refusal of John, and utters with dignified grace that single word, *Suffer it now!* Had He said no more, that would have sufficed to the Baptist, for its plainness and dignity were such as to silence all further questioning. It at once intimated,—I know what I now do; I am taught from above to submit to baptism, as thou art taught to baptize. *Now* for a time thou seemest to be the greater, who consecrates the less—soon, as it is fit, will our relative position be reversed! *Now*—it is only a transitional relation (as Neander has well observed): *Now*:—my hour is come, is the Lord's thought for Himself: perform thy function upon me, thou shalt afterwards learn what I do, is His meaning with regard to John. This promise, indeed, is already and instantaneously fulfilled, when, in order to remove all the scruples of this upright man, and to terminate this holy conflict of humility in him, by the sublimest and most commanding humility in

1 Presentiment, not full revelation as in Luke i. 43. So far, therefore, Braune is not *quite* correct, "As formerly the Mothers, so now the Sons stand before each other." Many suppose, contrary to the whole connexion of the text, that the Baptist spoke this after the Baptism and Manifestation!! ('Αφιήσιν Hieron. dimisit, which Sepp ridiculously maintains against Luther's false translation.)

2 Certainly with no such "arbitrariness, departing from simplicity and intended for reproof" as Schleiermacher finds here.

Himself, He proceeds to testify:—*for thus it becometh us to fulfil all righteousness.*

First of all, we cannot but be profoundly impressed by the lofty contrast between *this* avowal of righteousness and the *confession of sin* of all the others, who came to be baptized, ver. 6. And it is strange that Theologians in their search for testimonies of the sinlessness of Jesus, do not find here the first and most luminous dictum probans from His own mouth. This was to John the decisive declaration, which set him perfectly at rest:—Thy presentiment was true, in a deeper sense than thou canst now comprehend, *I am He* who knoweth no sin, *but for that very reason* come I in the likeness of sinners to this Baptism. And it is to all the world, that shall receive this word, an all-inclusive testimony of the Lord, concerning His own office and ministry as the restorer of righteousness to sinful men.

To fulfil *all* righteousness:—this has a large and lofty sound in the lips of a man, of an Israelite, who will speak the truth. And it shall be our righteousness, if we observe to do all these commandments before the Lord our God, as he hath commanded us. (Deut. vi. 25.) Because no man ever in Israel could say that on account of sin which yields not to the commandment, therefore is the Baptism of repentance for the remission of sins at the end of the economy of the law. He who now comes to this Baptism, is not a sinner, but a righteous man who neither needs repentance nor pardon. It is He who for us fulfils all righteousness, who, born of a woman and made under the law which was given to the unrighteous, has already hitherto observed and performed all the commandments of the Lord to Israel;—*and for that very reason* now subjects Himself also to that Baptism which was ordained of God as the concluding commandment of the Old covenant, through which is the transition to the New. He received circumcision, though born without the foreskin of the heart; He was redeemed as the First-born, though Himself the Redeemer; in all probability He offered every sacrifice which was required of an Israelite (as we see in one instance, at least,—that of the Passover), though Himself the Propitiatory and Paschal Lamb, the archetype and substance of all these shadows; He visited the Temple and the Synagogue, He humbly submitted to every custom and ordinance in Israel, and even, when no sin attached to them, to those which were not ordained of God; so likewise must He be baptized "into the coming Messiah" which is nevertheless Himself, just as He is the Prophet to prepare His own way. In this *now*, therefore, there is a terminating point, not yet absolutely the last, but certainly a typical and preliminary terminating point of His obedience to the Law. In this Baptism, inasmuch as it was the last external commandment of God to Israel, *all* righteousness was *fulfilled* by Him.

The Lord might now have said again, as He said before—*I must*—for the same innate necessity, in the obedience of the Father, prompted Him now; it belonged to the same unity of His whole life. Because, however, the question is now especially concerning an external transaction, and because He would obviate the scruple of John as to the *Propriety*, the Fitness, the Becomingness of that which was about to take place; He adopts this expression, *It becometh* us by all means! This embraces, besides the obvious reply to the plain question, a concealed testimony to the final principle of the whole course of His self-renunciation and self-substitution in the likeness of sinners. For all the first words of our Lord, especially, have so profound a background of meaning. The πρέπον is not simply used as it stands, Eph. v. 3, 1 Tim. ii. 10, in the New Testament, but in the full and sublime sense of Heb. ii. 10, vii. 26. It *seemed fit* to the righteous Father, that the Son in the sinner's stead should in a human obedience bring back their righteousness: within this boundary of thought did the Son Himself in His humanity ever reverently confine Himself, beyond it he knew and testified nothing. Thus it was also here, when the Baptist, who might not Himself become His disciple, but only send disciples to Him, was counted worthy to receive an early testimony of the mystery of His atonement which he then afterwards repeats—Jno. i. 29. The Preacher of repentance unto the Kingdom of Heaven expected, indeed, no earthly Jewish Messiah . he understood as Zachariah's son and the pupil of the Spirit in the wilderness, whatever might be understood by any Israelite, from the word of Prophecy concerning Him who was to come: but here at the very first does the Lord openly announce to him:—Placing myself in the likeness of sinners, *taking their sins upon me*, I shall and will fulfil righteousness for them. So might He have given back the Baptist's word literally :—*I have need* (χρείαν ἔχω) to be baptized of thee, I must be baptized with the baptism which is prepared for me (Lu. xii., 50). And so would He have spoken, if He had wished to speak of Himself alone : but He says not now: thus it becometh *me*—but *us*.

But how can He say this, and what does He mean ? we ask, and all the more earnestly because we have seen that the profoundest significance of this saying concerns Himself alone. The most obvious answer is that He thus replies to the separation between them which the humble scruple had expressed—*I* of *Thee, Thou* to *me !* He designs *now*, first of all, to induce the Doubter not merely to suffer Him to go down into the Jordan, but also to fulfil the external function of His office upon Him, and *baptize* Him, even as others. Thus it has this meaning as it regards John :—who art thou then ? The Preparer of the way, the Forerunner. Now *I am He* that cometh after thee ; thy presentiment is right ; we appertain to one another, each in his office and ministry. In baptizing me, thou fulfillest all righteousness and closest thine office : to be baptized of thee, is my righteousness, and belongs to my ministry and the design of my life. What majesty in this word, which immediately silences all scruple : and, at the same time, what a marvellous emulation of humility between the Lord and His servant ; just as afterwards in the eleventh chapter, where the Lord who was to come, places His servant by his side as one who was also come, and of whom the Scripture had also spoken !

But even this does not yet exhaust the meaning of this great Word. The baptism of which it speaks, is only in an external and *typical* sense the concluding point of Obedience for the Fulfiller of all Righteousness : it is truly and essentially the true *beginning-point* of that Obedience, the consummation of which, in the death of the Cross in order to the Resurrection, it pretypifies. The Lord does not say—*herein, hereby* it is incumbent upon me finally to accomplish all righteousness—but *thus !* That is an expression of comparison, which points forward to the thing compared. This Baptism to which the Mature man comes, who till now has loved righteousness and hated iniquity, is His *anointing* to that Sacrifice of Himself for sinners which now first properly begins. Ps. xlv. 7. As in this baptism by prophetic figure the Righteous One places Himself among sinners, so was He afterwards baptized with the Baptism of death, in which He as the Lamb of God bore our guilt; which was not to Him the wages of sin, but the highest meritorious righteousness for us all. As now the Father confirms His righteousness by a voice from heaven, so then in the Resurrection the Father justifies Him as His Son again. Rom. i. 4; Acts xiii. 33. It follows further, that as now the Spirit descends upon Him, so then also the outpouring of the Spirit for us all; that Baptism with the Spirit to which John alluded, without obtaining it below, and concerning which he unconsciously spake when he said:—I have need to be baptized of Thee. All this our Lord clearly saw when He came to the Jordan; and as He finally spoke of His sufferings as a Baptism, so does He now already contemplate in Baptism His sufferings. For now His wisdom is perfect, and He no more needs to increase in it. In that last word of His childhood the beginning of His consciousness concerning His own *person* broke forth; when this was grown perfect and finally sealed, this decisive *word of his manhood* utters His full consciousness concerning His *Work*. This honour is reserved for Him, to testify of Himself, before the sign from heaven seals His testimony. He presents Himself, saying—Behold I come, to do Thy will; before the Father's response—This is my beloved Son! This acceptance and obligation is to Him what the confession of sin is to the sinner. Therein our sins are confessed as done away in His righteousness, and *the future baptism* for the true forgiveness of sins, which should be ours by virtue of His Baptism, is fore-announced.

And because, finally, the Baptism which He *thus* prepares for us, finds its consummation only in the essential, actual fellowship of His death and resurrection; we remark, that the "us" in which He includes Himself in His humble condescension before John, means in its deepest signification, *us all.* He utters it as the *Son of Man* in the name of humanity, as the Forerunner in the name of His own, with whom He here, at the very beginning contemplating the uttermost end, most entirely unites

Himself.[1] He indeed is, pre-eminently, the Fulfiller; but all who become participators of His Righteousness, fulfil in Him and through Him the same righteousness and in the same way. *Thus* it becometh us to become like Him, as it became Him in our likeness to overcome sin, and render obedience. This will immediately become manifest in the wilderness of Temptation, where the Son of God not as the Son for Himself, but as *Man*, as the Second Adam and the True Israel, spoils, by faith in the Word, the power of Satan.

THE FIRST WORDS OF VICTORY OVER THE TEMPTER.

(Matt. iv. 4, 7, 10; Lu. iv. 4, 8, 12.)

These three words are, in their ascending connexion, to be reckoned as one; and, indeed, as a third *First Word*, approaching still nearer to the goal of His being, and drawn from the yet deeper depth of the mystery of God the Father and His Son. As the Son's first word of all concerning the Father, Lu. ii. 49, embraced the whole *inner* life of *His own* most essential personality; and the second concerning His Righteousness, Matt. iii. 15, the entire *work* of His active and passive obedience *for us;* so now the *fulfilment of all righteousness* in its three great branches, is maintained and asserted against the Tempter to unrighteousness. His Obedience approves itself in the renunciation of all Enjoyment, of all Honour, of all Possession in opposition to the Prince of this world: thus does He overcome him in the abasement of faith, to which he had descended from His Divine Power; and leads human nature back to God again, through the selfsame way, by which it had fallen from Him. Concerning the Temptation of Christ in itself, its innermost ground in the Father's holy justice, its redeeming might and typical signification for us, and especially the Satanic unity of design in the three temptations of the wilderness; we shall

1 "He desired and received baptism in the name of the *people*," says Nitzsch (Prac. Theol. i. 167) but too concisely. Mark, moreover, what is said there with perfect truth, that He who comes with Water and the Word of the Prophet to fulfil all the types must also come with *Blood*, then finally and fully with *Spirit*.

enter into no detailed description here. It is our purpose only to expound the words of Jesus, and to point particular attention to that which is unfolded in them.

But the words of Jesus on this occasion are not new, and distinctively His own; they are God's words long ago uttered, and taken from the ancient Scriptures, which he as the Fulfiller appropriates to Himself. This is, at the outset, of great significance. The child had grown and become strong in Spirit, had increased in wisdom; the man, arrived at the mature priestly age, and anointed for the Inauguration of His office, is now *full* of the Holy Ghost, Lu. iv. 1. But as afterwards the first word of the Spirit at the Pentecost was a proclamation of what had been said by the Prophet Joel, so here *the First Words of the Lord spoken from the fulness of the Spirit are only quotations from the Holy Scripture!* He has now learned them entirely, He is a Master in the use of them, and will prove Himself such first of all, against the enemy, whom the Word of truth, which he has perverted into a lie, must again beat down. What virtue and dignity in the holy letter, which, filled with the Spirit of Christ, now becomes only Life and Truth! Christ makes his appeal, when that old "yea hath God said" is brought against Him, not to the heavenly voice which He had just heard, but to the Word of God, written in the book of Moses. The living Eternal Word Himself vests Himself in the written word, which in its deepest foundation is written by Him and for Him. Let men think upon this! Let this be remembered by that theology, which refuses to accept, even from the consciousness of Christ, the entire and full authority of that which was *Holy Scripture* to *Him.*

But He does not confront Satan with any one of those many and clear words of prophecy which are written concerning the future bruiser of the Serpent's head. Satan well knows these, but does not understand the mystery hitherto folded up in them, the human abasement and self-renunciation of the Son of God, which is indeed the central mystery of all Scripture, and the essential secret of His victory over the enemy. That enemy must first perceive this in its fulfilment. Here in the wilderness for the first time, he earnestly scrutinises it, at once doubting and trembling; but does not thoroughly penetrate it, for he comes again at the Cross with his temptations, and once more foolishly brings forward his already repelled "*art thou the Son of God*, then save thyself!" The Lord does not permit Himself to meet him with an express—*I am He:* He was indeed, and would thus have shown Himself Satan's Lord, but would not then have been his conqueror *for us.* The first word which He opposes to him, says rather—*man!* It is taken, as is also the second, from the temptation of Israel in the wilderness, for Israel is a type of the Son of Man, the Servant of God for righteousness, that One to come, in whom alone that nature is consummated into perfect righteousness, which in all men else is ever sinking into deeper sin. Adam stood not,—Israel after the flesh stood not, when the Lord His God tempted him, but rather like Satan tempted His God: but now comes the second Adam, God's true Servant Israel, through whose obedience the way of life is made known, and actually thrown open—that man truly lives by the power and in the strength of the Eternal Word.

As Eve in the beginning rightly opposed the tempter with *God had said!* but alas, did not persist therein—even so now the Lord, but He holds firm. Satan knows well the word of God, and must admit its force; when in full faith and entire obedience it is used in answer against him, the might of his lying delusion is broken. Satan will challenge the wonderful power of God in nature—and His Son, if He be truly such, should make stones out of bread: but *this* is not the power which drives him out of that human nature, in which he now sees with doubting astonishment the eternal Son standing before him. *That* at least the bold challenger knew full well, and He knew it still better, who was come to be victor in this fight. Christ *answered and said*, placing Himself as man in the obedience of faith. Thus and not otherwise *does God reply to the Devil*, and indeed through Christ, the Son of God and the Son of man. He Himself in His humility—submitting to be tempted in order to conquer—is that living answer of God to Satan, which in holy right resists and casts out Satan's right to humanity. Satan must now learn this, and has not finished learning it yet; for he has not even yet betaken himself to his darkness again, but continues, and will continue to tempt the members of the Head with the same temptation, until he shall also in them all be overcome and condemned.

The first temptation, which through our earthly body is most obvious to universal human nature, is that of seeking the *enjoyment* and *nourishment* of *life* against the will of God and independently of His gift; to make for ourselves our *bread* in the misuse of God's power, entrusted to us over the lower nature and the creature. Our own age exhibits the development of this in those mimic miracles which seek the world's dominion by the industry which conquers nature. Adam entering into this temptation, would eat as the Son of God, that of which God has said —thou shall not eat of it. That was the case in paradise, even without hunger, and in the midst of the enjoyment of all the fruits of the garden of Eden which were not forbidden and in that first fall every other was wrapped up. It was exhibited again, especially, when Israel cried in the wilderness: if we are God's people, why have we not bread and flesh at His hands according to our desire? Then did God humble His son Israel, and suffered him to hunger, to show him what was in his heart. The true salvation from this unbelief could not yet then appear, it was only typically *made known* to the unbelievers, that man doth not live by the creaturely bread, but by the word of God. Here in Christ, who abundantly makes good what fallen man has turned to evil; who in voluntary abnegation fasts, in entire obedience hungers, and thus is released from the creature, in which Adam is sinfully held captive; here in Christ does that ancient word, written concerning manna, find its new and complete significance—that for the sake of which it was before provided in the Holy Scripture.

Man doth not live by bread only, but by every word that proceedeth out of the mouth of the Lord doth man live. Continually, and in a thousand ways, has the Spirit since then used and applied these words among the children of God, and every interpretation which the Spirit truly puts upon it, is included in its meaning. For this He caused it to be written in the prophecy of Moses, and then to be used in reply to the Arch-Liar by the lips of the Fulfiller. We seek now only to indicate briefly the leading principles of its interpretation.

Bread is in its general acceptation the food of man's life, regularly appointed for him as the creaturely instrument of the Divine word of creation and preservation :—thou shalt live thereof. (The Book of Wisdom (xvi. 26) says instead,—it is not the growing of fruits that nourisheth man). Gen. i. 29, iii. 19; Ps. civ. 14. To this stands opposed כָּל־מוֹצָא פִּי־יְהוָֹה that is, most obviously, as was demonstrated in the case of Israel in the wilderness, any particular word of commandment or will issuing from the power of the Creator and Preserver, which becomes what man may live upon ;—any kind of food given independently of the established order of things, as was the miraculous manna. But such manna itself, again, is only a veil of God's power; a pledge and symbol which is condescendingly reached forth to weak faith, in order that there may be something in man's mouth. Wherefore does God work miracles, and not leave man only and entirely to live upon ordinary bread, but thus oftentimes create a new thing for him? That He may make man know that even in the ordinary and natural course it is by no means nature and the creature which have and give the life, but Himself alone. *Even in bread* man lives not by bread only, for is not the life more than meat? Is not the Word, the Will, the Power of God in everything; so that we do not inhale our very breath from the air, but from the breath of God? *Word* stands not as such in the Hebrew text, but is taken here from the old exegetical translation. What is the מוֹצָא פִּי־יְהוָֹה of which Moses wrote? The breath of the creating effluence from the eternal Power and Godhead, the *Spirit*, in and of whom all *life*, even bodily life, consists, Num. xvi. 22; Ps. civ. 29, 30. But the Spirit goes out indeed only in one prepared form, and that form is the *Word*. In the deepest meaning of the essential and only truth, which ever contradicts the lie of Satan, all *Things* in the world, after their kind, are only variously embodied words of the Creator, inasmuch as by His mighty word alone they are upheld in being. (Hence דָּבָר and ῥῆμα in the Scripture signify also thing.) "God does not speak grammatical vocables, but true essential things. Thus sun and moon, heaven and earth, Peter and Paul, Thou and I, are nothing but words of God" (Luther). Thus the creature lives not by any other creature, any more than it lives of itself, but because, and how and whereof God will. Therefore the first meaning of the saying of Jesus here—obvious in its profoundness—is: "I commit the sustentation of my life entirely into the hands of God." Moses in the presence of the Lord needed neither bread nor water for forty days (Ex. xxxiv. 28). The man Jesus died not in forty days' fast; but then only at length, when the strength of the Spirit returned to Him that there might be place for temptation, felt He hunger.

But we penetrate deeper with the question, which is not always one of simple unbelief—how may this be? and how is this to be understood? Then may we reasonably ask—what is *Man?* Not the body with its earthly, animal soul, but the true and proper man, that is, the living spirit which came forth from God, which only *lives* in and by the Spirit of God, which continually goes forth as Word for the preservation of the creature. Even as the body—the abiding product of its soul—only subsists through a continual formative impulse of corporeity, so do the body and soul of *man*, as of a *living* soul in the moulded dust of the earth, subsist only by the *Spirit*. The outer man lives by the inner, as this again by the Word of God. Shouldst thou say—by *bread!* and determine in any case to have it, and in thy hunger to procure it for thyself, even at the cost of disobedience —any way thou canst or the Tempter places it at thy hand—then art thou captive in that idolatry and delusion, which serves the creature with and instead of the Creator (Rom. i. 25). Then art thou in the way to worship the Arch-Liar, who promises to give that of which God ever continues the sole giver and Lord.

Think not, too, that thou *livest* at all as *man*, that is, according to thy pure creation as a Son of God, in His image, if thou art finding a so-called life of thine own hand in the greatness of thy way (Isa. lvii. 10). For thou art dead in trespasses and sins, although the bread and the pleasures of the world should plentifully abound to thee. Here belongs, further, that most true sense of this sacred saying, according to which it is preached to those who only labour for the perishable bread of this world, and seek not the everlasting bread of God. But this leads us further and further; and "*not alone*" vindicates again the true life of man in God, against such as in their error cleave to any institution of the means of life, as if it was not God alone in them that gave them efficacy. As a general rule the word of God, externally written and preached, is given for the food of the inner man; but inasmuch as the living word of God in the word, is the true word, thou mayest, if it be His will, without Scripture and preaching, live by His Spirit; without intercourse with brethren, be connected with the Church; even without the physical bread of the sacrament, receive nevertheless the heavenly bread. Every manna given by God in the creaturely form, is a witness that points beyond itself to the immediate outgoing of God's life for the life of man, out of God's mouth into the *believing mouth* of man.

So does the letter of the written word testify here in the believing mouth of Christ, to its own most essential Spirit. And the Lord, at the same time that He avows himself to be man in the life of God, gives *to Satan* the true and mysterious answer as to *who Himself is,* and that is the last and profoundest sense which makes the old word His own, and transforms it into a *new* word, now fully for the first time exhibited in its truth. Christ, verily, is the *Original Man,* recovered from the fall, Adam and the Son of God in one. The Son of God gave Himself to human nature, and incorporated Himself with it; Satan's temptation would, for he now first half understands this, detach Him from it again, and thereby destroy His *mediatorial nature* through something, that *for it* would have the nature of sin. Art thou, poor hungry child of man, the Son of God? Then use thy might! But He has wrapped up His might in entire self-renunciation, in order to overcome the enemy, and thus does He overcome him in simple human faith. He is Himself the bread come down from heaven to give unto the world everlasting life, and shall He make for Himself bread out of stones for His own proper life? Against the Tempter's challenge—art *Thou*—He only binds Himself more firmly to us all: I am man, I am humanity, I am man-kind! (Just as that *us* is used in Matt. iii. 15). There is, indeed, a twofold nature in humanity, the earthly Adam and that which came forth from God in him; but both in their inseparable *unity* constitute the proper *man,* and as such he is re-established in Christ, the God-man. That *in Him Adam lives entirely by the Logos*—is the last and super-abounding fulfilment of the meaning of this word, which thus goes far beyond its application for the instruction of poor fallen man.

Satan has not yet fully apprehended what was said to him: for it penetrates too deeply into that eternal original truth, from which he is fallen, and which he no longer desires to understand: yet he is not repelled, but rather stimulated to a renewed and more earnest attack. The Tempter comes again—for this is his manner, and the second temptation proceeds very much like the former. The Deceiver had taken his position upon a word of God (thou art my beloved Son!) though only to pervert it as the deducer of false consequences;—he still persists in this method. Holdest thou so firmly to that which is written? Then I know yet another word, which will suit thee well. Dost thou expect, strong in thy faith, the miraculous help of thy God, even as only man? Then, instead of waiting and hungering here in the wilderness—for thou art, nevertheless, the Son of God, and to that I hold—wilt thou not spring down from the pinnacle of the temple among the people, as if Thou camest down from heaven, and thus announce thyself with becoming dignity? Thus both the half-mocking audacity, and the impious enticing cunning of the Tempter became more intense. He knows the letter of scripture, and may also use it for temptation, just as he has free access to the holy city and the temple. He takes his word from that psalm of faith's offence and defence against His own hellish might (Ps. xci. 5, 6, 13), which may have already in times past done him much injury; and designs in his malice and presumption to turn that well-known promise of angel-protection for mortal man, to the destruction of this wonderful Son of Man, who in this conflict will assume to be nothing more. But the Lord answers him, in words which are for ever the true defence and reply to every one-sided perversion of a saying of Scripture:—*it is written again!* This πάλιν means not contra, for no one word of the Bible contradicts any other: but it simply signifies that one Scripture teaches us how to understand and use another. We are only fully armed against the cunning of Satan, who presses upon us with isolated and wrested sentences of the Bible, when we are thoroughly grounded in a clear perception of the inner unity of the whole Scripture, which supplements itself and explains its own meaning. Our Forerunner teaches us here to use the word as our weapon in our own succeeding warfare, and teaches us especially to lay hold upon this—*again* it is written! Moreover, Satan's perversion consisted not in this, that he would have the *figurative* expression taken *literally*, for that is here actually permitted to faith in God's word, and Jesus acknowledges without contradiction this interpretation; but the *again* instructs us in the qualification which averts its abuse.

Jesus continues near to his first quotation. The Lord proved in the wilderness His people Israel (Deut. viii. 2), whether they would tempt Him or not, and alas! Israel many times *tempted* his God, so that afterwards in warning reference to the Past, it was said to him by Moses—*ye shall not tempt the Lord your God* (Deut. vi. 16). Wherein consists the tempting of God on the part of man? It is the complete opposite of the seeking in faith, of the waiting upon God in the obedience and confidence of trust, a self-willed demand of the mighty help of God; and, consequently, unbelief, disobedience, and distrust are its innermost principles. Thus did the children of Israel demand flesh for their souls (that is, according to their own lusts) and said: can God furnish a table in the wilderness? So limited they the Holy One of Israel (Ps. lxxviii. 18, 19, 41), and put Him arrogantly to the test:—so now, if He does this according to our will, it shall be well. The manna was before their eyes, and further supplies might come from the word and command of God: but they anticipated, by the word of their own self-will, the Word of God upon which they should wait; and this is tempting God. This would the Lord have done now, if He had challenged the angel-guard of His God according to the promise, in order to His passage through the air, which was not His prescribed way according to the Divine guidance. As He might not himself make bread for himself, so neither could he seek such a way. Satan's cunning omitted—*in all thy ways*;[1] our Lord, however, did not think fit to point out and dwell upon this omission: but instead of such discussion, set another decisive word of Scripture over

[1] St Luke omits this, though he has τοῦ διαφυλάξαι σε. When v. Gerlach supposes that this omission should have no stress laid upon it, as it was only meant to say, "wherever thou goest"—he most unjustifiably presses down the everywhere profound word of Scripture to the narrow limits of our ordinary human speech.

against that which he had quoted. The Lord knows His own way, the way of humility and not of vain-glory ; the way of waiting upon His God, and not of premature running and anticipation of His will ;—therefore, the word that is written, remains ever a lamp to His feet.

Every sin in its innermost principle is, properly speaking, a tempting and challenging of God: since he, who should obey, tests the Almighty whether the way of his own self-will shall not prosper. But then, particularly, when the unbelief and disobedience of self-will presses forward in what is false presumption, though seemingly only a firm confidence in promised assistance, as if God must and should hearken to it; this is the masked aggravation of sin, to which Satan here allures. Uncalled reformers, daring enthusiasts, even actual miracle-workers of their own will and for their own honour, have all fallen into this sin, because they have forgotten the Word of the Master spoken here in faith and obedience. What if before the eyes of men they have prospered at first in their airy way, it is not because angels have borne them up, but the Prince of darkness (who would, it may be, have carried the Lord also in safety down, even as he had lifted Him up), yet only to their final fall into the abyss.

Christ remains Lord over Satan in the simplicity and assurance of His human way according to the word of God. Power over His body may the Tempter exercise by the permission of the Father, His Spirit remains free and firm in obedience to the truth. If, as we perceived, the first answer struck the right point, and protested against Satan's fundamental lie, that in the creature of itself a life was to be sought ; the second answer advances still nearer to the crisis, even as the temptation advanced nearer. If the first answer had already sharply and clearly defined the boundary between the Lord God and His creature (in whose stead, and in whose nature, the Eternal Son here stands) ; the second defines it still more sharply, and gives to Satan a further lesson and one peculiarly appropriate *to him*, which indeed he may not be able to receive. For it is Satan himself who in the permitted abuse of his remaining angel-power, for deceit and destruction against the Word and will of God, absolutely and now in the most unreserved manner, *tempts the Lord his God*. Therefore did Christ change the letter of the Scripture, and say: *thou* shalt not, although it is written in Moses, *ye* shall not tempt. This is forsooth the *Spirit's* power in the weakness of the tempted one, that while he only thinks to cover himself and to hide himself in the sheltering, defending word; that same humble word approves itself as a sharp weapon of attack and of judgment against the Tempter's pride.

Then does the evil one begin finally to mark that in this *Man* he has to do with *the Lord his God*, who will maintain over him His right: yet is he unwilling to admit it. He gathers all his might and greatness for one more last and decisive onset; but the result is that he hears more decisively and openly pronounced that which befitted his own true character. Probably the Lord knew not immediately Himself with what kind of person he had immediately to do. In manifest bodily appearance Satan cannot, indeed, appear, for such corporeity in him, if it may so be called, would be for us the most frightful horror. Therefore does He disguise and mask Himself, now as he had from the beginning—yet still comes as a person. Probably the Tempter drew near the first time in human form as a *good friend* and adviser; the second time it may be he showed Himself as an *angel of light* who might bear Him up in his hands.[1] The Lord, without much questioning, had both times replied to the Satanic design in the temptation, and mediately therefore to Satan himself; but now the "God of this world" comes forward in his naked grossness with the horrible and undisguised demand—worship me! If thou altogether declinest to be the Son of God, then serve me for that recompense which is in my power and which I will give thee! He promises to give that which is not his, that which at least, when held and received from *him*, is perverted from glory into ruin: and the price which he demands is what belongs only to God. Then

[1] Lange, indeed, thinks that such mask-work and illusion must have been quite ineffectual upon Christ, the Pure One, just as children are not deceived by such jugglery in tales. But the self-renunciation of Christ, and the Father's counsel to give Him up to temptation, are on such a supposition quite forgotten. Might not the same argument be used against the anguish and the obscuration at Gethsemane and at the cross? To show all the kingdoms of the world at one glance was, undoubtedly, an illusion, for the letter of St Luke's account knows nothing of "highly coloured description, which turned a high and extensive prospect in the wilderness to a symbolical account."

does the Lord recognize the Prince of Darkness, the Archfiend, whom He has come to eject out of a world that he had usurped; and to whom He can now reply in *His own* might and dignity, as peremptorily as the demand was plain: *get thee behind me, Satan!* This is necessarily the last temptation and victory: for the order observed by St Luke, while it has a meaning of its own, must not regulate here the order of time. For the first and the second are so immediately and strictly connected according to St Matthew, that we cannot imagine anything intervening: and the Repelled One cannot be supposed to have returned again immediately after the third.[1]

This *away from me* might have been enough. But the humility of the Lord, which itself must have been the keenest condemnation of the Father of pride, does him a superfluous honour, and even adds a reason from Scripture. This word is found, again, near to the former (Deut. vi. 13, 14), but is here, in its entire appropriation, more severed than that from its literal connexion. In the words which had before fallen from the Lord's lips, *Ye* shall not tempt, had become *Thou* shalt not tempt, for Himself and at the same time for the Devil; but now it refers especially and in all its significance to the Devil alone; according to Christ's conscious purpose, when he fell back in this encounter, upon that great central word and fundamental commandment of the whole Old Testament, yea of the whole Scripture:—*thou shalt worship the Lord thy God, and Him only shalt thou serve.*[2] This answer forms one of the sublimest, most comprehensively significant critical moments in the history of His kingdom: and is the most distinc-

[1] The *apostolical* authority of St Matthew decides the literal truth of his connection: St Luke arranges the events, evidently, according to another point of view. Τότε παραλαμβάνει, πάλιν παραλαμβάνει, τότε ἀφίησιν in St Matthew import something more than St Luke's mere καί. He, in his account, has the two places in his view and joins them—first wilderness and mountain, afterwards returning to the second:—and he had brought him (already between the two) even to the pinnacle of the temple! The well-considered omission in St Luke of the ὕπαγε κτλ. is worthy of notice; for (as Alford remarks) he could not well have left these words in his inverted account.

[2] See the connexion Deut. vi. 4, 14: and Samuel's Serve him *only!* 1 Sam. vii. 3. Hence it is in the LXX. and Vulg: ἀυτῷ μόνῳ, illi soli. Even if this μόνῷ of St Luke originated in the LXX., yet we have it also authentically in St Matthew.

tive and definitive *Explanation* with Satan. Luther ventured with a good intention to add his well-known little word *alone* to the sacred text (Rom. iii. 28); and in justification of this addition, the Lord's example has been appealed to, who here does the same. But it is not entirely the same, even apart from the difference between our Lord and *Luther* as to supplementing the Word of God. The false emphasizing of "faith alone" wrought much evil in the Church from that time, till men learned to acknowledge, that St James' not strawy epistle is also right with its enforcement—not through faith alone. But to worship the Lord *alone*, to serve one God *alone* is absolutely necessary to the high and stern truth of this Scripture; and this *alone* can never be too rigorously brought forward in the contest with the lie of Idolatry in all its forms. It rejects all the Pleasure,[1] Power, and Glory of the whole *world*, as soon as this rises against its Creator; and here, at the close, upholds the *worship* of the One Eternal independently of and above the world. In the beginning of the Temptation this distinction between God and His creature was not so express, but in the "*not* by bread *alone*" the creaturely holds its proper place through the Immanence of the Creating Word.

Perhaps the most profound among the many views of the process and connexion of the history of the Temptation, (all of which may be more or less right according to its many-sided truth),—the most essential extract of its spirit, appears to us that of Zinzendorf, who deduces lessons from it concerning the *Mysteries, the Right Understanding, and the Fundamental Truths* of the Word of God.[2] The mystery—if thou be the Son of God—is brought forward at the wrong time and in a wrong application by the Tempter, therefore the Lord opposes to it that other mystery, which was suited to the occasion. The apprehension of the promised angel-protection, though right in itself, is used partially and turned to temptation, therefore the Lord shows the truth in its completeness, by exhibiting its other side. Finally, when the Arch-Liar overturns the fundamental truth,

[1] Not excluding even the remark, that Enjoyment entices the Youth, Honour the Man, and Possession or Power, finally, the Old.

[2] In the Discourses, which he delivered in 1742 as Pastor at Philadelphia in Pennsylvania.

that God alone is to be worshipped—the Lord can only re-erect it by asserting it simply again. For to quote Hamann: "The victory of men over Satan is then most easy, when he most plainly reveals himself. The ten commandments, if they are written in our heart, and we use them in defence against him, will ever drive him away."

Thus, for this reason, do the conqueror and the conquered separate—symbol and type of all future temptation of the Head and the members. The original fundamental truth, in which Satan stood not fast, and which he never more will learn or can, comes to him as his judgment from the mouth of this humble Son of Man. While the Son of God as man worships and serves with us, He reveals Himself as the Lord and God of the god of this world, who, instead of worshipping has tempted Him in vain. From this time forward the Devil knew Jesus. Mark i. 24—34, iii. 11, v. 7.

Thus also is the distinction established between the Redeemer from Satan's Power, the rightful King of the whole earth, to whom the ends of the world had been already given by the Father (Ps. ii.); and that false Messiah whom carnal Israel, through fellowship with the deceiving idolatry of the world, had learned to expect. What an earthly-glorious Jewish Messiah would then have been, Antichrist, the Man of Sin, will in the last days actually exhibit, and with an open rejection of the name of God. The time is come and now is, when the worship of the ancient, secular Jehovah, as He revealed Himself in the Old Testament and through His Incarnate Eternal Son has wrought our redemption, should cease; the Father of lies offers to men the *glory of this world*, and all who consent to His lie thereupon abase themselves to worship *him*, concerning whom, nevertheless, they desire to know nothing. But he has here thus early exposed and discovered himself, constrained by Christ: and *all* who abide in the way of Christ, are equipped with the sure armour of that word of truth which He Himself first victoriously proved.

THE FIRST WORDS OF THE MASTER TO THE FIRST DISCIPLES.

(John i. 38, 39—42, 43—47, 48—50, 51.)

All this was decidedly spoken and done *after the Temptation*, for the Baptism recorded by St John, ver. 32, was immediately followed by the Spirit's leading into the wilderness. This also was now past, and the mission to the Baptist in ver. 19, did not take place until the fortieth day at least, because the testimony, vers. 20—27, cannot have been uttered before the Baptism of Jesus. John deems himself not yet authorized to announce publicly Him who was to come: but waits till that Mysterious One who had retired from the Jordan into the desert returned to him again, which he probably did as soon as the victory in the wilderness was achieved. When he saw Him once more, He could *point Him out*, ver. 29. Further, those pregnant words, "there standeth One among you, whom ye know not," obviously imply, I *know Him* now as erewhile I *knew* Him not. So clearly is established the real harmony of the Gospels when they are rightly read. *Τῇ ἐπαύριον* in vers. 29, 35, 43 successively, can only retain its consecutive and unbroken sense when we regard them as following, not only the day of the Baptism, but the forty days of the Temptation also. To forget this, as the most recent expositors have glaringly done, and insert them between vers. 28 and 35, is entirely to contradict the chronology of our Evangelist, which preserves the strictest coherence.[1]

The vanquisher of Satan, to whom the angels ministered—the Lamb of God and God's own Son, walks in sublime silence by the Jordan, waiting for the further guidance and direction of His Father. He has come back to the Baptist, for He knows

[1] Hence the unbelieving criticism of *this* method of harmonizing protests that John makes the insertion of the history of the temptation after the Baptism impossible. There is but one true answer to this:—the baptism and the temptation precede ver. 19. The Evangelist confines himself here, as before in vers. 7 and 15, to the subsequent testimony of the Baptist. Compare Gemberg's remarks, in allusion to Schleiermacher (Stud. u. Krit. 1845 i. 105.)

that Himself must not first utter—*I am He*—in the presence of the people of Israel; but that His Forerunner must bear witness of Him, and that his testimony was now ready. The first day passes—John points to Him as He thus walks, and directing attention to His whole appearance and bearing, saith—*Behold*—This is He! not one of the marvelling and inwardly musing hearers, however, ventures to follow Him. But when on the next day the testimony to Jesus still walking thus, is repeated—behold the Lamb of God!—its meaning is then understood—the two disciples at that time with John begin to follow the Lamb. Only two indeed at the first, but in them we see the first strivings of the great impulse of all after *following*. Another new and sublime initiatory crisis! Beginning of the congregation of disciples, and inauguration of the great Teacher into His office; not indeed as yet in public ministration to the people, but according to the appointed and unostentatious procedure of His course, in gentle words to those who are first gathered around His presence. These *first words of the Teacher and Master* bear upon them that express and wonderful stamp of majesty in lowliness and lowliness in majesty, which is impressed upon the whole of His subsequent speech and action. They commence with the most simple utterances of human language, springing up, apparently, from the circumstance of the moment. What will ye? come, then, and see! But when we think *whose mouth* uttered these words, we perceive the beginning of the shining forth of His glory in them: and soon, indeed, does the Master-word rise to its full dignity in giving the new name, in piercing the hidden heart, in disclosure of what was secret, and in the promise of yet greater things. The whole, moreover, is brief and sufficing, simple and clear, with no more words than arise out of the occasion. But these are spoken in lowliness as profound as their majesty is sublime: while they have their simply human and external aspect, they have a profoundly significant and majestic background. These first words to the seeing and hearing disciples have their own glory, full of grace and truth—before the days of mighty miracles and preaching. These also verily are spirit, and they are life.

John saw Jesus *walking*, in silent meditation; waiting for His hour, and His Father's command: in full preparation for the world and its sin; equipped for His testimony to the truth with that armour, which has been tested and approved in his first great conflict; and for the utterance of those new Words of God, which the Father has given Him. The two disciples had heard the Baptist speak of Him, and have so far understood his words, that they now vehemently desire to be the disciples of the true, the higher Master. They follow Him in silence, venturing on no address, nor any introduction of their own. But Jesus is conscious in His spirit of the hour that has now come, and *turneth*—beautiful picture for the devout pencil of the artist! Will not some one now come to me? Such a question lay in that *turning*—springing from His consciousness that the time was now come, and from the longing of that love which would soon call all men to Himself. Then *looketh He* upon the two, as the first given Him of the Father, and opens His mouth in affectionate words. But however humanly and humbly He may begin to speak, yet must what He says become at this *crisis* and from *His* lips, an *involuntary revelation of the deep significance which lies in the high and peculiar presage of this crisis.* He cannot, and He will not avoid this: He knows full clearly with what deep meaning He speaks. If we may so stammer our human thoughts concerning Him, in whom all is human as well as divine:—a certain struggle between His dignity as God and His humility as the Son of man, resolves itself into a most profound concert of both. Like a true Master, He will not at the very first speak words of instruction to His coming disciples, but rather awake and excite their own consciousness. Thus will He commence their training as disciples. The *question-word* with which He begins will be found to have a latent fulness of meaning, conveying an essential truth which is applicable to all who ever come to Him; and leading immediately to that *word of invitation* which is the germ and type of all His future exhortation and teaching.

Τί ζητεῖτε; What will ye? that is, though He designedly omits to say so, of me? with me? Wherefore come ye thus behind me? Spoken with any other tone and look, this question would not have had more than the ordinary meaning with which we may suppose a man asking it in such circumstances;—it would have been even repulsive:—What would you seek in my footsteps?

leave me to my own way![1] With *His* look and tone, on the contrary, it already glides by a gracious transition into the following *Come!* Yet is there a distinction between them. That first word of all contained a solemn *question,* designed to penetrate the hearts of those who are coming: and this must not be lost sight of in the invitation. He whom they seek, and who is the object of the unconscious seeking of all humanity: He, who afterwards stands before the whole world and testifies, "come ye all unto me and find rest to your souls"—He says not now, *whom* seek ye? For whom do ye take me, that ye thus seek to be near me? Although this is involved in the matter, He does not express it, but as yet conceals that great "*I am He*" (which might have been the response to the Baptist's "this is He!"); and speaks apparently as if there were nothing in Him to seek, in order that they, again, may bethink themselves how all is to be sought and found in Him. He thinks not first of Himself, but first of those who are coming to Him. Those only who *seek* come truly to Him, but as they come they are met by the testing word—*what* seek ye? And wherefore from me? First must we in some degree know, by the revelation of the ground of our hearts through the face of the Searcher of hearts turned full upon us, and be taught by the question which He asks, *What* it is that we as men and sinners seek and need: then shall we more and more discover that it is only Himself whom we seek, because in Him all that man seeks is found. It is our Lord Himself, in general ever seeking the lost till He finds them, who meets us in our own way, with that first word of the Divine manifestation, which would not give the sinner up: Adam, where art thou? Strive not so hard after death in the error of thy life! Seekest thou to live? Thou shalt not find it in departing from me; return therefore to me as I return to thee. But here are Israelites coming to him, disciples of John, prepared in the old covenant of preparatory grace, by the hidden Christ, for the Christ revealed, when He should come. And now that He is come, they come to meet Him, and should know well the fit answer to the first question of the Lord. John and Andrew heard it,

1 As a late Bishop of the Moravian Brethren, when one following would join him as he walked, with the question, "Wherefore thus alone?" made answer, "I would rather be so." Not so the Lord.

too, but they reflect not immediately upon the inner significance of this startling question, as John may have understood it, from their subsequent report. They simply reply as well as they can to its most obvious meaning. They could not yet say—" we seek the Messiah, Thyself"—until they had already begun to find Him. That remained secret in the depth of their consciousness. But because Jesus stands so *humanly* before them, they are bold to speak in human language—" Rabbi,"—that is, we would be thy disciples. This would have sufficed as their self-dedicatory profession, Thou art our Master. His question, however, was so gracious, that they gather confidence to go farther — *where lodgest thou?* That is, we would this day enter into Thy nearer fellowship, we would be with Thee, hear Thee, and learn of Thee. The direct answer is concealed in their words, and it is from a right feeling of mingled reverence and shame, that they hold it back:— behold, Thou art the Lamb of God, and the Son of God; we are sinners of the world, Israelites who wait for Thee, and expect from Thee all that our souls yet need. If their counter-question seems to have in it something of uncourteous abruptness—yet how profoundly humble is it, and how full of *trust!*

He said unto them, *Come and see!* If that first word might have been construed by one who was excessively timid, or one who was insincere, into a repulse; this second carries with it its immediate tone of permission, and friendly acceptance—ye are welcome to me;—but its deepest tone is much more than merely *permission.* He who has come speaks in gracious invitation and with the gentle command of love: come! and we catch here already the key-note of all His preaching and doctrine. *Behold* —the Baptist had said—and now they shall *behold.* The challenge to come *and see* was an ordinary manner of speech in common life: but in some circumstances used with great solemnity, as of the grave of Lazarus (John xi. 34); with great majesty in the Canticles (iii. 11) concerning the magnificence of King Solomon; as in the Revelation (vi. 1, 3, 5, 7) of the heavenly visions—and in the Psalms (lxvi. 5; xlvi. 9) concerning the wonderful works of God. It was at the same time the common saying of the Rabbi to his disciples (as frequently in the Talmud, בּוֹא וּרְאֵה, come and let it be explained to thee). They came and saw *where He abode*—but their Lord had more than merely *where* in His view. They tarried with *Him*, as St John adds with emphasis: and saw all they might see in Him, His glory full of grace and truth; they tasted and saw that the Lord was gracious (Ps. xxxiv. 9): they beheld in faith the heaven open upon the Son of man, ver. 50, 51. All this the Lord promised them in that lowly-sublime invitation, which conceals His majesty, yet permits some rays of it to pierce through:—come, *and ye shall* see, experience, receive and find all that ye seek.[1] That is the rule and process of His discipleship; the immediate and self-evidencing testimony of the truth in Christ, as Philip, an apt scholar, begins already to use it against Nathanael's doubt, ver. 46. This is the sum of the apologies: the missionary appeal to all the world; the testimony of every true divine, of John the Evangelist as of John the Forerunner, who having himself seen, can bear his witness against all the perverse blindness of unbelief.

What the Two who came so readily, found or saw or heard at that time, is buried in silence: it was so much, however, that Andrew can already testify to his brother Simon — we have found the Messiah! When this Third, afterwards to be first, comes forward, we hear another word of the Master, still more authoritative and majestic. Jesus looked upon *him* and said—*thou art Simon, the son of Jonas*—I know thee, who and what thou art, from thy birth till thy present coming to me! The allusion which has been over-critically detected in the etymology of the old name in its allusion to the new, we mention and leave undecided:—the *hearer*, disciple, heretofore son of the timid *dove*, which flies among the rocks, shall become the sheltering *rock* of the dove. So lately, again, Lange,[2] although the reading Ἰωάνου, Ἰωάννου is not lightly to be rejected. Enough, that in this place, the design and reference is especially to the *new* disciple-name, and *such* allusion and antithesis can scarcely be deemed consonant with the dignity of the occasion. *Thou shalt be called Cephas:*—I now give thee thy new name; for I know what I shall make thee in my discipleship and for my

[1] Bruno Bauer's cunning eye detects here "feeble pomp, empty superfluity," and is sure that Jesus never could have spoken thus.

[2] Better, at least, than Sepp's יוֹנָה imbecillitas, oppressio.

kingdom! Be *my* "disciple" henceforth, and out of what thou *art*, thou shalt *become* something new. The new name which He gives is, first of all, the revelation in the light of His own countenance of Simon's peculiar and natural character, as in the case of the sons of thunder (Mar. iii. 17); it specifies his danger and the temptation of his inborn nature, and also its transformation and sanctification in the new birth. Thus it is given as a promise as well as a warning. He who receives his new name from the Lord, and well sustains it, will become that to which he is called. As in the Old Testament, Jehovah, in His supreme authority, gave the new names of promise *Abraham* and *Israel;* so also now does the Son in His father's power, and marks out *Peter* here as an originator, to lay the foundation, and as a spiritual progenitor of the new people of God in the similitude of those two great public persons. As "Israel" indicates penitent, wrestling praying faith, so "Peter" refers to the confession, and the building of the church upon the profession and testimony—although it is the Lord Himself who makes Peter, and all who are like him, the foundation upon which He Himself builds.

Rising still higher in its tone of authority is the Masterword to Philip; whom He finds and to whom He forthwith gives a direct summons—follow me! It appears, at first, like a second "come and see," but has a farther reach of meaning. It expresses in one word the whole disciple-life of all who have come and have seen: and is the early type of all that is wrapped up in the same oft-repeated call, and of that which is connected with it when it is last heard at the close of the gospel of St John. (xxi. 19, 22.)

And now comes the fifth in this rapid formation of the first circle of disciples[1]—Nathanael. He is not placed in the first rank of influence, but coming as he now does in virtue of the preparing grace which he had received, he may be regarded rather than Peter, or even than John (who has here faithfully recorded the praise with which his Master's lips greeted *him*) as the fittest type of all disciples—such as the Lord will receive and

[1] How and by what means? "Nothing but personal influences, few words, trust awakening trust." (So Nitzsch, Sermons vi. Select.)

greatly rejoice over when they come to Him. Ah that they all were such! The precipitancy of his hasty question which only catches at the last word—can any good thing come out of Nazareth? was redeemed from its error by its very sincerity. The error of prejudice, though indeed indirectly connected with sin, does not deepen into the sin of offence as in the case of the other Israelites. Nathanael in Cana, two hours from Nazareth, had no personal knowledge of Jesus,—that was certainly not his fault. Jesus now sees him coming just as man should come, seeking, seeking earnestly without guile. Oh how few such earnest seekers are there! Here is *a true Israelite in whom there is no guile*, whose sin is already covered, and his iniquity not imputed to him. It is not the humble man himself whom the Lord addresses, for that would not have been as appropriate as in the other instance—*Thou* art Simon—which involved a warning. He spoke to the others *concerning* him—(somewhat as the Baptist had spoken about Himself.) Behold, those who come like this man are my joy, these are the disciples whom I would have, thus might and thus ought all Israel to be prepared for me their Messiah.[1] Though still far from recognizing in the Nazarene the King of Israel, this upright man hears not in vain the "come and see," he goes at his friend's suggestion that he may see, and soon is his prejudice lost in his happy experience. This is the sure and direct way to that end. But he who would walk in it to Christ, like Nathanael, must first have gone, through grace, in penitent, wrestling, seeking faith the way of Jacob-Israel—in Jacob's nature before this first new birth, there is yet deceit and guile. If a sinner, like Zacchæus, believes, the Lord says of him—this also is a son of Abraham. When one who, like Nathanael waiting in preparatory grace for the perfect grace to come, frankly receives what is freely offered to him, the Lord terms him an Israelite indeed, in the purest sense of the word and name. So blessed a commencement of his ministry has the Father prepared for Him, that in two days five seeking souls are gathered around him:—the last, however, the

[1] Nazareth was even among the Galilæans held in small estimation, nay, despised. More surely is signified than—as *Alford* supposes—out of so small a place so *great* a thing! for it is added—τι ἀγαθόν.

loveliest, whose first misapprehension is at once requited with commendation from his Master's gracious heart.

Nathanael is ashamed and embarrassed; and the more so as he, in his still life, had been intimately known by only a few such as Philip. *Whence knowest thou me?* The doubt and scruple of his pure spirit which shrinks from the Searcher of hearts, is still less displeasing to Him than the first surprise on account of Nazareth. If He has seen and spoken to thee, and thou ask Him the same question in the same spirit as Nathanael; He will rejoice thereat, and thou shalt soon experience, how entirely He knows and has ever known thee. The inferior human life of the Lord reflects already the relations of His exalted state, and we see in it even His Omniscience and Omnipotence; although He was not actively, in His estate of self-abnegation, either Omnipotent or Almighty, any more than everywhere present. Whence knows He Nathanael? May it have been through an instantaneous revelation of the Father, even as on other occasions, for instance in the case of the Samaritan woman, whose husbands He reckons? Was it, besides this, through that knowledge of man which belongs to the First man, everywhere penetrating, by a true physiognomy, through the outer into the inner being, and which knows individual men because it knows what was in man? (ch. ii. 24, 25.) Neither of these must be entirely excluded here, yet the expression of the Lord, *I saw thee*, points in its simple meaning to something past. As the eyes of the Crown Prince have been wont silently to seek out the true men in the land, that he may collect them around himself when he ascends the throne; so also had Jesus, during His long eighteen years at Nazareth, the seclusion of which must at least have been broken by the festival journies to and from Jerusalem, most observantly looked around upon men. Hence he knows Simon, to whom he gives his name; Philip also, and Matthew, whom he calls to follow him; so did He also actually with His bodily eyes behold Nathanael under the fig-tree, but at the same time he read the thoughts of his heart with eyes opened by the Father. Therefore does he plainly tell him, — I see thee not now, as thou comest, for the first time; reminds him by the expressive *before that Philip called thee*—of the prejudice against Nazareth which he had manifested (at least thus does Nathanael feel, as the Lord knew); and thus gives him an answer to his question which mightly demonstrates His own Divine dignity; *a miraculous word* which goes straight to his heart, as if the all-knowing One Himself should speak—I know thee from everlasting, I penetrate thee through and through. And here is *pretypified* how *now* "Christianity grounds the claim to be entirely trusted in for the revelation of the Divine treasure to faith, upon the immediate experience of every conscientious man; since as soon as it is known, it seizes him by a glance that penetrates him through and through."[1] Nathanael's exclamation, "*Rabbi*,' thou art more than Rabbi, more than many in Israel deem the Messiah to be, "thou art the *Son of God*," is uttered with a feeling akin to that in Psalm cxxxix—Lord thou has searched me and known me! Thou knowest all that pertains to me, that which even Philip knows not, what I thought known to God alone.

An Israelite in the kingdom of the King of Israel was said to dwell under his fig-tree, 1 Kings iv. 25. But in speaking thus distinctively of the fig-tree under which He had seen Nathanael, the Lord's meaning went beyond this proverbial use of the expression, and signified more than merely—in thy habitation in Israel. Nathanael understands, as is obvious to remark, something special and mysterious, connected with a time when he had repaired to his fig-tree, not for refreshment and solace, but according to the pious custom in Israel, as a place of meditation, reflection, and prayer. There had been a solemn transaction with his God—quite alone as he thought: the prayer of repentance which left him *without guile*, the prayer of deep longing for the consolation of Israel, and what else Nathanael will reveal to us, when all that has been kept secret becomes known. I saw *thee*—said the Lord—thy inner man before God, the true Israelite in thee. We may receive His word, each one for himself, as the assurance:—I have known thee from the beginning in all thy ways! Let every one think of his fig-tree, of the places of his pleasure and his prayer, before he was called to Jesus. He whom his Lord can meet with the testimony: Thou art an Israelite indeed,—may and indeed shall cry out in joyful response: and thou art my King!

[1] Beck, Introduction to the Syst. of Ch. Doct., p. 163.

Then does the King and the Master, in the last and the sublimest of these His first words of kingly authority, bestow a still further commendation upon Nathanael:—He distinctly specifies and praises that one thing, for which His eyes have looked from the beginning and ever shall look (Jer. v. 3), with which man must come to Him, in order from Him to learn it still better—Faith.[1] New, great word of His mouth—*thou believest!* Well, thou art come in the right way; thou hast longed, and thou hast sought; thou art come, just as Philip asked thee, to come and see; thou hast seen and heard, and because I have said to thee what only I could say, thou believest;—then I say for thy further faith: *thou shalt see greater things than these!* Yes, verily, this promise holds good in its widest sense for all believers who abide with Him: — greater and yet greater things shall they continue to see, even up to the last "blessed art thou who hast believed!"

And now that all the relations of the Master to His disciples may, in this first history, be shadowed out, His words advance another step in sublime elevation; and we hear His first "*Verily, verily I say unto you.*" But He utters it as the Son of God in the unity of the Father, and not like the Prophets—thus saith the Lord. He utters it with His highest dignity, combined with the gracious condescension of the Son of Man. Hence He appends, as a testimony against unbelief, the Verily of swearing by Himself; though without it all that He may say must be believed, *even because He has said it.* What follows is spoken to Nathanael, but yet He says *to you,* for He addresses in the person of Nathanael all His disciples, and gives a promise which is recorded for all who, like Nathanael, come, see, believe, and in that faith abide with Him.

Henceforth—after ye have thus become my disciples—shall ye *see,* more and more intimately and gloriously experience, the full meaning of my first word, come and see. The coming in *faith* leads to the *seeing,* yea ultimately to the *highest vision* of all glory; but this is only through the *being seen,* the being penetrated by

[1] No shadow of "slight blame" here (von Gerlach)—for such "swiftness" to believe as this, is a precious simplicity, which should not be supposed capable of considering all at once the "necessity of higher evidences."

His eye. The genuine disciple-faith of the true Israelites, to which His praise and His promise are given, is that which needs no other miracle for its confirmation than the miracle-word of the Searcher of hearts;—such was found also in Samaria (ch. iv. 29).

But what is that miracle which, nevertheless, the Lord does here predict? *Ye shall see heaven open, and the angels of God ascending and descending upon the Son of Man.* Was this externally and literally fulfilled to those who heard these words first? By no means, assuredly, else would it have been recorded. We know, however, that both had just occurred;—the heaven had been opened upon the Son of Man when He was baptized, and the angels had ministered to Him in the wilderness. But the former was seen only by the Baptist—the latter by no man. They were secret and mysterious introductory miracles, designed as testimonies for the Lord Himself and not for the world; the visible attesting seals of the Father's voice, which by the Spirit ever more said to His Spirit—Thou art my Son. One includes the other as a natural consequence; there, where He now is, is heaven open upon Him and for Him (Jno. iii. 13); but where heaven is, there must also be the service and commerce of angels. So much we thus understand, that the Lord Himself, with all His humiliation and self-renunciation, must have had, since His baptism and temptation, an unveiled view of His Father in Heaven, and a sure experience of the presence of the angels around Him. What further voices and manifestations from above; what further appearances and interpositions of the ministering spirits occurred to Him in the mystery of His solitude, it is beyond our province to determine; but we are justified in presuming that there were such by what is recorded in connexion with the Mount of Transfiguration (Matt. xvii. 5) and the garden of anguish (Lu. xxii. 43). But of that Transfiguration only the three were the witnesses,—not Nathanael, Andrew, or Philip, not all His disciples; and that angel-manifestation was, when it took place, witnessed by no one. The notion that the disciples may have often seen appearances of angels around their Lord as He prayed, or slept, or retired into secret from His enemies, which they have not recorded, belongs to some imaginary and poetical Messiah. When the Lord here promises in general terms that those who had come to Him should *from that time forward* (that is, withal, since they occurred to Himself at the Jordan and in the wilderness) *see* these things with Him; we must not suppose Him to have intended it externally and literally, but symbolically. He takes from the first secret miracles, (especially from that first one of all, which the Baptist had made known to the disciples, and which the other followed as a consequence), the *expression* by which He signifies all the miracles in general which they should behold with Him; and were these not, too, heaven-openings and the service of angels? He teaches them that they are so to be regarded; for they are *signs* and tokens of that open communication which subsists between this *Son of Man* upon earth, and the heavenly powers and messengers. For that reason it is that He terms Himself the Son of Man, in the full and pregnant sense of that name, which He henceforward commonly assumes to Himself: thereby at the same time responding to Nathanael's confession, ver. 49, "Yes, I am the Son of God in humanity." He had made latent reference to Jacob-Israel's history when He spake of the Israelite without guile; He recurs to it once more, and refers to what once symbolically occurred at Bethel. It is written in Moses, concerning that ladder of heaven, that *the angels of God ascended and descended upon it*; and the disciples could not but think of it when the Lord uttered these well-known words. This first word of instruction, consequently, which begins to unlock the Scripture to them, was designed to teach them in the symbolical style of Holy Writ, "where I am, there is in the reality of its fulfilment, the house of God and the gate of heaven; and this ye shall all see and experience by faith. He who in the old time stood above that ladder with His elect Israel upon the earth below, has now descended, as the Son of Man, Himself the true and proper Israel, in whom the calling and regeneration of all Israelites is perfected. The angels of God, long round about man upon earth (wherefore it was there said—they *ascended* and descended) are all now gathered together around the person of the Son of God, and the Son of Man, through whom heaven is once more opened to all who believe in Him. Oh how often may we suppose them afterwards at sublime critical moments of the revelation of His glory, and not merely when signs and miracles are wrought, to have recalled these words ;—how often was it to their faith, as if they had seen that which He had spoken of! But what our faith thus sees, is truly and really more distinctly seen than with the bodily eye it could be. Fellowship with the unseen world is opened up once more in Christ. This is the first of all the promises which He gave to His disciples.[1]

THE FIRST WORD OF HIS DIVINITY AT THE FIRST MIRACLE.

(Jno. ii. 4, 7, 8.)

What was Mary's design in mentioning that the wine had failed? What would she thereby signify to her Son? Assuredly not[2] the expediency of now breaking up, in order to save their kind hosts from being thrown into embarrassment. Such departure before the customary and appointed time would have been still more unbecoming and offensive: besides which our Lord's answer, which certainly must correspond with Mary's thoughts, bears a different application. Neither does so decisive a rejection of His Mother's interference befit a simple suggestion as to the propriety of departing: nor *concerning that* can we suppose him to have said—My time is not yet come. Furthermore, Mary says not expressly—they have no more wine: but simply—wine is wanting. But that is not otherwise to be understood than as conveying a hint, question and supplication :—shouldst thou not have resources and help for this emergency? Is not this the fit hour, to manifest Thyself in might of miracle? (By supplying, may it be, the marriage-present omitted by us in our poverty?) Mary has very long, and with constant longing, waited for such manifestation of her Son. He has not yet accomplished any miracles,[3] though greater than Moses and Elias: and she is amply justified in expecting them, especially since the witness of John and His own public presentation of Himself.

[1] See Oetinger—Schrift von Auberlen p. 537.

[2] Though even Bengel thought so.

[3] For the apocryphal legends concerning earlier miracles are utterly discredited by a word of St John (ver. 11)—this beginning of miracles did Jesus in Cana. Ταύτην—who could have imagined *this*?

If the first disciples (in whose company they were at this time) had spoken ought of the promise—"hereafter ye shall see"—this would have stimulated her expectation to the highest intensity. She is even warranted to infer, from His acceptance of the invitation to the wedding, that He would not deem *such* a first use of His miracle-working power unseemly: she perceives, indeed, with exquisite discernment, the intention of the Lord; His will responds to her prophetic wish. It is her prerogative alone, to be capable of conceiving—before it takes place—the amazing grace and condescension of His *first miracle*.[1]

And does He, nevertheless, repel her? Does He, nevertheless, rebuke her suggestion, and in such wise as to prevent her from ever so speaking again? He actually accomplished afterwards, what she by gentle insinuation had asked of Him,—because she divined His thought as no other did—and yet, before He does so, there is this severe sharp word instead of the glad acknowledgment,—yes, thy thoughts are also my thoughts. Wherefore was this? Because with all that was sound and right in her motive, there is yet mingled a certain human impatience, an over-curious intermeddling with a matter, about which even His Mother must now keep silence and wait:—the slightest possible touch of the purest womanly-motherly complacency (we know no other word) prompting in her the desire to see *her son* honoured in her presence. Because, also, from this time forward, He, in His office and function, may no more be her son; and therefore takes the first occasion to tell her so once and for all. Here lies the deep significance of this *another First Word*, by which, conformably with that meet dignity with which His heavenly Father had invested Him, He releases and disengages Himself from every relation of regard and dependance which, as child, He had sustained to His Mother according to the flesh. The holy woman who, after having borne Him as Virgin, became Joseph's wife and widow, is nothing more than this throughout: nor ever may be more, as in heaven she is not, so neither upon earth. He who is not Joseph's son, but the Son of God, at the

1 Thus much we admit—but no more. That Jesus had previously given a hint of His intention, of which Mary only too prematurely reminded him, we hold to be quite improbable, as unsupported by any intimation whatever.

very assumption of His Prophetic office, and through all its functions, shows that He deems Himself not the son of Mary, but Him whom the Father had sanctified and sent into the world. How does the idolatrous fancy of His Mother's interposition with Him in heavenly mediation, fade away before this clear utterance at the outset! Yea rather, even when she approaches nearest to the inner comprehension of His divine-human purpose, even there will her fallible humanity betray its want of perfect harmony: and the Spirit of the Father in Him, provident for futurity, prompts this solemn, and earnest, and decisive utterance, as a witness against all the Mariolatry of His future grossly-erring church. Further on, this error is again most distinctly aimed at, in that other word—who is my mother? Whosoever shall do the will of my Father which is in heaven, the same is my brother and sister and mother. Matt. xii. 48, 50. And again: blessed indeed is she whose womb bare, and she whose breast hath nourished me; but only blessed because she hath believed, in common with all who hear the word of God and keep it. Lu. xi. 27, 28. In what way He addressed and how He honoured His mother, as her child and son, the Scripture records not; but it is recorded, that His first word to her in His ministry, and the last to her upon the Cross—though the testament of His filial love—terms her woman and nothing more.

The German translation "Weib, was hast *du* mit mir zu schaffen?" (Eng.: woman, what hast thou to do with me?) fails in many ways to convey the spirit of the original text. First of all, the appellation should close the sentence, because the reason why she is not termed mother, must at the beginning be indicated in order that such a repulse might be justified to all other women. Their "frau" (woman) bears quite a different meaning from the "weib" of our day:—it is an appellation by no means derogatory, but, under the circumstances, very affectionate, as in Jno. iv. 21, xx. 15. Lastly, *τί ἐμοὶ καὶ σοί*[1]—more correctly:—What have *I* in common with thee? since His person by right and honour

[1] This formula *e.g.* also 2 Sam. xvi. 10; 1 Kin. xvii. 18, signifies nothing hard or severe. Whether it was a common phrase of men towards women in general, and not at all for worthy gentlewomen, as Lange supposes, I much doubt, and can find nothing to corroborate it in *γύναι*.

must have precedence—involves no more, no less than this: when my office and its ministry are concerned, is it not for thee to retire, and forget that thou art my mother? "That which in me works miracles was not born of thee." (Augustine.)

This is the first part of our Lord's word, ever solemn and severe as a testimony for the truth in all nearer and remoter futurity. But no sooner has He, in holy submission to the Father, thus denied the affections of His human filial heart, than He changes His voice, and so modifies His speech, as to console her with all affection for the restriction and repression to which His words had subjected her. The other part of this saying, which is now adjoined, tends to assure her:—thou hast understood me, as I understand thee, I will and shall do what thou meanest. That Mary has so understood him, her own next words to the servants (clinging as they do to His last word, persisting in expectation of a miracle, and more confident than ever) most decisively attest:—whatsoever He saith unto you, do it! Yet does it become the holy dignity of the Lord to prescribe a set time, in order that Mary, and with her whosoever may read this *First Word at the beginning of His miracles*, should observe and take good heed, that all His works are done, only in the manner and at the time when the Son, under the authority of the Father, wills: that *their time and their hour* are fore-appointed, independently of human will and wish—My hour is not yet come! And though it were not even a matter of a day earlier or later (as afterwards when He repeats the same saying to *His brethren* concerning going up to the feast), but, as here to all appearance about something still less important: nevertheless, He doeth all things great and small alike, at their own critical moment. That is a word of divine value, which is written in Ecc. iii. 11. Hence did the Evangelist derive it, when he once and again testified:—His hour was not yet come, Jno. vii. 30; viii. 20. He Himself knew and bore witness when His hour had finally come (Jno. xii. 27; xiii. 1; xvii. 1; Matt. xxvi. 45.)

That was the last great hour of the glorification of the Son of Man in sufferings: but here He speaks not of that. Of what hour then? Does He refer *merely* to the right hour and moment for the performance of the miracle at the marriage in Cana? If we have felt the depth of meaning in all the other first words of the Lord, we shall be scarcely induced to believe that this sublime expression, so sublimely repeated by Himself at His passion, "My hour is not yet come," means no more *now when He utters it first* than just to intimate for the present occasion—a few minutes more and then is the right time. No, for we observe finally, that the error which was checked in Mary involved something more than the before-mentioned forwardness of motherly longing and interference. There was fundamentally mixed up with it the notion which was to the last shared by all the disciples, of the earthly glory of His kingdom. The error of supposing that He was come to supply all their need, to defend them from all want, to create around them happiness and joy, had in some degree contributed to the expectation that He would now furnish the wine. It is to this that the Lord's wisdom, which looks through the immediate occasion into the widest connexions of His truth, and contemplates in the individual circumstances of the present the last futurity which they pretypify, addresses itself now. When He says, My hour is not yet come, He is thinking, we may presume, in His secret mind (we dare so boldly to penetrate the depths of His thought) of that time when all shall be fulfilled, which the wedding-feast at Cana, and the cheerful wine—the first gift of His saving power and kindness—symbolically foretold. That hour of His established kingdom, when the fruit of the grape shall be drunk new, is *not yet* come—we must say this even yet[1]—but as surely as the sufferings of Christ did come, and in His church continue, the hour of glory will come after them.

Mary's confident faith after this humiliation hastened the hour; so that it was probably for the sake of *her* word that He turned to the servants. We may say generally concerning the words recorded as having been spoken to the servants, that they are an example of those altogether external, earthly, and merely human words which the Lord must have often spoken amid the circumstances of His life in the flesh, but which are in general not preserved. Yet when we look more narrowly into them, we find the reason why the evangelist who relates so

[1] And also learn, that the very last hour of need must previously come, when the Church will appear ready to give up the ghost. See the beautiful reference to the impatience of the "English apostles' in Böttiger's essay upon them, p. 102.

concisely, and with so much omission, the history of the miracles, has not passed them over: yea rather this example begins to impress it upon us that the Lord can have spoken scarcely any thing without some deeper meaning underlying the manner and matter of his words. He calls the *water* to bear witness of the existing gift and creature of God, which He will wonderfully change; for every miracle designedly attaches itself to something natural, which it may elevate and transfigure. Only Dr Paulus' infatuated perversity could suppose, that for a true miracle the wine ought to have been drawn immediately from the empty pitchers. Jesus commands that the whole of the six *waterpots* which were there for the *Jewish* purification (out of which the first manifestation of the glory of His new grace should come forth) should be *filled*, in order that not a little of the miraculous wine should remain over as a dowry: for this was as befitting on the present occasion as in Elijah's gift out of God's fulness, when the oil ceased not, till there was no longer a vessel to receive it. The servants fill them *to the brim*—strictly complying with Mary's direction, that they should do whatever He said unto them; and now they wait, looking at Him and not at the water, which *in the mean time* is made wine. Then speaks He majestically, precisely defining the instant of the creating miracle: draw out *now*[1]—and nevertheless in His humility discloses not what was transpiring. It would not have been possible for Him to say: draw out now the water, it shall have become wine;—or, the water which has been now made wine, as St John afterwards says. Finally, His directing the servants to carry the wine to the governor of the feast,[2] appertains to the entire and gracious condescension of the whole. It stands a solitary example

[1] This *now* manifestly indicates the critical moment; after ye have filled, look then at what ye will draw forth! So that by no means merely what was drawn became wine. Let the text be looked at, in which *τὸ ὕδωρ* in ver. 9, is parallel with *ὕδατος* of ver. 7. And why else the specification of the quantity?

[2] For we must insist that this *ἀρχιτρίκλινος* is by no means a table-server or kitchen-master (which for Cana is not to be thought of) but the *συμποσιάρχης* or magister convivii, chosen from among the guests to be president of the banquet, in order to regulate the quantity of the drinking, and to administer all the various usages of social festivity. Ecclus. xxxii. 1—3. How does this graceful mention and acknowledgment of the title of *such* an office put to shame all our pedants. This man, who is in no marvelling humour, and whose ignorance of the

in the evangelical history, of His most full and benignant approximation to human order and custom; and that in a matter which belongs rather to the slighter things of life, rather to its hilarity than its earnest work.

THE FIRST PUBLIC OFFICIAL WORDS TO THE HOSTILE GUARDIANS OF THE TEMPLE.

(Jno. ii. 16—19.)

The Lord spake more than the world itself could have contained, had every one of His words been written in books. Which, then, out of the multitude, should be committed to record for the world and the church? Those which beyond the rest had especial importance, although no word of the Word upon earth could be deemed unimportant. The selection and arrangement were not left with man, but were the prerogative of the Holy Spirit, concerning whom the Lord's promise was, "He shall glorify me, for he shall take of mine and show it unto you." That Spirit took a historical picture out of the Lord's whole *life and work* from His birth to His ascension, and so shewed it to the Evangelists that in their mutually supplementary records, the glory of the only begotten Son shines forth to us full and unimpaired. The Spirit of inspiration in his mysterious control over those records has also so ordered it, that we have likewise received through the remembrance of St Matthew and St John, the careful investigation of St Luke, and the simple ministry of St Mark combined, the substance of our Lord's *discourses*, in a

miracle warrants the goodness of the wine, even as the knowledge of the servants does the reality of the miracle (according to *Richter's* striking observation), makes a light remark upon it—half praising, and half in jocose blame. From this, as well as from our Lord's disguising manner of speech, ver. 8, we observe, of course, that all the guests were not likely to be acquainted, and were not acquainted with the transaction.

[1] Schmieder has some important remarks upon this in its relation to Scripture in his "Preliminaries to a fundamental vindication of the Biblical history." Haumburg bei Klaffenbach, 1837.

true and genuine abstract. The art and truthfulness of all historical writing, which aims to condense out of an abundance of events a succinct narrative, consists, among other things, mainly in this, that the beginnings and turning points, the buds and germs of development, should be made prominent with as much fidelity to their truth, as skill in their presentation; just for instance as we see it realized in that perfect pattern—the Acts of the Apostles. But where beginnings and turning points occur in the earthly history of the Lord's life, we may expect that His words will have an especially outbeaming character. Accordingly we find in the Gospels a preliminary series of First words, which the Spirit has selected as the most critical in their occurrence, and most distinctive in their expression. These are together the critical moments of our Lord's development until He reached the time of His proper teaching and testimony before the people and His disciples: each one of them is indicated by a profound Word which expresses the true nature of the crisis. The Lord did actually thus speak them, but His Spirit alone could with perfect fidelity reproduce them in the Scripture, and hand them over to the Church. What He spake to His parents as their child when He ceased to be their child and entered into the developed consciousness of His being the Son of the Father;—what He spake to the forerunner as a man at His anointing to His office, and what to Satan in that first conflict which immediately followed; how He received the first disciples, and at His first miracle released Himself once more from His mother according to the flesh, as He had before done in that word of His childhood, and gave Himself entirely up to that eternal Spirit who ordered all things in Him in their time and hour;—all this we have already seen. Now follows His first public official word spoken to the present *adversaries* of His life and teaching, to the desecrating occupants of the temple, whom He is constrained by His zeal for God's house to chastise, and who therefore crucify Him, by that very act paving the way for the resurrection of the new temple out of the old. Another great turning-point in His life, in which we discern, through the light thrown upon it by the accompanying Word, the infolded germ and symbol of a future glorious development.

How great is the contrast between the manifestation of His *lov-*

ing kindness before His mother and disciples at the humble Galilæan wedding-festival, and that of His *judicial severity* before the Jews and their rulers in the temple at Jerusalem. The glory that was full of grace was also full of truth. He who came to diffuse joy, is come also to fan the threshing-floor, and vigorously to correct all that is ungodly in God's people and house. Not here where the desecration reigns did He give the first of His signs; but before He begins in Jerusalem at the Passover to work miracles, He announces Himself with all His holy severity in His Father's house, by an act of testimony *and authority*. And with that act, which is itself, equally with the miracles, a sign, He speaks a prophetic *miracle-word*, which till this beginning had reached its end in the building of the new temple of the new Church through His resurrection—points to that great miracle as the end and aim of all others.

The messenger sent before His face had prepared His way. Now came to His temple the Lord whom they had sought there in all their worship, the Angel of the Covenant whom they desired, but could not abide the day of His coming. He began His refining and purifying by an act of zeal which every true zealot in Israel, whether with or without office, would have been justified and indeed was bound to execute; but no man performed it, the traders and money-changers sat in the temple, speaking signs of its decline and perversion. Then is His Spirit stirred by the holy indignation of chastising truth; He does not merely speak, for no simple *word* alone would have said enough duly to denounce this omission of duty; He begins Himself *to act*, drives with the scourge the men and their cattle out of the temple,[1] pours out their mammon, overturns those unsanctified tables in the sanctuary, which exhibited to Him at His very entrance the Jewish nation of traffickers; then in full self-possession, and by design He softens His utterance, and passes, after affectionately sparing the doves (in which He sees not mere sacrifices as in the sheep and oxen, but also the symbol of the Holy Ghost) to that word which illustrates and explains the

[1] He never drives *into* the temple with the scourge—as it is very thoughtfully remarked in the evang. Kirchenzeitung 1845, p. 93. That He, moreover, did not merely drive out the cattle with the scourge is expressly stated in ver. 15.

deed :—*Take these things hence; make not my Father's house a house of merchandise.*

In this first decisive command, beginning with three majestic words, He neither mentions the temple nor the objects which desecrate it, but merely accompanies the self-explaining act with —*these* things *hence!* He speaks the language of emotion and holy, divine-human anger, which must have excited within the minds of all who heard a response that would carry its own conviction—belong *these* things *here?* Remove them hence! This indignation has gathered in His soul from one festival to another, as the disorder met His eyes: the time is now come, and it breaks out in an act, which may partly be regarded as long before projected and prepared for, partly, as the instantaneous product of a sudden internal resolve. This first severe word is followed (as in Cana, to His mother) by one more gentle, which gives ample explanation of His conduct. It is not without a silent remembrance of that word which His Father gave Him on His first entering the temple eighteen years before, that He now publicly calls God His Father. He does not reveal Himself before the world, however, with an independent and self-asserting testimony—I am His son!—He avoids every appearance of bearing loftily His own honour, and utters it as the unpremeditated and self-understood expression of His inner being, arising, as in the former instance when He was a youth of twelve years old, out of the circumstances of the present occasion. It was, indeed, and must ever have been to all who heard it, a word of new and mighty significance, that any son of man should call the Jehovah of Israel simply and distinctively *his* Father. It should have been for all the scribes, who, like Nathanael, had learnt in prophetic Scripture concerning the *Son* who was to come, a full and distinct answer to the question :—who art thou, and by what authority dost thou thus act and command? But they who now first heard *this* word, the most important of all that He said, appear remarkably enough to have scarcely seized its significance, in the heat of their vexation and in the confusion of what was taking place. They stood, indeed, in silence, and listened to every word, when the Lord after His silent act began also to speak; but it was only afterwards that they found calmness rightly to reflect upon the word which they had heard. The Lord had withal referred to a passage of the Scripture, to that rebuke which the Lord of Hosts had administered to His people in Jer. vii. 1—11 : trust ye not in lying words, saying, the temple of the Lord are these! Is *this house* which is called by my name, become a *den of robbers* in your eyes? But it is only at the second temple-cleansing at the close of His ministry that He quotes this saying in all its severity; for the present He softens the expression, and says instead :—make not my Father's house a *house of merchandize!* Whether they detected therein the tone of that prophetic saying must remain a question. We read that *the Jews* (as St John always markedly designates the rulers of the people in Jerusalem) do not as yet lift up their contradiction—how callest thou God thy own peculiar Father? For *this* declaration they pass over for the moment; they must examine it again and again : it must first excite opposition in the reluctance of their rebellious hearts, before they can strengthen themselves to oppose it in words. We do not read, further, that they committed themselves to any justification of the commerce in the Temple, for which subsequent reflexion might have placed many arguments at their command. For the impression of His sudden act, and the irresistible conviction of the words which followed it—*take these things hence!* have so entirely overpowered them, that they can find no words of defence. But how this man, rabbi, zealot, prophet, or what else, should have the power to assail the time-honoured abuses which they themselves had tolerated and even established, and that so summarily, not merely in word but in act, *this*, although the most superficial part of the whole procedure, absorbs their thoughts, because it is an injury to themselves, an invasion of their official prerogative. Forgetting the word in the *act*, and in the act forgetting the right of the thing done in the right of the *person* doing it—as always happens in similar circumstances—they speak in pitiable folly while thinking themselves wise :—*what sign showest thou unto us*, seeing that thou doest these things? Not : is it then true that merchandize and money-changing become not the temple? but :—who art *Thou*, who bearest such vigorous witness to this truth? (Acts vii. 35). Though He has already told them :—I am the Son of God, whose house this is, they come as the official temple-police and rulers of Israel with their question: wilt thou arrogate to thyself the *right of a prophet?* Not further than this, but so far at least, must the Lord's act have moved them, that they were constrained to bring back to their thoughts those long-gone times when men of God appeared before Israel, condemning even kings and priests, and vindicating their right to do so by signs from heaven. John the Baptist had already brought the times of the prophets near to them: but he did no miracle, and his word, as the voice of a preacher in the wilderness, had left their temple-trading undisturbed. If now this man (who had been with the Baptist, and many reports of singular incidents in connexion with him were circulated) assumes the right to go so much further in reproof than he, his pretension must be justified in our presence, according to the law of Moses for the testing of prophets. Thus their question had the appearance of a prudent and righteous restraint within lawful bounds, when dealing with what was wrong; and yet it was full of folly and blindness. A right was conceded at that time to every zealot or earnest man for the removal of abuses and corruptions in Israel, without any miraculous assertion on his part of prophetical dignity: but what the Lord had now done, spoke sufficiently for itself: His neglected word was with the act itself a mighty and miraculous sign of divine authority.

The Lord did not now, as He never afterwards did, *show* the Jews a sign at their demand: he *gives* them a sign instead which, according to the word of Moses (Deut. xiii. 1, 2) should *come to pass* in its own time, and thus fulfils all legal righteousness, so far as their question was actually grounded upon that. He leaves unanswered the evil of their question, and yet says to them:—*destroy this temple, and in three days I will raise it up.* A second word of mystery, in which His enemies found much food for their speculation, even till under the cross, and at the stone of the sepulchre.[1]

That the comment of the holy evangelist—He spake of the

[1] Pity that Hauff (Stud. u. Krit. 1849. 1. p. 106) should spoil his beautiful and tolerably correct confirmation of the Johannean interpretation, by maintaining at the outset, that inspiration did not so far secure from error, as to make the meaning of the words of Jesus perfectly plain!! To wish to be better instructed than the apostles, is now-a-days the incorrigible—folly of the learned.

temple of His body—must through the Holy Ghost be the true one, admits of no doubt to a *believing* student of Scripture, however hard it may be to *understand* it. That the Lord when He said "this," should have *pointed* to His own body, is in itself a strange idea, and is refuted by the instant apprehension of the Jews :—forty and six years was *this* temple in building—rather, so long has it already been in building! They could not possibly have overlooked so manifest a finger-sign. It is equally certain, on the other hand, that the Lord must have spoken of that temple, of that desecrated house of His Father, about which the question then was; for He proceeds now as ever, from the present circumstance to the deeper truth which He attaches to it; He speaks to the understanding of His hearers, so that they might understand, even where they will not. But no man *could* have *immediately* thought of the temple of His body at that time, as even the disciples perceived that latent meaning only after the resurrection. How can the question be solved but thus, that the Lord speaks of *both at the same time?*

And so, indeed, it was. This mysterious wonder-word has not a misleading double sense; but the two sides of its deep meaning are in reality one. For what is the *new temple* built by Christ, after that old one, new-built by Herod, was destroyed, but *His church*, the new people of God, the house of the Father and the Son, the sanctuary of the Holy Ghost? And is not this church *His body*, raised up and nourished out of His *risen body?* Again, did not the Jews, in destroying His body upon the cross, cast down their typical temple, and effect and work out its destruction? For *this* temple on which they in hypocrisy rely, while they honour not its Lord and receive Him not when He comes to it, is a *shadow and type* of the body and the church of the Lord. This is the plain key to the mystery which the Lord's saying, in its sublime and profoundly simple wisdom, gives to the foolishly wise in Israel to think upon. His word points impressively, and, as it ever is, in strict harmony with the occasion, from the shadow to the substance, thus opening up the mystery of that substance. He prophecies in the beginning, while they are asking Him for proof of His prophetic office, concerning the end; He unveils to them, if perchance they might apprehend it in subsequent reflection, the entire relation of His sanctified person to them and their temple-service; tells them, as the Searcher of hearts, how well He knows that they themselves, who should be the defenders of the temple, would be guilty of its destruction; and yet, that by the marvellous pre-arrangement of the counsel of God, the evil which they should do to the temple of His body would subserve at the same time the removal of all shadows, and the resurrection of the new and abiding, out of the death of the old. I know what I have to expect from you, and whither things will tend, better than ye yourselves now know: my zeal will still irritate your anger till that takes place for which I came into the world: till through my death at your hands the veil is rent asunder, and in my resurrection through the hand and power of God, the foundation of the true and real temple is laid. For I am indeed not come merely to punish, but to renew: yea, to restore again what *ye* destroy.

As the obvious literal sense of the restoration of the destroyed temple in three days involved what was utterly inconceivable, and it was not possible that they could consciously and intelligently ascribe such a meaning to the Lord, as He now and henceforward manifested Himself to them,—it was necessary that they should think out some solution, and for that very purpose was this word given to them. That they did so is evidenced by their recollection and use of it at the cross and the sepulchre, where they show themselves to have finally approached very near to a right understanding of its meaning.[1] Yet there they distort it, however, and conceal the testimony of their conscience, by perverting the former part of His words in the testimony of the false accusers, as if it was himself that proposed to *destroy*, whereas He said "destroy *ye!*" and in this conscious perversion they betrayed that they had marked whither the Lord's words had tended. Therefore do they clamour Him in bitter mockery to the cross, thus actually performing what he had predicted.

Destroy! This was spoken prophetically and permissively. I know that it will be in your hearts, and that ye will be permitted

[1] What they affirm in Matt. xxvii. 63 the Lord had never uttered *in their hearing* in so many words—but it may be regarded as their right interpretation of the discourses concerning the building again in three days, and the sign of Jonas, taken together. *Lange* has well observed against *Hase* (ii. 3. 1625) how natural it was that *they* should understand earlier and better than the Apostles, the Lord's hint that they would put Him to death, and how then ex opposito the saying concerning His resurrection would make itself plain to them.

to do it—then be it so and let it be done! That their persisting in opposition to the truth of God might lead so far as to bring upon them yet another destruction of their temple, as the due punishment of their own act and guilt—so much at least must immediately have touched their *conscience*, and it was that which the Lord addressed. That this might take place as the consequence of their putting *Him* to death, became more and more plain to them in the after time. But that His death would issue in a *Resurrection*, and thereby in a demolition of the typical temple in order to the building of a new one, nay rather to the specific building again in its fulfilled design of that which had been abolished (I will raise it up)—this is the great prophecy which the Lord utters to them here; this is already the self-same sign which He afterwards *gives* at their demand, the sign of the Prophet Jonas, that one last sign which was chosen as appropriate to the wicked spirit that demanded it.

There remains now only the question whether the Jews then perceived a connexion between *this temple* and the *temple of His body*, as the central idea of the entire saying; and thence were capable of understanding the double meaning of His word. We must here take into account the whole nature of the case, and the tone of feeling between the Lord and the rulers of the people must be presupposed. John had announced the Messiah's kingdom as nigh at hand; afterwards boldly proclaimed that He who was to come after him was already in the midst of the people; and at last had publicly pointed out Jesus of Nazareth. Even if the heads of the people in Jerusalem had received no intelligence of this last open indication of Jesus (which is improbable) yet must that which preceded it have been sufficient to raise in them such a degree of expectation, that if any one should follow the Baptist and strikingly announce Himself with the authority of a divine call, this must be *the Messiah*. To such preparation rightly to hear and understand it, did the first word of Jesus—"*my Father's* house"—make its appeal; and yet that word is, in the unthinking excitement of their anger, and not without a wanton disregard, utterly disregarded. For it was most clearly and significantly spoken. But when their counter-question, losing sight of the "Son of God," only asks after His prophet-authority; such reply as this was in the highest sense natural:—I am more than a Prophet, as I have already told you, if ye had been willing to hear aright. This is the general tone of the second word, as it strikes their conscience in order to open their ears. It was not spoken to be understood at the moment precisely, but for their subsequent consideration, when calmness should return: but then the scribes in Israel might well understand, how the Messiah should speak of the temple and His own person in connexion, as if in a certain sense they both were the same. For it was a doctrine that was familiar in the more recent orthodox biblical learning of the Jewish writings,[1] founded particularly upon Dan. ix. 24, as generally upon that deeper understanding of typical relations which was not altogether wanting;—that the Messiah was Himself, and should be called the Holy of Holies. Consequently our Lord speaks, however enigmatically for the present moment, yet plainly enough for after reflection; and admonishes the wicked guardians of the temple to think, in connexion with the type and shadow—to which indeed its own honour is due—of that higher significance of meaning in them of which they were not altogether unaware. He deals with the *scribes* by their theology, with the *men* by their conscience. The process of thought, which would be excited by this striking and not-to-be forgotten word, was somewhat as follows:—"what meant this mighty one,—who acted and spake before our eyes and our ears in so marvellous a manner, that we had no spirit to reply to him otherwise than by the demand of a sign—by that strange saying which He so undisguisedly and with such dignity spake to us? Assuredly he spoke not as a builder, who could build anew the temple! That we should destroy the temple! Its ruin to be our guilt! Did He mean that it would be through our opposing Him, and laying hands upon His holy person? What if he were truly the Messiah! For he spake before indeed of His Father's house. But can then the Messiah be put to death, may His holy body—itself a temple of God—be destroyed? That second word, again, was so peaceful, so resigned to all that we might do to Him and through Him to the Temple: He appeared not, with all His anger and zeal, as if He would op-

[1] Here must be sought the historical ground of it—and not in those gnostic reveries, to which *e.g.* Hilgenfeld amusingly refers this ναός, (Clementin. Recogn. p. 111).

pose us with force. Well, we understand it:—it is that He himself is the Archetype of the temple, and He signifies, that if we destroy the temple of His body, this that is made with hands will fall with Him!" Had their thoughts proceeded so far, *then indeed* the remaining sentence would have intimated to them:—do this, *I shall nevertheless conquer*, and in a short time the destroyed Temple will be erected anew! I *myself*—by my own authority will raise it up. But this was more than their theology of the person of the Messiah was wont to attribute to Him.

In three days—is by no means a proverbial expression for a short time: but the Lord thus early declares, although like most other prophecy, it was only understood in its fulfilment, what He knew in His spirit from the Scripture;—that He should rise again, in order to raise up the church from His body, on *the third day!* 1 Cor. xv. 4; Matt. xii. 40, xx. 19; Hos. vi. 2. How clearly did He see the future from the beginning! How deep consciousness had He of the way and goal of His life and death, what an insight of consummate wisdom into the whole counsel and plan of His Father! He knows His relation to the masters of the present temple who opposed the truth, and with whom by this public signal He now begins the fore-appointed warfare of His testimony; He knows, that He himself is the true temple of which that typical one prophecied in its time; that He must yield himself up to receive death at the hands of the Jews, in order that the true sanctuary, after the shadow has in natural consequence passed away, may rise up from His resurrection. He is, finally, prepared to yield Himself up, for He knows that thus shall He bear the sins of those who slay him, and who thereby fulfil the design of the Old Testament in order to a new and everlasting covenant of grace, in which the essential truth of the old covenant comes forth to perfection. This still, calmly-sublime preparation for the dedication of Himself to that warfare—through blood leading to victory—with the blind ministers of that Divine counsel which indeed He only as yet penetrates; this clear all-comprehensive consciousness of the near approach of the end, and fulfilment, and glorification of the Old Testament economy, as also of the inner, essential relation of His own sanctified person to the whole; this is the central spirit of the Word which He utters at this great crisis of His life. He utters it, assuredly, rather for the hearing and understanding of the disciples who stood around Him, and who afterwards when the sign had come to pass, should think upon it, and should believe the *Scripture* and His words *drawn from the depths of Scripture;* than for His enemies, who neither would nor could understand Him. But He utters it, at the same time, with highest dignity, for the satisfaction of His own consciousness of what was just sufficient to that end. What the later teaching of the New Testament fully developes in the Epistle to the Hebrews, is already wrapped up as a germ in this early word of our Lord.

To prove them, whether they would understand, the Lord spake this to the Jews,—but they would not. They break out again in petulant, hasty, and vexatious objection—which only touches the surface of the matter; and treat the mysterious word which had been spoken in such majestic calmness, as unworthy of their silent attention and subsequent thought. He therefore keeps silence, in order, if possible, to force them to reflexion. They seem to desire no specific second reply, therefore He gives them none, and for this time they separate; He lets them remain, they let Him go. Thereupon He actually performs, after their arrogant demand had been repelled, those miracles in His humility which might bring many to believe on His name, although He knows that the faith which hangs upon miracles is not the true one. Thereupon one comes out from among the rulers, who has ingenuously pondered what he had heard and seen; gives his confession instead of all the rest of his colleagues who had suppressed it as it was rising in their consciences; and receives as the gracious recompense of his coming in the night, that new and impressive word of the Light of the world. Then does the Lord retreat with His disciples from the capital into the land of Judea, and baptizes them, as John had done, with a transitional baptism. When the enmity of the Pharisees begins to be excited, He returns back again to Galilee the second time since His appearance to Israel. He speaks in the way with the Samaritan woman, performs in Cana that other miracle, and begins at last *publicly to teach and preach in Galilee,* having His abode in Capernaum after His own

Nazareth had evil intreated him, and from thence making the circuit of the land and the synagogues. So that the strict chronological order would require the contents of the third and fourth chapters of St John, and even of St Luke iv. 16—30, to be inserted before we return to the Gospel of St Matthew. But we are disposed to leave the order of time, which soon becomes indistinct in the details, and is seldom of much importance for the understanding of our Lord's discourses; and for the present to follow each Evangelist singly, with references merely to the parallel places in the others, in order to anticipate in their connexion the whole of these profoundly significant *first words*. The Lord had already taught in their synagogues all round before His rejection at Nazareth (Lu. iv. 15); after that, He went forth still verging towards Capernaum. St Matthew briefly indicates this (iv. 13); and condenses the whole Galilæan preaching into one general expression, as what Jesus *from that time began* to preach and to teach.

THE GOSPEL OF ST MATTHEW.

THE SUBSTANCE OF THE FIRST PREACHING TO THE PEOPLE.

(Matt. iv. 17 ; Mar. i. 15.)

Again therefore another *First word*—the *seventh* as far as it may be connected with the sixth already touched upon—the first public word of *Preaching to the people*. There intervene, however, occasional testimonies to individual men, recorded by St John, and the first preaching in Nazareth ; which St Luke gives us, runs nearly parallel with it. It is not, further, so much a single utterance, once spoken on a specific occasion, as a compendious summary of his first preaching, which repeated itself in words of which these are a type. Thus it may be regarded as an introduction of that connected series of Discourses, which St Matthew gives us first of all, and with him St Mark and St Luke.

The Lord commences His preaching with the same words which the Forerunner had already uttered (Matt. iii. 2) ; in order that He may prepare the way for Himself and His announcement of the kingdom of God which had now appeared—the gospel gladtidings revealed to faith. For He is ever and throughout His whole preaching and prophetic office His own peculiar Forerunner ; the preparer of His own way to His mediatorial and kingly office. This is the first thing which St Matthew records, in order to indicate that same transition from John to Jesus, which we discern also in St John's history of the baptism (iii. 26 ; iv. 1). It is not immediately said—I, the King of this kingdom, am come ; nor is it, *My* kingdom ;—the Lord preserves the first utterance of this lofty expression for His disciples, in

His humiliation (Lu. xxii. 30)[1], and before Pilate; leading the way to it by the expression—the Son of Man and *His* kingdom (Matt. xiii. 41; xvi. 28; comp. xx. 21). The *kingdom of heaven:* —an expression which was hardly then already extant among the Jews, but probably originated in the Baptist's words as a most decisive protest against false notions of an earthly kingdom, and thence passed over into the *later* Rabbinical doctrine to denote the idea of the Messianic kingdom, which had indeed existed from the beginning. This expression does not occur in all the Old Testament, but is prepared for in such passages as Dan. ii. 44. The word of expectation which had been hitherto familiar—*the kingdom of God*—was taken from the Prophets, and indeed transitionally developed in the Apocrypha (Ecclus. x. 10). This continues to be the expression in the Gospels of St Mark, St Luke, and St John (only Jno. iii. 3, 5), and throughout the New Testament, with the exception of St Matthew, who, bringing into prominence the opposition between the true fulfilment and the Jewish expectation, joins with "the kingdom of God" the *kingdom of heaven*, in his record of our Lord's discourses. But the apostles use this word no more, as the Prophets have it not at all.[1]

It is *at hand*, says the Lord again, as the Baptist had said, and as His messengers were to say at their first mission in Israel, ch. x. 7. It is exhibited as just descending from heaven to earth, where a state of imperfection is, and the dominion of sin: afterwards it is said more decisively:—the kingdom of God is *come* to you (ἔφθασεν, ch. xii. 28), is in your midst, present within you (Lu. xvii. 21). But where the expression *kingdom of heaven* is used, the word always includes a reference to the Future of its true consummation, as connected with the secret preparations for that Future, as will be more fully seen in Matt. v. 3, 10, 20.

It comes otherwise than Israel supposed; therefore is the necessary condition of *repentance* prefixed. It demands a new and heavenly mind, with the rejection of the old spirit; it requires and brings with it, a new heart and a new spirit, Ezek. xviii. 31. That was the impressive, unexpected preaching of the Baptist: but only unexpected, because Israel had forgotten what was the

[1] For 2 Tim. iv. 18 is a quite different form of expression.

substance and result, the tenor and conclusion of all the prophecy and preaching of the Prophets. The last and greatest Prophet before Christ utters at the close of the Old Testament this great and comprehensive word: and Christ Himself as the Prophet of His new kingdom of grace, takes it up again, for it is the essential word of connexion betwen the Old and the New Testaments. It remains also the ever-recurring word of preparation for faith, and the reception of grace; for the kingdom of heaven belongs only to the spiritually poor and mourners in heart. All the apostles preach repentance and faith; purification from all former sins may never be dispensed with till the final entrance into the everlasting kingdom (2 Pet. i. 9—11); and even from heaven the Lord cries to His church below—Repent! Rev. ii. 5—16; iii. 3, 19.

Mark further this "*for*" between the two phrases, which is the true link between the preaching which demands, and the promise which bestows:—a word which, though it contains the pith of the sense, has been omitted, alas! from our German Bible in both places! "The desire for the kingdom of heaven should be the motive of repentance."[1] No true and perfect repentance can spring merely from the terror of the law; the law preaches no distinctive repentance, but life for the righteous and death to all sinners. But all the prophets and John had, on the ground of promised grace, exhorted to repentance: thereby, as in a word of mercy, offering also the gift of repentance unto life, even as the Lord and His Apostles do. Acts v. 31, xi. 18. Thus is folded up in this introductory word of the Lord the whole substance, the essential principle of all the exhortations of God to sinners. It binds in indissoluble and inscrutable connection the divine gift and the free acceptance of man:—*Will ye* and *Grace!* That is here foreshadowed which the Sermon on the Mount only further develops. But he who hears not and does not this, who is not made willing to repent in sincere poverty of spirit for the sake of the kingdom of heaven; to him the kingdom of heaven comes only *near*, alas! without being his portion and consolation (Lu. x. 11).

St Mark gives us another compend of this first preaching of

[1] Synod of Bern: Orders for the regulation of the doctrine and life of ministers and preachers in the town and canton of Bern, &c. 1632. A most weighty encyclical!

our Lord; and announces more fully what the Lord had said on another occasion, when He had advanced a step further into *His own* more distinctive preaching. The publican Matthew stops at the preaching of repentance, which the Baptist had made so emphatic to himself: he would now lay stress upon it for the people of Israel as the Messiah's preaching *also*. St Mark, on the other hand, takes up that addition which he had received from Peter, the man of faith, and represents the Lord as saying—repent *and believe the Gospel*. In that first brief exhortation, indeed, in which Christ and John hold the same language, *faith* was understood as the unexpressed middle-term; just as in the *believe* of the later purely evangelical preaching *repentance* is always presupposed without being mentioned, as preceding, accompanying, and following faith. Both are inseparably and essentially joined in the true μετανοεῖν, which in the very abandonment of sin presses on to lay hold upon mercy.[1] But yet Christ's ministry of grace more manifestly exhibits itself in this advancement in the expression: for the announcement of the kingdom of heaven comes forward into the *foreground* by this addition especially,—believe *the Gospel*. This is a new, fundamental, and principal idea. The *word* which denotes it is found in the Old Testament in a general human sense (2 Sam. xviii. 25); and in prophetic preparatory allusion (Ps. xl. 10, בִּשַּׂרְתִּי צֶדֶק—Is. xl. 9, lii. 7, lxi. 1; Lu. iv. 18); but as the most distinctive designation of the last and finished tidings of grace to human faith it is found first in the lips of *Christ*. That was also glad tidings which the Baptist announced (Lu. iii. 18 εὐηγγελίζατο); but it is the Lord who first preaches the Gospel of the kingdom, by proclaiming its actual existence, Mark i. 1; Matt. iv. 23, xi. 5; Lu. iv. 43; xvi. 16. For it was *His* alone to say:—*The fulness of the time is come!* Gal. iv. 4. The design of the Old Covenant is accomplished; the set time of waiting and preparation, which, according to the hidden counsel of God, was necessary for the sake of humanity at large, has

[1] It is not a proper use of the Lord's word, though otherwise applicable enough to a memorial of Luther, and only too significant for our own age, that upon the monument at Wittenberg the inscription is curtailed:—Glaubet an das Evangelium (believe the Gospel)—without the little word that precedes—Repent!

expired. The Son is born, has grown to maturity, has been anointed and tempted. The testimony of him who was to bear Him witness has been uttered, and now He bears witness to Himself. Now begins that last speaking of God by His Son (Heb. i. 2), *the Gospel,* which henceforth is to be preached in all the world till the end cometh, Matt. xxiv. 14. What a glance into the Past and the Future is this! What an announcement is this, wrapping up in mystery the deep things of the counsel of God (casting down every unlawful question—why not before?), and yet revealing to the penitent sinner all that is necessary for his faith! The time is fulfilled, the hour is come. I am come—come then all to me and see, but come with repentance, taste and see in faith! He does not indeed say openly at this beginning—believe in *Me!* but that this is His meaning was plainly to be understood. For what else could be faith in the coming *fulfilment* of all that had been promised?

THE CALLING OF THE FISHERS OF MEN.

(Matt. iv. 19; Mar. i. 17 [Lu. v. 4, 10]).

The Evangelists, according to the wisdom of the Holy Ghost, whose influence and direction they only unconsciously felt, were under the necessity of distributing in portions what was allotted to them to record. Thus here in the calling of the two pairs of brothers from their fishing-nets to the permanent following of the Lord. That their release from their earthly toil and calling was gradual and progressive, as we gather from St John, St Matthew, and St Luke together, might have been presupposed as more natural and likely; although St Matthew's call afterwards appears to present an example of an almost instantaneous enlightenment and separation from all. St Matthew, when he mentions Simon with the addition, "who was called Peter"—presupposes the giving of the new name at his former confession, of which he could scarcely have been ignorant: but St Luke's account, ch. v. 3—5, requires no more than that some such earlier relations between the Lord and these fishermen must be understood by his readers.

That Peter, especially, was designed for a distinctive personal position in this now-approaching kingdom of God; that the Lord purposed to form him into something especial, his new name, according to the analogy of such namings in the Old Testament, had sufficiently foretold. The preparation for this was indicated in the early beginning of the formation of a circle of apostles and disciples around the Lord in such a manner, that the command —*follow me!* now developed a still more comprehensive meaning. Yet those, who already surrounded the Lord as "His disciples" at Cana, went back in the interim to their fishing again; and it is at a subsequent critical moment that the Lord clearly reveals it to them, that the time is come when they must leave their ships and their nets as an ordinary occupation. Then they *followed Him* altogether, remained wholly in his company; as in past times the servants and disciples of the prophets had done according to custom and propriety, and in a later age the scholars of those who were called Rabbi among the Israelites (*Δεῦτε ὀπίσω μου*, לְכוּ אַחֲרַי, 1 Kings xix. 20, 21). This St Matthew significantly records, without relating more concerning the external occasion of it, than simply that Jesus walking by the sea *saw them* casting their net into the sea, and afterwards the two others mending their nets. Had anything more occurred at the time (as in Lu. v.), his account, as we now read it, would bear upon it the mark of actual untruthfulness. Thus the distinctive significance of this critical turning-point lies altogether and only in that internal glance of our Lord, which, regarding them as fishermen, contemplates in this lower calling which is revoked, that higher one, which He now for the first time clearly unfolds to them:—From henceforth leave this net; ye shall in my discipleship be prepared to cast the net of the kingdom of heaven into the sea of the nations (ch. xiii. 47); remain fishermen still, but in a higher style—henceforth ye shall catch men!

Two things claim our attention here:—how the Lord's profound wisdom lays hold of everything lower and external to become the *images* of things and relations in the kingdom of heaven; and also how familiarly His thought and language attach themselves to those *Old Testament typical expressions* in which the Spirit had already prophetically exhibited all the germs of the New Testament consummation. There is in the discourses of

Jesus much more of such reference to the language of the Old Testament than is discerned by ordinary exposition; so much, indeed, that we have never finished tracing it. It is not a casual matter, but a real though secret prelude of the Holy Ghost, that the Lord named in Jeremiah (xvi. 16), those who were sent forth for the restoration of Israel *fishermen*; and again in Ezekiel (xlvii. 10) spoke of the fishers who should gather exceeding many fishes in the new waters of the living. That which there pointed into the most remote futurity of the kingdom of God, is here beginning to be manifest; and the previous fisher-condition of the first Apostles was itself a pre-intimation; just as it has pleased Divine Providence in the case of *many other* important persons to shadow out their future calling in their earlier relations in life —in David's sheepfold, for instance, his own kingdom and that of his greater Architype.

Finally: I will make you fishers of men! This signifies not merely, I now by my prerogative appoint and call you to this; nor simply, I will from this time forwards, as your new master, train you for this; not merely even, I will qualify you for it, by creating you into some new thing, which I only can do. But there is included the promise: ye shall, with success and blessing, labour in the ministry of my word, which shall catch men, even as your nets the fish. This latter meaning comes out with especial prominence in the two prophetic draughts of fishes; at the outset in St Luke v. more remotely, but with perfect clearness; and in the latter after the resurrection, the symbolical import of which St John points out to us in his own manner, in all its full significance, ch. xxi. 6—11. I will make you into fishers of *men*, thou shalt catch *men*—these words are uttered by the Saviour of mankind with the same emphasis of love, with which He afterwards testified "I am not come to destroy men's lives but to save them," Luke ix. 56. How infinitely more excellent and lofty a calling! Whatever else His grace made of these Galilean fishermen, themselves sinful men who had been just by Him gathered and saved, even up to their thrones and crowns of apostolical dignity in the regeneration of the world; *this one thing* remains the climax and the crown of their honour and dignity, that they were made ministers and helpers of the grace which saved mankind.

Now they who would regard Luke v. 1—11 as merely a more specific account of the same circumstance which St Matthew has more generally narrated, do it at the peril of dealing with the Scripture as if it were not the holy word of God. This cannot we do. The positive expressions of the Evangelist, Matt. v. 18, 19, mark out definitely a situation which cannot be made identical with the account of St Luke, without imputing to a fellow apostle actual ignorance of these especial circumstances; or actual incorrectness, and not merely concealment, to the Spirit who inspired the Gospels, exercising a divine supervision and moulding the human element in them. The latter is to us still less conceivable even than the former. Peter continues to hold his house at Capernaum (viii. 14) and thereby his connexion with his property. He must not be supposed to have sold and given this to the poor, but only to have given up his ordinary occupation. Jesus many times afterwards sailed in his ship, sent him away as a fisherman with his hook, when there arose a necessity (Matt. xvii. 27); even after the resurrection Peter still speaks quite naturally of going a fishing (Jno. xxi. 3)—though nearer indeed than he then thought to the final call which released him from it for ever. All this makes St Luke's account sufficiently plain.

The Lord *prayed* Simon (ἠρώτησεν, as in St Lu. iv. 38, vii. 3—36), an interesting indication of the human lowliness with which the Master was wont to speak to his disciples on even such matters. His language only becomes imperative—though it would always befit it to be so—when He is about, in His wonderful promise, to bless and reward the service which He asked:—Launch out into the deep, yet further from the land, cast your nets down εἰς ἄγραν, *i.e.* not as on ordinary occasions, with the design to catch; but it is a promise as in Jno. xxi. 6: καὶ εὑρήσετε (comp. Lu. v. 9). Simon was already a disciple of Jesus, calls Him *Master:* now whether the Master better understands fishing, too, he can scarcely determine; but he soon turns away from all natural considerations, to simple faith in the word of

[1] This does not indicate, as Roos supposes, a slight alienation from Peter—for the Lord had certainly many times made requests to His disciples.

Him who had just been speaking the Word of God from his ship. The great multitude of fishes, whereas the whole night before they had taken nothing, rightly appears to him a miraculous sign; he feels his sinfulness, and shrinks before the power of God; calls his Master now also his *Lord;* and would as simply as foolishly remove himself in fear from His fellowship.[1] Yet is his meaning better than his language—he utters "the noblest feeling in the most unskilful words."[2] It pleases the Spirit of God to give him just at this instant such a deep consciousness of sin as for the time he could not control: and that is the characteristic moment which the Lord seizes for repeating, in order to its further and decisive confirmation, that which he had once before said to him: *From henceforth thou shall catch men!* Now is the *promise* which had been contained in the word which called them first, made more plain by the miraculous sign; which, occurring at the end of the Lord's sermon, was a fit type of that preaching itself. Now also is Simon's unworthiness and unfitness for that, which the Lord designed to make him, revealed out of the depth of his heart; and therefore further is that sublimely gracious word added, which the Lord has since then spoken to so many besides the first Apostle, which He speaks to us all;—that peculiar word of New Testament mercy, with which the angels in the time of consummation begin anew: *Fear not!* This word in His lips raises to its highest fulfilment of force and meaning, that which had been from the very beginning begun to be uttered in the old covenant, where the angels thus speak to terrified and sinful men (Dan. x. 12—19); and the revealing and witnessing Lord Himself, from the calling of Abraham down to the latest encouragement sent by the Prophets (Gen. xv. 1, xxvi. 24, xlvi. 3; Deut. i. 21; Josh i. 9, viii. 1; Judg. vi. 23; 2 Kings i. 15; Isa. vii. 4, x. 24, xli. 10, 13, 14, &c. down to Hagg. ii. 5; Zech. viii. 13, 15). Thus then is this word now uttered by Jesus, *at once* a word of *divine majesty* to the "sinful man" Peter (Fear

1 Lu. iv. 33—41. had *not* taken place just before in order of time, though in St Luke's Gospel it occurs just before. *Then* would Simon's conduct have been strange indeed—as Schleiermacher says quite correctly.

2 So far rightly Lange. But that he only feared for himself the continued oppressive enjoyment of this present blessing, does not appear. There is rather an actual putting away of the Lord's society.

not, Peter! as before Fear not, Abram!)—and a word of kindness from the *Son of Man*, the *Sinner's Saviour*, as if there had been already added, Be not afraid, *only believe!* Mark v. 36; John xiv. 1.

But when the Evangelist St Luke, further removed from the event, closes the history with—they forsook all and followed Him—he may be well supposed to have designed to record their special and distinctive call, without a clear knowledge of that earlier one: although his history itself obviously implies relations between the Master and these fishermen which must previously have commenced.

THE SERMON ON THE MOUNT.

(Matt. v.—vii.; St Luke vi. 20—49.)

We[1] deem it our duty conscientiously to abstain from bewildering ourselves in the strife of the critics, as to whether these sayings of our Lord uttered, according to St Matthew's testimony, when he was set upon the Mount, were indeed spoken as one connected Discourse. We may not unite with those, who, losing the simplicity of their attention to the one only Teacher in their oblique regard to this Doctor on one side and that Rabbi on the other, and sacrificing more or less the humility of discipleship to their overmuch learning; yet are skilful and sharp-sighted enough in their own eyes to come forward with their decisions upon what the Holy Spirit has written for the Church, and to decree:—"Here there is connexion, and there none"—"This or that cannot be accepted because inconsistent with the Lord's own style of thought."[2]

1 Not a formula merely, for we speak indeed in the name of many like-minded with ourselves.

2 On revision we retract not one iota of this. Wieseler, indeed, very summarily decides, that the *first glance of the eye* gives authentic evidence of its having been collected from many several discourses—but the glance of *our* eye beholds it very differently. Let the incorrigible sophistry of such, alas, as Lange persist in asserting—"This or that would be in this way or the other more appropriate,—the Evangelist intended or wished, &c., &c.":—I know by the testimony of my lifelong reading, that every thing is there alone appropriate, where the

We, for our own part, judge not those of our faithful brethren and friends who suffer themselves to be led by an unfaithful system of interpretation, so far from the firm foundation: but to us it must ever be matter of conscience and honour before the supreme judicial throne of the highest criticism, to abstain from putting our own self-willed construction upon that word which we read in common *with* the Church, and which should be jealously kept inviolate as the holy text of our preaching *to* the Church. Had not the chair and the pulpit in the present day been so unhappily sundered, the perception of theologians otherwise faithful could not have become so blunted as to allow them to rise from St Matt. v. 1, 2, vii. 28, 29, viii. 1, without asking themselves:—"Can I expect the simple laity, the believing congregation, to believe me when I tell them,—*this is not true in its seeming sense!* Will they be either willing or able to conceive, that St Matthew or any other could deliberately collect together into one, various discourses uttered by our Lord at various times, and then inventing an imaginary frame to the picture, report it in so many words, as one discourse uttered in one place and at the same time?" Let him believe this who may: to us the thought is incredible; and that as we are persuaded, not through wilful opposition to the light of truth which would enter, but through a true perception in their inmost minds of the self-evidencing truth of the holy word; not through their dulness which cannot understand the grounds of critical evidence, but from that clearness of discernment which sees into their groundlessness.

Yes, the Lord's Spirit so brought the Lord's words to the Evangelists' remembrance, that though they might not write them down always according to the strict letter and word, yet they were enabled to give us their substance and contents with perfect truth: but the Spirit of Truth could never have permitted the slightest untruthfulness to have occurred in their record. St Matthew and St John had the Spirit in apostolical measure; St Mark and St Luke, ministers to the Word, stand indeed at one remove from them. But even they, although liable occasionally (by way of distinction) to transfer or confuse things of no im-

Holy Spirit, who well understood and truly glorified the words of Jesus, has written and placed it.

portance, have never—especially in reference to the time, place, and connexion of the longer discourses—in the very slightest degree possible fallen under any such imputation. This every one must be constrained to admit. Much less can St Matthew and St John be thought to have presumed to treat in any such way the words of the Word, whose eye witnesses and ministers they were—arranging, adjusting, and working them up, contrary to actual and absolute fact.[1] The deeper we penetrate into the relation which here subsists between the human and the divine, the clearer we discern, having any measure of faith in our interpretation of Scripture, the miracle which must have been wrought by the Spirit in the furnishing of the Evangelists for the task of handing down the discourses and the acts of our Lord : so much the further must we recede from the unseemly thought that this or that was put in order simply by man ; or rather shifted and deranged, in order that we, learned investigators of later times, might be needed to set it right again.

We cannot conceive that St Matthew could have wrought up sayings of our Lord uttered at various times into one connected whole, as if they had been spoken at one time: for as the apostolical humility of his own spirit was incapable of such an impropriety, so neither was it possible that the Holy Ghost should guide and instruct him to record any untruth whatsoever for the Church. That which St Luke, ch. vi. 20—49, gives us as the Lord's discourse, with essentially similar notification of *place*, vi. 17, and concluding asseveration, vii. 1, as St Matthew's, is manifestly the same Sermon on the Mount in another epitome : whence we should gather that we have only in St Matthew also an *abstract*, though his is more complete. The passages of the Sermon on the Mount which we find repeated elsewhere in *St Luke* are simple *repetitions* :—the Lord did indeed re-utter them at the time and place which St Luke mentions : and a sound exposition will prove that their mention *there* is quite consistent with the connexion. That the Lord should have uttered more than once, not simply His briefer moral sentences, but also His longer dis-

[1] Even though the nun of Dülmen affirms it (Sepp. ii. 261) it is not true ! and though men of the highest repute have for a long time past (*e.g. Kleuker*, Menschlicher Versuch, &c., p. 223) maintained it—I will protest from the deepest conviction !

courses, is not unworthy of the great Teacher in any point of view; is conformable both to His human condescension and His divine wisdom, and puts to shame the vanity of many a poor preacher who is ever striving to bring forth what, at least in words, will take a novel form. Within the individual Evangelists such recurrence is incontestible. For instance, St Matthew repeats what was already in the Sermon on the Mount in ch. xii. 33, xv. 14 (comp. Lu. vi. 39), xviii. 8, 9, (Mark ix. 43—47), xix. 9 (yet again in another place, Lu. xvi. 18), xxii. 5. Further repetitions are to be found in St Luke :—xi. 2—4 the prayer given in the same words, but with a more impressive design and meaning: xii. 22—34, the longer discourse against care; similarly ch. viii. 16 (Mar. iv. 21), xi. 33, xi. 9—13, 34—36, xii. 58, 59, xiii. 24—27, xiv. 34, 35 (Mark ix. 50), xvi. 13—17. Finally, in St Mark, ch. iv. 24, xi. 25, 26. These very repetitions, which the expositor must first read in the place where they are found, and then refer to their connexion in the original discourse, serve to indicate to us the Lord's Sermon on the Mount as what it really is, the preliminary abstract of His doctrine : and He Himself in repeating them, points out to us the especial significance of this His first sermon for the instruction of all people.

The Lord spoke from a mountain—upon one of the level platforms of which He stood surrounded by His disciples—to His disciples and to all the people from among whom He would call His disciples. The choice of a mountain had reference to something more than merely a fitting pulpit; as the mind of the Church has testified in the fidelity with which this circumstance has been retained to designate the sermon itself. As the Mediator of the New Covenant bringing grace for the fulfilment of the law, opens here His mouth to preach to us for the first time *salvation* (Heb. ii. 3): we involuntarily and naturally think of that mountain of the law, which preached condemnation. The Old Testament placed foremost the curse; the New, being glad tidings, begins with blessing. It is not "a second law" which proceeds now from the Lord:—who as He then gave His testimonies amid the tempest and darkness of Sinai, now in His love to man, sits down among them that they may sit at His feet and learn

His words (Deut xxxiii. 2, 3) :—but it is the fulfilling of that one unrepealed law which is here offered by *grace*, and which is now *required* through the acceptance of that offered grace (ch. v. 17, 18). Thus the fundamental principles of this compendious first sermon are found in that mysterious word "the fulfilling of all righteousness," as also in that first public requirement :—"*Repent ye!*" We may further say that the Sermon on the Mount teaches us wherein that *repentance* consists, whereby alone we enter the *kingdom of heaven.* It preaches it, however, as *a Gospel,* since it commences with most gracious *promise*, with blessings pronounced upon the poor, and those who hunger after righteousness ; but it deepens into a *spiritual and strict interpretation of the letter of the law* (its only true interpretation as authoritatively established by the Lawgiver, the time being now fully come) ; and *requires* on the ground of the promised grace the righteousness of God for the kingdom of God : yea it closes with warning and threatening announcement of a future *judgment* before Himself, who here speaks and who already thus bears sublime witness to Himself as Lord ; before Him who comes to the meek and miserable with grace as their Saviour, and the power of grace as their Sanctifier, but will then as judge receive such only into His kingdom as have been restored by His grace to the *performance of the will of God.* This general view suffices to show us that the Sermon on the Mount embraces in its summary one connected design from its beginning to its end; and teaches us to perceive, between its most attractive commencement, where the kingdom of heaven is opened wide to all the meek, and its fearfully threatening close, where the strait gate is shut for ever against all evil-doers, the progressive advancement of a deeply significant development. The gradation of all preaching is here reflected:—from promise through requirement to warning; to which corresponds the progress of the life of the disciples of Christ, the children of God. All apostolical preaching of the Gospel must begin with the gracious commencement of this sermon, the conclusion of all apostolical warning and announcement of judgment must coincide with its awful conclusion; but intermediate lies all that progressive teaching and exhortation, which through faith in its fulfiller establishes the law in the believer. *This* arrangement of the Sermon on the Mount has been seized and reproduced to us with such simplicity and clearness by St Matthew—through the Spirit who, besides bringing to his remembrance what he had heard, now gave him to understand it likewise—that we can only ascribe the anxiety of expositors to find another connexion, or their inability to find any, to a lack of simplicity in reading and apprehending him. We may suppose that the Lord did not utter the individual weighty sayings in a manner quite so detached, but, as was necessary to the hearers of an oral discourse, that He assisted their comprehension by adding many explanatory and connecting remarks; and probably not without pauses at the turning points which would leave time for impression. But the Spirit has taken an exact epitome of its essential contents, and constructed it for the Holy Scripture into one new and as it were glorified word: so that we have, after all, through the intervention of the Holy Ghost, the entire actual Sermon on the Mount, which we may hear and understand even as it was spoken by the Lord Himself.

The whole contents of the three chapters of St Matthew fall, as we have said, into three sections. *The fulfilling of the law*, the perfect righteousness of those who, in becoming the disciples of Christ, may and shall become again the children of their Heavenly Father (ch. v. 48), and only through such righteousness shall enter the kingdom of heaven, is alike *promised* by Him who announced Himself as *come for its fulfilment* (ch. v. 17), and demanded likewise by Him who will only have such disciples, and only bring such children to glory, as receive and retain what He brings and imparts, even to the consummation and perfection of all. But both to the inner, gradual development, and the external patient progress of the disciple, there corresponds a progression in the teaching of the sermon—according to its three main gradations. First of all, there is the general *attracting promise*, then *law with its specific demands* (now indeed the law of the Spirit, through the life of grace which has been received); and finally the *warning*, which in its stern restrictions, rejects the impure and the disobedient. Thus the discourse proceeds from the *foundation* of sanctification offered as a gift at the outset, through its *outward manifestation* in the life, demanded as the acknowledgment and evidence of that gift; to the *test and proof* at the close of the disciples' course, which is exhibited as the most pressing of all motives.

The first division embraces ch. v. 3—20; in which the same three-fold progression already reveals itself as an undertone running through the general promise. Hence we have absolute and special promise, as the origin and foundation of all, in the Benedictions (v. 3—12); then on the ground of their assurance (ye are! ye have!) the evidence and manifestation of that new life and light is demanded (v. 13—16); finally, there is here also a warning, which in its emphatic restriction, and rejection, points forward already to the test at the end of all (v. 17—20). Even this last rigorous test indeed is still under the high note of promise:—I *am come* to fulfil!

At this point, viz. in v. 20, is the transition to the second division, which now proceeds to trace out in the form of a spiritual law, the *outward manifestation* of that righteousness, the foundation of which is the gift of grace:—ch. v. 21—vii. 14. This is pre-eminently the *main body* of the Sermon on the Mount. Here the Lord sets forth the righteousness of His disciples through *three great contrasts*, as they exhibit themselves in their inward organic progress. The *First*, and most obvious contrast, which at the same time is a representation of the spiritual fulfilment of the law:—*Not as the Pharisees*, the men of the letter of the law, and of external appearances which are, nevertheless, hypocritical. This is, in accordance with the fundamental principle with which the Sermon on the Mount set out, most strictly impressed and most amply illustrated from ch. v. 21 to vi. 18. This is the *basis* of a spiritual, correct, and cordial understanding of the law. The *Second* contrast springs with still sharper severity of truth out of the former; just as John the Baptist had placed Pharisaic Judaism on a par with heathenism;—*not like the Gentiles*, the self-seeking men of the flesh and of that good which is earthly and therefore perishable. In the former it had been already premised that the Pharisees were like the Publicans, yea, like the heathen (ch. v. 46, vi. 7); this is now more fully established, and in such a way that we can only understand *heathen* in a spiritual sense as the opposite of the new, true Israel of the Messiah, ch. vi. 19—34. This is the *procedure* of an obedient, undivided, and heartily believing endeavour after the kingdom of

God and His righteousness. Finally, what can the *third* contrast to true discipleship be, but its opposition to the imperfect, insincere disciples themselves, who even in the following of Christ bring with them their pharisaism;—*not as the half-disciples and mere professors*, the censorious ones who shamefully desecrate that which is holy! (ch. vii. 1—14). This is the *perfection* of pure love, as humble as it is wise; it is obviously, at the same time, the most stringent and severe utterance of Christ's law for His own people, and thus forms a fit transition to the third division which is wholly *admonitory*.

The spiritual fulfilling of the law, the perfect righteousness, has at length found its simplest expression, (ch. vii. 12), in a principle most easy to be apprehended, and which indeed our conscience confirms from our natural love of self; yet is this self renunciation but the turning of nature to the *strait gate* in order *to do*, and to the narrow way for continuance in doing. This leads, by a connexion not very manifest but very express and emphatic, to the third main division of the whole sermon, in which the solemn *warning* against every bye-path, and the threatening of judgment upon all who at the end shall be found not to have been doers of the words of spirit and of grace, reach their highest severity.

Here is shewn the test of true or false profession and life, and *not all* who have said Lord, Lord, and done many wonderful things, stand in the judgment. The fruits of the grace so freely and graciously offered in the beginning, are inexorably demanded; the one lawgiver who wills that every man should submit to judgment and judge himself in order to salvation, appears also as the condemner of all to whom he has not become a Saviour, (Jas. iv. 12). But here also, although all has the sound of solemn warning and severe threatening, there is yet heard once more a note of the fundamental promise in the planting of the good tree for good fruit, (v. 15—20). Then once more is the law of the Divine will stamped as a requirement, (v. 21—23). The exhibition of the certainly impending trial, awful in its simplicity, closes the whole; and the fearful fall of the house built on the sand forms a striking contrast with the invitation at the beginning! For the fundamental threefold progression evolved in the organism of life as of doctrine, repeats itself at every stage, as will be more manifestly shown in a closer investigation of the particulars from the beginning.

The seven Benedictions with an eighth (ch. v. 3—12), which contain the entire original foundation and beginning of *promise*, are also arranged in their order so as to advance from the first fundamental principle, through a progressive path marked out, to the full assurance at the end. The Lord lifts up His eyes on His disciples (Lu. vi. 20) — beholding in these immediately around him, the type and earnest of all those future disciples whom He would call out from the mass of the people—and proclaims what kind of men they must be whom He will receive, and by His further direction prepare for Himself; or what they must become, who shall enter the kingdom of heaven. Thus *first of all* there is the *internal state of mind*, which is the only, the indispensable condition of the regeneration which grace provides, and therefore the basis of discipleship. The promises, with all their perfect fulness of promise, are presented as the *objective supply* of a felt *necessity*, the sincere acknowledgment of which, together with the outgoing after help, gives already the certain right to *receive* them; the kingdom of heaven comes to the poor as a *free gift*. The *susceptibility* for this reception consists in the *knowledge of need*, in the mere knowledge and discernment of it first of all—a conscious poverty of spirit; to which must be added the grievous *feeling* of that knowledge quickened into life; and the instant and urgent outgoing of the *will* for help, this again being viewed as the mere *willingness* of a negative resignation (v. 5), and as raised into positive *longing*, the hunger and thirst after *righteousness*.[1]

Thus in the *second place*, inasmuch as they who thus earnestly desire it are invested with righteousness, the *outward and inward deportment* follows, which as that righteousness has been imparted,

[1] The transposition of the fourth and fifth verses in Lachmann's text, which Neander accepts as "logical" and "suitable to their aim as instruction," and which von Gerlach and others have approved of, we hold to be altogether incorrect. For the meekness here signified follows upon a mourning that has received consolation; and the poverty passes naturally into such mourning.

may be demanded as the *witness* and proof of discipleship in their after course. In the former series we have the strait *gate* of the kingdom of heaven, in the latter the narrow *way ;* as von Gerlach has so far well said. In this second series the promises become more definite as *conformable* to a corresponding *condition of mind,* the actual attainment of which with its manifestation in *acts* alone makes good the claim to keep, and increase, and to receive in all its fulness, that promised grace. The kingdom of heaven establishes itself in the heart as the *likeness to God* of those who seek that kingdom and exercise themselves unto it. The outward and inward quality of this advancing righteousness of life consists, first—in this *holiness of deportment* itself, as well in its *acts,* rendering to others *without* the mercy which has been received ; in that laborious love which resembles God's and is the beginning and end of all fulfilment of the law; as also in that *purity of heart,* which alone from the very beginning gives truth and value to every action, and in the deeds of mercy reacts *within* upon itself to its own perfection ;[1] and then secondly, as its result in the *efficiency* of such a holy deportment (concerning which it is both promised that it shall never be wanting and *commanded* that it should be diligently sought), to wit, in their diffusing peace as God diffuses it, when His children love as he loves, and are pure as He is pure. Thus have the spiritually poor become so rich in the possession of the kingdom of heaven that they are qualified to bring its peace, or at least to offer it, to the world ! (2 Cor. vi. 10.) Can it be true, as it has been maintained, that there is no *progression* to be detected here ?

Such are the *seven* Benedictions, which embrace the entire Christian discipleship, the regeneration in its development from poverty of spirit into all that is contained in the true and essential filial relation to God. But in the peace-making there was already presupposed a transition, finally, to the conflict and opposition of an evil world. There is added therefore in conclusion, *thirdly,* in the form of an eighth benediction extending beyond its imme-

[1] Here already, as afterwards in his exposition, Kienlen's hardihood contradicts itself, in transposing, to suit *his own* scheme, the seventh and eighth verses. The fault of " slight failures of memory " imputed to the evangelists may be exchanged rather in this case, for great failure of understanding in their expositor.

diate object, a declaration of the heavenly reward of God's children presented on earth, which is *admonitory*, testing, and points forward to the final ratification of blessing at the end of all. The *promise* which here also is the predominant note, refers only to the *confirmed assurance* of that first one—the kingdom of heaven is and shall ever be yours: it is at the same time the *contrast* of victory with warfare, a *reward conformable* to a worthy qualification for it. Indeed the persecution of the righteous by the unrighteous is the due and the authentic way by which the goal of persevering love is attained. This is further exhibited in the first transition to an application to the disciples—*happy* are *ye*—persecution injures you not, but is rather the proof that ye are true peace-makers, and not false prophets crying, Peace, peace (Lu. vi. 26)—yet here also we cannot fail to hear the undertone of *warning*—so they do it all *falsely!* Finally, the encouragement: your *reward* is sure, then be ye, like the prophets before you, and now much more, the salt of the earth and the light of the world! (The transition to what follows.) Thus have we exhibited our view of the order of the Benedictions: the reader himself must test it, and prefer, if he may, any other of the multitude of arrangements which have been essayed.[1] We think, however, that enough has been said to show that it is not our "preconceived determination, that the *seven-number* shall play their part here" (Kienlen) but that the eighth is really only supplementary to the seven.

We have already begun in these observations to pursue the whole into its parts, to point out the true position and the profound meaning of every single saying. In the light now thrown upon them the holy words will, even to their minutest detail, clearly and transparently unfold their meaning.

He *opened His mouth*[2]—Disciples and people solemnly waited

[1] See *e.g.* Zeller in the Monatsblatt von Beuggen 1847. No. 6, as before 1839 Nos. 9, 10 Compare therewith Kienlen (Stud. u. Krit. 1848. 3)—who indeed prefers quoting Lisco to Stier—where much is to the same effect and equally strange.

[2] Whereupon Lange says beautifully in his own way, "Man is the mouth of the creation, Christ is the mouth of humanity.

for the first word which, under God's heaven, with his eye upon the holy land upon earth, and after such a preparation for such preaching as had never before been heard among men, He would proceed to utter. And they were *gracious* words which here also at the first proceeded out of His mouth (Lu. iv. 22), although followed by those solemn and impressive utterances which brought the power and authority of God more plainly home to the sensual man for his conviction. The *first* word of His mouth is Blessed—and again and again He cries Blessed, before he could proceed to speak in that other style to which sinners and the ungodly constrained Him. For who is it that here speaks? He who is come to give *Blessedness.* But He also, who in speaking and dispensing blessedness from stage to stage, at the same time and by that means *sanctifies.* How shall we poor sinners be made happy unto holiness at the beginning, and holy unto happiness at the end? Here is the answer, here is the *doctrine* of all teaching for all people upon earth. The blessedness goes ever progressively increasing along that way, which the Saviour here points out to His disciples, if they continue by walking in it to become more and more *capable of that blessedness.*

Ver. 3. This first word of the Sermon on the Mount is, again, pre-eminently the "fundamental formula of the Gospel"—it demands *faith* in so joyful a message, without mentioning the word: it *awakens*, rather, and *attracts* that faith through its confident and encouraging assurance. And how can any one who is truly poor in spirit fail to apprehend and believe this message of mercy concerning the kingdom of heaven, as soon as it resounds in his ears? If the poor are altogether unable to believe in their being made blessed through grace, it is proof that, in spite of all appearances, they are not yet fundamentally poor enough. It may appear, on the contrary, sometimes as if a man could not yet believe, while there is actually in his complaining before God, in the seeking and longing after faith of his wretched heart, a secret faith already present;—such mourners, indeed, have pressed forwards already into the second benediction. In the first nothing more is as yet spoken of than perfect poverty of spirit, which may be so poor as not to have even a feeling of need, not even a becoming sorrow for sin. And this is indeed *that one thing* which the Lord at the beginning of his dispensation of blessedness may and must *presuppose;* nothing can the sinner bring with him when he is called by grace, but a *sincere consciousness* of his wanting before God everything that avails in His sight, of having no righteousness in himself, no life of the Spirit. Simple and easy is this one condition and requirement —but hard enough, alas, to the pride of nature! All the further requirements and conditions, which now follow as the objects of gracious benediction, are already fulfilled out of that first gift of grace to the poor—one after, and arising out of, the other. The quickening of the feelings into a deep and sorrowful penitence comes not from mere nature; he who can pour forth the tears of his eyes or of his heart, that is, the tears of sincere contrition for his *sin,* and not only for its shame and punishment, has previously received, though himself might not as yet be conscious of it, as one who has become poor, the spirit of grace and supplication for that purpose. And so further through the whole progressive series every succeeding condition is only required, because the preceding consolation has brought it. But no one step may be overleaped. We cannot begin in the middle: we can neither enforce a godly sorrow by any efforts of our own in order to bring this first to the Giver of blessedness, nor before the contrite surrender of sin attain unto the fervent hunger and thirst after righteousness: we can neither become pure in heart without the practice of mercy, nor again can we exercise mercy before we have received the comfort of mercy ourselves. The new life of the sinner derived from grace is indeed a living plant, which contains folded in itself at every stage of development all that is to follow; and as soon as the kingdom of heaven begins to sink into the needy soul, awakened to a sincere consciousness of its poverty, and aroused by the Spirit's influence in it, the germ of the peace of God for the making of peace among men enters with it.[1] But that one follows the other, as the Lord here speaks, even to the full unfolding and formation of the whole, takes place through the growth of time; and the field of man's heart, in which all such fruits by

[1] Lange says further, "and in the blessed peacemaking is still the poverty of spirit, in its essential excellence, transformed into the most blessed humility."

degrees through grace may grow up to maturity, is ever in itself nothing but—*poverty.*

The μακάριοι which with such gracious emphasis stands first, has not, down to ver. 11, either εἰσί or ἔσονται connected with it, although the translation gives it correctly enough for the obvious sense—*Blessed are!* In the sacred text it is a simple *proclamation* (like the Heb. אַשְׁרֵי), and contains as such the whole fulness of what mercy offers for the acceptance of faith, without any further definite announcement or qualification. It embraces *alike*, they *are* now, immediately blessed, and *shall be so* ever more and more unto perfection. Then as the promises attached look forward to the future from the second saying onwards, so does it also in the first—the kingdom of heaven is yours, it shall be, and will be ever more perfectly your own. The *kingdom of heaven* and *blessedness* are but one, so that the first *for* is a sublime assurance which bears its own witness to itself. Πτωχοὶ τῷ πνεύματι, עֲנִיֵּי רוּחַ, Isa. xli. 17; lxvi. 2; especially lxi. 1, to which Scripture the Lord here refers as again at His first preaching in Nazareth (Lu. iv. 18); yet πτωχοὶ answers rather to the Old Testament אֶבְיוֹנִים, (Isa. xxix. 19), so that *outward* poverty is actually included in it, as is manifest in the not incorrect version of St Luke. Only it is not merely the externally poor and wretched who are referred to, as the τῷ πνεύματι which is added emphatically shows: by consequence the rich and the exalted also, if they are only poor in spirit. But it must be observed, that the persons pronounced blessed are not the subject of the promising proposition: it is not they (as afterwards in ver. 20) who enter and attain to the kingdom of heaven, but the *kingdom of heaven* comes to them, and enters into them! Its whole fulness into every one, whose poverty opens to receive it! Yes truly, here is it come *near*, quite near to those who have it not. The first, bare commencement of μετάνοια may dare already to appropriate all to itself, in order to receive all; and thus through the shining of the beams of mercy into the soul, for the first time, and immediately, becomes awakened to a more lively perception and feeling of its own darkness.

Ver. 4. The Lord has further in view Is. lxi. 2, 3, and proclaims the great year of freedom and of grace—*to comfort all that mourn.* Were the *poor* (Matt. xi. 5) to whom He preaches the Gospel, actually in the most comprehensive sense of the general invitation all the miserable and the unfortunate, the toilworn and the heavy laden under the burden and need of life; so has this announcement of a general consolation a like unrestricted and extensive introduction:—Come unto me, all who suffer affliction, ye may and ye shall find help. But in drawing nearer to receive this comfort, it becomes evident that there must be added:—But be ye *truly* mourners, sorrow on account of the inner ground and first cause of all evil—sin! The outwardly poor are far from being always and in their inner spirit so *poor*, as to allow the heavenly gift of God room to enter into empty and destitute hearts: therefore is the impressive τῷ πνεύματι added, which, like the *kingdom of heaven*, manifestly casts down all Jewish expectation of the Messiah and *points within.* The same—as a kind of superscription to the whole discourse—is naturally to be understood also of the mourning (or something similar, as κατὰ θεόν, 2 Cor. vii. 10): it is not, however, repeated, partly because what preceded has made it sufficiently plain, partly because every mourner, in the pure sense of the word, as one humbled beneath the mighty hand of God, necessarily retreats within himself, and is very near at least to the susceptibility of receiving the true consolation. Seest thou one weeping, thou mayest securely address to him the heavenly message of a merciful salvation, in the sure hope and confidence of a hearing for your message. For "mourning and sorrow are in reality the acknowledged and felt contradiction of the nature that is in us, to the *Divine* life which will be revealed in us" (Nitzsch, Predigten, V. Auswahl). The mourners *shall* (sollen) be comforted, as Luther, meaning more than merely to avoid repetition of sound, has well expressed the future παρακληθήσονται, if they only will, if the consolation that comes only finds them true mourners, who will suffer themselves to hear comfortable words. Yea, as surely as the High and lofty one, who declares Himself, in His loving condescension to all misery and need, to be the *Holy One*, dwelleth with those who are of a contrite and humble spirit (Isa. lvii. 15), so surely is the merciful comfort of God immediately nigh to every troubled one in his affliction. It is but a commencement of *blessedness*, a specific beginning of consolation in the very sorrow itself, as even the world seems to suspect when it sings about the "sweetness of grief," and in its own way pronounces happy those who can weep. But that is only the shadow and slender beginning of that comfort which the Lord intends, and brings with Him. And if His unfading and true spiritual consolation is brought to those who sorrow in the world, it, alas, soon becomes manifest that they are very far from being willing to turn in sincere sorrow to the right consolation, they are not found to be *meek* mourners, who have broken down and given up their self-will, pride, and opposition. It is quite true what Nitzsch says, "I cannot be man, and not have the beginning of sorrow within me"—but the beginning follows, alas, very evil courses in degenerate humanity. There is a sorrow which is very lightly comforted with nothing: there is, on the other hand, a superstitious and proud sorrow, which *refuses to take comfort* with the consolation of God. To all such mourning as springs not from poverty of spirit, this promise is assuredly not given. For the Gospel which the Lord here preaches pre-supposes the work of the law and the discipline of preparatory grace upon the soul.

Ver. 5. Our previous general view and the immediate connexion have already shown how πρᾳεῖς, which is commonly interpreted falsely or at least superficially, is here to be understood. The mere external exhibition of a passive, unresisting mind is not spoken of here, it is to be understood (as Neander this time sees) only of the *internal disposition of heart*, into which the Lord's word deeper and deeper penetrates. Still less may we think of an anticipation of the entire and complete virtue of Christian *meekness*, for the gradual process of the inner preparation of mind is marked out here from ver. 3—6, before the conduct to which it leads is described ver. 7—9. The "patient endurance of earthly affliction" is not immediately here spoken of (as Kienlen supposes), but passiveness, and the breaking down of natural opposition, regarded strictly as an internal condition of mind. As the poor become mourners, when the consciousness of their need passes from *conviction* into *feeling*, so now is it, further, of still more importance, that they in their misery bend and incline their *will* to the coming consolation. The willingness to be comforted and helped, is indeed better than all outcry on account of necessity, if that go no further. It is, in a certain sense, as we have seen, the test of true mourning, which without it cannot be genuine: but then this *resignation* is more distinctively developed, when the Spirit-Comforter, in order to make the mourner entirely submissive begins at the very commencement of his consolation thoroughly to *correct* and chastise him. *Πρᾳεῖς* is found in the Old Testament answering to the עֲנָוִים of the Psalms and Prophets; and in the New Testament *πρᾶος, πρᾳΰς, πρᾳότης* indicates mostly (as besides in the Greek *πραΰθυμος, πραΰνοος*) an inner quality of mind. Observe carefully 1 Cor. iv. 21; Gal. vi. 1; 1 Pet. iii. 4; and especially Eph. iv. 2.[1] Thus is it a willingness and plasticity of spirit, in opposition to the proud, opposing obstinacy of the natural self-will. If those who are poor in spirit, and mourners, are found humbled and broken with the beginning of such a disposition, so shall they when comforted, by their *reception* of consolation, advance yet farther in this meekness of soul. For he who has experienced kindness is by it made gentle, so that he has become willing to be content with every thing, as Braune excellently says. Here Rambach[2] hits the right sense, much better than many later expositors:—"This is a fruit of the Spirit which is found upon the soil of spiritual poverty, contrition and mourning; a noble flower, which grows out of the ashes of self-love, upon the grave of pride. On the one hand a man sees his own utter ruin, his unworthiness and misery, on the other he contemplates the kindness and benignity of God in Christ Jesus (Titus iii. 2—4). The internal characteristic is a disposition of heart, which, through the keen perception of its own misery, and of the abounding mercy of God, has become so pliant, gentle, mild, flexible, and tractable that no traces of its original ruggedness, of its wild and untamed nature remain." Such meekness,[3]

[1] Where to *walk* worthy of our vocation in long-suffering, forbearance, love, and peace, is indicated as its end, but the internal fundamental state of mind by which it is aimed at is *ταπεινοφροσύνη* and *πρᾳότης* just in the same sense as Matt. v. 3, 5. *Μακροθυμία* and *ἀγάπη* are then the passive and active expression of such a disposition of mind.

[2] Observations upon the eight Benedictions.

[3] Not merely (according to Lange) "before men" as the result of mourning before God, but also and especially meekness before God! For are they not the "mourners" of the Psalter?

taking to itself the word of grace which dispenses blessedness unto holiness, in its correction as well as in its comfort, does St James also require (ch. i. 21); but only of those who are already new-born, in whom this word is already engrafted. With the requirement of this the Saviour could by no means have commenced. That would not have been the right message for poor sinners which should *begin* with—Blessed are the merciful, or the pure in heart,—so neither could this willing resignation be demanded from the natural man, before he has advanced to that point out of his poverty, which is all he has, through mourning and consolation.

With inconceivable grandeur does the promise which corresponds come forward, in order to allure our proud and stubborn natural mind to submit to that death from which it shrinks:—for they shall, they will, *possess or inherit the land, the earth!* Is this not worth the sacrifice of self, to be enriched with the free gift of such a possession, of such riches! It is an Old Testament promise, which, while it there clings to the typical land of Canaan, extends much further in the design of the Holy Ghost, see Ps. xxxvii. 11; xxv. 13; Isa. lvii. 13; lx. 21; even to the new earth which, with the new heavens, God declares that He will make, Isa. lxvi. 22. It is the ultimate and full meaning of the promise to Abraham—to be the heir of the *world!* (Rom. iv. 13). With reference to the hope of their faith, to the dominion of their spirit, it is already said of God's children—all things are yours! (1 Cor. iii. 22). But what will it be in the full fulfilment! The first promise was altogether for the present, the second already points to the ever-coming after consolation, the third stretches far away into the most distant futurity. The kingdom of *heaven*, ver. 3, which appears not at first in earthly power and glory, but comes into the hearts of the wretched for their consolation and righteousness, is nevertheless in its future, as it here at once openly proclaims, a kingdom of the *earth*. Thus does the great Fulfiller teach his docile hearers in his very first discourse, how the promises of the prophets, which cannot be broken, are to be understood; and at the same time teaches what it was the design of the law to create in their hearts, and that it is only given to drive the needy to Divine grace, in order that their hunger and thirst after righteousness should find its satisfaction. For already in these seven sayings of blessedness the *Law and the Prophets* are compendiously unfolded.

How manifestly do all these utterances of Divine truth, which bears its simple and majestic witness to itself, oppose themselves at once to the Pharisaic delusion and pride of self-righteousness; to the Sadducee contentment with the present, sensual delight of this world; and to the perverted thoughts of the world and the natural man! Verses 3—5 are three paradoxes, which with all their gracious invitation and promise, are nevertheless to carnal Israel, to the earthly, self-seeking, and sensual man, a stone of stumbling thrown in the way. For grace can only bear the testimony of truth to itself, and the Saviour conceals not, from the beginning, what kind of salvation it is that He brings. Happy the unhappy! Well for the mourners! This does violence to the world's sentiments, and constrains it, either to *press into* the true experience of so wonderful a doctrine, or even at this early point to pass it by for the broad gate, because this door is too strait. "Thou must assuredly be *converted* unto the *blessedness* which the Lord pronounces, as much as unto the righteousness:"—so preaches Nitzsch. The very first word teaches us that there is a blessedness which consists not in *pleasant* sensations, or joyful emotions, but that which is to *nature most displeasing.* The Lord points impressively from without to within, from the present time to the future, from the self of man to the gift and grace of God. Oh that the *richly endowed* and *worldly blessed* of our day, to whom the beginning of the Sermon on the Mount must come with the full force of most direct contrast and contradiction, would only meekly hear it, and give up their hold upon "this side" for the sake of that which is on "the other side," that kingdom of heaven which, in its time, shall also be upon earth, the inheritance of the despised, quiet, and patient ones of the land, the humble and meek of the "Preacher upon the Mount!" *Self-renunciation* is the way to *world dominion.* Give thyself up in passive obedience to divine grace, and it will present thee one day with a crown of glory, after having previously forgiven thee all thy sin, and healed all thy infirmity. But not otherwise! Thinkest thou in thine heart to rule, and possess, and to sway, and to enjoy, all things upon earth, at thine own will and in thy unrighteousness, under the eye of the God of heaven and of earth? Thou wilt be put to confusion, and bearest about thee already the silent witness thereof. The *vir fortis ac strenuus*, the hero or genius, the worldling or conqueror may strut in lordly pride with his evil conscience for a while upon earth, until he is doomed to go down into Scheol to all the other uncircumcised; but the meek in the school of Jesus have *a title of heirship* upon this earth, which no slanderer or persecutor will be able to cancel in the book of their Father and their King; and the day shall come when the *lambs* shall feed after their manner in *their* pastures and waste places, (Isa. v. 17.) The kingdom of heaven is a free gift for the poor, but only for the poor in spirit; a comfort for the mourners, but only those who sorrow with the right sorrow: it must ever be, and *will prove* itself also as a *kingdom*, a *dominion*, but only for the meek!

Ver. 6. Out of *humbleness, sadness, meekness,* (to use the words of Nitzsch once more) grows, finally, *greatness of soul,* the sanctified and right loftiness of desire which aspires earnestly towards that which alone is *right.* The future possessors of the earth, and its now rightfully installed heirs, whose is even now the kingdom of heaven with all its reversion, including the ruling upon earth, *hunger and thirst* throughout their whole course, even as they did at the beginning: just as the poor to whom the kingdom of heaven is imparted, mourn in the first repentance unto life which they receive as a bestowment of grace, and oftentimes after. But the Lord ever more and more comforts the mourners, ever more and more fills the hungry and thirsty soul with the good things of His *righteousness.* (Ps. cvii. 9, cxlvi. 7, lxv. 5, xxii. 27; Isa. xli. 17 [Bar. ii. 18]). He who created this hunger, shows by creating it that its appropriate food is also provided. There is a hunger and thirst in man which God did not create in him, and for that there shall be, after the brief semblance of gratification, the pain of an eternal famishing. But there is still deep, deep in fallen man, a little spark of longing and desire after righteousness; this faintly-glimmering flax, grace kindles into a clear flame, and that is the hunger and thirst which bears in itself the certain assurance that its supply will not be wanting. It is not, indeed, the *being made blessed* in itself and first of all, or "felicity" as man's doctrine runs, that the souls to which have been pointed out the way to happiness through self-denial, the strait gate of the doing of God's will, should seek and struggle after; but *righteousness*, the victory of the eternal, and just and good will of God upon earth and in humanity, especially, however, in themselves. Deliver *us* from evil! comes not till the last petition; but the first again and again cries out in longing, Hallowed be Thy name! *Thy* kingdom come! and utters in meekness, *Thy* will be done! They who thus pray receive the daily bread of their souls, and as much as they require it, of their bodies too. No willing and running, no labouring chase after it in our own strength and in our own way, attains unto righteousness; ours is to desire it, it is for God to give it. Yet observe, that as far as the kingdom of heaven is already set up in these poor, they in their new and inner man naturally, regularly, daily—"with the full force of the instinct of the sustentation of life"—hunger after righteousness, just as the old and outward man hungers after that bread, of which the *man*, however, does not essentially *live*. This hungering and thirsting is the sign of life of the new-born inner man, quickened from the sleep of death; hence it is the last thing by which the Lord can indicate the internal spirit and disposition of the children of God. The discourse now passes over[1] to the evidencing of that righteousness, which has been given to them who have desired it, and shall be more and more fully given even till their full and complete satisfaction, till the purifying of their hearts in love, till that is fulfilled which is written: As for me, I will *behold thy face* in righteousness, I *shall be satisfied* when I awake with thy likeness! (Ps. xvii. 15). In the new earth dwelleth righteousness (2 Pet. iii. 13), and they who one day inherit it, shall then hunger and thirst no more. He who now as a pilgrim citizen of the city to come, earnestly prays over the table of his house and of his heart:—Make us partakers of thine eternal, heavenly table, which thou hast graciously prepared and promised to us in Thy kingdom,—he shall be satisfied with the kingdom of God and His righteousness, even until the great feast

[1] As in the seven petitions of the Lord's prayer the middle one concerning daily bread effects the transition between the first and second table, between God's good and man's need; even so here the fourth of the Benedictions mediates between their two parts, and is the transition, inversely, from the need of the poor to the grace, which transforms and glorifies itself in them as righteousness.

with all the fathers made righteous in faith; shall be filled here with the supply of both soul and body from day to day, for what the necessity of his body requires shall also be given him, just as the soul's necessity, the special plague of every day, is provided for. So that the hunger for the bread of the soul shall never cease, until the perfect righteousness is come.

Vers. 7—9. Up to this point the promises have corresponded to conditions, but these conditions have been no other than the same *need* developing itself from step to step in increasing urgency, and outgoing fervour of desire:—in each case therefore that which is promised is most essentially a *gift*. Be poor, and the kingdom of heaven shall be thine! Mourn, and thou shalt be comforted! Give up thy will, thou shalt dwell in, and inherit, the everlasting sufficiency! Only hunger and thirst, thou shalt be filled! But now begins the unfolding of a new series. The beginning of this does not simply presuppose the end of the former and carry it on, but the outward expression and evidence of the inner principles, the fruits of these hidden feelings manifest themselves already simultaneously in the life; so that they who in their poverty acknowledge their need of mercy, and taste the first-fruits of the Divine compassion, begin already to exercise mercy; the mourners begin while they mourn to wash their hearts clean; the meek also spontaneously to make peace, the hungerers after righteousness to give themselves up to persecution, on account of that righteousness which they only as yet long for. Yet, inasmuch as all cannot be *spoken* in one word, which pertains to the many-formed unity of the development of the increasing life from its germ to its maturity, it is right to take the ascending order in which the discourse describes it. The eight Benedictions, with their conditions, are in a certain sense found united in every child of God, and no member of this wonderful series may be altogether wanting from the time that the first poverty of spirit has received the gift of grace; yet is there an actual and gradual growth of one out of the other. And here does the law apply in all its significance, that the gift received must be preserved, exercised, and increased; and that to him only who has, shall more be given in order to his having all, while from him who guards it not, and does not exercise and increase it, shall be taken away that which he has. Consequently the promises of the second series take now the form of *reward*, the recompense of grace to those who are faithful to what they have received. Be merciful, and thou shalt have mercy shown to thee ![1] Be pure, so shalt thou behold the pure one ! Make peace, so shalt thou be the manifest child of the God of peace ! Such *requital*, such *recompense* is not the less itself mere mercy and the reward of free grace ; the Divine gift is only in it going on to its superabundant fulfilment ; and the qualities, which are the object of recompense, were previously bestowed as a gift. For who can show mercy, without having first received mercy ? who can be pure in heart, without having contemplated the purity of God ? who can diffuse peace, except through that peace of God into which he has entered ?

But—and this is most important—there is here a possibility of the *withdrawal* of grace, from those who have received it but are not faithful to its corresponding exercises ; just as the parables, Matt. xviii. 23—35, xxv. 14—30, also teach. Therefore do the promises even now begin to *sink*, secretly warning against such a loss, while the conditions *rise*.[2] To the merciful, God has been, indeed, at the outset, merciful, but only they who thereafter forgive also as they have been forgiven, and love as God has loved them, *shall obtain mercy*, that is, at the final testing of their fidelity, finally and securely retain it. The pure in heart have purified themselves in the sight of God, have drawn nigh to him in living acquaintance with His name ; but only if they preserve and increase that knowledge unto the end, shall they who have come to God finally and fully come nigh to Him. Only they who as peacemakers have approved themselves to the end God's children, shall in the coming "*manifestation* of the sons of God," in the separation between the persevering and the apostates, actually *be called* the children of God, *be acknowledged* as such ! (which already presignifies ch. vii. 23). Thus does the gate become straiter and straiter, as afterwards throughout the whole discourse. He who sets out may in poverty of spirit con-

[1] What St Luke in another, briefer epitome of the whole Sermon on the Mount, in its few fundamental ideas, exhibits to us as blended with other sayings, ch. vi. 36—39 (Matt. v. 48, vii. 1, 2).

[2] Let a glance be taken *backwards* through the Benedictions in order fully to observe their organic connexion.

fidently believe, I have it! but the nearer he approaches the goal, the more will he utter another cry, Not that I have already attained!

Not a word is needed to prove that ἐλεήμονες in its compendious sense indicates the practical love of our neighbour, all that is done to our brethren from the inward principle of a communicating and helping charity. It is necessary, however, to observe that such rudiments of regeneration, as were to be found even among the heathen who, though they knew not Christ, yet through the pure impulse of a latent grace, exercised towards others what they sought for themselves, must be included here; in opposition to that narrow dogmatic limitation, which would despise the good works of such as Cornelius, though God nevertheless esteemed them. Mercy rejoiceth against judgment (Jas. ii. 13)—this impartial and holy law of eternal love graciously throws open the kingdom of heaven to many coming from the east and the west; even as it rigidly closes it against the children of the kingdom who, with all their vaunted faith, have never learned or retained love. This mercy, however, (as Nitzsch excellently preaches) is not that weak and sickly sympathy which ungodly selfishness cannot but feel, and is too willing to plead it in evasion as the true Christianity; not that false kindness towards one's neighbour which goes hand in hand with the most unbridled indulgence of one's own flesh. *Therefore* is purity of heart next spoken of as the test of true mercy; not the reverse, as if this presumptive mercy were the guarantee of purity in the heart. *Καθαροὶ τῇ καρδίᾳ*, בָּרֵי לֵבָב (Ps. lxxiii. 1, comp. Ps. li. 12, xxiv. 4—6.) Not merely pure in the Levitical typical sense, not merely of clean hands in a Pharisaical or carnally moral sense, but in the inner being before God, who desireth truth in the inward parts, (Ps. li. 8.) In the position where we find this here, it cannot be a disposition of mind that desires and seeks it, not even the struggle after it out of a deep sense of need, but an actual inner quality, a condition of the inner man that is ever advancing to perfection. The heart is purified through faith (Acts xv. 9); and in love out of a pure heart (1 Tim. i. 5), in faith working by love, to the perfection of which faith works co-operate (Jas. ii. 22), the purified heart goes on to the consummation of purity. The stimulant and impulse of practical mercy is the mercy of the Pure One towards my yet impure heart; the more diligently I now wash my heart in this mercy of God, and my hands by exercising it in return towards my neighbour, the more fully the sentiment of love within me is confirmed by the acts of love; so much the nearer do I come, in the way of a priestly entrance into the Holiest (which is, in its degree, an appearing before God already, a beholding of His face), unto the final and consummate fulfilment of that type—*to see God*, as it is expressed in 1 Jno. iii. 2, 3. Just as far as we are inwardly and essentially purified as God is pure, are we capable of a living perception of Him. But that perception, when perfect in the glorified, shall be also the actual *vision* of God; that is, be it understood, of the face of God *in the Son*, who has ever been from the beginning the face of God turned towards the creature. (1 Tim. vi. 16).[1] *Ἐιρηνοποιοί, βουλόμενοι εἰρήνην,* יֹעֲצֵי שָׁלוֹם (Prov. xii. 20) and more than that, for it is the last description of the high aim of discipleship, beyond which there is no higher step to be taken, for this makes the disciple as his Lord. Not merely are they contrasted with those who are ἐξ ἐριθείας (Rom. ii. 8), not merely do they keep and preserve peace, as much as in them lies, with every man (*εἰρηνεύοντες*, Rom. xii. 18; Heb. xii. 14), but they make, they mediate peace, they bring and offer to the world out of the treasure of a pure heart, the peace of God! Thus, finally, every disciple of our Lord is in his place, in design if not in effect, a messenger of grace, in word, in work, and in life, to all intents and purposes a bringer of peace in the ministry of the great reconciliation. *Such* shall, in the final separation and demarcation, *be called* the children of God, for they have been such in truth and worthy of the name: but *not* they who have proudly and unlovingly gloried in the testimony of truth against a miserable and sinful world, and just as little they who have, contrary to truth and righteousness, spoken peace when there has been no peace in God's sight.

Ver. 10. To the *seven* Benedictions, perfect in themselves, there is significantly added yet another supernumerary *eighth*,

[1] So that we may not limit the meaning of the promise to the manifestation of Christ only in this world:—the pure, the upright, perceive in Christ a manifestation of God. (Lutz, Bibl. Dogm. p. 48). Quite true, but not enough.

which proceeds no further with the development, but *confirms* and seals their seven-fold blessedness to the *righteous*, whose character is perfected through their peace-making in this evil world, against all the never-failing enmity and scorn of the unrighteous. And though ye also suffer for righteousness' sake, yet are ye, and shall ye be, blessed *notwithstanding*. (1 Pet. iii. 14.) Here is thus wonderfully blended the fundamental tone of promise and consolation, Fear ye not, rather rejoice! with the earnest note of requirement, that they remain faithful under so severe a test, yea, even of warning against hypocrisy and apostacy. For that *righteousness'* sake which has been now attained —by retrospect to ver. 6; and there is also a connexion with ver. 7—9—mercy *out* of a pure heart *unto* peace. The world will for the most part requite that love with hatred, will thrust this peace from them; and the Lord will by no means conceal this from His disciples in this most gracious first sermon to them. The essential idea of *persecute*, here, is to persist malevolently in seeking to withstand them; to transfer and carry on their enmity against God's righteousness, to its possessors and witnesses and ambassadors also. Thus is δεδιωγμένοι not only the highest honour ofthe children of God who are thus conformed to Christ, but also a condition of entrance into the kingdom of heaven not less absolute than the preceding. (1 Pet. iv. 13, 14; 2 Tim. iii. 12). It is the last and surest *token* of discipleship; and the tribulation of time becomes to those who persevere, a confirmation of their title to eternal joy. Thereby discern the peace of God in thyself and in others, that the world as such is opposed to it, yea, even rejoice in this, for as it is the natural consequence of thy charitable and peaceful walk, so it is also the testing proof which is needful to its consummation. (Jno. xiv. 27; xv. 18—21). According to St Luke vi. 26, the Lord further made this plain by a warning contrast. Thus does the Lord set the seal to His discourse, binding together its beginning and its end:—the kingdom *is* (and abides) yours, even as it was yours at the commencement in poverty of spirit. The ἐστίν presents a contrast with the *outward* and passing show of persecution, which indeed is more easily apprehended by faith than that first contrariety between the strong assurance and the *inward* poverty to which it was given. The *kingdom of heaven* is trancendantly elevated above all the transitory circumstances of this lower world.

Vers. 11, 12. The sentences which proclaim blessedness, are ended. There is now, through a final " Blessed *are* ye," a transition made to their *appropriation ;* and the *address* to the disciples begins, which continues down to ch. vii. 20. That this direct address was not used before, resulted from the tone of general invitation which marked the commencement of the discourse. The disciples of Jesus must not be supposed to be separated or distinguished from the other hearers ; but the discourse, in a manner, saw in them all, from the beginning, future disciples—graciously takes this for granted. Whosoever, among the people who heard the first sentences, is able and willing to appropriate them to himself, is referred to throughout what follows in the general *ye*, my disciples ! All other men, in sharp distinction from the children of God and messengers of peace who have been described, are included in the unexpressed subject of *ὀνειδίσωσιν*, &c. Quite correctly, therefore, though needlessly, does Luther insert *Men* (Menschen) ;—comp. ver. 16 with ch. x. 17. The children of God are in contrast with men, just as Israel, God's people, with the nations. For *my sake* : this is, likewise, the first coming forth of the personality of Jesus, the Master and Lord which corresponds to that first *ye* ; and its identity with For righteousness' sake ! is, at the same time, very significant. The persecution before referred to, is now more clearly traced in three stages :—first, reviling with bitter and hateful words generally, then more specific persecution in acts, and finally the pouring out upon the objects of their hate, in wanton *falsehood* and slander, *πᾶν πονηρὸν ῥῆμα*, whatever their wicked malice can invent.[1] The Lord manifestly refers to Isa. li. 7—8 ; in which chapter we find ver. 1. beginning with—" Ye that follow after *righteousness* ;" and immediately after in vers. 4—8, this is changed into " *My* people, my nation, my judgment, my salvation, my righteousness." Consequently, our Lord here already

[1] The daring disregard of truth with which the world is wont *calumniari audacter* the children of God, the Satanic cunning with which its lies are woven, would be altogether incredible, if it were not matter of fact.

in this lofty "For my sake!" speaks in the person of Jehovah, just as at the end of the sermon He reveals Himself as the future judge of mankind. The ψευδόμενοι about which there has been so much needless dispute, must not be connected *merely* with ἕνεκεν ἐμοῦ (as Tholuck thinks); but indicates in itself that most wanton wickedness and unrighteousness which has just been spoken of: though at the same time it contains, in order to obviate the too hasty confidence which this might produce, an undertone of *test* (as we observed above in the analysis), sounding thus—But look well to it in every case, that they *do* speak falsely! This expression, to return, exhibits the fundamental principle of all their hatred; which has its origin in the *lie* that ever opposes the truth of God, though the adversaries may not always be conscious of this. *Ye* must know it, however, and be firmly assured, that they speak falsely; or the benediction can avail you nothing. For, alas, all the way up to the high elevation of the reproach of Christ, may a man deceive himself; and too readily reckon that as slander, redounding to his own honour, which is but deserved blame. But if ye are surely convinced in your heart and conscience, that the reproaches of those who hate the righteousness of God, are falling upon you for its sake, then *rejoice and be exceeding* glad! (In St Luke, "*leap for joy*," spring upward in joyful hope towards your reward in heaven!) There is in this, as it were, a most emphatic command, *Be* happy! for which "Blessed *are* ye," in the previous verse, prepared the way. It is only befitting that the Lord, in His gentle condescension, should speak of recompense and reward (excluding, be it understood, all idea of merit from those words), oftener and more strongly than His apostles might afterwards do.[1] For *your reward*: that is, not merely the general reward of grace which in the kingdom of heaven awaits you; but in addition there shall be, for every affliction and for every wicked word which you have to endure as expedient for the confirmation of your faith to yourselves, a distinct, and precisely apportioned requital and compensation:—the *more* ye suffer, the *more* the reward. For thus royally will one day that righteous Lord and Judge requite His own, who on the other hand will not forget a cup of cold water that has ever been

[1] See Roos, the Doctrine of Jesus Christ, new ed., p. 764.

given to one of them! Finally, there is here graciously given to our weak faith another ground of joy in persecution, in that we perceive ourselves by this practical token to be companions of the prophets, the witnesses of God who have been before us; and thus become more and more assured of our citizenship in the kingdom of heaven, in contrast with the prevailing decay and destruction of all things. Christ gives, indeed, in these words an early explanation, that the kingdom of God was not among the people of Israel, as a whole, in the state in which it then was; that it was not what they thought it, after their way and manner; but that it was with the persecuted prophets, and as they taught it, in the misunderstood former revelation. The reward is reserved *in the heavens*, which is not quite the same with "in the kingdom of heaven;" but rather signifies the *interval* from the gathering of the righteous to the former prophets, till the inheriting of the *earth*, ver. 5. Him whom they tolerate no longer under heaven, Heaven will receive *into* itself! *Heavens*, in the plural, refers to the many mansions of Jno. xiv. 2, and helps our anticipation of the greatness and glory of the reward.

Vers. 13—16. The promise here already in the first part, as we have seen, advances into a demand, that the gifts of grace which have been received should exhibit and approve themselves. The danger of not persevering in persecution has been just before pointed out; but now the discourse strengthens its tone, and insists upon an indispensable continuance of *active influence* and *testimony* in the midst of an evil world. *Ye*—who have been described in vers. 3—10, who in your poverty have hungered for and have obtained righteousness, in order to the exercise of charity and peacemaking; *Ye*—who have been addressed in vers. 11, 12, as having to expect, like the prophets before you, the ingratitude, scorn, and persecution of this world as your earthly reward, but an everlasting compensation for all this, as your reward in heaven: *Ye are*, what Grace has made you—*be*, and in joyful confidence continue to be, *all that your new nature requires!* Let no hindrance prevent this; look well to yourselves, that ye become not again incapable and unfit! In these verses the three main ideas, with reference to which the whole sermon moves on in regular gradation (Promise, Requirement, and Warning), *are reversed*—from the point of their connexion with the preceding.

First, altogether warning—woe to the savourless salt! Then again, though in part a promise—the light *must* not and shall not be hid! Finally, with fuller grace—let then the light which is given you, shine forth!

The discourse, after having looked back upon the prophets of former times, turns at once to a prophetic contemplation of the entire *destiny of the new church*—the city set on a hill;—announces here preparatorily, what comes more plainly before us in the 10th chapter at the first sending forth of the messengers of peace; and already, just as at the close of this Gospel (ch. xxviii. 19), embraces the whole *earth*—the whole *world*. But what is the distinction which our Lord, who begins here to disclose the essential truth of those natural images which were originally provided for all human language, and to use them as the elementary letters of His own superhuman utterance, makes in this passage between *salt* and *light?* It would be superficial to regard it as a mere abstract distinction between life and knowledge. Rather is *salt* the *inner* essential power and virtue from which the *efficacy* proceeds by natural laws: *light*, on the contrary, is the *outward expression of testimony* viewed in itself. Therefore the *earth* is opposed to the former as a dead, corrupt mass which must be pervaded by it; the *world* is the object of the latter, as a dark region in which it must assuredly shine. The middle term between the two is *fire*, (Mar. ix. 49, 50, and Ps. l. 2, 3—compare Levit. ii. 13.)

The salt in itself is properly the power of life in its essence, the imperishable *permanence* of an abiding essence, inwrought into things as their principle by the Eternal. It can therefore no more become corrupted into saltlessness, than the light can become darkness, either in nature, or in that spiritual kingdom of which it is the symbol. Yet, inasmuch as our Lord has graciously condescended to say of those who have salt in themselves (Mar. ix. 50), that they are the salt; and to name those light who are only lamps or lightbearers; in this sense the salt may become indeed savourless, and the light in us become darkness (ch. vi. 23): that is, if we lose again the salt and the light. Salt alone averts corruption, and gives a good and savoury taste (Job vi. 6), hence it appears in the sacrifices as the seasoning, and a sign of the covenant of God. Without salt the earth is corrupt before God (Gen. vi. 11), and all who live upon it foul and stinking, an abomination in his sight (see Ps. xiv. 3) נֶאֱלָחוּ, comp. Job. xv. 16. But God gives to the corrupted mass a new salt, has checked the corruption from the very beginning by His grace, and will now in the fulness of His mercy and of His truth, salt again the whole earth—if it will receive it—unto life. The instruments of this great restoration are the children of God through Christ! They are the salt of the earth, for they bear God's truth livingly within them, which is made *their salt*, by which they should salt and season everything around them: just as in v. 16 it is also said—*your light*. They bring and they make *peace*, that is, in the full sense of the Hebrew שָׁלוֹם[1] for the healing of all corruption; for they bring the only living and abiding truth in righteousness; and only in truth is peace. (Col. iv. 6; Mar. ix. 50; Zech. viii. 19), Now, the healing influence of this sharply piercing truth, is foolishly resisted by human nature, and if it should therefore intermit its piercing, through unbelief, and indolence in its possessors, and give way before the resistance which it meets; if its point should become blunted in the attack, and that which through the might of God ought most powerfully to bear witness to, and approve itself, should in the bye-ways of false peace degenerate by degrees into a thing which only retains the outward appearance of that truth which is for man's peace, but from whence the power is fled:—then is the salt again become saltless, as church history has shown in the darkness of Roman Christendom, and more recently in the no less profound darkness of Rationalism.

The salt without savour has indeed the *obvious appearance* of being doctrine which has become impotent and unsound; yet, since this can only be the consequence of the loss of power and life in the salt-bearers, who themselves are termed *the salt*, it would be very false exposition to say that the Lord does not speak here also of *persons*. That he does speak of them, the treading under foot manifestly shows. It would be wrong to say, that though men once endued with grace may become weak and impotent for external influence in the awakening of others,

[1] What I have said concerning this in Jno. xiv. 27, and elsewhere (also in Isaiah) may be consulted and compared.

yet that they cannot themselves again be quite lost. That would be through prejudice to do injustice to the word which here, as elsewhere often in Scripture, expressly and incontrovertibly warns against relapse as only, alas, too possible. He only can salt the earth who is himself salted, has become salt; the abiding virtue within, and its energy without, are strictly inseparable. Now he who ceases to salt others, loses also the salt which preserves himself: and after such loss of the heavenly gift is no second renewal possible; there remains only the *consuming* fire of judgment, which is by no means the same with the *salting* fire of purifying, saving affliction. (Heb. vi. 4—6, x. 26, 27; Mar. ix. 49.) Only for the sake of the children of God who prevent its judgment, and co-operate unto salvation, is the *earth* preserved, though corrupt and full of wickedness, in order that it may be their inheritance of the Regeneration. But those who persist in their wickedness, will not abide that spiritual severity which would work out their welfare, that mighty testimony of the truth which is for their peace. Such salt is too fiery and biting for them, they persecute the righteous, and fight against the ambassadors of peace. Now, herein lies the temptation of these latter to become saltless; and the Lord teaches His own not lightly to despise this temptation! Contemplating the future of His church, He lifts up his warning cry, and proclaims what has since so often taken place. But Luther's translation here and in Mark ix. is quite incorrect;—with what shall we salt? wherewith shall we season? That would have seemed to refer to a *universal* apostacy, and have given to the question such an unsuitable meaning as this—if *ye* fall away, where will be God's children for the world's good? What the Baptist said (Matt. iii. 9), is the fit rejoinder to such view of the question.[1] No, the Lord most assuredly means:—If the salt loses its savour, wherewith shall *it*, the worthless salt, be salted again? What follows proves this—*it* is thenceforth useful or fit or good for nothing. The *casting out* is the lot of that which is useless, which can serve no purpose in the house, and the *treading under foot* further

[1] Hence with reference to Luther's text *Hamann* writes this vigorous application of it:—The salt of *learning* is a good thing; but if that becomes savourless, what shall we season with? With what but the μωρία τοῦ κηρύγματος, the foolishness of preaching? (1 Cor. i. 21.)

marks the perfect contempt of that which is thus cast out. No "mending of the way as by manure" is here referred to (as Lange thinks); but the Lord God casts the corrupt out of His house and kingdom again, and thereby gives them over to the scorn *of men.* The judgment upon Eli (1 Sam. ii. 30) has been ever fulfilled again and again in an unfaithful priesthood: and what the Lord here denounces has been true of entire apostate churches as well as of individual faithless men. If the world *persecutes,* it is because it feels the power of truth and righteousness: but when the saltless salt comes in its way, it *despises* it beyond measure, treads it under foot with scorn—and that deservedly!

He who Himself alone is in an absolute sense "*the light of the world*" vouchsafes also to call His disciples so, who yet are only bringers and bearers of the light (φωστῆρες, Phil. ii. 15; λύχνοι, Jno. v. 35; i. 7—9), only lights kindled from above. (Hence also presently ver. 15, καίουσι λύχνον). The light itself can no more be thought of as first lighted, than salt proper as salted. The children of light, heretofore of darkness, are light *in the Lord* (Eph. v. 8), the light of the world is the sun, and the Messiah is termed by Malachi (iv. 2) at the close of prophecy, the Sun of Righteousness. As such the Lord now proclaims Himself to all who hear Him even in this word, and before that great *I am come!* which follows ver. 17. But as instruction in the law is termed in the Talmud salt, and many a Rabbi a light of the world, the Lord may be regarded as taking up the Jewish doctrinal language which was already prepared for Him, and as announcing in dignity that He, the highest Master, designed to make His disciples also true masters and teachers. Yea, in His mouth alone is that quite true, which from human lips appears presumptuous;—the testimony and doctrine of His disciples should actually fill the world with clearly shining, true light of the Light. The *city on a hill* is not by any means a mere common figure of speech: the Lord derives the expression from Ps. xlviii. 2 (comp. l. 2, lxxxvii. 1) as afterwards that of ver. 35 from Ps. xlviii. 3. He speaks not of Saphet (as Sepp again says idly) nor of any other such hilltown in the land: but of His *Church* or congregation hereafter to be built, of the new *Jerusalem,* to which will be given the light of the sun, when the old Jerusalem, become saltless, the city upon the hill and all her dependencies around, shall be given over to be trodden down of the Gentiles. Now, however, in this period of development with reference to which the Lord is immediately speaking, His meaning includes all the true citizens of the city of God then living in the diaspora. Although as yet scattered abroad, they can no more with their united lights be hidden, than if the new city were already built upon the hill, and reflected God's light upon all the lands. Where light really is and continues to be, it must, from its very nature, shine forth. The same God, who founds and builds for Himself the heavenly city, and kindles for Himself its lights, places them moreover upon fitting candlesticks, each one upon its own. We must take the expression—do *men* light, and place, in ver. 15, in conformity with the general scope, as the action of men figuratively used for the action of the wisdom of God. The church of the Lord is to be no secret institution, like the heathen mysteries. The light of the pure word and of holy life is to burn brightly and loftily in it for the dark world, which also itself is, and shall be made a House of God. No human ordinance, no false shame or fear, may place this light under a bushel, which is designed to shine forth from word and work combined. What God has not done, man *ought* not to do: though, alas, it has been too often done in various ways, but only where God's light and salt are lost. Man's worst *bushel* upon the light of God is the bar and covering of "Temporals"—the bread and pay dealt out too richly or too sparingly for the ministry in the Church. Individually indeed the Lord will often cover up in His wisdom some small fresh-kindled light, that it may burn up in its time and order; but he who cannot tolerate that, and would himself prematurely ascend the candlestick, may easily chance (as St Bernard reminds us) to be blown out by the wind of temptation. This remains the essential matter, that the *placing* of the light be left to Him who kindled it. He will do it, assuredly, at the right time and in the right manner: for it was never His purpose when He kindled the light that it should be hid. Now he who, through fear of persecution or else through sluggishness, leaves his candlestick, and, becoming unfaithful to his calling, wilfully covers his light, shall have his light extinguished: yet *concerning that* the Lord says nothing further now (as in ch. vi. 22, 23); for he has already referred to this in what he says of the savourless salt. It is now His purpose, less as a warning than in promise, to encourage our shining, as that for which we were kindled. God only covers so long as is necessary for the better burning. But our short-sightedness, which we still retain though lights of the world, may often confound, when *self-will* blends with our testimony, the bushel with the candlestick. A proverb says very strikingly—the true light will burn, nevertheless, through the bushel.

It is of importance to observe, that it is not said, we must wish ourselves to shine; but as the translation well expresses it, that we should *let*, freely, without covering or hindrance, *our light*, that which has by grace been given to us, and exists within us, shine before men, according to its own nature and the will of Him who kindled it. The Lord says literally—so *let your light shine*, and thus expressly distinguishes the true, and only shining light of the Father, which has made us to shine, from ourselves, these bearers of the light. There is a *promise* in His requirement that we must without any co-operation of ours leave the gift of God to its own self-evidencing power, as if he had said: It *will of itself* shine, if you cover it not! That spurious desire to shine brings only darkness within and around us. It is not, shine *ye*, but let *your light* shine! Before *men;* as the explanation of the expressions earth and world: even before the men who persecute and revile you; for this must be your only retaliation—love and truth for hatred and lies. And now as to the good *works!* Are these not especially the *word* of testimony and confession of doctrine? This is not excluded, as will appear presently; but our Lord immediately refers to the *life*, because the good word without the good walk is of no avail; a lie before God it can bear no testimony to truth before men; with the appearance of light it has no power of fire; and tends rather to the temptation of the world, and the dishonour of God. That which, according to Rom. ii. 23, 24, befel Israel, is also repeated in the Christian community. The expression "good works," which explains the figurative "light," forms also the transition to what follows from ver. 17 onwards, where the righteousness of the disciples comes forward as the fulfilling of the law in act and in teaching. What kind of works? Here is already laid down before-hand, as it were, the theme, which is then developed from ver. 20. The external lustre, which proceeds from the inner light, and which alone can be *seen*, shines forth in genuine good works, that is, in works of light, of love, of mercy; so that here the salt may correspond to the *peace*, and the light to the *mercy*, of that pure life of love which was described before (ver. 7—9.) And certainly the *shining together* of all the works in the entire *walk* is here signified; which according to Eph. v. 8—13, neither should nor can conceal its revealing, witnessing, light-nature. Of the *individual* good deeds as such it is said on the other hand—do them *not* before men! (ch. vi. 1.) Isolated works or *deeds* do not properly shine; they are rather as flashes in the night, which make the darkness appear the darker: but the entire and persistent *doing* of all works of pure light and love is a bright light upon the candlestick of the office and calling. Again, to *men*, natural men, are these works principally and first of all to be shown: the brother already born of God understands our simple word, and God alone *sees* the faith in the heart, the inner light itself as such. (Rom. xiv. 22). *That* men should see our works is indeed the most imme-diate end of our letting the light shine; but the important end within this end follows immediately; *and* glorify your Father which is in heaven.[1] Not you yourselves, against which chapter vi. presently lifts up a severe voice—ye may yourselves be no more praised, than *yourselves* shine. Not that men, instead of all manner of evil (ch. v. 11) are to say nothing but good of you, but that the *Father in Heaven* (who is here named for the first time) may be acknowledged as *your* Father through your light, your good works; and that ye may thus be termed *His children* even now before the world. Whence arises a new and beautiful sense of the promise in ver. 9—as already ver. 7 had implied; they shall receive mercy from those, who, acknowledging their love, love them in return.

But now since men are wicked and for the most part wicked remain; as they reject the salt and hate the light; as they acknowledge nor honour neither the Father nor the Son (Jno. xvi. 3); as they consequently refuse the Father's honour in His children, by ascribing that incontrovertible righteousness

1 Roos has remarked among others, that here the Lord, after having hitherto spoken of *His* Father, for the first time appropriates the Father name of God to men.

in them which cannot be defamed, on the one hand to *human virtue* which they praise, or to the *gift of God* which they acknowledge; *therefore*, with the good and shining works *the testifying word* must not be wanting, which acknowledges the grace of the Giver, and cries out,—This is my Father's light through Christ, in whose name I do all this, (Col. iii. 17). Then are the clothes rent, and they cry to the people—We also are sinful men like yourselves, but the grace of God is with us, (Acts xiv. 14; 1 Cor. xv. 10). The life without the word is not enough, although the backwardness to confession often brings falsely forward this expression of Christ, as if to prove, that it is enough to let the light of good works shine before men. Thereby God's honour is not desired but our own; but when we glorify our Father in our life and in our confession, then we *constrain* men, at least as far as in us lies, to glorify Him also: first of all and at once, by praising the grace which has been vouchsafed to us, and then, receiving that grace also for themselves, by the selfsame good works and light.

Ver. 17—20. "Finally, there is here also a warning, which in its emphatic restriction and rejection, points forward already to the test at the end of all." Thus did we indicate previously, this conclusion of the first head, and discern now, again, the close of this conclusion in that most earnest *warning*—without a much better, a perfect righteousness, there is no entrance into the Kingdom of Heaven! (Here, beforehand, just as in ch. vii. 21, though not yet so fully established, but rather set down first as a paradox in order to be fully proved). This strongly protesting warning (either *all* the commandments of the law *done*, or *no* entrance *by any means* into the Kingdom of Heaven!) is preceded by one more gentle:—Not one of the least of these commandments must be broken, either in teaching or in doing, by any man, or he will be *least* in the Kingdom of Heaven! And *whence* then such righteousness in poor miserable man, to whom a Gospel is preached, yet with such a demand as this? The introduction of the Sermon has sufficiently assured us, that He, in whose coming the Kingdom of Heaven and His righteousness comes to the poor as gift, consolation, and food, Himself brings with Him His righteousness as His salvation: consequently we have here at the outset, as the true foundation of promise, on which alone the requirement is erected, that great, emphatic, and critical word—*I am come to fulfil* the Law and the Prophets, as first in myself, so also in *you*, my believing and righteous ones![1] Because, moreover, this whole conclusion of the first main division of promise is the transition to the severer tone of demand and warning which follows; therefore to this especial and most distinct *Promise* of the whole Sermon on the Mount (by which the Benedictions are first made intelligible) there is appended a warning and exclusive declaration—*think not* that it is otherwise, that the saving grace which hath appeared may remit or relax any thing of that whole will of God, which has been testified from the beginning, and waits for its full establishment and performance! Finally, that the whole section (ver. 17—20), may fall into the same threefold form which has become familiar to us, we have between its commencement of Promise and its excluding close, the natural middle term of requirement in the simple words :—All must be fulfilled! (ver. 18.) Every the least thing, every the most isolated precept of the great whole (the Law and the Prophets, ver. 17) must receive its fulfilment.

Thus will it be observed how the whole discourse, constantly rising and reaching forward, evolves gradually its deep meaning —each new utterance springing from the preceding as its immediate consequence. Truths ever new and fundamental, clothed in human language for human apprehension, proceed from the living Organ of the one all-embracing Truth (I am He, who bringeth to you Righteousness) which bears in it the mind of the Lord, and here gives an epitome of its first testimony. This (ver. 17), is the true and essential marrow of that testimony—its immoveable foundation of rock. Its clear and luminous declaration is essential to the right understanding of the whole Sermon on the Mount. It prevents us from being terrified by its succeeding *requirements* into a fear of condemnation: and teaches us *in poverty of spirit to seek and find, to ask and receive from Him who is come to fulfil all righteousness—who, while He demands, promises*

[1] It is true, but not by misunderstanding it, to be too straitly limited, that the Saviour here "indicated the object of *His own* life" (Beugg. Monatsbl. 1847. 9.)—for he designs at the same time to say :—The law must also by *you*—though only indeed through Me—be fulfilled.

likewise, and when He promises demands—all needful grace for the fulfilment of righteousness in ourselves.

And yet how wantonly do those err, who assert the Lord's sermon to contain only the mere so-called Morality which He taught, and would thereby get rid of what they call the dogmatic teaching of faith in His Person, its Divine dignity and sole merit! As they contradict their own heart and conscience, and will not feel that the Benedictions at the commencement set aside all righteousness and fulfilment of the law in our own strength, and speak only of grace for the miserable; so now do they entirely renounce their own understanding, shut their eyes and their ears that they may not perceive and read and hear, the inscription which is written upon the sublime portal which is once more erected in ver. 17 :—It is I alone who bring in and accomplish all! Yes, verily, the testimony which is found in St John's gospel, is anticipated here :—*I am He!* Are not all who hear His first word constrained to ask—Who can this man be but the Messiah, who thus announces blessedness, and thus by his own immediate authority administers the kingdom of heaven? His first words are in clear and profound accord with the most expanded predictions and promises of prophecy. And then that lofty and unrestrained—for *my* sake, ver. 11, which is so naturally uttered! So again immediately that first attribution to his disciples—*your* Father, ver. 16—springing from the communicating grace of Him who had already openly called God *His* Father, and continued throughout the entire Sermon (all being comprised in *Our* Father, ch. vi. 9) until that most impressive *My* Father, of ch. vii. 21, closes it! In conjunction with this is the sublime —Verily, I say unto you—which similarly pervades the whole, (ch. v. 18 and onwards) placing Him who utters it in Divine majesty above all the Prophets, in the unity of that only Lawgiver and Lord who spake *by* the Prophets: until at last, He who thus speaks announces Himself to be the world's judge in that day (ch. vii. 21—23), as He had in the beginning announced Himself as the giver of the world's blessedness. In ch. v. 17, we have the ground of all that high authority which speaks in the preceding and subsequent discourse, in the undisguised answer to the question :—Art thou *He that should come?* (ch. xi. 3.)

Twice with emphasis :—I *am come*—to wit, as one who was in

being before He came, and cometh *into the world* (Jno. iii. 19; xi. 27; xii. 46), knowing *from whence* He came: who is *come forth* from above (Jno. viii. 23, iii. 31), from heaven (vi. 33, 38), from God (viii. 42, xiii. 3), as the Father (xvi. 27, 28). This is much more than Nicodemus, drawing back in the paroxysm of his fear the confession which was springing to his lips, attached to it when he strangely enough called him only—Teacher and Prophet. For all the Prophets are but *sent*, He of whom they prophecy and He only, *cometh* from God. As elsewhere there is often appended to this expression—I am come! the aim and result of His coming in a variety of aspects (Matt. ix. 13, x. 34, xviii. 11, xx. 28; Lu. ix. 56, xii. 49; Jno. vi. 38, ix. 39, x. 11, xviii. 37), so here also it is directly given:—I am come *to fulfil*.

This, however, is attested with the negative warning—*Think not*, or *μὴ νομίσητε*, by no means be deluded into imagining that I am come to destroy the Law or the Prophets. Such an utterance presupposes testimonies concerning His person already received, and the existence of misunderstanding and false expectations in relation to it. Wherein did these consist? In a twofold error, as the Lord afterwards shows,—in false hope and in false fear. Especially, and first of all, the Lord testifies, in immediate connexion with the requirement of *good works* (ver. 16), against the delusion that the Messiah (*Himself* who assumed to be the Messiah) would dispense with the fulfilment of the holy *law*; for such a delusion more or less consciously pervaded the entire expectation of a carnal Messiah's kingdom, which might instantly be set up with its temporal prosperity and splendour, without repentance and regeneration unto holiness. (Hence once again the *μὴ νομίσητε* of ch. x. 34). The *kingdom* of God consists only in obedience to the will of God, only in and with God's *righteousness* (hence ch. vi. 33) the law remains inviolate—be ye therefore holy, for I am holy! (ch. v. 48). But for the other side of the error which understood not the Scriptures, whether of the Law or the Prophets, He who was come found existing a false *fear* of innovation, and the destruction of established and ancient institutions. In their blindness to the *Law* which must abide ever, they forgot the distinction between it and the types and the shadows which God's commandment appointed for their own time, and even between it and the precepts which had been added by man; they consequently inferred in their delusion that a Messiah who should invade the then extant Judaism could not be the true one of whom the Prophets had written; for they understood the Prophets still less even than the Law, and had utterly marred their promises by a carnal interpretation. Both kinds of delusion were in manifold ways mixed up in carnally blinded Israel; only that in the mass of the people the false hope of the relaxation of the Law in order to their supposed fulfilment of the Prophets, and in the pharisaic heads of the people the false fear of innovation rather predominated. There lay, in fine, in the hidden consciences of all the people—whose will and not their knowledge was at fault—*an absolute dread of the true fulfilment of the Prophets in order to the true establishment of the Law.* The Lord's mighty protest against each fallacy that ignorance or opposition of will might beget, embraces all this in its inmost connexion, so that every one might take his own reproof; and exhibits the *Law and the Prophets* in their inviolable unity, as one great prediction *of Himself* which waits for its *fulfilment;* as one great preparatory institute which reaches in *Him,* only in Him but certainly in Him, its end and consummation, that is, its perfect fulfilment and realization. Now as this preparatory institute was of God, of the self-same God whom the Messiah calls his Father, He could not speak of anything like a *dissolution* or destruction of that which was essential and true therein.

The superabounding fulness of meaning in this sublime testimony of Christ to Himself—whereby he places Himself between the Old Testament and the New as the living unity and truth of both — embraces thus the whole doctrine concerning His person and His work, is the epitome of all that *Christology* which is to be developed from them, as the substance of all theology, the sum of all true understanding of Scripture and revelation. To deduce this in all its amplitude is not the design of these our hints: we can only affirm and indicate how the understanding of such a saying as this requires an understanding of the whole Old Testament, as it goes back to its very beginnings and roots, and of the whole New Testament as well, inasmuch as it looks forward by anticipation to the entire fulfilment of those of its last predictions which have not yet been accomplished.

"*The Law and the Prophets*"—taken together are the name of the Old Covenant (as afterwards, ch. vii. 12, xi. 13, xxii. 40): yet not merely in the sense of the current manner of speech which divided the external body of the Scriptures under the titles תּוֹרָה and נְבִיאִים, but with reference to those two aspects of the Old Covenant upon which such a division was based—viz., *commandment* and *promise.* These two fundamental elements, however, so thoroughly interpenetrate one another, that the whole, the legal as well as the prophetic word, the legal as well as the prophetic institution, may be regarded as comprising both: the one element commanding the fulfilment of the fore-announced will of God, and the other, pointing in prophecy to that future, which alone will bring this fulfilment. He who does not thus understand the Old Testament, has not yet even begun to understand it: its double-name is its only right name. It is a law, which has not yet found its corresponding obedience, and which yet must and shall be done: it is a promise, which yet waits for its fulfilment. When this has come, it becomes an *Old* Testament, and gives place to the New. But this New Testament, again, is no other than the truth and reality of the Old, its *fulfilment,* which can alone bring it, as old and precursory, to an end. Oh that our critics of the present day would understand this; whose entire but idle toil is expended upon the vain endeavour to rend asunder the two Testaments of God, to unbind the Law and the Prophets, and then—to regard indeed Christ as one who has come, but who fulfils nothing and nothing brings![1] Let the Old Testament first be broken, then is broken also the New; as we have seen in the progress of Rationalism into all unbelief: let the *Christ* be taken away, who has come as He was to come, then is there no longer a Revelation and no more a living God.

To proceed, however, with a more specific examination of this subject:—What is *the Law,* of which the Lord here speaks? Assuredly not merely the unaptly so-called Moral Law of the Ten Commandments; for Israel had learned nothing in Scripture of any such improper division of that one, entire law, which the

[1] Instead of explaining away with their trifling the assertion of our Lord, they had better deal with it as the old heretic Marcion did, and reverse it at once,—as if He had said, τί δοκεῖτε; ὅτι ἦλθον πληρῶσαι τὸν νόμον ἢ τοὺς προφήτας; ἦλθον καταλῦσαι, ἀλλ' οὐ πληρῶσαι.

Lord had given them in various commandments, moral precepts and statutes. To that same law belongs, in inseparable unity with it, what we term the ritual or civil law; all is together but the one will of God, which is to be established in the obedience of His holy people. The typical ceremonies of the service of God, with all that appertains to them, are all appointed with reference to sin, just as they fore-announce its atonement; the external regulations of the polity of the people and the state which are not less typical than the former, are for the correction of disobedience, while they foretell the coming of a people and commonwealth of God, which should be the future realization of these forms. The commandments of Sinai, again, with all their condemning severity, rest upon the ground of that word of covenant mercy—I am the Lord thy God, who redeemeth thee and thus direct the hope of faith to go beyond their letter, and wait for that spiritual fulfilment, in which the law will not be given unto death but unto life. The law itself as such secretly testifies and predicts a righteousness of God, which should be made manifest, (Rom. iii. 21). On the other hand, the language and testimony of *the Prophets*, especially those who spoke after the law, with Moses himself at their head, is always in strict unison with all that word, which from the beginning had been a word of prophetical promise, (Acts iii. 21). They speak of the law, as the expositors of its spiritual meaning which the flesh cannot fulfil, and as most inexorable preachers of repentance, of woe, and of judgment—Elias and John the Baptist being their prominent types; but they also with most benignant consolation point to a coming grace—yea, to a grace which already began to be in some measure experienced, but reserved its full proof for the great futurity.[1] The law requires the *righteousness* of God in us (Rom. viii. 4), and at the same time *predicts*, as being given by a God of *grace*, that He will bestow it. The Prophets promise the *kingdom* of God, and the advent of one as its king—who will fulfil all, yielding a true obedience to the law as a servant, such as no individual servant of God, and much less the

[1] Thus the Benedictions themselves were all of them taken out of the prophetic word: see Isa. lvii. 15, lxvi. 2, lvii. 18, lxi. 3; Ps. xxxvii. 11, cvii. 9; Isa. xli. 17, lvi. 2, lxv. 13; Prov. xi. 25; Ps. xxiv. 4, 5, xxxiv. 19; Isa. li. 7, lxvi. 5.

whole people had been; offering a true propitiation for sin as a Priest; bringing in the fellowship of God's covenant in all its fulness and reality as the Mediator of the Covenant, and the Lord our righteousness: but at the same time every word of the Prophets *requires*, as given by the God of *truth*, the coming of that future one, and the fulfilment by Him and through Him of all that was written concerning Him. The law is a prophecy pointing to Christ, prophecy is a law, a will of the Father for Christ to do. Of both together in their unity He who was to come speaketh:—What is written in the volume of the book is written of me, and all is obligatory upon me, I must come to do the will of God, (Ps. xl. 8, 9). *Did no such Christ come*, then would the entire Old Testament, which declares itself to every candid mind to be the marrow of the world's ancient history, and to contain the revelation of the most essential truth of humanity, remain a beginning without an end; a before without an after; a riddle without its key; not merely a longing of the human spirit without its fruition, but a testimony of the spirit of God without truth; an incomprehensible nothing, making an incomprehensible pretension to contain in itself a living germ—a germ however, that never knew development, withered up in this modern Judaism, the miserable and worthless remains of the religion of that man, who once believed in God, and sought after righteousness in vain!

But Christ *is come*, and as He now at the first by this most sacred "I" bears true and absolute witness to Himself as the end of the Old Testament, so has the history of His kingdom and of His work since then, of the institution founded in the New Testament down to the present day, borne witness to the truth of His word. The actual and surely progressing *fulfilment* in the history of the world and the Church since Christ of all that waited for fulfilment in the old world, cannot be entirely mistaken, but by such a delusion from the abyss, as knows of no fulfilment either of man's longings or of God's commands and promises, simply because *it dissolves all things* in the Indian Maja, or swallows up all things in a bottomless grave. Or rather would dissolve and swallow up, but cannot: for the *Law* of God still abides, testifying against *sin*, and urging men ever to the word of the prophets concerning the fulfilling and atoning obedience of one man for all. Yea, Christ Himself is still in His Church, and asks most earnestly: If I am not come to fulfil, what then is humanity, history, God?

Has Christ, then, in any sense, brought a new, a better, a more perfect law, than *the* law, to fulfil which He avows Himself to be come? By no means, as the whole Sermon on the Mount, His whole word, and the virtue of that law itself in our consciences, attest. All the Prophets representing the conscience of the people, which again represented the conscience of humanity, knew of none other than the one, eternal law. But this, through the Spirit of God, they went on to predict, that one was coming, whose salvation should consist only in the establishment of this law, and its righteousness, and further also, in the establishment in its true meaning and fulfilment of the entire typical ceremonial and political law of Israel. *The Law and the Prophets* are at all points internally *one*. Therefore the Lord does more than merely place them in juxtaposition—the Law *and* the Prophets; but with deep emphasis, think not that I am come to destroy the Law *or* the Prophets, that is, neither the one nor the other, neither of the two which are yet but one. The requirement points to the promise, the promise to the requirement: the latter predicts the Spirit, as the Spirit enforces the latter. But inasmuch as the *first* and *most immediate* delusion, to which the entire connexion of His discourse is opposed, was only that of supposing that he would relax *the Law*, He orders His words for their conviction upon that subject:—*No more* will I destroy the Law than I will destroy the Prophets! If ye expect a Messiah, such as the Prophets fore-announced, and yet suppose that He will come as a Relaxer of the Law, ye do greatly err, not understanding the Prophets in their central harmony with the Law. If I did not fulfil the Law, then would the Prophets also fail in their fulfilment.

Thus does the Lord disclose the deep common foundation of *all* that delusion and error, which withstood Himself by a *perverted expectation of the Messiah*. It was simply the Jews who destroyed the prophetic word, by a carnal interpretation of it. It was simply the Pharisees, who likewise destroyed the Law:—by teaching it without performing it themselves (ch. xxiii. 3—4), by sacrificing one part of it to another, omitting the weightier matters, judgment and mercy, while they cared for the externals of its ceremonies (xxiii. 23); by neglecting the spirit that was required, while they were exact in the letter and work of their conscious hypocrisy; finally, by making the most important fundamental commandments of God of none effect through their superadded traditions (ch. xv. 3—6). Therefore He is no Messiah to these Pharisees, who in their evil imagination call destroying fulfilling, and fulfilling destroying. Therefore must the righteousness of His disciples, and of the subjects of His kingdom, be something exceedingly different from the so-called righteousness of these Pharisees:—it must spring from the power and grace of His own true *fulfilment*, which has come, and is ever coming.

What is this, in fine, and *how does the Lord fulfil* the Law as well as the Prophets? He fulfils the Law as its first perfect teacher and performer (ver. 19); who releases the Spirit, which though in it was bound in it, by the confirming testimony of a spiritual interpretation, and the living exhibition of it in word and work; who, as man, made of a woman and made under the Law, as minister of the circumcision bound to all the ordinances of Israel (Gal. iv. 4; v. 3), fulfils in perfect obedience all righteousness; and satisfies every righteous obligation which human nature and the creature sustains in relation to God (τὰ πρὸς τὸν θεόν, Heb. ii. 17). But because this obedience, which was freely undertaken in the incarnation of the eternal Son, is fully accomplished in His sacrifice for us sinners who could not render it; an obedience not merely imputed to us, but implanted in us through our actual union with His humanity; therefore Christ in His entire obedience, suffering in doing from the beginning, and doing in suffering to the end, is the one meritorious and living sacrifice, finally and fully presented in death, the true object of the whole typical law, which testified of the necessity of such a sacrifice between God and man on account of sin. He is the righteous one, who bears and overcomes in enduring love the sin which rages against Him in temptation; yet the *curse of the Law* is withal fulfilled in Him through His mysterious substitution in our stead, but only in order to make way for the blessing. In this is realized the true use of the Law, that for which it was given to sinners; that they through the Law may die to the Law; that the power of sin may be broken in its conflict with inviolable righteousness; that God may conquer in judgment, aud yet man not be lost, but be redeemed to a new life in living righteousness. In Christ's flesh, which is our sinful flesh, and yet, which is through the eternal Spirit without sin, the flesh is put to death, the enmity is abolished, sin is judged, the judgment of God against sin is executed even unto the securing of a new holiness. He sanctifies and offers *Himself* for us, and in this act of obedience unto death He is the servant of God, the Prophet and the High Priest of whom the Law and the Prophets foretold. As in His death sin is abolished and its curse is repealed, so also every vain delusion of erroneous expectation in which the blindness of sinners have enveloped the promise, is revealed and destroyed as such; his cross is the death of all Israel's carnal hopes of a Messiah. The covering falls from the eyes of those who refuse not to see this, the shadows fade away, the veil of the figure is rent, for its reality is come and is set up. Its further consequence and efficacy is immediately fulfilled in the *Risen Redeemer*, the servant is glorified as the Son, the kingdom of the King and the Lord, of which also all had foretold, begins to appear. The Lord who died especially for the fulfilment of the Law, though to that also the Prophets contributed their testimony, *liveth* now especially for the fulfilment of prophecy in its stricter sense; although the promise of the Law—He that doeth these things shall live! is realized also in Him, who as the Righteous One has voluntarily accomplished in Himself the command of the Law—for thy sin shalt thou die! even to the attainment of a superabundance of righteousness. This life, thus by right as well as grace obtained for us, is one with the *Blessing* of the first promise to Abraham; and thus the righteousness of the Law itself, which was for ever beyond our own attainment, turns in Christ into a righteousness of faith for us (Gal. iii. 8—14). The circumcision of the heart which the Law required, the profound truth which was borne witness to by the whole sacrificial economy of the tabernacle (for the veil and the foreskin are the same in the inner spirit of the man before God) is, through the obedience rendered by Jesus in His perfect humanity, brought nigh and within reach of us all (Rom. x. 6—10). The Law is far from being relaxed, and our being released from it is eternally impossible. We are delivered, rather, from the curse of the Law in order to its being established in its due honour. For the power of sin in the flesh is taken away, and the influence of the life-giving Spirit is shed upon us in unrestrained abundance from the glorified God-man (Isa. lix. 19).

When the Lord, in the Sermon on the Mount, said—I am come for such fulfilment as this;—all was not yet accomplished in Himself which was incumbent upon Him, but he had only within Him as yet the resources of power and willingness for all. His whole *work* is developed and consummated in and with His *person*. When He cried upon the cross—It is finished—then was His great work truly accomplished, and all that remained even up to the ascension was but the manifestation and completion of the victory which he had obtained. When He had risen again and reached his consummation He fully explained all that the Prophets had spoken of Him, and in what sense all had been imposed upon Him as a sacred necessity (Luke xxiv. 25—26). But that which is in Him accomplished and established *for us*, must from this time be also accomplished and established *in us*: in order that the righteousness demanded of the Law may be fulfiled in us, and the Law be established through faith (Rom. viii. 4, iii. 31). He who thus has shown Himself the *end* of the Law and of prophecy, has become thereby the new and living *beginning* of a new covenant and kingdom, the old covenant and the old kingdom of Israel having risen again in their great and high reality. There remains yet for fulfilment in the new Church no less than all that is written in the Law of Moses and the Prophets and in the Psalms (St Luke xxiv. 44): and since the time that the heaven received Christ, He intermits not the influence of His spirit, nor will He till the restitution of all things which God hath spoken since the world began. (Acts iii. 21). The new creation of the Spirit begins immediately upon the day of Pentecost, in simple and gradual fulfilments of what had before been written: the whole typical history of Israel is reproduced in its essential reality in the true Israel of God, and will go on till the new heaven and the new earth are created, wherein dwelleth righteousness.

The ordinances of men, however, which were not the *Law*, are utterly abolished, as well all the mere human expectations which answered not to the meaning of the *Prophets*. And not only so, for the actual *fulfilment* of the old Scripture is at the same time to some extent an *abolishing* fulfilment, inasmuch as that which was preparatory ceases through its completion, the shadow retires before the substance, and the shell which enclosed and concealed the kernel, drops from it. The servant of Israel, the minister of the circumcision, the Messiah of the Jews, becomes a Saviour of the world, as it was indeed most plainly predicted. (Rom. xiv. 8—12). That which through the imperfection of the prophetic vision was only uttered with restriction and limitation, is expanded now into most abundant and glorious universality, and thus only fully corresponds with the meaning which the spirit in their letter had signified from the beginning. Yet more! As the *prophecy* has found its *end* when fulfilled in Christ, so that no more prediction shall go forth concerning Him, and we are released from all expectation of another than He who is already come, and of anything else than what we now have, from all the imperfection of fragmentary prophecies which have not yet found their unity; so also is Christ, as the fulfiller of the Law, likewise *its end*, that is, the *Law* in contradistinction from its fulfilment (and as such only secretly predicting a future righteousness of grace, while condemning present unrighteousness) has altogether lost its force for those who are justified in Christ through faith. We are no longer *under* the Law, for through Christ it lives within us and works its own accomplishment; its requirement no longer presses upon us as a commandment from without—Thou shalt! Whoso doeth not all these things, let him be accursed and die! The *punishment* of the Law is no more contemplated than its rewards, by those who through the Spirit of grace in Christ, are made meet to be the people and temple of God.

Finally, there is another sense in which both the Law and the Prophets continue still, and cannot fail till all things be accomplished. Grace itself retains the office of correction, and Christ as the living and life-giving law of the Spirit, chastises sin, indeed, even in His own, until He finds it no longer; but His chastisement is only unto life and peace. (Isa. liii.) The old law viewed as preparative, also, is not gone out of the world; but still exercises, as ever, its open or secret office wherever the Christ who has come is not yet preached: and even in conjunction with the work of the Spirit in evangelical preaching, the work of the letter continues upon all hearts and consciences in the outer congregation, before Christ comes into it. The Lord Himself as Prophet preached the Law, to prepare the way for Himself; and His servants follow his example.[1] Similarly Christ Himself, in His Person and history from His birth to His ascension, is a still-continued prophecy of the fulfilment of His work, of the reproduction of His person in His Church: as the Church again, in its beginning and progress, is still a prophecy of His matured body, of the Temple finally completed at the end of the world. This is, indeed, a living prophecy, bearing in itself the power and security of its own fulfilment, but still a prophecy pointing to the Future. *Waiting* has no more ceased than *Duty*: only for all who are in Christ, the former is a progressive possession and attainment, the latter a progressive ability and willingness. Similarly the prophetic word continues to be a standing witness to all who have not acknowledged the Christ as come, even till they acknowledge Him. And all things thus go on, till the Law and the Prophets have reached their fulfilment in the perfect Church, the body of the great Head; until the final decision and separation of the judgment has come, which is every where attested to be the goal of all law and prophecy: and thereby the end returns back to the beginning again, the entire Old Testament appears spiritually yet visibly in the tabernacle of God among men, eternally new; and after the last rejection of the unbelieving, and the glorification of the faithful, nothing more remains to be commanded or threatened, and nothing more to be foretold.

Thus have we, to some little extent, pointed out the meaning of our Lord's utterance in Matt. v. 17—the enlightened reader will discover how little only of its inexhaustible fulness. But we have not once as yet fixed our attention upon the *second* sentence of this great saying, in which He so emphatically repeats—*I am not come to destroy but to fulfil.* Is this really a repetition only for the sake of emphasis? Assuredly so in part, so far as it is

1 The Law and the Gospel go ever hand in hand, and jointly increase in the clearness and profundity of their revelation. The Law reaches its fulfilment in Christ, not only in His bearing of its curse, but also in His more perfect revelation of its demand, through His own word and act—even till the final judgment and the kingdom of grace are at once and together fully brought to light. So Schöberlein, Stud. u. Krit. 1847. I. p. 26. 27.

the Lord's design to impress a more vivid conviction of the infinite contrariety of these two things, and to place in a more striking light the folly of that delusion which expected any *abrogation* from *Him*. But there is also something new in His meaning, something wider and greater, when He now omits the "Law and the Prophets," and testifies in general and comprehensively: I am *altogether and absolutely* not come to abolish anywhere any thing that is right and true, but my coming is throughout and entirely to conserve, to expand, and to fulfil all the rudiments, preparations, and tendencies towards the kingdom of God in humanity. Hereby does He throw His unrestrained glance over Israel even into the whole world of Heathenism, for which also He is come, and in which also there will be found elements of preparation for His coming, which His new revelation may seize upon; for He comes not absolutely to create anew, but rather to fulfil. He looks into the deep things of humanity in relation to God, and surveys its history as presenting a universal aspiration towards Himself, and waiting for His coming. And do not these very Scriptures concerning the future Christ, which were given by God to Israel, that copy of humanity, also disclose the self-same preparation for Him, though more hidden and darkened, in the other nations of the earth? Is there not something in them all, which we may also term *νόμος ἢ προφῆται εἰς Χριστὸν?* The heathens have a law in their conscience, a worship of God through sacrifice in their religions, codes of morals and rights in their political economy, longings and presentiments in their wise men and poets who are also their prophets. (Tit. i. 12; Acts xvii. 28.) The Lord brings its fulfilment to every such expectation in the ancient world, and destroys nothing in all this which testifies to the righteousness and truth of God; only its sins and its delusions He destroys everywhere as being the work of the devil, in order that He may help forward to its development, every, the most secret, germ implanted of God which still existed among them. How gracious and full of encouragement is this word for all in the world, who, as poor as they are sincere, are waiting for righteousness! How solemn and admonitory is the instruction which it gives to all the Lord's servants, His missionaries among the heathen and His preachers in Christendom, that in every relation internal or external, they must not teach and labour in the spirit of such entire abolition as their Lord here signifies, but bring in everywhere a universal *fulfilment* through *Him who came to be* the Spirit of all forms, the consummation of all beginnings, the answer of all questions, the satisfaction of all necessity.

But *let not the world think*, even the Christian world down to this day, that He came for any other end than to establish the whole Will of God, as the Law and the Prophets in Israel especially enforced and foretold it :—let this be declared to the world continually in the Lord's own words, both for its encouragement and its warning. *Fear* ye not this new thing which Christ brings, as being a subversion of all established customs, a casting down of your own vain righteousness, and an interruption of your own cherished peace: He does indeed destroy inexorably the Old, which was not from God and avails not before Him, but only as the fulfiller of all aspirations towards a true righteousness in God's sight! But *hope* not for that grace as bringing a false freedom from law, wait not for His Kingdom with expectation that savours in any degree of the blind delusion of the *Jewish* expectation of Messiah: He does indeed make all things new in the spirit, brings grace, peace, life and blessedness, but only in order to righteousness in the obedience of God's will! Would you rather have a Saviour who should not establish the law of Sinai, because your evil conscience recoils from it; a Saviour who should leave behind much of the Jewish word of prophecy, because your foolish fancy in the unbelief of a sluggish heart opposes it;—then does He most decisively answer you, *Such an one am not I!*

Ver. 18. For *all* must and will be *fulfilled*, that is written in the ancient *Scriptures*, even to the tittle. Of this the Lord gives His yet stronger assurance, and confirms it with His *Amen*, which was heard first in Jno. i. 51, and had since then been often used to individuals as in Jno. iii. 3, v. 11, but now for the first time occurs in His public teaching of the people. The Prophets who testified of Him who was to come, and Moses, the mediator of the Law, might only say—Thus saith the Lord! But here that Lord Himself is speaking whose way they all as servants had prepared; who, greater than a prophet, expounds the true meaning of the Law which Himself had given (vers. 21, 27); withdraws those condescending concessions which it had made to the hardness of their hearts (vers. 31, 33, 37), and re-establishes and reimposes it in all the perfection of its original integrity; who, indeed, thus early declares Himself (vers. 19, 20) to be the one Lawgiver and Judge who receives into or rejects from, the kingdom of heaven. He it is who thus preliminarily asserts His own authority and the authority of the whole subsequent discourse: *I say unto you!* Here at once His peculiar method of instruction begins to become more distinctly manifest, in which He excites the deaf ear to attention by *striking proverbial sayings* which have the appearance of hyperbole, and yet utter nothing but the actual and literal truth, of which no tittle shall be abated, and which He can seal with His *Amen!*

We perceive immediately, if we will only give heed, how far-reaching had been the Lord's preceding word concerning the *fulfilment* of the Law and the Prophets; since the fulfilment is to take place not merely in His own person, but further and ever increasingly through Him *in all who are His,* through the whole yet future history of humanity in all its ages down to the end of the days of heaven upon earth (Deut. xi. 21.) He now mentions only the *Law,* as the more common name in popular usage, which employed both interchangeably; but its connexion with what has gone before shows that it embraces also the Prophets, whose prophecies *must* as certainly be fulfilled as the commandments of the Law,—see the repetition of this at a later period in St Luke xvi. 16, 17.[1] Yet, when we mark what follows, we perceive that there is a transition in this expression, and that the Lord is proceeding now to bring into prominence the Law in its narrower sense, the *commandments* of righteousness. *Heaven* is not the heavens of ver. 12; as *earth,* here, is not the same which is promised in ver. 5, as an inheritance; but the present heaven and the present earth, which await a *passing away,* παρέρχεσθαι, a vanishing, a growing old (as 2 Cor. v. 17; Jas. i. 10; Rev. xxi. 1), the

[1] *Schleiermacher* would very erroneously (on Luke p. 207) strike out of the Sermon on the Mount ver. 18 as an interpolation from St Luke —because it makes the whole uncertain and ambiguous! vers. 17 and 19 immediately connected are so very plain! Surely Schleiermacher finds some σκάνδαλον here to remove.

being changed and renewed, according to the predictions of the Scripture, which clearly announce this in such places as Ps. cii. 27; Isa. xxxiv. 4, li. 6, lxv. 17; and even in its earliest revelation had occasionally made it known, as in Gen. viii. 22; Job. xiv. 12. The first *till* is just as certain and as necessary as the second —compare the direct assertion in Lu. xxi. 33. Thus the substance of the word of God, written before Christ and in Him to be fulfilled, with the development of this His kingdom and work, stretch forward to the final passing away of all that is perishable and changing of all that is mutable; then first when the world passes away, will the fulfilment of all be complete and established!

Heaven and earth, the form of this present world, are but a transitory creation to endure for their season (1 Cor. vii. 31; Heb. xii. 26, 27); but the word of God abideth for ever (Isa. xl. 8). The world passes away entirely and as a whole; there is coming another heaven and another earth; but the word of God, the slightest minutiæ of which are here compared with the whole universe, must remain even to the smallest point. There is in that word, rightly conceived of, neither small nor great; nothing in it can be lost, for it is, and must ever be, a living whole. And this applies to the word *which is written* in the letters of human language, to the *Scripture* which cannot be broken (St John x. 35), as the ἰῶτα ἓν ἢ μία κεραία incontrovertibly declares. The iota is the smallest letter; the tittle, little horn or point, is the smallest part of a letter, which appertains to the true and established Scripture.[1] That this strong expression refers figuratively in its special meaning to the least important of its contents, is plainly to be understood: and this saying therefore teaches us that while with the change of the heaven and the earth there will follow also, finally, a change of the form of the word of God, a *passing away* of the letters and points in which it must till then be contained, its full accomplishment yet remains:—till *all be fulfilled.* This *all* comprehends every ἓν καὶ μία which now exists in the letter, and shall remain in its reality; and assures us of such a fulfilment of everything in Scripture, whether great or small,

[1] And by which alone many Hebrew letters are distinguished, as ר and ד. The iota is often superfluous, yet even then the Jews ascribed to it a peculiar signification.

first or last, in its pure and actual truth, as we cannot now apprehend. The *manner* of this establishment of the written word in the eternal permanence of the new world, our Lord leaves in obscurity, even as He does the *manner* of the old world's passing away. Thus much, however, He says, in passing to His subsequent discourse, that this *fulfilment begins* in His disciples' *performance* of it unto righteousness.

Ver. 19. He therefore now turns more particularly to the *commandments* of the Scripture, and asserts their inviolable continuance as a whole and in their individual precepts, in opposition to the destructive error of the *Pharisees*. They are obviously referred to here, though without being named, as He presently afterwards places His disciples in direct contrast with them. The Pharisees understood not that the Law is a living whole (Jas. ii. 10), though the many threads united in one border upon the fringes which Moses appointed (Num. xv. 38; Matt. xxiii. 5), might have pretypified it to them. They counted the single commandments as single, just as even yet a blind misunderstanding has nothing better to say than—this God has commanded to us, and this also, and yet further this. They investigated with subtilty which were the greater and the greatest commandments; and which as being the least might be left unperformed:—just as even now dead systems of spurious morality and ethics speculate about a collision of duties, in which one must give place to another; and dream furthermore of grosser and more venial sins. It was their custom to compare what they regarded as the *least* commandments with the smallest letters of the Scripture, י or ו, and to this folly the Lord had alluded in the previous remark. They at last, in the excess of their perverseness, treated the especial precepts of holiness (which the Lord Himself, more strictly defining his present expression, certainly terms *τὰ βαρύτερα τοῦ νόμου*) as slight and insignificant in comparison with the external ordinances and customs, in the frivolous fulfilment of which they sought their righteousness. (Matt. xxiii. 23, 24). In opposition to all this, the Lord asserts the equal validity of the smallest of *these* commandments also, as being uttered always with a like "Thus saith the Lord," and from among *them* He presently afterwards takes His examples. By the admonitory

Whosoever, therefore, shall break one of these, He does not so much aim at the Pharisees, as at His own disciples, appointed to office in His kingdom, who are warned against doing as they did. This *breaking* takes place, as the connexion shows, through a spurious, enervating exposition which *teaches* it as something unimportant, leading as a consequence to an entire disregard of it, so that the requirement of the commandment is annulled, and it is left altogether *unperformed.* Whosoever of His disciples deals in any such manner with the Law, in this or the other department of its precepts, and teaches the people so, let him know that he is a bad teacher, who himself has understood and received but little of the perfect righteousness of the kingdom of heaven. Since he has not scrupled to term some commandments the least, he shall in just requital, here, in the true records of the church, and hereafter, when every man's praise or blame shall be righteously dealt to him, himself *be called the least.* This is obviously not to be taken in a good sense (it is severer than μικρότερος, ch. xi. 11), but has an almost scornful tone, and verges upon not entering the kingdom at all, though it is not altogether the same.[1] For the Lord does not refer to full and absolute Pharisaism, but to an intermixture of it in His disciples with error of judgment. But whosoever of them, on the other hand, is zealous with all his might and before all things, *to do* the apparently least commandments of God, and in this spirit *teaches* the Law, shall be called *great* in the kingdom of heaven, shall be acknowledged as a genuine teacher and master (Rabbi is equivalent to great) in the final and just judgment which shall give to every man his due. Ye must be Rabbis, in a better sense and in the highest truth of the name! Mark, then, accordingly, who are in the sight of Christ the little Rabbis, and the untaught doctors; and who are the great and genuine expounders of Scripture and masters of the Law! But art thou disposed to press the matter so far as to cleave to the minutest letter as such, or even to accept this most important expression of our Lord so strictly in the letter as to deduce from it the perpetual, external

[1] There is *to us* more of *irony* in the tone, than (as *Braune* thinks) of love and gentleness, such as might yet consider the object of it to be in the kingdom of heaven. More correctly *von Gerlach*:—"To be called the least, is generally an expression of contempt, and rejection."

obligation of all those Mosaic precepts, which He, nevertheless, elsewhere has by His Spirit annulled,—then hast thou not yet rightly understood the Master, who speaks, indeed, of an abrogation or establishment of the commandments, very different from that which may take place in the letter. We shall henceforward find many more such paradoxes in the Sermon on the Mount, which penetrate into the profounder meaning and harmony of truth. He who, in his exposition of any one commandment, which was written for Israel in the books of Moses, has nothing else to set out with than, "this is now obsolete"—is one of those who destroy the Law. But he who discovers in the whole, for himself and for others, an inner abiding meaning and import which even yet applies to us all, is the genuine teacher of Holy Scripture.[1] He only who interprets it in harmony with the Old, is a true interpreter of the New Testament.

Ver. 20. How great is the contrast between *this* declaration, which closes the first part, and the promises which commenced it in vers. 3 and 6! The Lord utters it by way of transition, as a general superscription for the whole development of the second part:—Let yours be a sound and genuine and perfect righteousness, and it is specially now said for the first time:—not like that of the Pharisees! If that contrast between the beginning and the end is rightly regarded, and the entering of the kingdom of heaven into us is taken in connexion with our entering the kingdom of heaven, we cannot but perceive that even this severe utterance has an essential promise within it. For it then runs thus, being reversed—Unless the kingdom of heaven enter into you with its gracious gift, ye can have no righteousness at all! If ye receive it in your poverty, ye shall be filled with righteousness! But just at this point the discourse passes over to a more rigid *requirement* that this gift of righteousness be both received and preserved. The strong expression, *οὐ μή*, in no case enter, goes further than the previous comparison of least or greater in the kingdom of heaven. It is similar to ch. xviii. 1—3.

Not all the *scribes* were at that time *Pharisees* likewise, or the reverse;[2] but the Lord blends them together according to their

[1] *Richter's* Family Bible asks, "Art thou not afraid because of thy past treatment of the Old Testament?"

[2] At least not according to the more general idea which holds good

internal points of union, and thus exhibits under two aspects the absolute opposition between every kind of insufficient and false righteousness, and the perfect, genuine righteousness of His own disciples. This opposition is ever the same to the present day, in all ages and in all places, for the developments of the Jewish people down to the age of Christ are but a mirror of that humanity into which He enters as a whole. The scribes are everywhere those who are *learned* in the letter (γραμματεῖς) and who teach it; and the worst delusion is that of supposing that such knowledge, without corresponding action, is righteousness;—it therefore stands first. But it is no better, when even such doing is added as that of the Pharisees. These are in all times the *doers* of the work in appearance but not in reality, retaining now as ever the disposition to add the ordinances of men to the commandments of God, to substitute their *opera supererogationis* and ἐθελοθρησκεία for the weightier matters which they have lightly dispensed with. The book-learned and letter-sifting γραμματεῖς reckon up the precepts of God, as if they were no more than mere letters and points: they determine with keen subtilty which are the greater and which the less, and it is all that they can do, to *give instruction* in these matters. The Pharisees are zealous, also, in the work; but with the same formal, blind, dead cleaving to the mere work without any life in it, as that of the former to the letter without any spirit. Though the two are sometimes distinct, they generally run one into the other; and therefore the Lord here unites them together. What then is *the righteousness of the Scribes and Pharisees?* First of all, knowledge and teaching without doing: then the doing without heart, as in the accustomed offerings, tythes, their own self-invented washings, &c., and even in the case of the commandments: Thou shalt not kill! Thou shalt not commit adultery! and yet shall this, wherein all is hypocrisy and the lie of pride without any the slightest approach to poverty of spirit, be termed a "*righteousness!*" The Lord so terms it indeed, but with that severe scorn of sharply penetrating truth and love which He must ever feel towards all such as they were, down to the end of time. These *righteous ones*, these *especially holy*—as the name Pharisees sig-

here. But it will be seen to follow from ch. xxiii. 2, that only the orthodox Pharisees held the seat of Moses.

nifies[1]—think themselves to *exceed* other people, and to possess abundant righteousness: but the Lord casts them down from their eminence, when, in ironical allusion to this, He cries to His disciples: Let *your* righteousness *exceed*, let them be the common people and sinners in comparison of you! The tone of this is more severe than what was said in ver. 19; for it means no less than that their righteousness is *none at all*, since it gains them *not even* an entrance into the kingdom of heaven.[2] On the other hand, that first righteousness which is attained by the justifying faith of those poor and wretched ones to whom mercy graciously inclines, is a *true righteousness*, although the mourning and the hungering strictly speaking should come after, and their hearts be not yet purified in all holiness. The Publican goes down from his first prayer of penitence justified *rather than* the Pharisee: and if he proceeds in this righteousness, if he, now that the kingdom of heaven is come into him, constantly seeks the full establishment of the kingdom of God and His righteousness within him, then will the Fulfiller fulfil all in his experience, until he is perfect, as his Father in heaven is perfect. All this is effected through asking and receiving (ch. vii. 7), through that process of self-denial before God and before men, which, though easily apprehended by the mind, is only possible in act through Divine grace, (ch. vii. 12, 13). The spiritual law of our Lord, as it now proceeds on from ver. 21, ever anew casts down throughout the whole way to its full accomplishment, every presumption of perfection already attained; reveals the still-existing heathenism of nature in the hearts of the children of God: puts to shame all precipitate judgment of others, while self is not judged, all rebuking of the Pharisees without the much better righteousness than theirs, as sheer hypocrisy; and cries to all disciples from step to step, for their encouragement and warning, in order that all Pharisiasm may be extirpated:—Let your

[1] פְּרוּשִׁים according to the Rabbinical writings, those who assume to be separate and holy, so that it might be seen from their very garments that they held themselves different from עַם הָאָרֶץ, the common people.

[2] Similarly in Heb. xi. 4, Abel's better or greater offering than Cain's.

righteousness be yet better still, let it yet more and more exceed, until it become absolutely perfect![1] This let us do and teach even as our Master did, and take good heed that we abate not His word by a single tittle anywhere, nor invalidate His "verily I say unto you" by any falsehood of our own.

Not like the Pharisees, the men of the letter of the Law, and of hypocritical outside appearances! This is the first great contrast, by which the perfect righteousness of the disciples of Christ is further delineated, that righteousness which is required as the fruit of the grace which has been previously received. The two other contrasts, as we said above, *develope* themselves out of this :—Not as the heathen! Not as the half-disciples, who, being disposed to remain in an imperfect righteousness, fall away again entirely as a consequence, and are put to confusion as hypocrites and evil-doers!—*Not like the Pharisees!* The Lord thus, in the manner of the Prophets, connects His teaching with the characteristics of the men of His age, embracing and illustrating by them general and permanent relations. But how is this seen? As the development of these words proceeds into detail, they evolve *three* other contrasts which disclose and explain themselves organically, advancing from the original principle of Pharisiasm to its consequences, and tracing that *right understanding* of the Law which is opposed to theirs into its essentially voluntary and actual *obedience.* His disciples' understanding of the Law is *spiritual;* to this is opposed the merely *literal* understanding of the Pharisees: that of His disciples is consequently *correct,* and is opposed to the *false exposition* of the Pharisees: their right understanding approves itself, finally, in a *voluntary and hearty* reception of the Law in order to *do* it, in opposition to the *hypocritical* legality of the Pharisees. This is the internal arrangement of the discourse from ch. v. 21 to ch. vi. 18; which cannot, indeed, be viewed otherwise, since it corresponds with the most profound relations of the matter upon which the discourse dwells. The error of the Pharisees proceeded from their

[1] At the utmost possible distance from the picture which Zeller (in the Monatsblatt) draws of the proud saints who imagine that the paper-money of their own good works must be current, also, in heaven, and be reckoned there *at par,* at least, if not indeed *above par.*

merely literal acceptation of the Law (ch. v. 21—32): and in its origin was to some slight extent excusable, inasmuch as the letter of the commandment was obviously most prominent before them. But if man's sinful heart would sincerely and humbly permit the Law to enter, it would soon reveal its spiritual and inner meaning as designed for the conviction of the spirit, it would thus spiritually expound itself, just as all sincere souls have ever understood it; for we must not suppose that Christ gives now an altogether new publication of its meaning.[1] But in the wickedness of the Pharisaic mind, on the contrary, this literal understanding of the Law produced, and, indeed, had for its foundation, a *false interpretation* (ch. v. 33—48), which, finally, in the progress of perversion, disannulled it entirely; so that, Thou shalt love! became in the destroying gloss—Thou mayest hate! In the *detection* of their error we find its *principles* becoming more evident as we go further into its *outward exhibition*. The Law is literally understood from the beginning because it has been falsely interpreted. And, finally, as to the third? The Law has only been falsely interpreted because it is read and heard not with a view to the simple and sincere *doing* of it: since the design is not to obey the Law in spirit and in truth before God who seeth in secret, but only for the sake of man! Hence, thirdly, and quite correctly, we have the *hypocritical seeming-legality* of the Pharisees, which developes itself from this false interpretation, and is also found to be its source (ch. vi. 1—18). With which is brightly contrasted the genuine, internal fulfilment of the children of God before their Father in secret—which alone avails and will receive reward.

If after this general glance we enter more into detail, we find that the Lord further illustrates *each* of these three contrasts by *three examples* taken from the precepts and duties of righteousness, and evidently according to a fundamental and necessary order of selection. And here we are met by the division of the Law into moral, ceremonial, and civil; a classification which, notwithstanding the essential unity of the three, is based upon truth, and now will be exhibited in its propriety. From the

[1] To suppose this is most fundamentally to misunderstand the relation of the Sermon on the Mount to the Law. Christ says even here, only what Moses and the Prophets have already said.

ceremonial law, or the law of the Sanctuary and Divine service, the Lord takes no particular leading example, because that was given not so much for the conviction of sin, as for the typical satisfaction of an already awakened sense of need of a propitiation. He contents Himself in relation to this with merely adding to the first example an impressive caution, referring back to the instance of Cain, against the unhallowed *offering of gifts* with an angry and implacable heart. On the other hand, He very distinctly brings forward, in connection one with the other, the civil law or the law of the *political economy* of Israel, and the more distinctive law of *Holiness*, as we prefer calling it, instead of the moral law. He begins naturally with the latter, with the *commandments of Sinai*, the heart of the whole divine legislation; and presents as the three examples of the first contrast, *two* from Sinai and *one* from the civil code. In the second contrast this is reversed: *two* are taken from the civil code (concerning swearing and judicial retribution), and *one* returns again to the summary of the moral law,—the love of our neighbour. In the third contrast, finally, He very significantly abandons the written precepts of God's word, and takes His illustrations from the three main works of righteousness according to the human Pharisaic idea: —almsgiving, prayer, and fasting. The details of this arrangement will exhibit and justify themselves, when we examine them more narrowly.

We now proceed in our more direct exposition to vers. 21—32. The two commandments of the Law given from Sinai, are such as exhibit the literal and spiritual acceptation in their rudest collision, and Christ, by His full disclosure of the latter, lays open the very ground of man's evil heart. The civil enactment which follows, concerning the *letter of divorce*, is one which exemplifies the preparatory character of the Mosaic ordinance, its accommodation to men's hardness of heart; and Christ exhibits His fulfilment of this law, to those who possess His spirit, as being a cancelling of that which was imperfect, and a re-establishment of the original and right ordinance. The two first commandments are united: Thou shalt not *kill!* Thou shalt not *commit adultery!* for the pride of self which towers above all others (involving the denial of all that is not I), and the sensuality of entire devotion to the flesh, are in their essence just the two poles of the same sin. *Hatred or murder* and *lust* are forms of corruption in the heart, mysteriously reciprocal and interwoven one with the other, which the two keen commandments of the letter, Do no murder! commit not adultery! penetrating to the secrets of the heart, will draw forth and reveal. (Let Lamech of the race of Cain be called to mind, Gen. iv. 19—23. Reflect upon the sensuality of vengeance and the murderousness of sensuality, and that both constitute the perfect opposite to that unselfish and pure *love*, which the holy law of God requires.) But the civil regulation, which permitted divorce, is plainly shut out by the prohibition of adultery, inasmuch as every divorce pre-supposes an act of adultery which is either committed in it or revealed by it. Consequently the essential *spirit* of the command—Thou shalt not commit adultery! testifies *against the letter*—Thou mayest practice divorce! so that the Law of Moses in its integrity and unity itself contradicts the temporary imperfections of its own ordinances, and at the same time demands and predicts in its fulfilment their establishment in perfection. Thus much at the outset,—and now for the details.

Vers. 21—26. When the Lord designs to cast down the delusion of a legal righteousness, resting only upon a literal and false apprehension of the Law without understanding its spirit which judges the inner disposition of mind, He begins, here as elsewhere, with the *second* table of the Decalogue (ch. xix. 18). For our conduct to our neighbour lies most accessible to conviction, and he who feels that he loves not his brother, may deduce from that conviction that all is not right when, before the Searcher of hearts he says, "I love God." That the discourse in its further progress does thus penetrate to the revelation of the heart's *idolatry*, will be manifested from ch. vi. 24. On another occasion, when the Lord points out the disannulling of the commandments of God by the traditions of men, He uses for that purpose the last precept of the first table, which is the middle-term of transition to the second (ch. xv. 4). *Here*, where the whole discourse, according to the note which ver. 7 had already struck, is to reach its climax in—Be perfect in love, as God loveth (ver. 48), the first commandment of the second table naturally takes the lead, the spiritual significance of which is no other than this:—*Thou shalt not hate!* The Lord lays down first the letter of the command, and its merely literal apprehension, ver. 21; in opposition to this, He expresses the spirit of this letter, and yet, in order to awaken and excite a spiritual apprehension of it, He employs figurative language which cleaves to the letter still, and is not to be understood in its literal import. Ver. 22. From this follows, finally, the direct exhortation to love, without which even the offerings upon God's altar are nothing worth; expressed first, in terms of simple exhortation, vers. 23, 24, and then vers. 25, 26, of solemn denunciation, in the figurative exhibition of the *judgment* which is taken up and continued from ver. 22. This judgment, however, can only be fully understood when referred in its higher sense, as the preceding intimation in the "offering" shows, to the highest and only Judge.

Vers. 21, 22. The Lord by this *Ye* addresses His disciples as before, but at the same time all the people, in as far as they belong to Him, may learn what His teaching will be, and this is in a sense the beginning of discipleship. Ye have *heard*, not *read:* this latter could only have been spoken to the Scribes, and the Lord does not now at the first address them at all, but warns the people, to whom He speaks, against them. The people only heard out of the Law which was read and expounded in their hearing; but, alas, were obliged also to hear their teacher's manner of apprehending and interpreting it. (Jno. xii. 34; Rom. ii. 13, 18). That *it was said*—by whom? According to the earlier and customary acceptation, which *Luther* follows, this was regarded as designedly left indefinite, because the Lord's—But I say unto you! was intended to oppose all false teaching generally, from whatsoever source it might come; and it was only defined as the doctrine which had come down from antiquity:—hence, that it was said *to them of old.* Others think that these ancients were the contemporaries of Moses, and that the Lord places His own word in direct contradiction to that of Moses. This supposition is conclusively refuted by vers. 17, 18, after uttering which it is not to be imagined that the Lord would immediately say: Moses has said thus, but I now say otherwise! For that purpose, also, the standing form of speech, "to the *Fathers,*" would have been used (Lu. i. 55, Jno. vi. 31; Acts iii. 22, vii. 38; Heb. i. 1) from whom the ἀρχαῖοι here are clearly distinguished. Does not the Lord expressly confirm, in ch. xxiii. 2, 3, all that the Scribes who sit in Moses' seat teach conformably with the word of *Moses?* Does He not everywhere throughout this Sermon prudently avoid stating in contradistinction to His own words, that *Moses* had said —even, for example, in ver. 31, where this is actually meant (comp. ch. xix. 7, 8), where a preparatory, imperfect ordinance of Moses is abrogated? But here it is *God* Himself, not Moses, who spoke the inviolable word, *Thou shalt not kill!* The Lord does not say any thing in opposition to *this word* in itself, but it is against the merely literal interpretation which was immediately attached to it that He contends:—"This means no more than that whosoever *kills,* inflicts a death-blow, shall be in danger of the judgment." Just as in ver. 43 it is not the commandment of Moses, but its altogether disannulling interpretation, which is spoken of:—Thou shalt love thy neighbour, and *hate thine enemy!* We quite agree with Lange, that "the first corruption of law is exhibited in its not being developed according to its spirit, but *bound down* to its *literal* meaning." Our Lord enters into conflict with all such glosses and teaching as tend to *relax* the commandments (ver. 18); whatever has been said beyond the Word of God, and in false exposition of that word, He contradicts by His own sayings: and thus by the same Divine truth and authority He confirms and establishes the true meaning of all which before Him had been written or spoken as the Word of God.

The notion that Christ contradicts Moses, could only be endured by such orthodox theology as that of our day, which holds so feebly to the Old Testament as immediately Divine! The most tolerable presentation of this view, which is very generally embraced, and, alas, has been latterly maintained by the sainted Neander, in the "Deutschen Zeitschrift,"—that which could alone recommend it for a moment to our consideration, is the notion that Christ only designed to oppose the law *as law,* the "legal relation and expression" as such. But the truth of this view must be much more clearly and appropriately unfolded than, *e.g.* it is by Dietlein;[1] and, moreover, the discourse does not deal dis-

[1] Das Reich Gottes. Berlin 1846.—What *Rauh* also throws out (Deutsche Zeitsch. 1850. p. 360) is more apparently profound than it is well-grounded.

tinctively with *this* point at all, but speaks, rather, in most rigid terms of an unconditionally necessary fulfilment of the Law and its commandments—and, indeed, with a yet more exacting rigour of legal expression of its own. The old Fathers with whom Neander briefly declares himself (in the "Life of Christ") to agree, meant their *correctio legis* in a very different sense from that of the Socinians and moderns, as Tholuck (on the Sermon on the Mount) has very properly observed.

Most certainly it is not the design of the Sermon on the Mount, if we only hear it and read it aright, to *contradict the Law*, but to *expound and glorify it in its fulfilment.* Hence it is not said: Ye have heard, that it has been *read* in the Law. The common people, whose knowledge of the Law was only indirect, would have said with regard to whatever they heard, even though not found written there—We have heard *out of the Law ;* that which was written, and that which was said, being blended together into what was *popularly valid* as "law." But it is our Lord's design now to put a final end to all such intermixture. By the expression which He uses, He indicates the entire system of *erroneous interpretation*,[1] which not merely might, but which actually had to the greatest extent crept in between the true meaning of the letter (ver. 18), and this *hearing* of what had been *said* concerning it. The Scribes read the word "kill," as if it simply meant murder, and as if the limiting addition was strictly proper: but thus they *read* not aright either what was written, or how it was written; as the Lord elsewhere, in referring to the right manner of reading the Law, emphatically expresses Himself:—What is written in the Law? *How readest thou?* (Lu. x. 26). Further, they did not sincerely *tell* the people even what their own awakening conscience, in spite of their system, must ofttimes involuntarily have perceived in the Law. In like manner the people, on their part, did not listen to all that was said to them, but received just what pleased their ears; and thus they limited and weakened it still more, so that the error which understood not the Scripture (ch. xxii. 29), increased as it passed from the saying of the Scribes to the hearing of the people, just as it has ever happened even

[1] The Pharisaic *caricatures* of the Old Testament—which they made not as the *opponents*, but as the *exponents* of the Law—as *Richter's* family Bible has well hit the point.

down to our own time, wherever the people may be said only to hear out of the Gospel. Thus, after having given His assurance that He will not destroy one tittle of the Law, if the Lord should say any thing different from what thou hast hitherto heard "out of the Scripture," look well to it, and see where the error lay, whether in thy hearing, or in what thou hast heard; and then in the right spirit of hearing let Jesus Himself *tell* thee *what is truly written in the Scripture.*

Τοῖς ἀρχαίοις must certainly be translated as meaning that it was said *by* or *among* them of old time,[1] namely, that it had been handed down by the masters and doctors in Israel, by the Rabbis of a former age, with the false semblance of antiquity as an immemorial statute. For thus runs the thalmudical formula of teaching adopted by the learned caste, under cover of which they transmitted from age to age error and truth united, under the seal of their own supreme authority:—אמרו קדמנינו our forefathers have said, or merely איתמר, אותאמר *it has been said;* which was then as firmly established as if it had been the eternally valid *γέγραπται.*[2] In opposition to all this, and rooting

[1] As the ablative, equivalent to, *ὑπὸ τῶν ἀρχαίων*, which construction is preferred by very many, indeed by most expositors. Tholuck regards it as supported by "reasons which deserve notice," though he himself does not accede to it. For ourselves, we regard it as the only possible one, and rejoice that now, in the corrected German Bibles at least, it stands—bei den alten. These ancients are *not* "the fathers" (Heb. i. 1) to whom God had spoken. It was not *Moses* (whom the Lord, moreover, would not have referred to by a mere general *ἐῤῥέθη*!) that had said: Thou shalt not kill, commit adultery, &c., but the God of heaven upon Sinai. (Comp. Matt. xv. 3—6, and all those passages in which Christ places the "commandments" so high, and confirms them so strongly. We cannot conceive why, as *De Wette* thinks, our interpretation would have required *πρεσβυτέροις* to have been written for "elders" (which, however, does not exactly correspond with קדמונים), any more than why, as *von Gerlach* thinks, *our* view would have been expressed—"Ye hear, that it is said in the schools and synagogues." Did they not then refer in these synogogues to the *παράδοσις* of antiquity?—alas that *Alford* also, in his penetrating work, should have failed here. Of a contrasted "imperfection of the *Law* and its ancient *exposition*" (what an unseemly conjunction, as if the latter necessarily sprung from the former) He cannot have spoken who had just asserted ver. 19.

[2] Correctly and beautifully is it observed by *Lange:* "This *corruption* of the Law was gradually and slowly produced by the joint errors

out all tradition and precepts of men which God hath not planted, stands the mighty Ἐγώ δέ λέγω ὑμῖν, which is one with the כה אָמַר יְהוָה or נְאֻם יְהוָה of the Law and the Prophets. Had the contrast been instituted, not with those who had said, but with those to whom it had been said, it would have been ὑμῖν δὲ λέγω.

The false teachers declared to the people the commandment of God—Thou shalt not kill! but with an explanation which coupled the Law of Sinai with a mere criminal statute concerning the execution of a murderer (Lev. xxiv. 17; Ex. xxi. 12), and made the two parallel: as if the Lord God did not in the first place speak of that which came before *His own* special tribunal, and signify by *Thou* the true murderer, the inner man! Thus they lower the commandment of holiness to the level of a civil statute, just as, on the other hand (ver. 38), they improperly elevate what was only spoken with reference to human judicature, into a commandment of moral obligation. To this exhibition of the literal interpretation of a law degenerating into gross error, our Lord now sets in sharp contrast His own explanation of its spirit and meaning; yet in a manner as attractive as it is emphatic. He most *emphatically* declares the concealed *anger* against a brother to be no less criminal than the open offence; or as it might be further illustrated in the popular catch-word—Thou hast heard it said, and supposest that the gallows is the end of a thief, but know that he who only covets his neighbour's goods already deserves the gallows! But He speaks this also to *conciliate* and win them to the spiritual understanding of the Law, since the impossibility which was immediately discerned of carrying this principle into civil jurisprudence must have tended to direct their views to the higher government of God, and to the spiritual law of the Searcher of hearts, whose prerogative alone it

of ages which engendered this false tradition. It was not the work of any particular person, but of a general spirit of interpretation (ἐῤῥέθη); but this tradition was ever received and gathered up with diligence by the elders, or those who were antiquity-minded." Correctly as to the matter in hand, though we cannot but regard this so convenient construction of an *absolute* ἐῤῥέθη with a *dative*, as too artificial. It is a strange, and almost impossible construction. It was so said to the ancients,—by those yet more ancient? Who then were the first of all these ancients, the especial depositaries of this *tradition?*

is to convict the sinner of his secret guilt before his own judgment-seat. Moreover, the Lord here utters nothing that is actually new; it had already been written by Moses in the same sentence, from which He afterwards extracted the summary of the second table (Lev. xix. 17, 18; comp. Deut. xix. 6). Brother is an intenser word for neighbour; Moses used it as such in the passage referred to, and by no means with that restricted meaning of the Pharisees which our Lord condemns in ver. 47. It has been hotly disputed whether εἰκῆ (whosoever is angry with his brother *without a cause*, needlessly, to no purpose[1]) is or is not the true reading: such contention, indeed, is needless. The proposition is correct with εἰκῆ, if this is rightly understood; and, indeed, without this qualification, if ὀργιζόμενος is rightly understood, that is, as signifying a righteous and holy indignation (Mark iii. 5; Eph. iv. 26; Jas. i. 19) which is not only not forbidden, but commanded (1 Sam. iii. 13). It is observable, that such a various reading just here was designed to teach us, that the matter of essential importance is the spiritual understanding of the sense and not the mere letter of the word. Bengel's expression: *plane humanum hæcce glossa sensum redolet*—is not satisfactory, since critical authorities are in favour of this glossa. It appears, indeed, more conceivable that a Rigorist should have struck out this little word, than that its so frequent addition should have been permitted. We rather hold with *Grotius* (who quotes *Aristotle* on unrighteous anger): *Merito* ἐικῆ *additum*. As also *Euthymius* before him: ἡ γὰρ εὔκαιρος ὀργὴ ὠφέλιμος. *To be angry* and *to hate* are not indeed one and the same, though *Bengel* confounds them. He who *hateth* his brother is assuredly a murderer (1 Jno. iii. 15), and Moses said directly, Thou shalt not hate thy brother in thine heart. But there is an anger springing from holy and jealous love, existing as in God so also in men of God; and we may suppose that our Lord in His severe declaration left room for this *by an express word*, in order not needlessly to harass the consciences of His disciples. He does not concern Himself with the possibility of a still further perversion on the part of the Pharisees, who would never be at a loss to find adequate cause

[1] *Lange:* "ins Eitle hinein."

for their unrighteous wrath: for all that follows must also be spiritually understood. The letter even of Christ's word demands an interpretation which adheres not to its letter; for *a letter that may not, without the Spirit, be misunderstood, is a thing impossible*, as is manifestly shown by such subsequent sayings as vers. 29, 30, 34, 37, 39—42. Whosoever should literally follow out all these, would be at the furthest distance from the Lord's meaning. St James addresses the fool, who boasts of his faith without works, with an ἄνθρωπε κενέ, which is literally equivalent to this forbidden ῥακά.[1] Jesus, like John, termed the Pharisees a brood of vipers, and the Jews even children of the devil (as St Paul did Elymas), which goes beyond μωρός נָבָל, godless. Thus it may be seen that εἰκῆ, which it is sought to take away from the anger, must be supplied in this case also:—he who, out of the anger of hatred, and not in love, calls his brother Raka or Fool (vain fellow, scoundrel, madman, heretic). The Lord designedly conjoins the slightest invective of a rash but half-jesting petulance,[2] with the worse and indeed most malignant insult that the language afforded: but it is not His design to bring this word itself into judgment, but the word as springing from the evil heart. The Pharisee, indeed, asks when he hears this most plain and evident saying: Who is then my *neighbour?* and goes on with his abatements and qualifications till no one is included whom he thinks his enemy. In like manner he asks—What, then, is *anger without cause?* by the same process finding means to stipulate for all his ungodly wrath. The Quaker, at the other extreme (to which he has come, notwithstanding his boast of the Spirit, through the self-same want of the true Spirit), also reduces the spiritual law to a letter again, swears not at all, lets his coat and cloke be taken, and fulfils the Sermon on the Mount in all external gestures and acts. But all this is no more right than Origen's mutilation of himself as a safeguard against adultery, or the unconditional rejection by our latest zealots of any divorce, however necessary still in the Christian state for the people's hardness of heart. But He who will read and hear aright, cannot fail by this first precept of Jesus to learn what

1 Which *Matthäi* thinks proper therefore to intrepret "Grüzkopf."

2 Which "has nothing to do with the morality of one's neighbour at all." *Braune.*

relation the directions of the Sermon on the Mount bear generally to the external laws of the state and the church : that they are given only for free and most spiritual fulfilment in those who have the Spirit within them to that end. Was it the Lord's purpose to erect any human tribunals before which secret anger and the saying of Raca may be brought ? Where only a brother might always sit in judgment upon a brother concerning the anger *without cause?* He does not reduce the spiritual law of divine judgment to a criminal code after the manner of men, as the Jews of that time did; but rather elevates all the external ordinances which Moses gave at God's command, into the region of their most central truth, not in the letter, but in the spirit, even as Christians should now do !

Thou shalt not *kill*, that is, thou shalt not *hate!* This is the fundamental meaning of our Lord's words, according to the saying of Moses to which He tacitly referred. He does not, however, once directly express it, but would awaken in their consciences the remembrance of that word, and the consciousness of His meaning. He therefore points out three degrees in the expression of the spirit of hatred or murder. First, the *inward expression*, if we may so speak, the rising up of hatred in the heart, as an unrighteous and unloving *anger*,[1] selfish and self-willed (for it reads, *Thou thyself* shalt not hate !); and then the progressive outbreak of it in the milder and in the severer word. But the Lord does not go beyond the *word* of anger, for even the Pharisee would admit that the laying a violent hand upon a brother was amenable to judgment. Although he interpreted "to kill" as merely signifying the act of murder, yet was he compelled by reason and conscience to extend the literal meaning *so far* at least, even at the expense of contradicting himself. Judgment, high council, gehenna, were the three degrees of penalty in Israel. We read that in the tribes there were inferior courts of judgment, (Deut. xvi. 18); in the holy city the so-called council of the Sanhedrim (Deut. xvii. 8), which might cast out of the congregation; and, finally, as the deepest ignominy, the

[1] Which He certainly does not "presuppose as something unavoidable by the sinful subjects of His kingdom," as *Dietlein* ventures to maintain, so that this intensification of the Law would *only* lead to the acknowledgment of our sinfulness, and not also to its fulfilment.

the being cast out into the valley of the dead and of all abominations. (Valley of the children of Hinnom or Valley of Hinnom, where had been the service of Moloch, 2 Kings xxiii. 10; Jer. vii. 31. The corpses of malefactors were burnt subsequently, and all the most filthy refuse thrown there; whence in the Prophets we find it used as a type of the place of condemnation without the city of God, Isa. xxx. 33, lxvi. 24; and the symbolical Jewish style of teaching, the truth in which our Lord always appropriated to Himself, had yet further carried out the figure.) But these three degrees of punishment are, as the Lord here utters them,[1] only intended to convey an increasing emphasis of assurance in the expression (he already deserves the judgment, yea, even more than that!) and by no means the idea of degrees in the actual guiltiness.[2] For how could the word be more guilty than the disposition? A sincere though forward Raka which might escape from a Peter might well be a less evil than secret wrath concealed behind the blandishment of words: and in ver. 25 we hear only of *one* punishment, and that the highest, for the implacable. So that most assuredly there is here only an advancing energy of expression (though degrees of guilt are not necessarily denied): κρίσις and συνέδριον cleave more closely to the transitional figure, εἰς τὴν γέενναν points to the ultimate and fearful signification of all these figures taken from human judicature.

Vers. 23, 24. Who is my *brother?* Every fellow-man from Adam downwards, every Abel to whom I must not act the part of Cain, and who is called to glorify the Father in heaven (ver. 16) if I let the light of His love shine before him. Yea, even *my adversary*, who has, whether justly or unjustly, any thing against one in the highway of life (though he were as Cain himself), and who at the end of it will bring his charge against me before the highest tribunal, if I should have retained anything against him in my own heart. Thus does the Lord

[1] Who does not (as *Von Gerlach* thinks) merely follow here the usual forms of the judicature of the time, in order to make Himself intelligible to the people who expected from Him the establishment of an external kingdom; but speaks *figuratively*, in the long-established Jewish manner of teaching, as we observe in the use of *Gehenna*.

[2] Against which *Roos* (Lehre Jes. Chris. § 138) very well protests; and also speaks with full correctness of the "heavenly Council" of the divine judgment which was typified in the "Synedrium."

explain His own meaning in the strict connexion of His words; and it would be a great mistake to think that vers. 25, 26 do not belong to this place, simply because they are repeated elsewhere. The Lord here lays the deep preparatory foundation for what is fully set forth in vers. 43—48, where the general conclusion reverts back again to the commencement of the discourse.

It was observed above that in vers. 23, 24, the entire *ceremonial service*, the law pertaining to which is here referred to, is denoted by the *offering*, which is its centre. It is not, as *Luther* has it, *upon* the altar, but, if thou *now* (consequently, in a state of condemnation before God on account of the anger in thine heart) bringest thy gift *to* the altar, and unreflectingly preparest to offer it, as if it could then be acceptable. This is spoken once more against the Pharisees, who omitted the weightier matters, while exact in ceremonial observances, and violated the most sacred rights of filial obligations and love to man through their own superadded *corban*, (ch. xv. 3—6.) The Lord only re-utters what all the Prophets had said, especially that most important passage which He more than once quoted, (Hosea vi. 6); yea, what Moses had already borne witness to in his history of the first offering. He reproves all idea of palliating the lack of charity to man by attention to the service of God, as a remnant of Pharisaism in His disciples. Until He has brought in by His offering of Himself the abrogating fulfilment of all types and shadows, He retains in His language to the people the altar and its gifts, but His *meaning* goes forward to the reality which was implied in these figures. It is not *τὴν θυσίαν σου*, but *τό δῶρόν σου*, because in the New Testament the offering up of ourselves in spiritual consecration is continually realized. This is now the true Christian service of God, with prayer as its centre: the fundamental petition of which for a perpetual sense of reconciliation is a self-contradiction unless there accompany it a placable disposition towards our brother. Hence our Lord at a later period (Mark xi. 25, 26) illustrates His present words, or more fully in this New Testament meaning repeats them. And *there* rememberest: before thine and thy *brother's* Father, with a collected and self-examining mind, in the sacred place of atonement and forgiveness, thinking of the way of life and the end thereof —this being the germ of the thought in ver. 25. Its being *first* there remembered is not, indeed, approved of, but rather censured. That thy brother hath *aught against thee:* designedly put thus instead of: that thou hast something against thy brother. For as I must ask: whose neighbour am I? in order to know who is my neighbour (Lu. x. 36): so it is not enough quickly to justify one's self with hypocritical inconsiderateness—I have nothing against thee; while possibly my brother may have well-grounded cause of complaint against me. Probably I have too easily forgotten that there rankles in his mind some Raca of mine uttered yesterday or the third day: or there may be some anger in my heart against which he *would* complain if he knew of it, as that God knows it who looks into the heart which I have brought before Him. Yea even if my brother had any thing against me εἰκῇ, without cause, had spoken against me as a ψευδόμενος, (ver. 11)—this also should I remember in my charity before God (though *Braune* improperly denies this), and show myself, as a disciple of Christ, in the intention of my heart an εἰρηνοποιός (ver. 9; Rom. xii. 18). The signification of this "aught against me"[1] thus grows, as the sensitiveness of my conscience increases: and the letter of this declaration which fully expresses its own spiritual meaning, tolerates no hasty and partial dispatching of the matter, but pierces to the ground of the heart, and rigorously looks for that pure spirit of love with which alone I can abide in the presence of the Lord, and erect in the consciousness of an accepted offering, behold His face with joy. These are fundamental principles which were already embodied in the history of Cain and Abel, to which undoubtedly our Lord here directs our thoughts: so profoundly one is His new word with the most ancient revelation, and so manifest is the folly of those vain enthusiasts who impute to Him in contrast with Moses a new and purer ethical system of charity.[2] *Leave there* thy gift *before* the altar, and lay it not thereupon! Without any delay leave every thing lying, if it may be possible, in

[1] Compare the Apostle's word (Col. iii. 13: ἀνεχόμενοι ἀλλήλων καὶ χαριζόμενοι ἑαυτοῖς ἐάν τις πρός τινα ἔχῃ μόμφήν.

[2] Which folly finds now again acceptance with Christian theologians and expositors:—a lamentable sign, whither this crypto-rationalist, yea, this crypto-pantheist treatment of the Old Testament must infallibly lead.

the holy place: there is such danger in deferring it that even the service of God, which till then is worthless, must be interrupted. Thou standest as Cain before God if only this *aught* justly cries out against thee in thy brother. How inconceivably strict does the law of love thus become, though only fulfilling its own original meaning! What we wrongfully call a *little thing*, condemned equally with the *great!* By the same Spirit of Christ St John likens him who only *loveth not his brother* to the first murderer (1 Jno. iii. 10—15). Many a disciple might be disposed to rebel against this precept of the Fulfiller, and mitigate it by saying: How can I answer for every matter that any man may bring against me? *Am I my brother's keeper?* Assuredly men (ver. 11) have many things to say against Christ's disciples falsely; and the Lord of course does not mean that we must be answerable for all that they may perversely say. *But* it is nevertheless true on the other hand, that it is our precious vocation to be our brothers' keepers in love, and to be messengers of peace to them; that in Christ not only should the world be crucified unto us and we unto the world, but in the selfsame cross the world should be reconciled unto us and we unto the world. *Go thy way!* Thus speaks the Father to that child of His who would approach with an offence in his heart against His holy love: *Away from me*, thus mayest thou not see my face! Thus will the Lord dispense, as it were, with His own service and honour until we have rendered to our brother what love demands as his due! *First* be reconciled to thy brother—the imperative requirement that for ever recurs as long as there is any, the slightest flaw in this reconciliation. Διαλλάγηθι, forgive or obtain forgiveness, do at least thy best, that so nothing may be set against *thy* account by the great Judge. For to "mitigate thy neighbour's wrath"[1] may not be always in thy power, and is not always to be attained. Pray for them which despitefully use thee and persecute thee, when thou bringest thine offering, that so thou mayest have a vital fellowship with that dying settlement of a great reckoning—Father forgive them! which accompanied the One Offering through the virtue of which alone we may bring our offering to God.

[1] As *Von Gerlach* at Rom. v. 10 explains this place.

And *then come* and offer they gift! The first coming avails nothing, now first thou *comest* aright. The offering itself, however, must not be omitted. The Lord expressly guards against that other aspect of Pharisaism, the Pharisaism of practical virtue: which with equal impropriety sets the duty we owe to our neighbour above the requirements of God's worship, and supposes that *this* may be dispensed with if that misconceived charity to man be not forgotten.[1] Whence hadst thou then thy mercy towards thy neighbour, supposing it to be genuine, but from the mercy of God? *Thank Him* that thou canst love, and let that be thy offering! The Lord also discountenances every attempt to compound for a deficiency in the worship of God, by deeds of charity to our neighbour: such charity, indeed, being no more genuine than the Divine worship was in the opposite kind of compromise already referred to. For "that is not the most acceptable homage, which is offered to God by a man who loses sight of his neighbour altogether, and seeks to sink wholly and entirely into a consciousness of nought but the Highest Being, forgetting entirely the testimony urged against him by the whole time past of his life, in all relations of right, propriety, and love." *(Braune.)*

Vers. 25, 26. The reconcilable and in Himself reconciled God, to whom we bring our offering, becomes a *Judge*, or rather continues to be only a Judge to all those who would fain merely be the objects of His holy love without receiving it in their hearts, and rendering it back in charity to their neighbours. This is that rending of his one law which is the last and most subtle Christian Pharisaism. There is an economy of judgment and punishment at the end of the way, corresponding to the provision for offering and reconciliation in the way itself. The penal laws of ver. 22, *which are explained in what now follows, being referred to the tribunal and period of their award*, assume there their full severity. *Now* they only hang threateningly over our heads, to

[1] Over the door of a Dessau church is inscribed "Preiset Gott *hier und* durch gute werke" (praise God *here and* in good works); but there are many who not only altogether leave out the "here and," but "God's praise" also, inasmuch as their hypocritical way of speaking of good works being the only worship of God must be understood in the same sense as when they say: Cease from Revelation, Reason is the only "revelation," that is, none at all is necessary!

drive us to that *grace* which will take away all our guilt, and extinguish all our hatred and anger. And whereas after the mention of appearing before God (though God is designedly not named, but only the altar, before which man's conscience should think of God Himself), the language of ver. 22 is reassumed; we are thereby assisted to perceive its meaning, and the due relation between grace and justice. The *adversary* (ἀντίδικος, accuser, a judicial term which had been received into the Jewish phraseology) is by no means the *Devil* (who presently appears for the first time as the keeper of the prison), but simply and obviously the ἔχων τὶ κατὰ σοῦ, my fellow-man in the journey of life, whom I must regard as a *brother* (ch. xviii. 35) whether he reciprocate it or not. But inasmuch as every man who may charge me with omission of the rights of love, does not this by any right of his own (being himself equally guilty), but by the authority of the Divine law which takes up and corroborates his complaint; this complaint and this complainant may be regarded as representing the accusing Moses (Jno. v. 45) or *the Law*. Hence in the repetition of the parable, Luke xii. 58, 59, this meaning appears more distinctly shadowed out. Be *disposed to agree*, ready on thy part for reconciliation, and proposing it to him; thus is the previous διαλλάγηθι now fully explained. According to the Roman law, which the Lord thus recognizes in Israel, the complainant carries the defendant before the judgment-seat,—in *jus rapit*; on the way thither, however, an amicable accommodation, *transactio*, being possible. So is it with us all on our way to the highest tribunal; and inasmuch as this way is short and precarious, the exhortation has a most urgent fulness of meaning: agree with thine adversary *quickly*, before it may haply be too late! If I have done my best towards my brother in the advances of reconciliation, the amicable disposition will be set to my account, even though the other would not respond to it. It is not always possible to go actually to my brother and speak to him; in that case this inward reconciliation will avail for me at the very place of offering and of prayer. But when this is neglected to the last, then comes in the rigour of the righteous law; the just complaint of the complainant, even though himself guilty, has its force, and the blood, not of Abel but of another Cain, cries out against Cain. So, finally, adversaries mutually bearing testimony against each other meet in one common prison.

Who is then the *officer*, if God is the Judge? In chap. xviii. 34, βασανισταί are mentioned in the plural, but here it is Satan, the chief of the tormentors, the minister and executioner of the Divine judicial wrath—a profound intimation, though only thus given by the way! *Verily*—here comes in the second great *Amen* of the Sermon on the Mount, the first having previously confirmed the Law, ver. 18. But as the prison of the Devil and of those delivered over to him has its threatening Amen appended to it, so has also the kingdom of the Father in heaven, and of those who are redeemed into it from all evil, with all its power and glory, its Amen of promise, (chap. vi. 13). The Amen which confirms the fulfilment of the *Law and the Prophets* unites both. Besides the three main Amens, there is only found the threefold Amen which seals the recompense of the hypocrites, (chap. vi. 2, 15, 16). (A contribution of internal criticism in favour of the genuineness of the doxology, as well as testifying to the connexion of the whole discourse!)

By no means come out *thence*—an ἐκεῖθεν which forms an antithesis with ἐκεῖ in ver. 23. If the *Judge* and the executioner of His wrath were not so manifestly before us, and if the whole was not a representation of strict *justice* in opposition to grace, the φυλακή might have been here as elsewhere regarded as Scheol; and in the admonitory *till* an actual period might have been traced when the sins carried forward into the other world would find forgiveness (ch. xii. 32). But the connexion will not permit us to regard the Lord as *here* speaking of any such prospect. Though not to be excluded in other connexions, here it would be quite out of keeping. They who thus interpret the paying of the uttermost farthing, pervert its meaning; for if there be any deliverance in Sheol it can take place only through *grace*, in the way of *forgiveness* and *atonement*: it is absolutely impossible that *needy* man, possessed of nothing in the sight of God, should ever legally *pay* the slightest instalment towards the extinction of his debt. He has not even the first farthing, to say nothing of the last (ch. xviii. 34, 35). *Bengel* wonders that the *uttermost* farthing is not urged in the argument by those who think otherwise, rather than the *till*: but when we closely look into it, the reality of the ἀποδῷς τὸν ἔσχατον is immediately withdrawn by the ἕως ἂν, and marked as an impossibility in such terms as we are wont popularly to express what is impossible. To be cast into prison remains thus just equivalent to the entering *in no case* the kingdom of heaven (ver. 20).

In the discourse upon the Second Commandment of Sinai, which now follows in its order in the second table (according to Matt. xix. 18, not as reversed in Mark x., Luke xviii., Rom. xiii.), we find the same process observed. First, we have the letter of the Law, the merely literal acceptation of which does not need to be more particularly pointed out: against this is set the rigorous vindication of its spirit which judges the heart, now exhibited more briefly and plainly than in the former case: finally, the corresponding exhortation to an earnest endeavour after purity of heart (as before to love or mercy, ver. 7, 8), with the warning once more of the prison of hell for the unclean, in which verses 22 and 25 are blended into one.

Vers. 27, 28. The doubtful reading "by them of old time" is, by the authority of internal criticism, *now* more properly left out; for thus there becomes evident a descending abbreviation of the words down to "it hath been said" in ver. 31; after which the new section begins again (ver. 33) with πάλιν and the full formula. "Ye have *heard* that it was *said*," is immediately understood as in the former case to signify that they had been taught the Divine Law in its merely literal acceptation; as if he only was guilty of adultery who committed the act of carnal uncleanness. Such conciseness in His words was adapted to open the ears of His hearers, and would test them, so to speak, on the second occasion, whether they understood the first aright. Those, however, who were dull of apprehension must have understood clearly enough what had been intended by the "said" and "heard," when the Lord uttered His own contrasted words:— But I say unto you, *that whosever only looketh upon a woman* hath committed adultery already. Job long ago declared, in making a covenant with his eyes, (Job xxxi. 1, comp. Ecclus. ix. 5—8), that the first provocation to carnal lust was in the eye full of adultery (2 Pet. ii. 14.) The first spiritual adultery, which was the principle and type of all carnal adultery, began with looking (Gen. iii. 6). In βλέπων γυναῖκα πρὸς τὸ ἐπιθυμῆσαι αὐτήν is condemned that *active* lust, into which the will enters. This, indeed, only is sin, not the passive involuntary impulse of that flesh which is our *nature*, not the "spontaneous observation of the greater beauty of another man's wife"—as *De Wette* expresses himself.[1] He who experiences at a first glance this desire, and then, instead of turning away and withdrawing from sin (2 Pet. ii. 14), throws a second glance with lustful intent and in order to retain and increase that impulse, *commits* the sin. He has already committed adultery in his heart: for the proper *deed* begins earlier than the Pharisees suppose. It is in word or look before the act itself is performed, yea in the *heart* before the look is cast, for it is there that that inner act of the will takes place, which alone gives its significance to the outer deed. This is a stronger and plainer utterance than in ver. 22, where it is not directly said, "he hath killed him already in his heart." It is the *perfect formula applicable to all the commandments*, and it was not necessary similarly to quote those which followed, as: whoso desireth his neighbour's house, has already stolen it in his heart. But so profoundly internal is its application, that it goes yet beyond this:—Whoso, only in thought, by a glance of the imagination, *looketh on a woman in his heart*, who is not present to his eyes! The Lord says simply "*a woman*" (even if not the wife of another), and "*whosoever*" looketh (even if himself not any woman's husband.) Just as conversely (Job xxxi. 1), speaks of a maid when the married woman is also signified. (In like manner it must necessarily be understood:—Whatsoever woman thus looketh upon man, &c.) Has *committed adultery*—how then, if both man and woman are unmarried? The Lord speaks according to Old Testament usage, in which *adultery*, in the sixth commandment and everywhere, indicates and includes whoredom in general.[2] Marriage is the making one flesh, and consequently every carnal lust which seeks its gratification independently of the union which God has appointed in marriage, is

[1] *Matthai* has further and rightly mentioned, that as we must in order to marriage, look upon a woman to desire her; so that only the adulterous, sinful "desire" can be referred to.

[2] As in ver. 32, fornication stands, conversely, for adultery.

a breach and offence against this sacred order. He who has not recognized a spiritual meaning in the Law generally,[1] must at least discern it here, where the Lord evidently includes every concupiscence under the letter of the commandment. And the unmarried by this offence commits adultery by anticipation, sinning against that future marriage for which he should reserve himself: and further in the deepest sense is guilty of infidelity to himself, and the Lord to whom his body belongs.

Vers. 29, 30. Contemplate it now more closely and observe that there is a desire which, springing indeed entirely from the body, becomes an offence which thou must involuntarily endure: but that, at the same time, there must be a continual victory over this desire and casting away of this offence, or a consent to it which implies the actual sin of positive and active lust. The commandment stands in terms which already explain its meaning (Deut. v.) לֹא תִתְאַוֶּה, *suffer thyself* not to desire! The Lord mentions the *eye* and the *hand*, and means, as He explains Himself, *one of our members*. This He does, partly for the sake of a decorous concealment of the member to be further alluded to afterwards; partly on the ground of what had just been laid down, that the impulse of lust usually begins with the eye; and partly, because of the general importance of these *two chief members* in every impulse to every kind of act. (For in the profoundest sense all sin is here included as being uncleanness, spiritual impurity; hence the repetition of this saying with this wider meaning in ch. xviii. 8, 9.) The *eye* is both the organ of reception through which sensual, and therefore already spiritual, enticement enters, and the most certain betrayer of that conceiving lust which will bring forth the act of sin; the *hand* is the general organ for its performance and practice. Casting the eyes upon a forbidden but desired object leads directly to the stretching out of the hand towards it (Gen. xxxix. 7, 12, 13) and the rest follows. The eye—the light, the lamp of the body, its most precious and dearest member (Gen. xxxii. 10): the hand or arm—

[1] Although the last Sinaitic commandment already and expressly forbids *coveting!* No one but *Ernst Meier*, with his universal perversion, could have *concluded* that *because* Christ brought in a *purer* morality than the Old Testament, therefore he could not have spiritually understood this לֹא תַחְמֹד!! (Dekalog p. 73).

the strength, the support, the defence of the body, its most indispensable instrument. Now it is quite evident that objects and persons around us may be, through our close connexion with them, like an eye or a hand, on one of our own members, and that if any of these should become a stumbling-block to us, they must be resolutely cast off (Deut. xiii. 6—10; xxxiii. 9). But it is folly to take that as the only meaning, which is only a right application of it; since this very application must rest upon the internal, intrinsic truth itself. The first and most obvious meaning of the expression is doubtless to be sought in the words "*looketh* upon *to lust*" (to long for, and then to reach forth towards) with which it is directly connected, as well as in their manifest antithesis—*thy whole body.* The expression which is so readily termed figurative, is, as usual, very literal and real in its meaning, though obviously not in the bare literality of an external accomplishment. It is not the eye or the hand that we are to pluck out and cut off, but the *offending* eye, the *offending* hand, and this leads our thoughts to those members of that inner body, of that internal organism of *sin*, which corresponds to the external members, and which might continue all the more vehemently to look and to lust and to strive, if those external members were actually plucked out and cut off. (As an eunuch embraceth a virgin and sigheth. Ecclus. xxx. 20). They are the πράξεις τοῦ σώματος (Rom. viii. 13) which we are to mortify, and this, indeed, is only possible through the spirit of life, without whom the body of this death brings us into captivity to the law of sin in its members. (Rom. vii. 23, 24). How it is to be accomplished we are taught by the experience of grace, of that grace which, preparatorily given, had taught men before the coming of Christ; having from the beginning placed enmity between the woman and her seed and the serpent, and from the time of Cain downwards provided, in the very exhortations which it uttered, a certain gracious power to resist sin in the will and conquer it. But that such inward mortifying of the members which in idolatrous, adulterous desire mind and aim at the things of earth (Col. iii. 5) is demanded by the rigorous voice of the Law —*Thou shalt not!*—and that the ceaseless process of sin from within outwards can only be checked by the suppression of that lust which is the root of all its acts, must be manifest to every sincere hearer of the Law who observes that his eye is not himself, and yet that the commandment of God says—*Thou shalt not!* The important word is not ἔξελε or ἔκκοψον, which are figurative, but that which is attached to both βάλε ἀπὸ σοῦ—renounce in thy will and deny the ὀφθαλμός σ ο υ and δεξιά σ ο υ, declare thy member to be *not thine*, place thyself as far as may be in contradiction to thy member, *hate thyself*, that is, thy flesh, thine own life, so far as it is bent upon sin! Yet *cast from thee* with earnest detestation the offence in thy own dear body and life! Every unconditional *thou shalt not!* is accompanied by the tacit addition —not even if thou must die![1]

But because every creature in every condition, and fallen man also in his ruined estate, cannot and may not cease from *loving self*, so that even the self-murderer only destroys himself from a conviction that it is *better for him* to die, and the diseased man will undergo amputation rather than his whole body should perish; therefore to the commandment—hate thyself! there must be appended—only by so doing *dost thou love thyself* in truth! The requirement to cast from us an eye or an hand must derive its force from—*It is better for thee!* Not merely—" it is good for thee" (συμφέρει carries with it a comparative sense);—still less is it merely—" it will hurt thee not." *Thy whole body should be cast into hell*—that fearfully greater evil, to avoid which the lesser evil becomes an advantage; that essential *death* in death, from which only a " dying to sin" before death can redeem us. *Thy* whole body (which significant repetition is lost in Luther's translation); just because thou regardedst it with false kindness as *thine own*, and wouldst not kill its sinful members! *Cast out* thyself from Jerusalem, because thou wouldst not *cast from thee* thy offending members! *One* sin developed into dominion draws the whole man after it. The *body* is the organ of sensation for future punishment at the last, when the prison of Gehenna opens to receive the eternally corrupting and burning, who in dying

[1] Which might literally be the result of an instant cessation from some accustomed vices. How profoundly spiritual, moreover, the application of this mortifying of our members may be made, and how comprehensively it may meet every man's distinctive individuality, may be seen in *Oetinger's* exposition of the plucking out the eye:—Does thy studying offend thee, lay it by for a while, just as Paul was blind for a season.

shall never die, even as it is now the organ for the commission of their sin. Hints are here given us in passing, the far-reaching significance of which we can only now forecast. In *everlasting life* even the body has become spiritual and enjoys the life of God received through the Spirit: in *everlasting torment* even the last remains of spirit are entirely absorbed in the body, and thus the condemned man experiences bodily that death, which is the wages of sin. This death is something very different from that *perishing* of our members, by which the casting them from us is immediately explained. Their present perishing is the means of avoiding that eternal death. And the member which has offended in the sinful life withers away, but is spiritually given back as in a present resurrection.

Finally, let it be observed that the sacrifice of "one of thy members" is demanded, definitely and inexorably it is true, but yet with a certain forbearance towards cases in which man's soft nature would shrink from the exaction of an eye or an hand. He who does not shrink but accepts it in all its rigour, will evermore experience that it is through many such acts of mortification that the way of life is won. He finds, indeed, at the same time that this exaction does not proceed once for all from the eye to the hand, but that it is ever beginning anew. As it is intimated in these words, which simply mark the commencement of it, it advances from the hand to the arm, from the arm to the heart, and thus *all* the members and the *whole body* must submit, lest as the body of sin it should be cast into hell. And yet such dying is not death, but tends to true *life* in the overabounding restoration of all that is thus sacrificed. What the Lord says in chap. xviii. 8, 9, concerning the entering into life maimed or with one eye, is spoken in yet stronger and more striking proverbial language, and with yet more condescending accommodation to the position of those addressed; but it has its own deep truth which may be viewed under two aspects, as the hearer may accept it. The old body as *the old* must undergo *entirely* the process of healing destruction; thus viewed, the language is that of severe irony—shrink not at the beginning of their entrance from becoming maimed or from losing one eye! The *new* body, however, will be perfectly restored, for all who inherit eternal life, and thus viewed, the language assumes a character of affectionate appeal to their shame—art thou then foolish enough to think that thou wilt remain halting in the resurrection, or that anything will be wanting to thee in the kingdom of God, which thou mayest have given up in order to enter it?

Vers. 31, 32. When the Lord turns from a commandment given by God upon Sinai to a *civil ordinance* connected with it—which latter may be regarded as given by Moses in God's name, but the former rather as given directly by God through Moses—when He passes into another region of the Law, where its precepts in the nature of the case assume a more transitory character, He designedly adopts that most general and concise expression—*It hath been said.* Neither Moses is mentioned nor the ἀρχαῖοι, although Moses actually spake what is here briefly quoted from Deut. xxiv. 1. Thus vers. 31 and 43 stand in conjunction: in the former a Mosaic law and in the latter a human ordinance immediately attached to God's commandment and entirely perverting it, are joined under one general "it hath been said." For the Lord's *saying* opposes itself in the most comprehensive sense to every kind of false reading, or teaching, or hearing, out of the Law. We have already observed above that the Mosaic precept concerning the letter of divorce was closely connected with the Sinaitic prohibition of adultery, and by it only could be rightly explained, the fulfilment of the Mosaic ordinance in its spirit being itself the abrogation of its letter. Marriage is the most sacred of human relations, in which pure love, that in which one person loves another as himself (Eph. v. 28) finds its highest expression, and impure carnal lust, which conceals in itself the spirit of hatred and destruction of another's personality, its most perfect cure and prevention. So that this question of divorce most appropriately follows in strict connexion with ver. 27, as well as with vers. 21 and 22. Marriage is the foundation and nursery of all social relations, and therefore the bond of that *civil order* which, deranged by sin, is to be re-established through Christ according to the design of the Creator at the beginning of the creation. (Mk. x. 6). It was quite natural that the letter of the Mosaic Law in relation to this would be miserably perverted by sinful men, since every law, in proportion as it descends more directly into the details of common life, becomes more liable to abuse through the spirit of literal interpretation. And here we are encountered by an actually *false exposition* of the law in addition to the merely literal acceptation of it; the transition being thus effected from the first to the second department of examples. For what was only a permission is regarded as a law, as if it had been said, thou shalt, and not merely thou mayest, be divorced! (ch. xix. 7, 8): whereas divorce was in no other sense tolerated than that in which polygamy was, which still more directly opposed the design of God's original creation. The precept was read, expounded, and practised as if it had been written כָּל־דָּבָר (κατὰ πᾶσαν αἰτίαν) instead of עֶרְוַת דָּבָר; and thus it was altogether falsified, everything being made to depend, according to the mind of Moses thus interpreted, upon the observance of the mere *formality* of divorce! But as Moses at the beginning took care, in immediate connexion with his precept, to prevent that wanton and abominable divorce and remarrying between the same persons which would have been the worst consequence of such perversion (Deut. xxiv. 2—4); so also the last prophet Malachi, who at the close of the Old Testament (iv. 4) enforces the whole Law of Moses with its statutes and judgments till the coming of Him who was to come, bears similar witness against polygamy and divorce, alleging the high example of Abraham. Deal not treacherously, he says, with the wife of thy youth, who is thy companion (helpmeet!) and the wife of thy covenant, for the Lord hath been witness between thee and her, that is, in effect, what God hath joined let not man put asunder! (Prov. ii. 17). Take heed to your spirit, he says, that ye apologise not by the letter of the Law for your sin against its spirit. "If he hate her, let him put her away, saith the Lord"—that is the wicked language of your own spirit, *but* it is *also* said, "evil will defile his garment, saith the Lord." (Mal. ii. 14—16). Mark here again, that the Sermon on the Mount utters or lays down nothing new, even where it seems most to do so; but where in any sense it annuls the commandment, actually fulfils it in its harmony with the Prophets.

As, further, in the Sinaitic commandment the letter of the Law was first laid down, which expressed the extremest development of the evil in act, (kill instead of hate, commit adultery instead of lust), thus manifesting a *condescension* to the position of that hardness of heart which would only thus apprehend it at the first; so do we also find it in the further statutes and ordinances of the civil law. The spirit of the ordinance to which its letter must give place, is not an abolition of it, but rather its re-establishment in the spirit of the original command—Thou shalt not commit adultery!

Hence we shall sufficiently understand in what sense the Lord speaks when He proceeds—It hath also been said (by Moses), but I say unto you: *Divorce* either presupposes past adultery, or contains and involves it, ye shall not in any case practise divorce! (as ver. 34, to which indeed this is a transition). He who is divorced from his wife, *saving for* a λόγος πορνείας (equivalent to דָּבָר in Moses or ἀιτία) that is, the cause of fornication in the woman which had already taken place, not only *himself* commits adultery by his *unjustifiable* divorce (which is not mentioned as being self-evident), but *is the cause* that *she also commits adultery* through another marriage or illicit intercourse without marriage. Especially, however, in the former case, which therefore is additionally explained. The man himself sins who puts away the divorced woman, the woman so divorced sins, and, in addition, the other man who marries her thus divorced: so that from this wantonness of divorce nothing but perpetual fornication can follow—nothing but the *weakening, disannulling, and contempt of the inviolable sanctity of marriage*, which is the essential and distinctive meaning of "adultery."[1] It is clear that the Lord here designedly says *fornication* instead of adultery, just as in ver. 28 adultery, on the other hand, included fornication. Yet the expression has a wider scope, and does not, for example, exclude the incontinence of the wife before marriage, if she should not be found a virgin by her husband, or impose upon his paternity an illegitimate child.

But let us see to it that we rightly understand the Lord, and fall not into the same error of a too literal understanding of His new law! Let us take heed that, while He in abolishing fulfils the old law, we do not conversely, in thinking that we fulfil it, abolish the new law which he has given us! What then is the

[1] It is clear to us, that ἀπολελυμένην signifies only the unlawfully divorced, and thus that the re-marriage of one put away because of adultery lies under no prohibition here. We find in this no such obscurum, as *Augustine* in the place here cited by *Alford*, de fide atque oper. c. xix.

relation of the New Testament age to that of the Old Testament in regard to the law of outward ordinances? It belongs to the *perfection* of the New Covenant that it contains no longer any external statutes immediately given by God, no theocratic constitution for society and the nation. And wherefore not? Because those who are in the fellowship of the New Covenant stand and live in the *Spirit.* Thus *for these His disciples,* so far as they are, or aim to be, perfect, the Lord lays down the original commandment of God's pure ordinance as His own new commandment, doing away with all that conventional license which had been given in condescension to an imperfect state. But only for these, as they have His Spirit for its fulfilment. Now if any should pervert the letter of the *new legislation for God's spiritual commonwealth* to an external use, instead of spiritually subjecting himself to its judgment and rule; if he should impose it as a yoke upon the neck of those who have not yet received the requisite spirit, and thus transform the law of liberty into an ordinance of bondage again; could he be said to deal with it on New Testament principles, and according to that love, which is the abiding and true spirit of all fulfilment of the law and application of the commandment? That would be rather the re-appearance of a New Testament Pharisaism, the *Quakerish* observance of the Sermon on the Mount, which, in the corresponding aspect of the opposite extreme, coincides with the *Catholic* externality of the Church of Christ. And the well-meaning zealots who would elevate the Lord's command into a Church ordinance, have by no means escaped the Catholic error, which goes only one step further beyond the express letter of the Lord's word, and holds every marriage to be indissoluble, forbidding every re-marriage. Wherefore then do they not expound the whole Sermon conformably? Is it the Lord's design then, as the letter of His word plainly seems to run in ver. 34, to abolish swearing as a necessary regulation in imperfect human society? He Himself swore! Is it His design in ver. 38 to banish the *jus talionis,* which is the Divine basis of all requiting justice, from the tribunals of Christendom? No, He will not abolish *in matters to which it must ever appertain,* the rule laid down in Lev. xxiv. 19—20, any more than what is said in Ex. xxi. 12: he that smiteth a man, so that he die, shall be surely put to death. As the Law in its Sinaitic letter *condemning* sin continues its function in the Gospel, so also does the Law as wisely *restraining* sin in the Mosaic ordinances. It is the Lord's design to forbid to His disciples in his discourse (ver. 39—42) all protection of themselves, their interests, or their property: and to impose upon them such *all-endurance* and *all-abandonment* as would require them to go out of the world in which they must nevertheless live? He has himself obviated this gloss, for He did not turn the other cheek! and as all this is to be understood, so also is His word concerning divorce. The unconditional ordinance, which the Mosaic account of the creation reveals, runs in simple terms,—*Let not man put asunder!* (ch. xix. 6). Now, if sin or fornication has sundered, may not enduring patience and forgiving love join them together again? God Himself in His covenant of grace takes back again that which was separated from him. Or, if adultery has been committed, *may not* the unoffending consort retain the offending one in the bond of love, and receive her back if penitent? The Christian Church from the beginning has determined that he may, and practised accordingly.[1] And God Himself takes back His adulterous people to Himself, becomes anew the husband of the adulteress (Hos. ii. 1—20), and continues to do Himself what He has forbidden in His precept (Jer. iii. 1). But we should, and we must love perfectly, as our Father in heaven loves. So *if thou wilt be perfect, thou must not divorce even on account of fornication.* Wherefore, while we find once more in Matt. xix. 9, *παρεκτὸς λόγου πορνέιας* (in another expression), it is *wanting* in the parallel passage (Mark x. 11, 12) as well as when the Lord a third time alludes to it (Lu. xvi. 17, 18.) This is not accidental, but an intimation of the Spirit which goes beyond the letter. The Lord constrains us, by this change of the letter, to understand its meaning spiritually: for both are true; on the one hand that fornication, or any infidelity, gives the right of divorce, since that has already in effect taken place, but that also on the other, neither the man nor the woman in the church of Christ ought, generally speaking, to exercise that right.

[1] Though not always, for in the Const. apost. vi. 15 we find: Ὁ *κατέχων τὴν παραφθαρεῖσαν φύσεως θεσμοῦ παράνομος·* Luther on the other hand confidently urges that the unoffending party should forgive. *Hengstenberg* (on Hosea) speaks of great criminality on his part, if he do not use every means to bring about repentance and reconciliation.

When the Apostle, again, having the Spirit of God, quotes the Lord's words with emphasis in ver. 10 of 1 Cor. vii., and then immediately after, in ver. 15, gives his more liberal decision, (not *by commandment*, but, on account of sin and infirmity, by *permission*), that a separated person, having been left and repudiated by the unbelieving partner, might marry again; is not that also a no less manifest intimation how this commandment of the Lord is to be understood, and that it is not to be carried out literally in all its rigour and literal compulsion in the external church, mixed up as it is with heathenism? What then, finally, is *fornication* and *adultery* in our Lord's mouth? Shall we be willing to limit the word just in this place to the gross act, after He Himself has in ver. 27, 28, immediately preceding, expounded it otherwise? Will the Lord abate from the עֶרְוַת דָּבָר which is written in Moses, one jot or tittle; will he not rather provide for its being retained, like the whole Law, but for right use? (Ἐάν τις αὐτῷ νομίμως χρῆται. 1 Tim. i. 8.) What other shameful things of various kinds might not in Christian matrimony be brought forward as ground of divorce equally valid with the accomplished act of infidelity![1]

Our Lord's new law of marriage, consequently, like all the laws of the Sermon on the Mount, is not uttered with design to abolish the wholesome relaxation contained in the Mosaic institution of divorce, viewed according to its original *spirit*. It does not intend to do away with it once for all by a compulsion which works from without inwardly, but by a fulfilment of its design working gradually from within outwardly. This is its true relation, conformably with God's will, in every external national church down to the present day. The secular law of the state (albeit Christian), and no less the ecclesiastical statute also (which should not be violently sundered from the state), not only *may* exercise a Mosaic forbearance, but *must* do so, where the same reasons are presupposed as those for which the Lord by Moses exercised it. "Divorce may no more be removed than the oath." It is impossible that Christ should command mar-

[1] Maintaining this we are not perplexed by any such rigorous views as *Sixt* has lately once more defended (Stud. u. Kr. 1845. 3.) The Kirchliche Vierteljahrsschrift declares its agreement with us, and *Rothe's* Ethik quotes us often with approbation.

riages sinfully contracted, such as were properly no marriages and therefore dissolved themselves, to be made binding by force: and equally so that He should intend to oppose the sin which might afterwards break in, by any thing but the power of the Spirit. When severity, through the infirmity of the flesh, might aggravate the evil, He still may relax the law. For such *ordinances of nature,* as this—Man shall not divorce! are in their *externality* not on a level with the commandments of holiness uttered on Sinai, which are fulfilled inwardly in the spirit, and which alone unconditionally admit of no relaxation. The external church, which in a sense is still partly after the spirit of the Old Testament, condescends, like Christ Himself, to sinners in many ways, with all its severity of testimony: and has for the unconverted a confirmation, for the unworthy (whom she in most cases has not the power to judge) a Eucharist, a marriage service for those who come in wanton carnality to marriage; but she must give up all this, and by a licensed civil marriage separate herself in this also from the state, if her doctrine of divorce were otherwise. A Presbytery, Synod, or Consistory, standing to mediate between the Law and the Gospel, *bears witness* of the *commandment of Christ,* with all the spiritual force of His word, to the consciences of those who should hear *it;* but those who insist upon separation, even when no future marriage can take place, are sundered and granted a bill of divorce:—for their hardness of heart! and the church under certain circumstances may have a blessing for the second marriage of those who are thus separated, bestowed upon them in the hope that *now* the true grace of matrimony may find its true New Testament entrance into their hearts.

The *false interpretation* of the law more distinctively considered now follows, as the developed result of this literal acceptation of it. Of the *three examples* which are given in illustration *two* are taken, as we have already shown, from the civil code, and *one* from the law of holiness. Viewed yet more closely, the two first deal with our *words* and *deeds,* the third with our *disposition of mind.* Thus the error is exhibited as advancing from a too close and insincere straining of the letter of the precept first, onwards to the complete perversion and destruction of its meaning, such as is seen in the antithesis which is unscrupulously added in ver. 43, and which entirely subverts the precept of love with which vers. 21—26 set out. The first example concerning our *words* goes back in its ultimate allusion to the Sinaitic precept—Thou shalt not bear false witness, *not speak falsely;* but conjoins this with the commandment of the first table which forbids the taking God's name in vain; and mentions particularly *swearing* or a protesting use of that holy name. The false exposition or application of this Mosaic ordinance borders upon a too strict adherence to its letter: but the perfect disciple of Christ in reality stands by that ordinance. In ver. 33, we have the letter of the ordinance, with an *intimation* of that abuse which being well-known is not directly mentioned: as was the case in vers. 27, 31, after the pattern of ver. 21. Against this is set, vers. 34—37, what in a certain sense may be considered a new and severer rule, yet perfectly in the spirit of the old one: the disciple of Christ need not in general swear at all! although He may, on account of evil (having to do with the sin and untruthfulness of the world), swear *by God*, yet is he never to do this without strict necessity and solemn earnestness. By *things independent of God* (and here was the Pharisaic abuse of swearing most manifest, particular examples being named of their perversion) *he may not swear at all!* Neither by things *out of himself* (heaven, or earth, or Jerusalem, the place in which both meet), which are altogether God's; nor by any thing *in himself*, since his *head* (his life) and even his *hair* (the highest individual thing belonging to him) is also and only God's. For the disciple of Christ must speak the simple truth in its most simple possible expression.

This general analysis would give a clue to thinking minds for all that should follow; but however anxious we might be to keep these hints within concise limits, they must become here a little more diffuse, on account of the evil of false interpretation, which underlies, even in Christendom, the word of Christ.

Ver. 33. The πάλιν which now meets us, equivalent strictly to *weiter* in German, indicates the commencement of another series of examples of a different kind, as an arrangement of the discourse has already shown. It speaks once more of our *words*, as ver. 22 did, for in word as well as in deed our holy dispositions must manifest themselves, and perfection excludes every sinful word as well as act. (Jas. iii. 2). Our speech must be sanctified in truth, as our deeds in love! But that which the *ἀρχαῖοι* in this matter taught the people, as if out of the Law, did not immediately and directly refer to the decalogue, but to the Mosaic ordinance concerning oaths and vows given to the holy commonwealth of Israel. This, indeed, is yet more closely connected with the second (properly the third) commandment of the first table, than the ordinance concerning the letter of divorce was with the seventh. Thou shalt not commit adultery! Yet the Lord does not directly cite Ex. xx. 7 as He had done Ex. xx. 13 and 14—but He makes what we may term a collective-citation of the Mosaic ordinances, designedly changing the expression[1] in doing so, because it is not what was written there that He opposes, but its incorrect apprehension. He refers to Lev. xix. 12; Numb. xxx. 3; Deut. xxiii. 21, of which the last two places deal more especially with *promissoriis* or vows. The first passage connects itself immediately with the decalogue—Thou shalt not desecrate the holy *Name;* in the other two also *τῷ κυρίῳ* is expressly inserted: hence arose the false interpretation, that an *ἐπιορκεῖν* consisted *only in the express mention* of the Divine Name, and the consequent shameful abuse of other kinds of frivolous and deceitful protestations. This unrighteous limitation our Lord indicates in the concluding sentence which He cites:—*ἀποδώσεις δὲ τῷ κυρίῳ τοὺς ὅρκους σου*—thus you have heard it said out of the Law, as if only to the Lord was signified! If we place *οὐκ ἐπιορκήσεις* in juxtaposition with *οὐ φονεύσεις*, ver. 33 will here have a meaning similar to that of ver. 21. Ye vainly think that killing only is murder, and only a lying and faithless abuse of the Holy Name is perjury. But as the letter of the law in the former case had reference in its spirit to perfect love in disposition, so in the latter it refers to perfect truth in word.

Vers. 34—36. *Μὴ ὀμόσαι ὅλως*, that is, assuredly, *by all means*, generally or absolutely swear not. To expunge the comma between *ὅλως* and *μήτε*, and read: absolutely not by heaven, earth, Jerusalem, or the head,—is, whether we regard the language or the matter, extremely forced, yea decidedly false, for it

[1] *Επιορκεῖν* is not found in the Sept. canonical Old Testament—only in Wisd. xiv. 28. Similarly the LXX. have never *ὅρκοι* for נְדָרִים, but *εὐχαί*.

overlooks the sharply defined antithesis between μὴ ὅλως taken by itself, and the simple οὐκ ἐπι—ορκήσεις. And in any case there would still remain in ver. 37 the unconditional prohibition of every word that went beyond Yea and Nay—consequently of any oath. To say with *Stäudlin* (Geschichte der Vorstellungen und Lehren vom Eide) that the Apostles afterwards in their permission of the judicial oath deviated from the Lord's interdict, does not touch the point. But what is, then, the relation of these, one to the other?

That Christ forbids *to His disciples as such*, and in their intercourse one with another, every form of protestation, including God's name; that He abolishes them all as useless, because without their aid his disciples should speak the truth, is most manifest, in spite of all invalidating misinterpretation; hence St James (ch. v. 12) thus repeats the Lord's commandment, yet more irrefragably strengthening His μὴ ὅλως: μήτε ἄλλον τινὰ ὅρκον. But are we therefore, with a Quakerism which is only the re-appearance of Pharisaism on the spiritual side, to set up externally the spiritual law of Christ alone and contrary to its spirit in the midst of an evil world; to apply the perfect ordinances of Christ for His perfect ones to the regulation of churches and states which are in a condition in which imperfection so largely mingles? and may we, similarly, thus summarily *send abroad* peace in the earth (ch. x. 34), where yet the angels' word (Luke ii. 14) must *excite conflict* among men? The Christian should not divorce, but on account of fornication he does it, and it is then not a divorce which proceeded from himself, but the outward expression of one that had already unhappily taken place. The Christian should not utter Raka or Fool, as the language of hatred or anger, but, nevertheless, on account of the vileness and foolishness of men, he may, in his holy hatred of sin and in the anger of his zealous love, term them what they are, even children of the devil. So also he swears and confirms his word by oath on account of the deceitfulness and incredulity of men, and the strife which thence arises: and this he can all the more readily do, as all his words should be and are yea or nay, words of truth spoken before God, that is to say, oaths. Consequently in the perfect kingdom of God the oath-ordinance ceases simply because the oath has no longer any distinctive or especial force, beyond any other utterance of a man's mind. Hence, again, it is written by the Apostle, and his words are not a relaxation of the Lord's prohibition, but when rightly understood actually include it, just as that prohibition itself includes some such abatement as the Apostle's seems to be. "Men verily *swear* by the greater, and an oath to them is an end of all strife"—a *confirmation* of truth and love, only the yea and nay more effectually said (Heb. vi. 16). That can by no means be wicked or sinful in itself, since God Himself, on account of our unbelief, oftentimes swears by Himself (Heb. vi. 13, 17, vii. 21; Isa. xlv. 23, &c.), since the Son of God incarnate not only takes a judicial oath (Matt. xxvi. 63, 64), but even in this Sermon on the Mount, as also elsewhere, appends His Amen to His words; since the holy angel (Rev. x. 6) swears by Him that liveth for ever, and the Apostles frequently by the Lord whose coming they announce. As Christ, according to ver. 17, does not destroy the Law and the Prophets, so neither does He abolish that unconditional toleration of the oath which we find in the Old Testament. The Sinaitic commandment permits and *enjoins* the right use of the name of God, in that it condemns its profane abuse; in Deut. vi. 13, x. 20, the swearing by His name is actually commanded to Israel as the avowal of His worship; in Ps. xv. 4, swearing and changing not, is attributed to the true and spiritual Israel; and, finally, in the Prophets, Jer. xxiii. 8, Isa. lxv. 16, swearing by the God of their deliverance, by the God of truth, is vindicated for the distant future of His kingdom. Consequently the εἰκῇ, too harshly rejected in ver. 22, may be added also in this connexion, if it be rightly and spiritually understood. As pure love would prefer to say brother only, if for that brother's sake Raka is not necessary, so pure truth would prefer the simple yea and nay, if stronger confirmation were not necessary in order to its overcoming the falsehood to which it is opposed.

We should certainly be very far from discerning or exhausting the full meaning of Christ, if we regarded Him as *merely* prohibiting that profuse and frivolous swearing to which the Jews were addicted in common life, in contradistinction to judicial swearing. That might be the preparatory instruction for catechumens, whose apprehension could go no further. There might, indeed, be light swearing even in a court of justice, and the Christian man "in common life" may stand and make his appeal to the judgment-seat of God, if there be need. Yet assuredly Christ in what follows does take account of the customs of His age, and draws His examples from them. It is His design to exhibit and to condemn Pharisaism in the aspect which it assumed before His eyes. "As Heaven and earth pass away, so pass away all vows by heaven and earth," was a saying uttered in Israel at that time. Thus while they abused the name of His throne and footstool, yet because they barely evaded the name of God itself, they dared to think that they avoided the lie and the sin! Thus they forgot that heaven and earth should be changed but not pass away; that they were rather to become more plainly manifest, the Heaven as the throne of God's glory, this lower earth as His footstool, before which all his enemies should be bowed down. Hence Christ, designedly sustaining His word by Scripture (Is. lxvi. 1), traces back all such formulas, here as in chap. xxiii. 16—22, to the name of God; and by so doing gives us in His wisdom much else to reflect upon. (Let Isa. lxvi. be only read carefully again). After heaven and earth have embraced the whole universe of the first creation, He most significantly mentions further the holy Jerusalem (Rev. xxi. 1—2), as the type of the new creation of grace which brings heaven down to earth, designating it out of Scripture as the city of the great King, which is Himself.[1] It is in direct contradiction with the rightly understood meaning of the oath generally, if I, instead of mentioning His Name, *by whom we swear*, simply because heaven and earth, and Jerusalem especially (as a citizen of which I know His Name), are His; if I, instead of naming this great Ruler of the Creation and King in His City, make mention of some particular portions greater or less of His Kingdom, and think that I thereby avoid mentioning Him, and that this affects Him not! As if aught could have significance when conceived of independently of God, so that to swear by it without thinking of God were reasonable and right, or that such an oath might

[1] *Hamann* contra *Mendelsshon* (see his works by *Roth* vii. 120), found, and not without some grounds for it, a far-reaching meaning of general significance in this prohibition to name *Jerusalem* needlessly and irreverently.

innocently be trifled with! The God of Truth, who will not let His name be falsely used, will not permit any particle of dust in all His universe to be thus dealt with. If I indeed know His name, then must I also know that heaven and earth are His, as well as I know that my head and its hair belong to me, though not essentially and only to me. When I pass from things out of myself (things which in their true sense are holy, being sanctified by God), *to myself*, and *swear by myself;* there is more significance in this than the former, though that significance is altogether godless, since I thus regard myself as my own, pluck self from the authority of God, and wickedly usurp God's own prerogative—to swear by Himself.[1] By my head—borders closely upon—by my life! by my soul! as I live! and then the sin becomes most manifest, for none of us liveth to himself. But even the smallest hair of the head or the beard (by which they also swore in the East) is not mine, as I may soon discover if I attempt to change its colour by my own power, though this is still less than making one hair grow.[2] I may indeed with deceitful dyes give it a brighter or darker tincture, but nature reasserts its original colour in the hair which grows afterwards. I can no more make other hair to grow the length of a line, than add a span to the measure of my life, (ch. vi. 27). We see, consequently, that Christ here *interdicts* to His disciples *first*, all swearing generally, even by the name of God, inasmuch as it is enjoined upon them as their perfection to speak perpetual truth in the name of God, without the necessity of any confirming appendage whatever. As the consequence of this, the oath which protects truth is supposed to be abolished in the intercourse of Christians by an influence working *from within outwards*, just as the locks and bolts which protect against thieves. *Secondly* and especially is forbidden all swearing by things independent of God, be they appertaining to ourselves or otherwise, because we should think of God and give His name its honour in the mention of all His creatures; because He only has and He only is the confirming *Amen* of all truth; because His name

[1] As Cæsar by the fortuna Cæsaris, and the younger Doria in *Schiller's* Fiesco with his " Donner und Doria!"

[2] But we much doubt whether this is to be regarded (with *Sepp*) as meaning that they swore " may I become gray, if it be not so."

only is above the yea of any creature.[1] *Finally* is prohibited all *inconsiderate* and *useless* swearing, all confirmation and corroboration of our yea and nay without cause. As this was miserably current in the Pharisaic Israel of that age, so it attests the hypocrisy of men in every age; for by adding such strengthening appendages to our discourse, we confess ourselves to be, without them, untrustworthy.[2] But when adequate reason for an oath occurs, it is not only *permitted* but even *commanded*, as a service to God and our neighbour, to corroborate our plain words by such confirmation as may maintain the truth and advance the cause of charity. Consequently the judicial oath of the Christian citizen is justified under such circumstances, as well as the oath with which the Apostle, the Preacher, the Disciple may solemnly confirm His testimony.[3] He who, in what he is constrained to say before man, looks up in his spirit to God as his witness, may and indeed ought openly to avow it. The true New Testament oath, however, must ever retain its own formula—*I call God for a record upon my soul.* (2 Cor i. 23). On the other hand the formula—So help me God—if it mean, otherwise may He not help me! May God punish me! though under the old covenant of the Law's severity it might have been tolerated (The Lord do so to me!), must under the covenant of grace be absolutely avoided as being a self-willed invasion of the future, like the language of Cain (Gen. iv. 13).

Ver. 37. Our communication should be Yea on the lips, where Yea is in the heart, Nay on the lips where Nay is in the heart, and therefore *sincere*, not like the devils' or the liars', or what according to *Shakspeare* is "no good divinity," consisting of yea-nay and nay-yea. This is the first and most obvious mean-

[1] To swear by the life of the *King*, Pharoah or Solomon, was in a sense tolerated in the Old Testament as being a type, which referred to *the greater*, the only great King. (Ps. lxiii. 12).

[2] It is worthy of remark that the ἐπιορκεῖν which is here used meant originally to swear merely, or to swear often, and thence naturally passed in its signification to *false* swearing—just as oaths, the more frequent they are, the more frequently are they perjuries also.

[3] Indeed "the sanctity of the solemn adjuration is exalted by the prohibition of common and gratuitous swearing," as *Von Gerlach* says. Compare also *Rothe's* theory in his Ethik iii. 576—586, which agrees with my exposition.

ing. But then it must be *only* yea or nay, that is, of course, not just necessarily this little word, but *affirmative* or *negative* without any thing περισσόν, without any superfluous corroborating additions, therefore *simple* and definite :—what I say I say and believe, and let me be trusted! St James' expression embraces both (ver. 12) :—the more sincerely we speak, the more simply also shall we be able to speak, since others will have learnt to rely upon our word. Further there should only be yea or nay in our speech and in our heart, where there is yea or nay in the thing itself, as it is before God, as the eternal truth of God says yea or nay: consequently our communication must be *true*, according to the reality of the matter we speak of, so far at least as with our best ability and in good conscience we can discern it. Finally, for this cannot be excluded, more particularly as the discourse had just run upon the keeping our word and vow; we may not afterwards say nay, where we had previously said yea, or the reverse, and consequently our communication must be *consistent* and stedfast and trustworthy (2 Cor. i. 17). Thus does the Lord set before us, Himself using the simplest possible form of words, the ideal model of what the holy speech of God's children might be and should be, if the sin that is in the world and their own remaining sinfulness be left out of the question. It does, indeed, exclude even the oath by the name of God, and relatively abolish it; but it is not unconditionally done away, for after the preceding words μὴ ὀμόσαι ὅλως, *this*, as being the only oath permissible, was not expressly mentioned. What then is the meaning of the following position? It evidently modifies the former part of the sentence. The literal observance of the former clause is necessarily connected with a false interpretation of the latter, as if the Lord had said—*Whatsoever is more than these is sin.* But this He did not say, nor could He have said it, without subverting the system of the world as arranged since the entering in of sin, and reflected in the law of Moses; nor, indeed, without condemning Himself. Not only is every oath a περισσόν, but so also is the *Amen* of Christ which strengthens the yea (2 Cor. i. 20), and even that second yea which on this occasion the Lord adds to the first. Every confirming addition of any kind may be said to be only a second, more emphatically repeated yea. All this *cometh of evil*, the Lord says, and we are not to understand ὁ πονηρός as immediately referred to in this place. (As also not in ch. vi. 13; Jno. xvii. 15; comp. Rom. xii. 9; 1 Thess. v. 22.) Often enough it does, indeed, spring from the sin, the evil that is in the speaker himself, just as Raca springs from his malevolent anger, and divorce from his own infidelity. But *not always;* the speaker may thus utter in truth and in love, *what is forced upon him by the world's sin, with which he has necessarily to do:* just as the manifold and incessant protestations which pervade the entire Holy Scripture must be accounted for. Such conformation is consequently permitted and necessary, that is, where and so far as it is directed *against* evil. The yea, yea, and nay, nay of God which His servants must maintain and protest against the nay-yea and the yea-nay of wickedness, comes not, therefore, in an evil sense from the evil of him who utters it, although it is spoken on account of evil and therefore may be said to originate in evil, it is essentially good in itself and cometh of good, even of the very zeal of the good to overcome the evil.

The *second example,* which passes from the word of truth to the work of love, has reference to the Mosaic *judicial ordinances* concerning *revenge,* which had been subject to a still worse interpretation and application than the former. For although before the tribunal of the sinners' judge a strict and righteous *requital* or *retaliation* of evil inflicted will find place; yet it is both perverse and perverting to appropriate to oneself the prerogative of such requital in private life. The Lord gives a fundamental example, which illustrates strikingly the relation of the external, legal ordinance, to the internal fulfilment of the Law according to its spirit,—to Christian love. The disciple of Christ should, in *patience* or *passive* love to his enemy, rise superior to all revenge for the evil inflicted on him: and this forms the wisely preparatory transition to the injunction which follows, of *active* love of our enemies, as being the sum and the end of the spiritual law, loving as God loves! The Lord first specifies the falsely applied and wickedly misunderstood Law of Moses, by simply quoting its letter just as in ver. 31: presupposing and intending, that misunderstanding and perversion of it, as the contrast which follows makes evident. He commands His disciples rather to *endure* evil or injustice: first, by a general prohibition of resistance, and then by a corresponding command, which expressly and precisely indicates the *Spirit* which he requires, by the act which is the test of it. To do this He lays down *three* significantly chosen examples, and closes by a requirement, ver. 42, which being in its letter incapable of being fulfilled, draws our minds from the literal to a spiritual acceptation of it, and leads the way to the active love of our enemies.

Ver. 38. These words occur thrice in the Law of Moses. First, among the first fundamental precepts given to Moses immediately after the decalogue and still upon the Mount (Ex. xxi. 23—25; where it is defined by what rule the arbitrators shall be guided in a particular case, (and the proverbial maxim goes on, hand for hand, foot for foot, wound for wound). Then in Lev. xxiv. 19, 20, where the general judicial law for injuries, and their compensation is laid down—if a man cause a blemish to his neighbour; as he hath done, so shall it be done to him. Finally, once more in Deut. xix. 21, where this principle is laid down with reference to a particular case, not being one of injury, as a rule of proportion to be rigorously applied: Thine eye shall not spare! To administer this compensation of like for like, is entrusted to the judges as אֱלֹהִים; for it is and must ever be the fundamental law of the eternal and divine government of the world, and as such is confirmed afterwards by our Lord in ch. vii. 2. Consequently it is not our Lord's design in what He now says to condemn the application in every commonwealth of this perfect rule of justice,[1] which provides against all excess or deficiency in punishment; for Judgment and Justice are to be administered in the name of God by the magistracy in every human society, and the pattern of that administration in every State must be sought in the government of the Great King over His people. What He designs to condemn is the reading and enforcing and obeying the statute, as if it had been written:—*He*, the injured man, may exact like for like from his neighbour, in the exercise of a private revenge which is

[1] Especially, of course, directed against the *excess*, though not that alone as *Augustine* supposed: non fomes sed limes furoris est. Contra Faust. xix. 25.

guided by hatred and anger. As even king Solomon in his time, though not unmindful of what appertained to magisterial authority and judgment, knew how to teach it in his exhortation: *Say not*, I will do so to him as he has done to me: Say not thou, I will recompense evil: but wait on the Lord and He shall save thee! (Prov. xxiv. 29, xx. 22; comp. Ecclus. xxviii. 1—3). So that the Lord here again utters nothing new, but that which Moses and the Prophets had already uttered; in confirmation of which consult further Lev. xix. 18, and mark what is there said in connexion with that other law which the Lord is about to bring forward in ver. 43. Our exposition may now become more and more brief, since this example has found in part its illustration in the two preceding; and the three great fundamental principles for the understanding of the Sermon on the Mount are now firmly established on our minds; viz., that the Lord does not abolish the Law, but fulfills it; that He only demands a perfect obedience to it from His own, through the power of that grace which His fulfilment of it has obtained; and that His requirements to that end are by no means to be externally and literally put in practice in this evil world and mingled Christendom, but all the Mosaic laws and ordinances continue also to hold their place. And if in these we find the idea of *Law* as opposed to Gospel, and of strict right as the antithesis of patient, forgiving love, made prominent; so also will it be made clear that in the present condition of this world, love can only very gradually and in restricted measure have its perfect exhibition; nay, rather, that while the children of God are supposed to possess the spirit of patience, they must, even for love's sake, maintain and enforce punitive and protective Law.

Vers. 39—41. τῷ πονηρῷ is not to be understood as in the masculine, the Evil one, the Injurer, any more than in ver. 37. The expression is indeed related in the two verses, but it advances in meaning here, for τὸ πονηρόν is not so much evil or sin, as the *evidence* of it in the injury and injustice actually inflicted upon myself. We must of course oppose the sinner as such, and his sin, even as we resist the Devil, the wicked one whose malignity shews itself in each individual sinner, (Jas. iv. 7). *Τὸ πονηρόν* is the fundamental principle generally of that evil which opposes, injures, oppresses and burdens the children of God in the world. Hence is chap. vi. 13 to be understood, where *misery*, and sin its cause, are united in one grand and comprehensive expression; as, on the other hand, in Rom. xii. 21 τὸ κακόν makes prominent the *evil* distinctively, as sin, yet not without including its consequent suffering. The fundamental words and ideas of Scripture must be apprehended in all their depth and universality of meaning first, and then their distinct and critical meaning in individual passages will obviously and naturally present itself. *To resist not* evil! So does the Lord absolutely, in the infinitive mood, lay down the law of His kingdom for His disciples. What means this ἀντιστῆναι, to resist or to oppose? Were the word expunged, we should probably, looking at the connexion, supply its place and its meaning by *render back* like for like, or retaliate: and this is the actual signification of the passage. As we might say: ye shall not *put yourselves in opposition* (ἀντιτάσσεσθαι, Jas. v. 6), not strike again, not revile again, not take again (ver. 38), not inflict injury, in retaliation for injury, *or in defence* against it. This latter is necessarily involved, inasmuch as he who thus defends himself, anticipates the functions of the magistrate. (If we could requite without reference to self, not in our own person but in the stead of God, *then might* every man be his own blood-avenger and arbiter). The *three examples*, which illustrate the general position, are so selected as to descend from the worse evil to the less:—actual personal assault, spoliation of property, forcible constraint to a service not due. The Lord, indeed, refers only to things comparatively unimportant, in order that His words may find their easy application to ordinary life. He does not begin, for instance, with the dashing out of the eye or the teeth, or with any such wounds and bruises; for the sentiment and conscience which His word necessarily awakes, testifies against the instant exercise of private personal vengeance in such cases, as being sinful and like the haughty violence of Cain, (Gen iv. 23; I have slain in my retaliation a man who wounded me!); but he would teach us, that we must also patiently receive the smiting on the cheek, without permitting ourselves even in things so slight as this, *any measure* of self-

[1] Hence *Braune* speaks at least without sufficient precision when he says that bodily injury stands first, because it is hardest to bear and most swiftly provokes revenge.

revenge or retaliation. This is one side of the case: according to another view, however, the slighter injury is oftentimes more irritating and more fraught with temptation than the greater, since we are led by the natural impulse of fear to retire before the enkindled rage of one who would assault us, unless our own rage be as hot and violent as his. In this case it is not so much the pain which is to be taken into account, as the shame of a scornful insult: hence among all people, and in all times, smiting upon the cheek has been in proverbial use in such a sense as this. See in the Old Testament Lam. iii. 30; Job xvi. 10; Isa. l. 6; and in the New 2 Cor. xi. 20. The general usage which puts the members of the right side first, will explain the circumstance that the right cheek is mentioned first, and not the left, which would receive a blow administered by the right hand: in St Luke *the one* and *the other* are used instead. Immeasurably more important than such a remark as this is the rigid and most impressive contrast which must be noticed between the requirement: —turn to him the other also! and that heathenish law of honour, which will not accept the very slightest indignity, but even in the midst of modern Christendom, demands the duel itself. To this *point d'honneur* stands opposed the patient acceptance and endurance of insult, as the genuine Christian courage and knightly honour. Offer him the other also—that is, in thy heart, and in the disposition of thy mind; calmly and patiently wait if he may strike thee another blow, and be ready to receive that also:—so far let thy spirit be from opposing, or declining or avoiding it! This is all that the Lord intends to say by this emphatic expression, the figurative, proverbial letter of which must be understood in its spirit, just as we saw in a similar case before; for the actual turning of the other cheek might be no other than a challenge to continued sin, consequently itself sinful, and opposed to the love of our neighbour. There might even be a proud despite in it, or a mere hypocritical affectation. Christ interprets His own word by His own act in Jno. xviii. 22, 23, where He gives to the rude officer a gracious word of gentle admonition in return for his blow, which, according to Isa. l. 6, the Lord's Spirit would, however, have suffered him to repeat.—The enquiry in the next example is of little importance as to the relation between the χιτών and the ἱμάτιον, used conversively in

Lu. vi. 29, which gives a slightly different presentation of the discourse. We must regard St Matthew the Apostle as giving the more precise words of our Lord; the Spirit in St Luke, in another grade of inspiration, teaches us that literal exactness in such details is not strictly necessary. St Luke's view is more general, referring to an actual *seizure* (ἄιρειν), and this begins from the outside garment (Mic. ii. 8 Heb.); but St Matthew's refers to an unrighteous process at law (κριθῆναι) to obtain possession of the property; and the closer body-garment is therefore first mentioned, because the law of Moses contemplated the taking of the outer garment also, as the last and most aggravated evil[1] (Ex. xxii. 26, 27). So that it means: if any one would unrighteously rob thee (τῷ θέλοντι), and aims to do it under the impudent guise of right, even if it touches thy necessary clothing as nearly as the blow on the cheek touches thine honour, thou must rather be entirely stripped than manifest a disposition, in the spirit of discord and violence, and personal enmity, to defend thy rights at law. We cannot but understand, however, that this speaks of express outward *conduct*, (which could not always be externally maintained,) only as the figure and the test of an inward *disposition*, which should ever be prepared so to act. To every one who would go to law revengefully, selfishly, stubbornly, or out of a weak devotion to this world's good, it may be said, as the Apostle wrote to the Corinthians: There is yet utterly a fault among you (ἥττημα); why do ye not rather take wrong? why do ye not rather suffer yourselves to be defrauded? (1 Cor. vi. 7). But if thou art conscious of the indwelling of forbearing love in thy heart, that very consciousness will enable thee, with all the more propriety, to *withstand* the *sin* which would wrong thee by defence of law, and hold fast thy property, as God's steward, for a better use.[2] The ἀγγαρεύειν, again, (to

[1] *Roos* thinks, that perverters of the law having no conscience, might have taken away the lesser garment, imagining that so the letter of the Mosaic Law would not be transgressed.

[2] *Kleuker:* "Where Christ's aim is attainable, there the means to it becomes a duty, that is, though Christ specifies it not, where such means are means really to that end; and where the spirit of Christ's aim cannot be attained, the mere mockery of the means to it, is unreal and unnatural, even though seemingly coming under the Lord's specification."

demand service as messenger or guide, to lay claim to it by force as the only right; a word which passed from the Persian usage and speech into other languages, since the same thing everywhere takes place, Matt. xxvii. 32, where this word occurs, being an example), violently trespasses upon personal rights, so that a high spirited and unloving man might well defend himself against it with all his might, on the common principle—Thou hast no authority to demand this of me, I am not under obligation to render thee this! It might indeed, in some circumstances, interfere exceedingly with one's own wishes and business. But yet it is, in comparison of the blow on the cheek and the robbery of one's garment, the lesser thing, and therefore the Lord's injunction is more imperative—Art thou compelled to go one mile, go with him twain! Shouldst thou serve any one for an hour in any matter, add yet another hour! This goes beyond the mere negative endurance that went before, and with ver. 42 begins already the transition to the exhibition of *active* love. Ver. 44. Say to the impetuous maker of the demand, but say it with thy heart as well as with thy lips—although I am not bound by any obligation of external right or law, yet am I, according to the spirit and law of love, both willing and obliged to serve thee and every man; that which thou art disposed to enforce from me, I will do for thee in free will and in double measure, preventing thy sin by my kindness!. Such conduct is actually practicable in many cases; and how effectual is the rebuke it administers, how it tends to peacemaking and the prevention of sin!

Yet it is not the Lord's will, when such a motive is out of the question or anything else might stand in the way, to impose it upon his disciples as an absolute necessity to render every service that may in this evil world be demanded of them, any more than he requires them to allow all their property to be taken from them, or to tolerate every kind of personal insult He enjoins only the requisite disposition of mind. As He Himself often before His hour was come, withdrew from the sinners who assailed Him and hid Himself: as He counselled His disciples to flee before persecution (ch. x. 23); as St Paul availed himself of his rights as a citizen, and made his appeal unto Cæsar; so it is permitted also to us to do in all respects the same, and even indicated to us as better so to do, for the sake of the world's sin, even though we would sincerely prefer to suffer. The Jews made the regulations of public justice the rule of private life: but Christians must not elevate the sacred private prerogatives of love into statute law before the time. The spirit which this would require being absent, nothing but disorder can follow. As the office of the magistrate continues in existence for punishment of evil and protection from wrong, it is our right and our duty to avail ourselves of it. However willingly I might suffer myself to be smitten, as far as myself and my cheek are concerned, yet must I maintain also the honour of that office, and not let presumptuous outrage go unpunished. I have not the less fulfilled the Lord's command in its spirit, though I make my appeal and go to law for my right, being *compelled* thereto by another's wrong, and resigning myself patiently to litigation, which is directly opposed to my principles of forbearance.[1] Even absolute self-defence is not excluded, where a man assumes the office of judge himself: it is observable that the Lord did not say—if any man will kill thee, defend not thyself, but let it be so! There remain cases quite sufficient in which patience may have her perfect work, and Solomon's word may have its force: wait on the Lord and He shall help thee; as well as Christ's example, who committed Himself to Him that judgeth righteously. "A father says to his children: bear what your brothers or sisters may do to thee, and hurt them not in return; will one of them take away thy fruit, give him thy bread also rather than engage in quarrel with him. But it is tacitly understood that the father means—I will presently compensate the patient child, and visit the wrong upon the other."[2] The Lord will render

[1] *Rud. Matthäi*: "The *disposition* to reconciliation must be as strong as life, unquenchable as the soul—the *act* of forgiveness should be as discriminating as the distributing of any pearls. If thou wouldst actually heap coals of fire on the head of an enemy, and thus confirm the neighbourhood in faith and love, thou mayest also literally turn the other cheek, and go the two miles, &c. But where thou wouldst only cast thy wheat amid the hemlock which would choke it, keep it for better soil, and stand upon thy right."

[2] Philosophische Vorlesungen über das sogenannte Neue Testament. Leipzig, bei Junius 1785. An original book of *Pfenninger*, too much forgotten.

judgment and justice to all who suffer wrong; vengeance is His, He will repay, and that in the full measure of the most rigorous *jus talionis.*

To these three examples of deepening wrong which is inflicted upon us, the Lord adds yet another word, which requires a more profound consideration than at first sight appears. *Asking* appears obviously after *demanding* to be an inversion of the order: for it is the gentlest kind of desire, which acknowledges my right and submits to my volition. The Lord's saying, indeed, is in the same strain with that of Moses in Deut. xv. 7—11, where it is commanded to lend and give to the poor brethren, and forbidden to harden the heart or shut the hand against them; just as it is commanded by the Apostle, 1 Jno. iii. 17. Compare also Ecclus. iv. 4, xxix. 2; Tob. iv. 7, in harmony with which passages we have here the admonitory: *turn not those away!* Yet this asking may be in an imperative style, and many ungodly ones are eager enough to borrow, who never think of repaying (Ps. xxxvii. 21). Must I then be ever giving and giving, contrary to all propriety encouraging every hardy beggar; and must I suffer to be begged and borrowed from me all that I have for mine own proper use, to the glory of God and the true service of my neighbour! Here becomes most manifest the utter impossibility of a literal accomplishment of all this. He who should thus give, would indeed give no good gift to such unrighteous one, but would violate the law of love to individuals and to human society at large. Consequently we must regard our Lord as only laying down this saying of Moses and of Sirach, in order that He may point out and enforce the spiritual and not the literal fulfilment of this commandment of love, which has become a maxim among all nations; He speaks *figuratively* as in the former instances. The transition from them to this is plain in this obvious connexion: do to him who violently *compels* thee, what he asks, just as if he had *requested* it.[1] Whom does the Lord, in his deep meaning, intend by him who asketh of thee? No other than the Whosoever of vers. 39—41, just as the Adversary of ver. 25 was the brother of ver. 24. Not merely he who

[1] Which connexion in Lu. vi. 29—30 is yet more obvious: Let the taking away and robbing be like asking from thee.

expressly and in words asks of me:—that would be a Pharisaical cleaving to the mere letter, so interpreting I might let my benevolence wait till asked, and keep the commandment by not turning from one who never asked me; or with hypocritical, proud, or heedless dispatch send him away with "There thou hast it," which could only do him harm. (Give also to him, who asketh not of thee—is as valid against this as, on the other hand, Give not to every one who asketh of thee!) The asking, which I must be accessible to, is *need* itself; the seeing my brother in want. The needy one speaks by his very presence to my heart—Help me to the best of thy ability! And, finally, in the spirit of the word—what is it that he who injures and constrains me seeks of me, without saying so or being conscious of it? Nothing less than the best and highest gift I could bestow, the proof of my love, which he in his hardness of heart so pressingly needs as an example for his reproof and amendment. And that I should give him in the form which may seem best to the wisdom of my charity; either by enduring or resisting, by giving or withholding. Thus much remains certain after all is said: whosoever opposes the evil which comes against him by any the slightest exhibition of evil, that is, does any thing to the evil-doer which is opposed to the spirit of enduring, forbearing love, himself commits evil, as far as in him lies, aggravates instead of amends it on the other, and denies that example of righteousness and of love which his neighbour's unrighteousness and uncharitableness demanded at his hands. That is the most profound significance of the "*but*" in ver. 39. Oppose not πονηρόν to πονηρόν, but good to evil, patience and love to evil-doing! Every enemy as an enemy asks of me to overcome him with love, to heap coals of fire on his head: that thus I may take away his enmity by the requital of abounding love, according to the highest examples of my Father in heaven. (Vers. 44—48; Isa. lix. 17, 18; Ps. xli. 11.) It may probably be found to be only a lending of love, which will come back to me in rich return: but I should be disposed to impart it also to the ungodly who *would borrow* it without ever repaying; and unweariedly to impart to every one from the inexhaustible capital of my love, and that without hope of interest in the return of love. Consult Lu. vi. 32—35, which, in a more extended discourse, perfectly confirms the view that *lending* is a figurative expression for *love.*

How abundantly has the Sermon on the Mount hitherto drawn out of the depths of eternal wisdom its fundamental far-reaching principles of truth! In what luminous words of its own has it set before us its new teaching, which is yet only the kernel of the already extant word of God in the Old Testament released from its shell, and in the unity of fulfilment is one with the Law and the Prophets! How majestic in its independence does every isolated word stand, and yet how does one hang upon another, and spring from it in a living, harmonious organic progression! Could the Publican Matthew, or any other hand, successively have woven together this fabric from detached and single words, after the manner of men? Or could the Spirit of Christ Himself have blended them altogether by the Apostle's instrumentality *under the untrue superscription*: He went up into a mountain, opened his mouth, and taught them saying—? No, the Lord did verily speak from the mountain, and in this very manner did He open His mouth for His first most solemn discourse.

It may be hoped that we are now more able, the farther we proceed, to enter into the meaning of the Lord's words and manner of teaching. The two examples taken from the Mosaic statute and penal law were intended, in opposition to the Pharisees' false exposition of the Law, to point His disciples to such a fulfilment of it in its spirit as should, by working from within ontwardly, render those ordinances useless; while at the same time it should assign to the legal, judicial element in them, its proper place, and vindicate for it its true use. Now follows the third example, which returns again to the Moral Law, or law of holiness. As this is to close the distinctive reference to the commandments, it is not one of the individual commandments of the Decalogue which is introduced, as the first quotations had been; but the epitome of the whole second table, as Moses had already specified it; viz., the law of *love*, of that one central *disposition of mind*, which should evidence itself in every word and every work. In this case, in which the wicked principle of natural selfishness *not willing* to understand the law, comes into direct collision with its clear and unmistakeable terms, the mischievous perversion takes the form of an arbitrary *addition*, which mutilates the precept and entirely disannuls its meaning. The misinterpreting appendage at ver. 21 was actually a precept of the Mosaic ordinance; the error consisted only in bringing down the Sinaitic—Thou shalt not kill! to the level of a mere sentence upon homicide. But the daring addition to the Divine precept—*and hate thine enemy!* is nowhere found in holy writ. This human and wicked selfishness, which would assert its hatred in the very face of the commandment of love, is met and opposed by the fresh disclosure in its clearest expression of the central spirit of the old law. Thou shalt *love* just as God loves, that is with the love of *mercy*, with the *active love of thine enemy*. That is the holiness which is to be established in thee. The whole aptly fits in with that which commenced in vers. 21—26; where the *adversary* was manifestly a *brother*, with whom I should be reconciled in the love of God. Ver. 44 merely lays down the command to love our enemies with its evidences, as the express opposite to the perverted addition; ver. 45 immediately follows with its foundation in the example of our heavenly Father; then the importance of the subject demands a reference once more to the contrast of those who, with all their selfishness, yet make their talk and their boast of love (vers. 46, 47). This is, however, no love; but the *Pharisees* prove themselves to be no better than the *publicans*, the arrogant self-righteous ones in Israel no better than the despised sinners, yea, even, the *heathens*. (This latter paves the way for the second main contrast in chap. vi. 19—34: not like the Gentiles!) These are two convincing *questions*, which presuppose, notwithstanding all their hypocritical perversion, a right understanding in their consciences: the one points forward to the *reward*, which will presently be discussed (chap. vi. 1, 4, 6, 18), the other points back to the *exceeding* righteousness which in chap. v. 20 was required. Ver. 48 forms the sublime conclusion—the first of those *three fundamental laws* (or in the superficial language of modern times, *principles of morality*) which are laid down by the Sermon on the Mount; the second and the third being found in chap. vi. 33; vii. 12. This first one points toward heaven, and the fountain of mercy in the Divine love to enemies (Rom. v. 10), as the source whence our love should flow. It also at the same time prepares the way, in passing, for that which chap. vi. introduces: let your righteousness be *in the sight of the Father*, who looks to the hidden thought of the heart; and not terminate in hypocritical acts in the sight of man.

Ver. 43. The beginning of that wicked and wanton misunderstanding which is here condemned in Pharisaic Israel, was their restriction of the commanded love of our *neighbour* to their *own people* only, and their contempt of the heathens as enemies whom they might, and indeed should hate. This was the all-pervading false interpretation which their uncircumcised hearts put upon God's revelations and institutions for His peculiar people. But as the Jewish, like all other national pride in general, is only an expansion of the selfish haughtiness of the I into that of the We, the limitation did not tarry at that point, but the "neighbour" became more narrowly interpreted even within their own bounds as a people. It has been assumed that Moses does indeed often so speak as if the neighbour was only the fellow-Israelite; but this was only so far the case as such was naturally the most obvious application of the term in common life among a people so isolated and self-contained. Let it be noted, moreover, how expressly, in the very chapter from which our Lord derives the compendious law of brotherly love (Lev. xix. 18), the *strangers* are included in that law (vers. 33, 34); just as in ver. 10, they are coupled with all other poor.[1] And does not the constantly-recurring רֵעֲךָ point back to the *Decalogue*, the commandments of which are recapitulated in the beginning of this chapter (Lev. xix.)? But where is the expositor who would venture to say that it was lawful for Israelites dwelling in heathen lands to bear false witness against the heathen man outside the land of Israel, or to covet his wife or his house? Thus in this chapter (Lev. xix. 18), "the children of thy people" and "thy neighbour" cannot be one and the same; but the latter part of the sentence is the general law upon which is based the more limited application in the former:—Thou shalt not bear

[1] Zech. vii. 10 includes the stranger among others, who are called *Brethren.*

grudge against the children of thy people, *for* thou shalt love every man! and no less than *as thyself!*[1] It is in the highest degree characteristic that the Lord imputes to Pharisaism the omission of just this word: though the doctors of the law tolerated and included it in the dead letter, they utterly disregarded it in effect. What means it other than this,—that I should place myself in thought in the place of the other, and do to him what I would desire to have done to myself? (ch. vii. 12). Thus apprehended it gives itself an immediate and sufficing answer to the cavilling question—Who is my neighbour? Every one, assuredly, by whom I would be loved; and would not the Jew, needing charity and its kind offices of help, desire *them* even from Samaritans and Gentiles? (Lu. x. 29—36).[2] But here, instead of *this* rejected appendage, which condemns all selfishness and opposes all limitation of the precept, another is substituted which absolutely sets *self* upon the throne, *above* our neighbour and *against* him, with all its bitter wilfulness—*and hate thine enemy!* Who then is my enemy? Every one, in fine, whom it pleases me so to term, for cause of enmity sinful man will never be slow to discover or invent. But the Law says rather—thou shalt not hate, that is, *on thy part* thou shalt have no enemy, thou shalt regard and treat no man as such. Thou shalt not hate thy brother in thy heart (even when he sins against thee), but rebuke his sin in the spirit of sincere love,[3] thou shalt not bear grudge nor avenge! (Lev. xix. 17, 18). Even the adversary in judgment is continually spoken of as a "neighbour." (Ex. xviii. 16; Lev. xix. 15). But the Pharisee who will insidiously evade the Law without tampering with its letter, gives its meaning a rash and narrow

[1] There can be no more mischievous perversion of Scripture, or slander of the Old Testament, than what *Dietlein* maintains:—that the Law commanded hatred of an enemy, not merely permitted it—and that the enemy whom the Mosaic institute commanded to hate was every stranger! Formerly the Rationalists only spoke thus, and every Christian man contradicted it.

[2] Observe hence once more, how falsely Christian theologians impute hatred of an enemy to the Old Testament Law. Against *von Gerlach* let the great difference be remembered between hating "*the* enemy" and "*thy* enemy." Where in all the Old Testament is the latter found?

[3] "The enemy is just so far our neighbour, as he most of all harasses and occupies us."—*Lange*.

interpretation, until, finally, nothing remains but—my neighbour is he, *who loves me* (ver. 46). And since this love, so eagerly desired, very easily admits of any cause of interruption, *he* is only my neighbour so long as no offence causes me to declare him my enemy. Thus is the godless perversion of the precept perfected in an express contradiction to it; just as now-a-days the proverb too often runs among Christians—Every man is his own neighbour!

Ver. 44. In sublime contrast to this is the mighty re-assertion of the Law which must be fulfilled:—*But I say unto you!* What terms more entirely harmonize in the natural mind than *enemy* and *hate?* It is the full, undisguised heathenism of the carnal mind which the Pharisees condensed into an express precept, a genuine essential precept of man, and then appended it to a commandment of God as its exposition! But when that commandment said—"Love thy neighbour," it also signified no less than *Love* thine *enemy!* impossible as it may still be to human nature to reconcile the two. All heathens have been *conscious*, that the love of an enemy was a beautiful and a noble thing: and it is actually asserted throughout the Old Testament, in its histories, proverbs, and precepts; see, for example, only Ex. xxiii. 4, 5; Job. xxxi. 29; Prov. xxiv. 17; xxv. 21, 22. Thus it is not anything new which the Lord announces as His Law. He only brings new grace for its right fulfilment, as He thus already erects brotherly love into a new spiritual commandment. After having, in the impressively simple antithesis—*Love your enemies!* laid down first of all the internal sentiment, which was of chiefest importance; He exhibits its progressive operation in three degrees, which through word and act lead back to the inner disposition again. As enmity advances, must the maintenance and proof of love keep pace with it. Bless them that curse you, oppose words of love and peace to words of scorn and insult! If the word of blessing suffices not (which is mostly the case), proceed further, to deed answering deed; do good to them that hate you, that show themselves by more than a single curse, by persistent conduct, to be your haters! And when the good deed is not sufficient (which again, when rightly understood, is always the case), continue nevertheless to preserve that disposition before God, which was the *love* spoken of at the beginning:

pray for them which despitefully use you[1] and persecute you! Bless them not merely in words but in acts—which is more difficult: the answer of kind words might be in vain without the proof of deeds. Let it not be thought enough to say—I will not revile again, but will speak affectionately; yea, not enough to dispatch it quickly by saying to God—Let them curse but bless *Thou!* But there must be a real earnestness in the prayer, as it is uttered in the prophetic Psalm (cix. 28):—Bless thou *through me*, by my well-doing to them! and when even this does not overcome the enmity, and cause the despiteful treatment and persecution to cease, continue, nevertheless, in intercession: Bless *Thou!* This is the last and severest test of the pure spirit of love, without which the blessing and the doing good could never in God's estimation bear the name of love at all. The putting one who hates to confusion by abundant deeds of kindness might even be a matter of Pharisaical and hypocritical pride, a sweet revenge under another form: but he who can pray for his enemy, loves him indeed. This already penetrates that secret region of which ch. vi. 4—12 speaks more at large, and is the transition to what immediately follows concerning the Father in heaven, who looks in his children's hearts for love like His own.

Ver. 45. That which in vers. 9 and 16 was preparatorily spoken, is summed up in one word—the children of your Father which is in heaven! The regeneration that underlies this, and is procured through the grace of the Son (John i. 12), is in the Sermon on the Mount a mystery unspoken, but which betrays itself to our notice, or at least to our anticipation, in the very foundation of the discourse. For the faith of any one who heard it might have concluded:—He who discloses and condemns with such severity the sin of the heart, and exacts such lofty requirements, Himself designs to bring the kingdom of His Father to the poor, and with it satisfy those who hunger and thirst after God's love as their righteousness. That the Lord sets up the perfection of

[1] 'Επηρεάζειν is not "slander" or "revile," for that would be no advance in meaning upon cursing and hating, but according to *Hesychius* it is equiv. to βιάζειν, inflict injury. The persecution points back to ver. 10. Or we should have with *Lange* (iii. 386—389) to oppose the secret intercession to the secret and quiet vilification—but how could this be philologically established?

merciful well-doing after the example of the Father as the high *aim* of an ever-growing *exercise* and *appropriation*, was already intimated in the progressive series of the benedictions, as it is now again in the ascending stages of ver 44. The mercy of the Father comes to us freely and preparatorily: he who exercises to others that which he has obtained, experiences thereby more and more the purification of his heart from every thing which is contrary to that mercy; as we there apprehended and expounded it. So that we may here also, without hesitation or fear, lay the stress either upon the ὅπως—*in order that* ye may be so ever more and more, that ye may approve yourselves more and more fully, and at last in absolute perfection as children resembling their Father, or upon the γένησθε—in order that ye may *be so*. Our Lord designedly does not refer to the spiritual exhibitions of mercy to sinners as the pattern of the divine and fatherly benevolence; but, in order to work a more instant conviction, appeals to that general testimony of nature which was as open to the heathen as it was to Israel (Acts xiv. 17): for it is His purpose to reduce Israel and the heathen to the same level, in relation to the Law and to grace, even as the Baptist had done before Him. Moses and the Prophets had demonstrated the goodness of God from His sending down *rain* and the blessing of heaven which made fruitful the earth: (Deut. xi. 10—15; Ps. lxv. 10, 11; Jer. v. 24, xiv. 22). The heavens cannot rain of themselves, and we should not be content with an unmeaning "*it* rains" which places Nothing in the place of the living God; for it is God who rains, or who causes rain (as Israel sadly learned in the frequent shutting of the heavens), even as it is *His* sun which He causes to rise. His manifestation of Himself as the mighty Creator and Lord, is also, as such, the revelation of His goodness: "for he is mighty and despiseth not any; for he is mighty also in strength of heart." (Job xxxvi. 5). His loving-kindness in nature is further the type and the promise of the spiritual gifts of His grace for the innermost necessities of the heart of man. Rain, in the prophetic Scriptures, is often referred to with this meaning, (Ps. lxxii. 6; Isa. xlv. 8; Ezek. xxxiv. 26; Hos. vi. 3, x. 12), and also the light of the sun, as the Lord had already intimated in ver. 14. Christ Himself, according to the concluding promise of the Old Testament (Mal. iv. 2), is the sun of righteousness, and in Him beams forth in its fullest radiance the Divine *love towards enemies.* (Rom. v. 8—10.) We who now know this, detect such meaning in His words: but He then spoke, even while the light of grace was graciously beaming in His face, only of the light of the natural sun. He did not say: that ye may be *my* disciples and *my* brethren (as afterwards Jno. xiii. 34, 35, as I have loved you; and the Apostles, Eph. v. 1) —but in His labours and His lessons of love glorified His father in heaven. He blessed those who reviled Him, even in rebuking He blessed them; He persisted in works of benevolence and healing in spite of all opposition; and He openly prayed for the evildoers, who inflicted upon Him the last injury, as He had prayed for them all His life long in secret (Ps. xxxv. 12—14, cix. 4). That He here magnifies the Father's goodness to *the evil and the good,* the just and the unjust, is to be understood partly as referring to the relative proportion in a mixed multitude between the seeming good and bad; and partly as if it had been said—on the evil and the unjust, who deserve it not, as if they were good and just, without any reference to merit and worthiness.[1] For who is good and just in *His* sight? We are none of us worthy that His sun should shine upon us. Hence St Luke briefly expresses the fundamental idea—He is kind unto the unthankful and to the evil.

Vers. 46, 47. Returning once more to the contrast of the Pharisaic spirit, we have an advancement in the idea, a full revelation now for the first time of their unrighteousness and lovelessness. Before it was that they hated their enemies, thinking that that was lawful, provided only they loved their "neighbour." But they really *love* not at all, in strict truth, these their so-called neighbours, friends and brethren. They have so far narrowed the circle, that not merely those who hate them are excluded from their love, but also those who love them not. But if ye only love those *who love you,* can this be indeed called love, which is in its very nature anticipating, and abundant, and universal, like the shining of the sun? Is it not rather a seeking of your own, and in its principle simply a loving of yourself?

[1] Which is also indicated by the interchange of the leading word—the evil are mentioned first in the former, the just in the latter.

This *question* the Lord presses upon their consciences, which cannot refuse to give back a true answer. If He speaks of this as "love," it is with that severe irony which He may use towards hypocrites: they are said to love, in the same sense as they are called *righteous* and have *righteousness* attributed to them (ver. 20). This is, indeed, the sense of all mankind: no man ever yet hated his own flesh; he that loveth his wife loveth himself, and seeks his own personal comfort (Eph. v. 28, 29); he that loveth friend and brother is not impelled by any voluntary disposition of his mind, but by the mere natural feeling that it is *his own* friend and brother that he loves. This is the so-called love of his neighbour which the natural man is said to entertain. If he attempts to plead it in justification, however, in the presence of strict law, the mask of "more than others" is plucked away by the Lord, who shows it to be only the common *Pharisaism* which extends even to publicans and heathens. No man is so wicked and abandoned, no sinner is so essentially devilish, as not to have some objects of his selfish election, of whom he may say—I love them because they love me. Do not even the *publicans* the same? In St Luke this saying is expressed in another form, which simply gives the general principle involved in it—sinners also do even the same. But here the Lord's expression deepens its emphasis in the second question—do not even the *heathens* the same? (which reading is both on external and internal grounds to be preferred.) For the Pharisees always placed the publicans on a level with the heathen (Matt. xviii. 17); as they were seen to be no better than the publicans, the second contrast (afterwards again in ch. vi. 7) is ready to be introduced, by which the Lord will teach His righteousness—not like the heathen! Therefore He had not said that the Father caused His sun to rise and sent His rain upon Jews and heathen: because this pharisaically-apprehended antithesis is merged in the one, true distinction of just and unjust. *'Ασπάζεσθαι*, to count worthy of greeting and friendly intercourse, attaches itself to the *εὐλογεῖν* of ver. 44; not without allusion to the fact that a Jew only gave his שָׁלוֹם to a Jew, a Pharisee, certainly never to a publican. Your *brethren* is ironically spoken, even as the love here apparently conceded is to those whom you regard and acknowledge as such: whereas (vers. 22—24), from the days of Cain and Abel every man is every man's brother! Alas that the disciples of Christ in the present day should need so much to be warned against a Pharisaism still extant—let not your brotherly love fall short of love universal! (2 Pet. i. 7, τὴν ἀγάπην simply, which is alone the truly catholic love). What *reward* have ye? A precarious and transitory reward in man's praise and in his fleeting favour, but none from the Father in heaven; which prepares the way for ch. vi. 1, even as it looks back to ch. v. 12. Similarly τί περισσόν refers to ver. 20, where a περισσεύειν of righteousness was required, beyond that false one of those "saints" who were like all other sinners. Thus progressively the inner connexion of the fundamental ideas of the Sermon on the Mount exhibit themselves to our view!

Ver. 48. Τέλειος is primarily, according to the usage of the LXX. תָּמִים, but ὥσπερ gives it such an elevation of meaning that it becomes equivalent to the קָדוֹשׁ of God. It is used here in the sense of that fundamental commandment which comprised within itself the whole Law of Israel, as well the external ordinances as those moral precepts with which they were inwardly bound up:—Ye shall therefore be holy, for I am holy! (Lev. xi. 45, xix. 2, xx. 7, 26.) It is to this that the Lord now refers on closing His *citation* of separate commandments, reducing the sum of the second table to the sum of the first table and of the whole Law. *This* is the distinctive περισσόν of the children of God (Deut. xiv. 1) through which they are sanctified and separated from an evil world to the honour of the ever-praised Father. But what is that virtue of His *holiness*, of which He will make His children *partakers*? God is holy as the condescending and Merciful One: His highest, most perfect praise is that it must be said *He is Love*, in a sense in which it is not, and cannot be, said He is Omnipotence, He is Justice. Love is even in Him the bond of perfectness, the essence of all His other attributes and perfections. We may be, and we should be, not almighty as God is, but *merciful* as He is, and St Luke with perfect propriety uses this word instead. This is *our* perfection, this is our being entire and complete before God and in God. For children are indeed only perfect as children. This is set up by our Father as the goal of our attainment—*Be ye* therefore; and as this command contains a latent fore-announcement that the Holy One designs to make us holy, the Perfect One to make us perfect, so now in the Son is the fulness of the Godhead, the plenitude of Divine love brought down, in order that it may enter our needy souls through the Spirit. If we believe on His Name, we are already regarded, through the imputation of righteousness to our faith, as πεπληρωμένοι ἐν αὐτῷ. (Col. ii. 10). If, apprehended of Christ, we press towards the mark with full earnestness of spirit and walk according to the rule, we are now τέλειοι in the principle of our mind and will, though not yet τετελειωμένοι in consummation and attainment. (Phil. iii. 12—15). But the living Law of our Lord gives us a sure and comforting security in this ἔσεσθε—*Ye shall be* perfect, if ye abide and increase in love. But this does not set before us a general prospect of an unending progress towards perfection, without a definite goal of completed perfectness; but the God of peace will sanctify us until we are actually ὁλοτελεῖς (1 Thess. v. 23), until in the perfect work of patience we *have become* ἐν μηδενὶ λειπόμενοι. (Jas. i. 4). To that end it is said, Ἐι δέ τις λείπεταί τινος, αἰτείτω παρὰ τοῦ διδόντος (Jas. i. 5)—as also in the Sermon on the Mount our Lord opens up to us the path of prayer which leads to the fulfilling of all the commandments.

The discourse, which set out at first with the most deep-drawn, fundamental principles of truth, the pregnant language which embodied them demanding most rigorous attention for its exact interpretation, becomes henceforward more easily intelligible in its phraseology, and descends to a more popular style of teaching. There follow, however, at intervals, sayings the meaning of which is somewhat disguised in figurative and obscure expressions, and is not immediately obvious, such as chap. vi. 22, 23; vii. 6. The section chap. vi. 1—18, may be termed a sacred example of popular Reformator-Polemik—if it is allowable thus exactly, though in unidiomatic German, to express our meaning.

The third contrast with the *Pharisees* fully discloses, as our general survey showed us, their *hypocritical and external lega-*

lity, as the complete development of that false system of exposition which originates in an adherence to its mere letter. This is exhibited, to wit, as the original internal principle, and essential quality of their *pseudo-righteousness*. There is designedly and appropriately no further reference to individual commandments of the Divine Law and their fulfilment: the appealing reference to that which is written, and to what they of old time substituted for it or perverted it into, was brought to an end in ch. v. by a most searching and comprehensive contrast. The *three leading examples*, however, which now are to follow in conformity with the Lord's prescribed plan, are taken from the three meritorious works of righteousness, so to speak, the highest acts of all so-called righteousness according to *universal human estimation*, heathenish as well as Pharisaic. For this whole section aims, in transition, to exhibit the Pharisees as, in their natural state, heathens in the true sense of the word. These examples are the three works which even Christian Pharisaism, especially in the Romish Church, has on similar grounds reproduced:—*Almsgiving* to our neighbour, *Prayer* to God, *Fasting* for ourselves. See them thus united in Tob. xii. 9. It may probably be thought that prayer would have more fitly been placed last, as thus the contrast between the hypocritical and the sincere performance would have been more direct, and the transition more immediate to the fundamental idea which follows in vers. 19—23:—viz., the single-minded aim and pursuit after God's own righteousness! But the order in which the Lord places them is, however, that of their natural development, whether in the good or evil intention of man. He who seeks righteousness, begins with external good works (instead of the right commencement which is directly in prayer); then proceeds to prayer, that his God may regard his good deeds, pardon their deficiency, and be pleased to strengthen him for their performance; and finally, in order to further the devotion of prayer, he fasts and exercises himself in keeping under the flesh. Thus we find it with Cornelius, Acts x. 2, 30, 31; and precisely the same with hypocrites, although in caricature of the truth. Yet at the same time almsgiving was most immediately included in the divine statutes for Israel (ch. v. 42; Deut. xv. 11); fasting, on the contrary, was for the most part optional, since there was only one fast-day appointed to Israel, the day of atonement, to which very early were added other times of general fasting (Zech. viii. 19), till in process of time came the fasting twice in the week of the individual Pharisee. (Lu. xviii. 12).

In ver. 1, there is laid down a general warning against such a performance of the duties of righteousness, such a righteousness of works, as consists only of hypocrisy and semblance, inasmuch as it is exhibited only *in the sight of men*, and to be seen of them. An apparent contradiction to ch. v. 16, which, however, really explains it. The preliminary—*your righteousness!* of ch. v. 20, here recurs again. The reference to the Father in heaven, and the only standard of worth and of reward in His sight, is here continued, following ch. v. 46, 48. He who was there in ver. 45 exhibited as the highest *exemplar* of perfect holy love, is also the *Rewarder* of all true righteousness which consists in similitude to Himself. ("Before thee nothing else has any value, but thine own likeness.") He is merciful to the merciful, and gives the pure in heart to see His face. Hereupon follow in their order, first of all *almsgiving*, distinctively by the Pharisees termed "righteousness," but here taken as a general designation of all good works towards our neighbour. Now occurs for the first time the expression—*the hypocrites*—so often cast in the teeth of the Pharisees down to ch. xxiii. For they are no better, who are like the publicans, and yet arrogate to themselves a special and exceeding righteousness, throwing the veil of an apparent sanctity over the wickedness of their hearts. The same is uttered, again, in connexion with prayer, ver. 5, and fasting, ver. 17. Thus it is the leading idea of this section, although in the central part of it concerning prayer, ver. 7, the reference is extended—like the heathen. In opposition to this our Lord tells His disciples, that they should, as far as possible, perform their good works *in secret even to themselves*, to avoid all imagination of having by the deed in *itself* done any thing. For deeds of charity by their very nature neither can nor should be altogether concealed; they cannot indeed admit of concealment at all. It is somewhat less so with prayer to God; hence afterwards, enter into thy closet, and shut thy door! Finally, exercises of self-restraint and discipline cannot by their nature be concealed from ourselves, and they should on that account be all the more closely hidden from others, for here is the greatest danger. Ascetic discipline, not hidden, loses all its value; consequently, in ver. 17, there is commanded even a holy disguise of fasting, as the only and effectual antidote to a wicked hypocrisy. These are the three stages of concealment before man, which the righteousness of Christ's disciples admits of.

Prayer, again, is the centre and soul of all acts in general which pertain to the service of God. In connexion with this, as the point of most importance, the contrast developes itself more plainly as twofold:—not before men first, but also not before God and men together,—which is the consummation of these Pharisees' hypocrisy, and of the wretchedness of the blind people who follow them,—*by much speaking!* Word-making, instead of prayer from the heart, whether before men or only in the closet, is ever the direct opposite of true prayer. Our Lord sets against this His own sacred *model of prayer for the children of the Father;* which teaches how that they must in the simplest terms, before and after, and in connexion with all their earthly necessities, pray for the establishment of His Kingdom, in the doing of His will, to His own glory (*the fulfilling of His Law*), as *the gift of His grace;* that thus *through prayer they may fulfil the commandment.* We see this in a very different light from *Neander*, to whom it appears *evident* that vers. 7—16 are altogether *foreign* to the organism of the Sermon on the Mount. *To us*, on the other hand, it is manifest that this prayer, inserted in the very midst of the second division of the discourse, is its proper *centre*, the key to all the mysteries of its demands, by which the way to their fulfilment is pointed out. To ask is all that is required *of us* in order to the performance of every requirement (ch. vii. 7—13), and the *command* thus to pray with the *promise* involved in it, is *the heart of the evangelical law.* Hence the Lord's prayer, as we shall see, is arranged as the counterpart of the Ten Commandments. Here does our heavenly Father exhibit Himself the third time as the hearer of prayer and *giver* of righteousness: as in ch. v. 45 He had shown Himself to be its pattern, and in ch. vi. 1, 4, 6, its rewarder. In vers. 14, 15, the fifth petition is again repeated with the most solemn emphasis, for in it is especially fulfilled the law of love through the asking and receiving of the love of God; yet, as is strictly appropriate here, with a *warning* against the hypocritical conceit, which might lead them to imagine that such prayer as this is already heard even without any such condition.

Finally, in vers. 16—18, concerning which we have almost said enough already, we have *fasting* as significative of all asceticism and *abstinence* of every kind. There is a simple repetition of the terms of the first contrast, which thus, after the apparent interruption of the pattern-prayer, closes the section as it was begun.

Ver. 1. *Δικαιοσύνη*, for which ἐλεημοσύνη has been substituted as a well-intentioned but mistaken gloss, does not here convey the meaning of liberality or almsgiving; as צְדָקָה does in the Pharisaic usage which pervades the whole Talmud, though never in the Scriptures of the Old Testament.[1] The Lord speaks assuredly according to Scriptural usage only, and *δικαιοσύνη ὑμῶν* can be no other than that of ch. v. 20, to which this fundamental position looks back before it is followed out into more specific detail. It is consequently quite similar to ch. xxiii. 5; *all their works* they do for to be seen of men. Therefore is added the *admonitory* *προσέχετε*, take heed! as this was also contained in ch. v. 20; and the third contrast with the Pharisees now deepens, according to the general fundamental plan of the sermon, into a tone of warning. Yet does the Lord at the same time address Himself generally to the poor misguided people who blindly followed these hypocrites, as well as to His own separated disciples, in order that He may open their eyes the cunning treachery of their guides and examples, and thus awaken and secure their desire for His discipleship and its better righteousness. A slightly ironical ambiguity in the expression, which rather lay in the word as understood by His present hearers, than in the Lord's own design, paves the way for the mention of that ἐλεημοσύνη which to the Pharisaic Jews was the most eminent δικαιοσύνη. It is not the "before men" which is

[1] The transition is seen in apocryphal passages, such as Tob. xiv. 9, φιλελεήμων καὶ δίκαιος, xii. 9, ἐλεημοσύνας καὶ δικαιοσύνας, where also in ver. 8 the whole three occur together, prayer with fasting and alms.

forbidden as such, but making that the improper aim, in opposition to the proper aim in ch. v. 16. Hence θεαθῆναι in this passage is quite different from ὅπως ἴδωσιν in that, and contains a bye-reference of an evil kind to θέατρον and the like, to mere *show* before the world. Hence afterwards, in vers. 5 and 16, the yet more severe ὅπως φανῶσι, which plainly expresses an empty *appearance* without any truth within. But the reference to the everlasting reward of the Father in heaven detracts not by any means from righteousness, but rather belongs essentially to its reality, since it is wrought *for God's sake*, for His approbation, and in order to blessedness in communion with Him.

Vers. 2. As the *you* had already in ch. v. 23, 29, 36, 39, passed over into the *thou* of a more specific application, so does it uniformly now in each part of this section. The Jewish over-estimation of almsgiving begins already to show itself in certain otherwise well-intended apocryphal sentences, such as Tob. iv. 11, 12, xii. 9; Wisd. iii. 28, xxix. 14, 15, which themselves seem to lean on such canonical sayings as Prov. xix. 17; Dan. iv. 24. The truth which lay at the foundation of this error, but which was, alas, perverted and altogether lost in Pharisaism, Christ Himself acknowledges, for instance in Matt. x. 42, and also His apostles, 2 Cor. ix. 9. The sounding a trumpet or letting it be sounded cannot, in harmony with the connexion, be regarded as a mere figure, denoting, it may be, "loud and shrill begging-litanies" (according to *Lange*), but also an actual custom of that age, of which nothing further is distinctly known to us:[1] for the Lord is now describing the hypocrites and their work right strictly after the life. Before *thee*, the saintly man, the great benefactor—as descriptively as it is scornfully spoken—that thy name and fame might be trumpeted forth! This were then also thy reward, dismissed with which no other awaits thee.

Vers. 3, 4. But *when thou*, a child of God, doest alms—which must no more be omitted than the offering of the gift according to ch. v. 24—let it not be with ostentation, but keep it rather, so far at least as the act of giving will admit, a secret from the world; no artificial concealment is necessary, however, or that

[1] Compare, however, Sepp, Leben Christi, ii. 183. Moreover σαλπίζειν is not merely *tuba canere*, but *tuba cani curare* also, according to a general usage, which Meyer cannot well deny.

thou shouldst show that thou art ashamed of it by false anxiety or affected modesty. Especially take care—for that is the main point—not to glory in thy act, which should be as natural to thee as shining is to light. The saying concerning the right hand and the left is manifestly proverbial: forget it, if it may be, even while thou doest it; let it be far from thee, while the right hand is giving to hold in thy left a trumpet, or to stretch it out for reward and praise. If the hands know nothing of it, the soul knows nothing—we may say with von Gerlach. That is at least more simple than to regard it with Lange as referring to the solicitous counting from one hand into the other before the gift, and the clapping of hands afterwards. Take ch. xxv. 37 as its best exposition. Be not afraid that thy good work will be done so secretly, that even God will not know it and find it again for its reward. He forgets no work of love (Heb. vi. 10). If thou thinkest of this, and at the same time of the strong temptation on thy part to forget and to lose it while receiving the praises of men, thou wilt prefer ever to do thy work in secret: thus shalt thou be more sure of that secret and true estimate in the sight of God which alone gives its value to what may be termed good. Not as the Chinese proverb runs:—Give thy alms in the day, thy reward will come in the night—but just the reverse: Give in secret, and thou shalt openly receive the true Divine recompense, partly even in this world (Eccl. xi. 1), but in all its fulness at the resurrection of the just (Lu. xiv. 14). As again the Mohammedan proverb says: Hast thou done a good deed, cast it into the sea; if the fish finds it not, yet will God see it. He reckons to thee capital and interest in rich return: for every deed of love, done from a pure heart, as unto Him, bears its fruit unto everlasting life.

Vers. 5, 6. Sincere worshippers pray, indeed, in the *synagogues*, and there is nothing wrong in that: but they who *prefer* to pray in the congregation, instead of the closet, are thereby convicted as hypocrites. How much more so when it is *in the streets*, to which, with rare exceptions, prayer is not appropriate,—and even *at the corners* of the streets, where is the greatest concourse of passers by. There *stand* they, the wicked ones, who pervert the most holy act of secret, interior communion with God,—concerning which, therefore (according to Braune's deep and striking remark), Moses gave no direct precept—into a mere matter of *ostentation* before the world. They have artfully so watched their opportunity as to be at the street-corner at the hours of prayer; they then continue standing there as if it was a matter of conscience not to omit, even there, the holy hour. For without any such pretext and occasion, to stand in the street for prayer would appear even to the world to be such frenzy as the essential, indelible feeling of truth in the most wicked hypocrite would be ashamed of: manifest as it is that prayer is out of place in the street, hypocrisy itself requires another cloke to hide the shame which clings to it. They have their reward: they pray not indeed to God, and seek not to be heard; therefore they have only just what they desire and seek. But thou, if thou truly prayest to God, must know that while the temple is a house of prayer, and the synagogues places of prayer also, this does not prevent the equal sanctity of all other places, where the Lord may be near to all who call upon Him, and dwell in the heart of the contrite ones. Thou shalt not be ashamed of the public prayer under fitting circumstances, but shalt in addition *especially* and *habitually* retire into solitude, where nothing must interrupt, hinder, or tempt thee in thy devout abstraction. Go into thy closet, if thou hast one (Judith ix. 1, viii. 5; Tob. iii. 12); or else seek one under God's own heaven, which may become to thee a Bethel. Shut to the door, if thou canst and it should be necessary (2 Kings iv. 33); but in any case the door of thy senses and thoughts, that no distraction may interpose between thee and thy Father. So pray to thy invisible Father, Himself concealed to thy sense (τῷ ἐν τῷ κρυπτῷ as before in ver. 18), and He who out of His secret place looks into secret, will openly reward as well thy prayer as thine alms, each in its kind. Reward is here the common middle term between the ideas of recompense and simple grant.

Vers. 7—8. Frightful and shameful, but alas true, was it that the Israelites, the holy of Israel, in their *very prayer* to their God, have become like the *heathen*, because they actually do not pray *to Him* at all! The heaping up many words is essentially the manner of all heathenish prayer, which supposes that God must be awakened by human cries (1 Kings xviii. 27) as all the babbling of the heathen shows to the present day. This is, however, so deeply rooted a mischief in the heathen mind of the natural man, that it may well follow the disciples of Jesus even into their closets. Therefore it follows: and *when ye yourselves pray in the closet,* before God and not before men, beware of this same folly, which would convict you either of hypocrisy in your own hearts, or at least of unbelief in a present and living God. Even Sirach (vii. 14) said long ago: "Make not much babbling when thou prayest!" and the Jewish teachers abounded in good maxims to this effect, though they were neutralized by others of opposite tendency, such as,—He who multiplies his prayers, is sure of a hearing,—Whoso lengthens his prayers, will not return empty,—Every man should daily repeat at least eighteen prayers—and so forth. To these clung the hypocrites of that age with their long prayers (ch. xxiii. 14): but the same evil breaks out in every age where simplicity and truth decline, as the confusion of Paternosters, Ave Marias, and Rosaries among the Catholics bears witness; and no less the pious babbling of many a pietist keeper of the hours, of many a devotee in the closet relying on his enforced *opus operatum.* Nothing indeed is farther from the Lord's meaning than to repress the prayer which is ever welling from the full heart, the spirit of persistent wrestling with God. But the *multa locutio* wherein there is not *multa precatio* (to quote Augustine), the *words* which are not urged from a vehement and overflowing heart, He esteems a vain heathenish work; and condemns as a vain delusion the imagination that any words, as such, might contribute to the acceptance of prayer (Isa. i. 15). For our object in prayer is not to inform the Omniscient of what he knew not before. The universal subject and matter of our prayer is,—that which we have need of for body and soul, in general and in specific things. This *knoweth* the Father before we ask Him, yea better than we can ever ask or conceive; for poor fallen man *knows no longer what he is in need of*, first, generally for his soul, and then in particular, at least very often, for either soul or body. (Rom. viii. 26.) While before God we are thinking *what* He may know to be our real need, we shall also remember to trust it entirely to His hands. In this utterance, finally, so stern in its condemnation of all that is not simple in prayer, and yet so encouraging to all that is so, the Lord solves that ever-recurring doubt:—Will God, in deference to our prayer, interfere with the order of the world? He has already in its arrangement provided for the answer of every prayer, as generally for every foreseen expression of human freedom, and for every necessity of His creatures known to Him from eternity. Superstition, which can only take root in hypocrisy, supposes that words must do this; unbelief into which superstition ever degenerates, for it is essentially one with it, expects no help to acceptance from the words of prayer. Neither knows aught of the living God, in whom true faith only can confide for the knowledge of its need and the willingness to help it, and therefore alone can truly *pray*, even as children ask of their father.

THE LORD'S PRAYER.

(Matthew vi. 9—13).

Vers. 9—13. But where shall we begin and where shall we end with the exposition of the *Lord's prayer;* not His own, that is, (after this manner pray ye!) but *our* prayer who are and would be the Lord's, *given to us* as the children of the Father, by His Son our Lord?[1] What has exposition to do, we had almost said, with the words in which the wisdom of God descending upon us in perfect love, has condensed and enshrined for us neither more nor less than *all*, *all* which ever has ascended, does now or ever will ascend from human hearts in *prayer* to heaven? Yes, verily, whatsoever may not be included in this, cannot be fit subject of prayer, and may not be asked. Such unlicensed prayer is indeed no prayer at all in spirit and in truth, for God's Spirit hath not prompted it; neither can it be real communion of the heart with the living God, for presumption and error have never the confidence of faith. Think of and utter aught which it is in thy will or thy power to ask, and thou wilt find it already spoken for thee in this prayer of prayers. Whatever from the beginning, since

[1] How *Braune* can suppose that *the Redeemer* Himself often used this prayer is to us inconceivable; particularly on account of the fifth petition, and also on account of the sixth and seventh—for "evil" must be *pre-eminently* sin, from which Christ redeems us, but never needed Himself to be redeemed from it.

men first, on account of sin and evil, lifted their hearts and hands to heaven, has been in their minds to ask, is here reduced, in the simplicity of the new and everlasting covenant, the last utterance of God to us in His Son, to one word, which will remain man's last utterance also to God, until heaven and earth are divided no more. All the cries which go up from man's breast upon earth to heaven, meet here in their fundamental notes: and are gathered into words which are as simple and plain for babes as they are deep and inscrutable for the wise, as transparent for the weakest understanding of any truly praying spirit as they are full of mysterious meaning for the mightiest and last struggles of the spirit into the kingdom and glory of God. Whatever Israel may ever have prayed in words given by the Spirit of God or shaped by the spirit of man ; whatever there was of just and sound in the contents of any Jewish formulary or collection, any Kaddisch or Machsor, which was extant in the time of Jesus, was but the preparatory aspiration towards this most living of all formulas, full of spirit in its letter; this most comprehensive of all epitomes so marvellous in its brevity; into which our Lord and Master condenses now for His own, all that those words imply :—*When ye pray say !* Thus has His spirit expounded it for nearly two thousand years to those who have prayed in his name : and all that it has ministered to their thoughts and they have derived from it, is the comprehensive fulness of its real contents. Learn to make it *thy prayer*, and it will interpret itself to thee with ever-deepening impressiveness, from the Fathername which it places upon thy lips down to that Amen of faith, which, having first impressed it upon thy heart, it draws to thy lips, that out of thy own mouth thine heart may be strengthened : but all through the power of God the Spirit, without which the most consummate words to those who resist it—remain but words. Let the reader receive the exposition which will now be given, only as a finger-post to indicate where the paths of profound thought go on to their endless development ; especially as giving some very necessary hints for the *unity* and the *harmony* of those paths, which as the individual petitions open them up, proceed in compact and harmonious progression towards the one great end.

After this manner then pray *ye*—the Lord says, in immediate connexion with the prohibition of heathen babbling. In the most obvious meaning, therefore,—thus briefly and simply, embracing in plain and sound words whatsoever thy heart prompts thee to utter before God: not going round and round for the mere sake of saying many words, as if He did not understand. But when we see presently after that the Lord, in giving a pattern of its *form*, incorporates in it at the same time the *substance of all prayer* for which words can ever be required;[1] and in so doing goes entirely out of and beyond the immediate connexion of His discourse in order to condense the whole meaning of the Sermon into this prayer as its kernel;—we shall not be disposed to agree with many who unwisely think that He *only* designed to commend to us by an example simplicity and brevity in the *expression*. He who should cordially assent to this might well despair of matching this by any other prayers, and therefore rest entirely in the given form itself. Did the Lord by, "after this manner," signify these very words, or only their substance and their manner? No rational man can think that it was His meaning that we should use these words exclusively. But that it was His design that they should be adhered to and used, as His church has understood Him and acted accordingly, we have most decisive proof in the *repetition* of the same words upon a *subsequent* request of His disciples for a *form of prayer*. (Lu. xi. 1—4.)[2] For there they wished for a directory and form for daily use:—as *John also* taught His disciples. The Lord did not refuse it, but most emphatically referred them in their need to that which He had given a long time before: He knew nothing and had nothing better for them, and now says more distinctively than on the former occasion:—When ye pray, and have need of prescribed expressions, then *say ye* the same words! There is a prayer of

[1] "Not so much a sacred formulary as for Divine instruction as to what petitions are universally good, universally necessary, universally acceptable," says the *Beuggen* Monatsblatt with perfect correctness, although it cannot be gainsaid that the Lord set out with the *immediate* design to inculcate simplicity and brevity in the expression.

[2] As certainly as the Sermon on the Mount was spoken by our Lord in the form in which St Matthew gives it, and the Our-Father is an essential part of it, so certainly St Luke's is not merely a "more particular account of the circumstances under which the prayer was given." Alas that the excellent *Harms* should thus express himself upon it, from whose valuable expositions in his Sermons we have elsewhere received much that is useful.

the heart without word, but let him who should think himself so qualified and capable for that at all times, as to be able to despise the prayer of words, reflect upon this saying of our Lord:— When ye pray, *say!*[1] Further, the Spirit of prayer does give the special and ever new and appropriate words of prayer; but this does not remove the necessity of the weak to fall back upon a given form of words, yea, even of the strongest who are, sometimes at least, equally weak, and know not either what they ought to ask or how to ask it. In any case, there remains, finally, the great necessity of a *common* prayer of general consecration and promise. Therefore, the Lord's commandment—Pray thus, and say! is the actual appointment of a letter sanctified and blessed for the church's spiritual prayer, the institution of an almost sacramental word-element resembling that other—*Do this!* For as we have need of the Lord's Supper, *well nigh in like manner*—I say not more, for there is yet assuredly a difference—have we need of a word of prayer full of promise to be placed in our lips, that we laying hold of it may by the word excite the Spirit, in the name of Jesus, who has Himself commanded us thus to pray ourselves from the poverty of receiving faith into the full confidence of being heard and accepted. And this confidence is especially strengthened by this, that we offer the same prayer in fellowship *one with another,* whether in external or internal communion. In that request of the disciples a purely human need uttered itself which the Lord could not have left unsatisfied, yea, well knowing what they needed had already provided its satisfaction. If, on the one hand, alas, this most sacred prayer has been desecrated into a most profane formality of babbling by the misuse of it in endless Paternosters and Our-Fathers in the many tongues into which it has come; yet on the other hand an unlimited experience attests the gracious and condescending will of the Lord to bless these words, with which He has connected, and into which He has inwrought, a sanctity beyond that of any other prayers that we may use. In them the little child begins to spell out the rudiments of its prayer, and when the church unites, in its loftiest festal assemblies, to pray, these words and none but they are still its most perfect

[1] As Dr *Schurf* answered some such one.

concerted utterance, sufficient for the most sublime occasions, and beyond which nothing can be expressed. All that is needful for every act of Divine service, and all that any man may have especially in his own heart, is comprised in this prayer; as the ecclesiastical formulary (which we do not blame as *Nitzsch* does) so excellently says.

Thus the Lord over and above the *how* teaches us abundantly the *what*, and not merely *teaches* it, but *gives* us the petitions which He commands us to pray, as simple *promises*, for the encouragement of our confidence in asking, if we lay hold upon them in faith. But it is indeed only a prayer for *us* poor sinners, who have need of forgiveness and deliverance. He Himself, as the Son, prayed otherwise to the Father, and has opened a way whereby we, having become children of God through Him, may have liberty to pray to His Father as *our* Father too. Thus does He turn our asking into receiving, and makes our *prayer* the way and means of our *fulfilling the commandment.* This is the meaning of its position here in the Sermon on the Mount. Jehovah cried upon Sinai amid the thunders of His majesty—Thou shalt be holy! Jesus on the Mount of Blessedness gives to the people, who sit down at His feet and receive of His words (Deut. xxxiii. 3), the word of living power from His own mouth:—Ask and it shall be given you to become holy, yea, finally to be holy for ever in your finished redemption to the glory of God!

Hence it may already be presumed that this central word, containing the very heart of the Gospel as the *life-giving, self-fulfilling law* of grace, would stand,—through the marvellous wisdom of the Holy Ghost which has *so ordered* it, that all things in the great whole of Revelation correspond and are fitly joined together,—in immediate relation with the *Decalogue*, the authentic expression of the *law of commandment* for all ages. And so it manifestly does. First of all it is obvious to every one that in this as in that there are two tables, and indeed in a similar manner referring to God and man. As the commandment begins—I am thy God, thou shalt consecrate thyself to Me alone, but not in any forms of thy own devising, and regard as holy My name, My day, and My representatives (My image, in their united human life, thy father and mother), and then first descends into the circle of man's relative duties and obligations; so also in the prayer, after the invocation come first the petitions, which, as they ascend to the Father, utter only "Thy," and afterwards the others which may also say "Our." If even there the gracious covenant-word—Thy God—preceded the commandments, how much more must all the petitions here have that first word of appropriating faith before them—*Our* Father! Further, as there the precept concerning parents (according to right reckoning the fifth), while it essentially belongs to the first table, is yet the middle-term of transition to the second, so also here the fourth makes such a transition from Thy to Our. It does, indeed, say "*our* bread," but at the same time—*Give* it to us as *Thy* good; while in the following petitions we ask only for the turning away of *our evil*. *To honour* God in the person of men, is the internal principle of the loving our neighbour as ourselves (submitting one to another in the fear of God, in honour preferring one another); the filial feeling is the foundation of family-life, from which society and the community grow as a more extended home in which thou shouldst do thy neighbour no harm, because he is thy brother. So also the filial petition for the true bread from the true Father is the beginning and foundation of all further petitioning for all our need, as will presently be shown. Finally, as there we have *ten* words (עֲשֶׂרֶת הַדְּבָרִים), so here, though the petitions—to distinguish the new above the old—are contained in the holier number Seven (repeating the most holy *Three*); yet the prayer itself is found to be also comprised in *ten* words, or sentences, if we include not only the invocation and doxology, its commencement and its close, but also, as is fitting, the single *vow*, which appears as the condition of the fifth petition. It is that "as we forgive," which is in itself something distinctive, as the Lord's immediately following repetition teaches us: yea, in this member of the prayer is its essential heart to be found, for we attain to this love, which is *the fulfilment of the law*, only in the way of asking and receiving from the love of God.

Thus the one prayer runs through both: Be *our God* and *give* us all *Thy* good—*take* from us all *our* evil, in order that in us also *Thine* may be the glory! Give Thy grace, take our sin—give Thy glory, take our evil away. But as the prayer bears the relation to the commandments of an abounding fulfilment of them, the *invocation* does not merely correspond with that first word of the covenant—I am thy God, but at the same time transforms the two first commandments into a prayer which fulfils them. Every other God, and every self invented likeness and image, is already excluded, when we cry in faith—Our Father which art in heaven! The first petition for the hallowing of the *name* embraces in itself the true principle or beginning and the final end of all prayer, but it aptly corresponds also to the next commandment—Thou shalt not take the name of the Lord thy God in vain. The New Testament order of conception, however, enters here. Now in the great fulfilment we pray down from heaven to earth the *kingdom* which is come and is coming, and we pray the good and gracious *will* of the Father into the hearts of ourselves and all his children. The three first petitions are inseparably *triune*. The Old Testament already contained at the law-giving in the hidden back-ground of its word,[1] reference to the sacred Three in God, but now comes into clearer prominence the name to be hallowed, of the *Father* just now invoked, of the *Son* whose kingdom is to come, of the *Spirit* through whose inworking the children of God are disciplined to do His will. The three petitions are inseparable, while each introduces and includes that which follows; yet do they, at the same time, exhibit the development in which they are fulfilled, through beginning, middle, end. For the first invocation and petition already hallows the name, then comes the kingdom more and yet more, until in its perfection the will is fully done.

Such is first and essentially "*that which we have need* of" (ver. 8). The following supplication grounds itself on this, and follows from it, as *Olshausen* rightly seizes the connexion between them; "*In order that this may be*, give us daily the bread of life." Thus may we understand the true meaning of the fourth petition, which mediates between the two tables, though so often, alas,

[1] Namely first: אָנֹכִי יְהוָֹה the Father, אֱלֹהֶיךָ in the Son, אֲשֶׁר הוֹצֵאתִיךָ through the Spirit's power. Then again: No other gods before Me, the Father; no likeness besides the Son, in whom my *Name* is; the *Sabbath* for a sign that I sanctify thee, and will carry on in thee the work of my Spirit (Ezek. xx. 12).

wrested from its connexion :—give us Thy good! It is, in some sort, as a condescension that it begins with the expression of our earthly, bodily need! it designs to signify more than that, however, elevating bodily need into the figure of spiritual. Impart that to us whereof we live, give Thyself to us for the good of our hunger, for the satisfaction of our desire. This is essentially the central word of all prayer: *supply our need!* Here is also the proper meaning of the much contested ἐπιούσιος, in its plain position before us: that which is necessary to our οὐσία, the sustenance of the creature derived from the power and gift of Him, who alone is in Himself ὁ ὤν. But man lives not by bread alone: and as the Lord has spoken at the commencement of the Sermon (ch. v. 6) of a hungering and thirsting of the inner man, so now in its centre, yea, in the innermost heart of the prayer which is its very kernel, He most assuredly does not bid us pray *merely* for the need and nourishment of the body, but speaks also of the *bread*, which the Father giveth from heaven, just as in John vi. 27—33, iv. 34. The details will follow upon the individual[1] petitions.

We also plainly see how the three petitions of the second table further describe and explain that bread of life, for which we, on our soul's behalf, must pray. As the first table of petitions is from above downwards, invoking all from heaven, to which *he who prays has risen in his invocation*, until the earth in re-established obedience becomes like heaven; so now the prayer returns back, rising from the confessed and expressed necessity, into which the Lord's merciful answer descends, towards full satisfaction and accomplishment, and, indeed, in the order of a sacred three, corresponding to the former :—our *trespass* is that we have

[1] It may be taken for granted that it is no design of ours to exhibit the commencing petition for *bodily* necessity as a "*common* petition among the other more elevated" (*Rothe's* Ethik p. 339), but admit, at the outset, its full significance and justness as such. But the position of *Karrer* (our Lutheran critic, to whom we shall revert again), that the true meaning is *only* the earthly bread, and that it is perpetrating robbery upon poor Christians if they are not allowed to use the prayer in that undivided sense, seems to be pushing the matter to an extreme. I am entirely misunderstood, as if I only tolerated the most obvious and bodily reference, with little approval.

15

not done the *will* of the Father, and reconciliation is the bread which we first and most inwardly need; then comes *temptation*, opposing through the might of the wicked one, the coming of the *kingdom;* then the *evil*, under which we sigh, to the very last opposing the full glorifying and hallowing of the *Name* of God in His saints. All that we here pray for is indeed embraced in order in the Son; the true *wisdom* of the children of God which is to pray for bread from their Father (in the four first petitions, but especially expressed in the fourth), is taught in the *doctrine* and *life* of Jesus; this leads us to His *death*, which is our justification from guilt; then to His *resurrection* in order to our *sanctification* against all temptation; finally, to His *ascension* and return for our full *deliverance* from all evil. Yet are these petitions on the other hand inseparably three-one; so that in the first we already perceive the last, and each prayer petitions for a spiritual sacrament, in which there is forgiveness of sins, and also victorious life, and salvation to blessedness in hope. Thus pray we for health and life in place of decay and death, for that true and only *deliverance*, in which the *Father* forgives His children for His name's sake (1 Jno. ii. 12); the *Son* strengthens those who are His against the evil one; and the *Spirit* perfects the deliverance unto glory.[1]

As, consequently, the *fourth* petition sets out with the expression of *bodily* need, which is to be developed into a spiritual meaning; so the *seventh* petition obviously first of all refers to *spiritual* evil in its principle, sin and temptation (as the connecting ἀλλά evidently intimates); but it also includes all the external, bodily evil which sin has brought and is bringing, and authorizes us in this legitimate way to pray for deliverance from it.

Thus has this general view placed the two petitions concerning which opinion has been divided in the true light, which harmo-

[1] The reader must consider whether this disposition is the logical construction which *Theremin* deprecates (Abendstunden p. 439), and also whether, besides this not absolutely necessary arrangement, other quite different combinations are supposable, as is there conceived But we very much doubt whether the parallel with the commandments, which our critic *Karrer* gives (Zeitsch. für die luth. Theol. 1848. 3) can be regarded as preferable.

nizes all differences: and pointed out our way for the right understanding of the particulars, to which we must now direct our attention.

How much more is that which the Son now puts into our mouth—Our *Father!* than that former—I am *thy God!* He graciously tells us—thus *say ye!* well knowing that the permission—thus may ye say! would have been by far too little for our diffidence. Would the disciples have been able after the Sermon on the Mount to lay hold of that permission and diligently avail themselves of it? It appears not from Luke xi., and therefore must the Lord repeat for all, what that one had not heard or had not understood and embraced. We may place our little children's hands together, and teach them—say ye. Well for every one, for whom this is early done: it is not too soon, as early as the child can cry—My father, and my mother (Isa. viii. 4)—and lift up his eyes to heaven as a child of humanity. How perfect is the *simplicity* of this beginning of all prayer, descending to the root and principle, already naturally present in the heart, of all sense of love, and trust for gift and help! In "Father" the Creator is at once included, but the glance towards heaven immediately adds: Who hath made all these things! Me, *with all other* creatures This beginning of all prayer given by our Lord Himself should be proof enough to all, that it is His will to build up His church in families and in nations from the very commencement of life, and every Our Father in the mouth of a child of Christianity (and should we then by any means suppress it?) asks the question—Can any man forbid water, that these should not be baptized, who are already taught by the Spirit to cry Abba? But again, if the simplicity of childhood has departed in after time, and sin has broken out, how hard is the return to it and the becoming again as little children! We might almost without qualification say that he who has never trembled at that invocation, and confessed that he dared not take it upon his lips, has never yet learned to utter it from his heart. Then does the word of grace attract the spirit and overcome—Have I not brought it down to thee in thy sin and misery, do I not give it up to the common use and even desecration of all men, in order that those who receive it in faith and are willing, should *learn* to use it in spirit and in truth? Then hear we the appeal to those who are parents

—If ye then, being evil, know how to give good gifts unto your children, how much more shall your Father which is in heaven! And then comes that knowledge which can never be enough learned, that we, through the Son, have also a Father, who is never weary of coming and laying hold of us through the power and impulse of His Holy Spirit. Only begin with this encouraging assurance, and let every Our Father anew from your lips to your heart declare—that He who hath given thee the word, gives also the faith, the grace and the spirit of prayer to use it. Thus the Gospel goes forth among the heathen in this prayer, laying hold of their innermost and first natural feelings after God—"On high above the stars a good Father dwells!" and transform the presentiment into assurance, in every one who receives it to his heart.

Further, what an inexhaustible meaning is there in the conjunction in this first glance towards heaven, of the Father-name, which is inborn and sweet to every child of man, with the universal compass of all things and the hosts of the universe! He whose are all the heavens, and not thy own earth merely, is the Father, is thy Father! All true prayer from under heaven goes up to Him, even though eyes and hands be not lifted up, even though the heart should return into itself to seek the Thou of prayer. Whosoever, however, would in the wilful delusion of his spirit seek it there *alone*, is at the very first appealed to by this prayer of our Lord: Not so! Not in thyself! Every good gift cometh down from above! The heavens give not showers (Jer. xiv. 22); the sun, and the moon, and the stars have no power in themselves and can impart nothing, but the Living God in His own world. By this is all Pantheism condemned, which, having first miserably compressed and shrivelled up this universe of things, knowing no other spirits than the spirit of man, knowing nothing of secret things beyond the history of the earth; then proceeds to make this scanty "all" into the god of its idolatry. Every child who can utter "Our Father which art in heaven," may put to shame such vain thinkers, and teach them a lesson of faith. (Heb. xi. 3).

But the Lord at the outset does not teach us at once merely to say—in heaven, as afterwards in the third petition it is used in contradistinction to earth (Matt. xxviii. 18): this would have been ill adapted to inspire the confidence of prayer, and would have removed Him who is nigh at hand to far distance again. But he teaches us to speak according to the language which described the creation: *in the heavens.* It would be well if the Lutherans would take that again from the Reformed. Where God is there is heaven, and where is God not? When these first words are more deeply pondered after this first upward glance, there is found to be no antithesis in them to the *here below* of him who prays, but they rather suggest a responsive descent of heaven to earth, and into the heart of the petitioner. I dwell in the high and holy place, with him also that is of a contrite and humble spirit! Here is the heaven of prayer, which opens to the petitioner when the High and Lofty One, whose glory is sung by all principalities and powers in His temple, and in His house of many mansions, bows down in His holy mercy to the abject ones, who otherwise could never by any struggles and endeavours rise to Him. He whose are the heavens is the Almighty Father: as He *can* help as God, so *will* He help as Father. He is the true Father, in a sense beyond that of His faint images—the fathers upon the earth. He is the universal Father: high and extended as the heaven is above the earth, so universal is His presence to praying hearts, opening up in them everywhere the countless heavens of His manifestation, like the suns in the drops of dew. The Lord had, however, previously said: But thou, when thou prayest, enter into thy closet, and pray to *thy* Father—for the "thy" must have its own prior claim, and it is obviously understood that he who prays, first of all prays for himself. Yet He now gives us a *common* prayer—*Our* Father! And even in the most essentially personal supplication and wrestling, which would only cry—My bread—my trespasses—deliver me—we must ever bear in mind that we do not alone thus pray. If faith utters the word Father, love, without which faith cannot be, immediately associates with it *our*, that all its prayer may go into the great fellowship of supplication, and all its petitioning be *intercession* also.[1] Here is there already an anticipation of the

[1] As *Lange* says, "even childhood is not without its distinctive feeling of human brotherhood," though this expression seems to embrace too much, when "all good spirits" are incorporated into this great brotherhood.

subsequent—as we forgive our debtors. (Mal. ii. 10). I with all others, but also all others with me and for me, in the presence of the one common Father of us all! Just as if thou wert to enter in diffidence and fear the audience chamber of thy King, and foundest there hundreds else with whom His majesty was kindly speaking; so should thy closet be large enough for all to enter with thee who pray under heaven, that thy faith may thus gather strength :—Where all are will I be, I will wait with them and with them be heard and be blessed!

But now to the *petitioning!* Between every word of true prayer, which does not remain the mere converse of the heart *before* Him, but becomes communion *with* Him, God speaks in answer. Listening to these answers the soul is moved to the most inward progress of its utterance. Thus now, after we have boldly uttered the invocation, the first voice of Majesty speaks from His throne—Am I a father, where is mine honour? (Mal. i. 6). Then comes the confession, in common with all who pray, and on behalf of all who pray not: Alas we are not yet thy true children! We are yet under the Heaven, and where the Holy! Holy! Holy! of the highest Heavens fills not yet all lands and all hearts. *Holy* is the first word, which we are taught to learn in the Lord's prayer, the vocabulary of all fundamental and elementary ideas in which man must speak of God and to Him; and it can only be learned in speaking *to* Him, out of the *invocation* that is first uttered. He has not made us shrink back terrified by His—I am holy! He has indeed by anticipation impressed this upon our hearts in the Father-name, but He now demands that which he has given, not indeed as yet by His solemn—be ye holy! but by the prayer of His own Spirit proceeding from our spirit: we would be holy, oh that we were so and might be, help us, good Father in heaven! *Hallowed be*—the race of thy fallen children, mankind, upon earth, which calls upon Thy name, and which does not call upon it, yea knows it not as yet? This is its meaning, but it is not so said. Not for our own sake do we pray, so much as for *His name's* sake. We have taken it into our lips with all the boldness of permitted and commanded confidence, and now meets us the solemn—not in vain! Befitting lowliness and reverence are joined with this childlike confidence, and we only pray for the honour of His name. Not unto us, O Lord, not unto us, but to thy name give the glory! By this is the self of the natural man, which even in prayer would ask and have for its own sake only, cut up from the roots; and the first and last principle of all prayer, is laid down in the *first* petition which so far includes all the rest. The prayer proceeds from the individual heart, and then goes forth, with a —hallowed in *us*—which must be understood, over all the world, even as far as the "Our Father" reaches. It has its degrees of meaning, and three in particular. For children who begin to learn it, as for heathens and all who know it not:—Reveal Thy name that we may know it, and utter it! For all who know it, but hold that knowledge in error and human delusions:—take away man's lie, which hangs around Thy name! Finally for all, who know it but deny it in act, who acknowledge it, but not from their hearts:—take away that most grievous dishonour of Thy name, that those who call upon it, sanctify it not in their lives! Thus do we here for ourselves and all the world lift up our confession and our vows: Glory be to God in the highest! In this all is included in one compendium: and the Pharisaical *mine* be the glory! which has a tendency to rise in God's children's hearts, for ever anew condemned. For the *name* is, indeed, not merely the word of appellation by which we address God; neither is it (as a false catechetical tradition in its pretended wisdom runs) God Himself in His being and nature, but the *acknowledgment* and the praise of God, *revealing* Himself to us and in us.[1] But He reveals Himself through Him, *in whom His name is* (Ex. xxiii. 21), the Son, in whom the Father Himself is honoured, in whose coming God's *kingdom* comes.

The kingdom *is come*, as the Lord's first preaching announced in another sense: but He here teaches us also that it is not yet come, but ever continues coming until the time when there shall be no more room or reason for such a prayer upon earth. The

[1] Assuredly the first petition goes out from the previous invocation "Our Father," continuing its invocation and adoration, yet it is not the same with it, in the sense of being its explication, or, as it were, a customary doxology appended to it. It has an actual petition of its own. We cannot concur with *Laufs* (Rheinische Monatsschrift, Nov. 1847), who, following older precedents, would deny this, and refuse to admit that *veneratio* and *laudatio* may be made, in any sense, *petitio*.

kingdom of God, by which He rules the world, is not here signified; that stands unmoveable and admits of no coming. But it is His kingdom of grace, which not only judges but extinguishes sin, and re-establishes His honour, His Father-honour again in the sinner. It comes, indeed, of itself without our prayer, inasmuch as if it did not descend as a free gift for the poor in spirit they could never have prayed for it, much less have drawn it into themselves by their prayers: nevertheless it comes not without our prayer; but in it and with it. The supplication which is excited and nourished upon earth—*Thy kingdom come!* is itself the evidence of its coming, its fruit at once and its seed in continual mutual co-operation between God and man. Thus it begins to exist, and goes on progressively until the kingdom of grace is consummated in the kingdom of glory. Until this is accomplished, the prayer thus given to us retains its value and force as a promise. Again, as it is not *we* who are hallowed but the name of God in us, just so it is not :—Help us that we may come into Thy kingdom, but let *Thy kingdom* come to us! Whoso with a kind of selfishness supplies in his heart—to *me*—and seeks even in the kingdom of heaven *his own* blessedness as his, is at once and always condemned by the language of this petition, which does not here mention "to us" at all. It does indeed belong to it, and not merely in the sense of the narrow "even to *us*" of the Lutheran Catechism (which without the Mission-glance is very faulty here), but, *in earth*, yea upon the whole earth, where as yet far other than Thy will reigns! That Christendom has prayed this second petition so long, and prays it now so much, without the corresponding Missionary impulse, and Missionary work, is the most mournful evidence that could be adduced of the great blindness which opposes everywhere this prayer and its clearest words of light. Where, however, this blindness is only that of the understanding, the horizon over which the eye may range being limited upon this subject, the prayers for the coming of the kingdom which have issued from believing hearts may, notwithstanding, co-operate to the good of the heathen. From the beginning they may have been sowing secretly and unconsciously the seed of future harvests, even as the children's Hosanna contributed to the destruction of the Adversary.

Finally, where is the kingdom, and where does it come? Where the *Will* of the King is done. The three petitions, without any "And" interposed, are inseparably three-one, as was said above; and as we pass from one to the other, we become more and more convinced of the deep principle that underlies them all. Thinkest thou that His name is hallowed at least in this place or that, so that one might confidently cry out concerning it, Lo here or lo there? Look narrowly whether the kingdom of honour and glory be indeed fully come, and pray on! Thinkest thou that the kingdom, too, is come here or there, question profoundly whether it be indeed *inwardly* set up in the children of the kingdom, whether they do the *will* upon earth as it is done in heaven, *voluntarily*, and entirely without any evil will or device openly or secretly contradicting it, and pray on! *As it is in heaven:* there there is no disobedience, nothing disorganised, nothing but the will, the kingdom, the honour of God; as in the courses of suns and stars, so among the morning stars and sons of God (Job xxxviii. 7), there is the festal service of those who, active in rest, shout for joy in their ranks of blessedness. So should it be *upon earth:* vast is the meaning which carries the promise in this prayer far above all the stir and tumult of humanity, inviting and urging all the children of God to restless wrestling in praying and receiving, and fervour in doing His will! By this petition, if he ventures to take it into his lips, the godless man condemns himself; with it the sufferer comforts himself, and is assured that through the gracious will of God all evil shall loose its hold upon the meek, who already have in hope the earth for their inheritance; by it the slothful man invigorates himself, the self-willed rebukes himself, and by it the will of the Spirit, which must conquer, prays itself through all the impediments of an opposing flesh, to perfect victory. The Forerunner Himself, in the weakness of our flesh, prayed *this* prayer before us, yet *without* sin.[1]

Thus have we, arrived thus far, prayed down and prayed away through the invocation and right confession of God the Father, all *false* selfishness of mine and ours, though without naming it,

[1] *Hamann* to *Herder* calls this *Fiat voluntas tua* the true *lapis philosophorum* in our Pater Noster.

from the most impious and devilish pride of self-glory which reigns in the world down to the slightest and merest volition of poor individual humanity. Let him who has not in this sense used this prayer, *begin it entirely anew*. In the three first petitions all that follow them were profoundly included: where then was the need of these after the former were fulfilled? The gracious giver of our prayer permits and requires us to *speak more plainly*, and, after having spoken of the honour of God, to unfold our own need, and our own plague. The prayer, which aims to lift us up to heaven, does not accomplish that at once, but we still sink back in our misery—*still on earth!* it therefore sets out again afresh, taking its stand *on earth*. Well might we in the former have essayed: "I would go up to Thee in faith!" —the attempt could not be in vain and without profit: but its best effect was to strengthen and excite us still more urgently to proceed—"Come down to me on earth in love!" This is the central turning-point of transition between the two halves of this prayer; the fourth petition in the heart of it indicates that transition.

How runs it? Give us this day what we need, the *bread* which pertains to our being and life! *Bread* as such? Poor man in the flesh upon earth thinks immediately of the wants of his bodily life, the supply of which it is not in him to create; he may think of it, for the gracious dictator of our prayer designs not to prevent *this* petition, nay rather puts it in his mouth. Yet is it, according to man's fallen nature, the *first* genuine prayer, with which we all commence, whereas the prayer for God's glory *should* be the first. With a profound reference to our earthly condition and our earthly need, does the second portion of the prayer commence: and sets out afresh, by teaching us, as the first elevation of man's head toward heaven, the table-prayer, as *Claudius* incomparably lays it down: "Man is not a cow or a horse, but he is among cows and horses, and must eat with them: therefore when he is fed, he rightly lifts up his head above them, conscious that he is thus fed and in order that he may never forget that he is." Are ye not, in your heavenly Father's sight, much better than they? They who would altogether take away the earthly meaning of the fourth petition, scarcely know what they say: is it not necessary that they should thus pray, and can we suppose the Lord not to have included so necessary a petition in His all-comprehending prayer? In this sense the simple words have a large and profound meaning. It is immediately evident that "bread" here means what man absolutely needs, excluding the slightest superfluity, and as opposed to all "not being content:" including, however, according to its proverbial use, food and shelter, in addition to nourishment. (1 Tim. vi. 8). *Επιούσιος, ἐπὶ τῇ οὐσίᾳ ἡμῶν αὐτάρκης, ἁρμόζων* is not the *daily* bread (Chrysost. *ἐφήμερος*) which is already included in *σήμερον*, whence it is in St Luke *τὸ καθ' ἡμέραν*. We may not care for the morrow, and never pray into the future! Still less, therefore, is it *to-morrow's* bread, *ἄρτος τῆς ἐπιούσης ἡμέρας*—in Gosp. of the Hebrews מחר.[1] But it is just a translation of לֶחֶם חֻקִּי as it runs in Prov. xxx. 8,[2] only that here in the Gr. *ἐπιούσιος* the idea of *need* is somewhat more prominent than that of appropriate, proportioned, and sufficient. Both, indeed, concur in one, according to the parallel cited by *Lange* out of the Gemara: "To every man what he needs for life, and to every body as much as is needful for it." We are also, in addition to this, reminded by *σήμερον, καθ' ἡμέραν*, of the uncertainty of our earthly life, that we might with every to-day reach the term of our course, and know no morrow: and thus there is already reference to a need that goes beyond this earthly life. But that we *need* our food for every *to-day*, the *ἐπιούσιος* boldly acknowledges. The Father *gives* it without prayer, even to the evil, and adds to it much more besides: but His own children may not only thus receive it, they bring with them the prayer to which they are bound as the expression of their *thankfulness*, as acknowledgment of their obligation. They also should remember that God may at any moment withdraw what He hath given, and consequently their "give" includes—continue to us and preserve! Thus poor and rich are alike petitioners before God's gate, all the care of poverty, and all the security of possession alike dissolved in this daily asking and receiving. Finally, the "our" in this more outward meaning, gives rise to two very important thoughts. It points

[1] Comp. upon this *Delitzsch* in the luther. Zeitschrift 1850, 3, p. 469.

[2] Which *Meier* too (die ursprungliche Form des Dekalogs. p. 42) has this time rightly seized.

to necessary *labour*, the true way of asking and receiving according to God's original appointment for man in Gen. iii. 19, independently of which we eat not *our own bread* (2 Thess. iii. 12; 1 Thess. iv. 11—12) but another's.[1] Similarly, it points to the obligatory communication and fellowship, since as we in "*our*" and "*us*" pray with and for one another, so we may not hold any thing that we receive exclusively and covetously for ourselves alone. (Isa. lviii. 7, break thy bread to the hungry—comp. 1 Sam. xxv. 11). Thus not as in that old hymn-book: "gib Regen und gib Sonnenschein, für Greiz und Schleiz und Lobenstein; und wollen andre auch was ha'n, so mögen sie's dir selber sa'n!"

But with all this it is only admitted, that earthly bread is included in this petition: and by no means, that the children of the Father are not to think of more than this in the word of Jesus. A petition *only* for earthly bread, we insist, would stand alone, interrupting the course of the whole prayer for spiritual gifts; and would neither have connexion with the preceding, nor be a fit transition to the following, petitions. What the Lord says in Matt. vi. 33, must be the key to the exposition here: it is in the sense of that saying that He commands us to pray for *bread*. As certainly as the weak beginners begin with the earthly bread, a prayer which is granted to us all; so certainly must the petition have a wider meaning for such as no longer, at least in *many* an "Our Father," care for or ask for earthly bread, because they know that it already falls to their portion. Or are there none who thus petition, and who find out what further the Lord intends, their hunger and thirst after righteousness interpreting the word:—Give us the bread of Thy strength, the gift of Thy grace, which we need that we may live in Thee and to Thee! To them indeed the distinction between the one and the other vanishes, and this may indicate the truest and most consistent use of this petition: they care only to say, Give us Thy gifts, O Father, that we may possess and enjoy them, fill thou all our human need, whether of body or of soul! But as much as the soul is more than the body, we should learn to give the pre-

[1] Man lifts his imploring, empty hands to heaven, and God lays work upon it—thus hast thou thy bread!

eminence to the spiritual in our thought and in our prayer.[1] Thus are we taught by the sacred three of the following petitions, strictly united as they are by *and:* they assuredly are designed to give us a more detailed explication, and individual exhibition of the general *Give us* which preceded.

This *and*, which from this petition forwards, unlike the first three, forms a link between each (in the concluding one passing into the still stricter conjunction of *but*), thus appears to have in the first instance a twofold sense of connexion, and that whether the one or the other meaning of bread is assumed. If thy thoughts rested simply in the idea of bodily necessity, this *And* comes immediately to excite the acknowledgment which is needful in order to the humility of that prayer:—But we are altogether unworthy of what we ask, we have not deserved to receive, but must expect it only from thy mercy. Thus the prayer placed in thy lips *constrains* thee, immediately after thou hast paid thy bodily need its tribute, to bring to God thy soul's need likewise: the continuous "and" becomes a self-recollecting "also," penetrating forcibly the heart and conscience. But of what avail—shouldst thou say in thine heart—is the food which perisheth, if Thou didst not *in addition* and *more especially* heal the hurt of my soul, in order to life and refreshment of my inner man? But if thou hast, on the other hand, as a disciple of Jesus, lifted up thy prayer, according to His instruction and exhortation elsewhere, for the "bread which cometh down from heaven," then is the And which follows a mere transition to the more express acknowledgment and specification of that which thou meanest, and requirest, and prayest for, and receivest by that prayer for the bread of the soul.

The *forgiveness of sins* is and must ever be the first nourishment and refreshment, the first gifts of God's grace even to His children. To them indeed the whole prayer is properly given, for only they *can* truly say "Our Father." The first cry and supplication of a returning prodigal son, does not so appertain to the Lord's Prayer as to find its place first of all in this fifth petition. *That* has been uttered *before* and independently of it:—

[1] We cannot understand how, as *Alford* thinks, this higher, mystical meaning of ἄρτος is excluded by the addition of ἡμῶν, for it is just the inner man, who prays for himself, even in the case of bodily need.

I am not worthy to call thee Father! The confidence of an enjoyed reconciliation is presupposed in the invocation, and the three first petitions which are developed from it. He whose conscience is first aroused to repent of and turn from his sins and misdeeds by the fifth petition (though it may, indeed, condescend to the exertion of this influence), has at least uttered all that precedes without sincerity and truth. This itself has added to his sin, and it would have been better for him to have begun with "forgive me" before and in the first "Our Father," in order that he might truly be included in the "Our." Hence the Lord does not say here: our sin and iniquity or our transgressions (παραπτώματα, as afterwards in ver. 14), but he uses the much milder expression ὀφειλήματα. We may indeed strictly say that his first forgiveness every man must supplicate alone, for himself (*my* sin, *my* sins!); he may not include his own absolution in the wide and general "Our," and should not cast in his sin at once with the petition which the congregation of God's children here present. This refers rather to a daily-recurring need like the fourth petition, and all that daily repentance for daily forgiveness which is needful even for the children of God. Here then the prayer comes close home to that which is our own, that evil in us, which the Father alone can take from us, while He imparts to us His own good: for sin is essentially *our own*, and must be considered as *our guilt*, before we can speak of a further healing. Under this ὀφειλήματα is included all that over which the saints have yet to mourn, down to the minutest shortcoming and intermission in doing good and the practice of mercy, down to the most secret defect of unholiness or imperfection in good works. It teaches us to ask forgiveness even for our "secret faults," and for that very reason, *because they are secret to ourselves*. And if we should imagine that the overlooking of such infirmity in us is necessarily to be supposed and taken for granted, this petition strikes down all such rising thoughtlessness, presumption, and pride at once, by teaching us that the remains of sin in us require the same *forgiveness* through grace that we received at first. Hence the Lord, when in Lu. xi., He repeated the prayer, solemnly *explained* His meaning by substituting ἁμαρτίας, and it would be well for us sometimes to impress it upon our memory by changing the term: Forgive us our sins!

And now, in the very heart of this prayer for that mercy on which we all daily live, and that acquittal which we all daily need, stands the single *vow*, which the Lord has inserted in direct contrast to all the vain and precipitate conditional-prayer of man's invention. It is only in the spirit of gross and presumptuous misunderstanding and perversion that a nameless author (die Evangelien, ihr Geist und ihre Verfasser, Leipz. Wigand) maintains that no subtlety can explain away the Pharisaic self-righteousness from this appendage to the prayer. For it is not any thing that we bring with a view to merit forgiveness when we say we forgive, but our purpose, and that we are *now willing* to forgive. While in all the petitions such vows lie concealed—we would fain have it so, we will let Thy name be hallowed in us, we will do Thy will in thy kingdom—there is here, though only here, an openly expressed—We will! That ἀφιέμεν is in this place, *first of all*, such a vow, viz., to render the mercy we receive to others, and to do to others as God to us, is quite evident; for who ever forgave his brother from his heart, who had not previously learnt by receiving it, what forgiveness is? But the promise further, even while we are praying, becomes a present fulfilment, in the joyous avowal: yea, we do forgive. Whoever brings his sins before the mercy-seat of God in genuine contrition, consents by that very act to the death of all his revenge and all his wrath, and is already reconciled to every one, who might be termed his debtor. Here is the root of the Law's fulfilment in us through the power of Divine grace entering our souls; this love, thus forgiving, can *do* no evil to a brother which he would have to forgive. This is so entirely and essentially necessary in itself, that it required no express statement or resolution to be uttered, no legal—I will because I should, I will not what I should not. As the first invocation put away all idolatry and image-worship, so is all murder and anger, adultery, stealing, slandering, and whatever other evil to our neighbour there may be, put away from the heart and will of him, who prays the fifth petition, and abides in it.

But that abiding is of the utmost importance, and thus, finally, the added sentence assumes the character of a warning *condition:* If ye forgive not, neither will your Father in heaven forgive! Here lies the emphasis of—*As* we forgive. In this all living dogmatic theology, which has *faith* in order to justification through grace as its vital heart, and all living moral theology which knows only of *love,* are *joined together and harmonised* in that one word which *the heart utters to the Father in secret,* a word so simple that the weakest may understand it, yet at the same time a word of inexhaustible meaning, the applications of which know no end. Who has sufficiently admired the wisdom of the Lord's love in the placing of this petition ? A little child, who has just learned to distinguish between good and evil, and to feel sin in the conscience, may apprehend it: again, the congregation of the saints, having sin and discord within it, needs only to urge the fifth petition in all the fulness of its meaning, peace is re-established, and the sin put away. On the other hand, he who forgives not his brother, testifies against himself that his "as" must be turned against himself into a frightful imprecation—Forgive me also not ! Dares man, then, pray to God : Forgive me my sin, but this man or that, mine enemy, forgive not ! If we say: Forgive *us*—we have already included all for whom God's mercy waits, and have therefore prayed for our enemies, as the Lord requires. And should we refuse that love to those, whom we acknowledge to be prepared with ourselves to receive the common mercy of God as His enemies and debtors ? It is only, however, in condescension to our estate, that they are regarded as *our* debtors. Sin is not committed against us, but against God alone, with whom forgiveness is; and he who duly remembers this, will only say to his enemy in accommodation for the sake of his importunity: *I* forgive thee—but must also at the same time say, in effect, with Joseph : Am I in God's stead ? (Gen. l. 19). Finally, if thy heart be thus rightly affected, and yet thou art troubled with weakness of faith, doubting whether God will forgive thee this thing or that, then does the fifth petition give thee strong consolation; assuring thee that there is forgiveness with Him in heaven, even as there is with thee on earth, and that God's heart is not harder than thine own, which, indeed, His grace only hath made so soft. (1 Jno. iv. 7, 16).

Have we now reached the end of our petition ? We might have put this question at each of them, for every one in a certain sense includes all the rest in itself. We should, indeed, have reached the close *now*, after having received mercy from the Father, and rendered it again in love to our brethren, were it not that sin, as it is guilt, so also it is corruption in ourselves and in the world. What lies in the past we have put away, and may forget it, even as God no more remembers it; and so even for the future, we have pledged ourselves to a continuance in the life of love, wherein no sin shall more find place. But, however sincere the heart that has done this, there remains the sin still, harassing us from within and without, so that we may yet again fall into a state of guilt before God, and trespass again against that neighbour with whom we had confirmed our peace before the mercy-seat. We extend our thoughts towards what awaits us in the future, and that same sincere heart is constrained to acknowledge that God's grace alone can protect, preserve, and sanctify us. The evil world in which we live is full of *temptation*—the *tempter* is its prince—and in ourselves there is yet the evil concupiscence, the treacherous infirmity, the fleshly susceptibility: should we not fear the world, the devil and ourselves, should we not betake ourselves to urgent prayer for help and salvation? The more fully we experience, day by day, that we yet need the fifth petition, the more fully do we press forward, in watching and prayer, into the realization of the meaning of the sixth.

But how does the Lord ascribe temptation to the Father, who tempteth no man to evil? Partly, because all things which may befall us are under His dominion and permission, and then because He would have the uncontested right to permit our falling, to subject us to tests which we could not sustain, and trials in which we could not stand. This *right* we humbly concede to His justice, but we know, that while we ask according to His command and promise, His *mercy*, the same which forgave our sin, will not leave us to our corruption, to contract fresh guilt. Although He sees fit to prove, to discipline, and confirm His children through conflict with sin, so that we, as His children, may not altogether pray against and deprecate temptation; yet may we say in humble confidence and encouragement—*Μὴ εἰσενέγκῃς*, lead us not so deeply *into* temptation, that we must succumb to it, not beyond what we are able, that no way shall be made for our escape (1 Cor. x. 13). (Comp. *ἵνα μὴ εἰσέλθητε*, Matt. xxvi. 41). And in our thus praying are we secured. This prayer suppresses all that presumption and pride which threatens us, and which would say with Job: when he hath tried me, I shall come forth as gold (ch. xxiii. 10)—but also removes all despondency lest confidence and strength should fail: the Lord knoweth how to deliver the godly out of temptation! (2 Pet. ii. 9). Further exposition of this comprehensive and significant petition, would lead us away from our object (which is here only to exhibit the connexion and train of thought), into all the depths of the Christian doctrine concerning sanctification and its appointed means. We make only a few further remarks which are obvious, and immediately derived from this petition. He who thus prays, yields himself not up to temptation, but, when it comes, uses the armour which God provides; he who thus prays for himself and for others, desists from all condemnatory judgment of others' sin, since he in himself only too well knows, that the Searcher of Hearts alone can estimate the might of temptation.

Thus has the sixth petition at length led us, in language increasing in plainness and significance, to the root of all our misery and corruption, the eradication of which alone will make us perfectly sound, and holy and happy: for the most internal, persistent temptation, without which no temptation from without could do us harm, is the lusting of the flesh against the spirit. Now at last does the Lord comprise in one finished *concluding* petition, which is itself the *sum* of all prayer, our sin and the whole world's, with all its connexion and consequences: one great word embraces all—*τὸ πονηρόν*—and from it we are taught to pray to the Father for full salvation and deliverance.[1] The *ἀλλά*, which closely connects this petition with the preceding (lead us not *into*, but entirely *out of*), teaches us, indeed, so much as this, that the real evil which is *first of all* referred to, is that sin which is still present in temptation: but it does not by any means forbid us to extend our view further. The Reformed divines, in reckoning six petitions, not only break the sacred number seven which should certainly be held fast, and the yet more express arrangement of the prayer, as we saw above, in relation to the Ten Commandments; but they further intro-

[1] Our request to be preserved from temptation *rises into* the longing for full redemption, as *Laufs* well expresses it.

duce an unacceptable *tautology* in making the two sentences into one. When, further, they understand τὸν πονήρον in the Masc. as the evil one, I trace the same lack of *liturgical* feeling and perception which attaches so much in other respects to their church. This is the liturgy of all liturgies, and here it reaches its sublime close, which through the deep lowliness of the believing—*Deliver us!* immediately passes on to the heavenly doxology—Thine is the kingdom! And just at this point must the conqueror confer that honour upon the vanquished enemy, to name him with his threatening power? Are the believing children of the Father, already redeemed, for ever to be subjected to the contumely, at the end of every private and common prayer, of mentioning him? Let him believe this who can; our inmost sense of holy propriety recoils from it. The Redeemer has left His own name unmentioned, though Himself the ground, and medium, and end of every prayer; and can He be thought to have expressly mentioned Satan? We may and we must, indeed, have *thought*, as at first of the Devil's kingdom and will, so now of the tempter and original of evil: but none of this was uttered in *word*. I would suggest to such interpreters:—Try the experiment, close your prayer at any time, let it be in the most joyful festival of the Divine service and at the sacrament, by uttering in plain words the *cry of distress*—Deliver us from *the Devil!* and would you not instantly feel how harshly that sounds. Further, there is nothing *personal* in the whole of the second part of the prayer, the πονηρόν must correspond with the ἄρτος, ὀθειλήματα, πειρασμός: and should we be disposed to understand thus also τὸν πονηρόν in Jno. xvii. 15, against the accompanying ἐκ (other than 2 Thess. iii. 3), and the internal connexion of the discourse in that place? We rather look there for the true explanation of the last petition, as also yet more definitely in 2 Tim. iv. 17, 18, where, according to our conviction, the apostle, just after he had mentioned the raging lion, passes on to the all-embracing ἀπὸ παντὸς ἔργου πονηροῦ—and (as the ῥύσεται shows) quotes actually and expressly the last petition of the Lord's prayer with the Doxology and the Amen pertaining to it.[1]

[1] *Lange* has recently, very cheerfully and disinterestedly, admitted the interpretation of τὸ πονηρόν which we have espoused.

What is then the *evil* which we finally name? We can only apprehend it in the same way as מָוֶת and *θάνατος* elsewhere in the Scripture are understood: it is sin itself and all its consequences, from the first pang that it inflicts, through all the necessities which it creates as long as it remains, to the damnation where it rests for ever—no less than the whole of this combined. Thus it is the fit conclusion and sum of all petitions, and the deliverance which is asked for is a full redemption into the heavenly kingdom, *σώζειν εἰς τὴν βασιλείαν τὴν ἐπουράνιον.* It tells us that only by the taking away of all sin can this evil be taken away (as the position of the prayer after all the others also indicates); it points us most impressively, when the *ἀλλά* is rightly understood, to the fundamental evil of all, bids us think of that, and to ask no other deliverance than the being delivered from *it.* But does there not follow from that deliverance from all guilt, all need, all care, all strife, yea from every kind of pain and suffering? And could an all-comprehending prayer, which gives a place to every petition of human infirmity, exclude *that? Make us happy! save us!* Take all need from us, and every plague! This is a prayer equally permitted and equally indispensable to God's children upon earth, as that for daily bread. The natural selfishness and blindness of men lead them to begin with this prayer, without reflecting how and in what way it can alone be answered: in His wisdom the Lord has, therefore, placed it at the close. And as He in the weakness of our flesh used this prayer for the taking away of His bitter cup, so will He give words to His disciples which shall express their weakness, their sighs, and their sorrows. But when a member of the Reformed Church cries to his Father in any lesser, though violent, trouble Take it away! and finally in the agony of death—Put an end to my pain! where does He find such perfectly justifiable prayer in *his* Our-Father?

Moreover, we Lutherans know as God's children the prayer which preceded: Thy will be done! We know full well, that happiness and rest before the time without the *κακία* of every day (ch. vi. 34) might be an evil, which the Father would not and will not give us, even though in our ignorance we should ask it: that good days may well be more full of *temptation* than evil ones, and we have prayed against all temptation. We do not therefore say: Father, be no Father to us, chastise us not for our profit, that we may be partakers of thy holiness! (Heb. xii. 10). We know that external, temporal, salutary evil both is and brings *deliverance* from evil properly so called, eternal evil: and we are able to give such a meaning as this to the petition—Strike hard that we may be saved, give us the cup of our healing which we must drink to the dregs! But this does not prevent us from rejoicing in the prospect of deliverance from all need, leaving it to our heavenly Father's righteous will with perfect confidence: in our infirmity we may with His permission offer it with our thought fixed especially, at some seasons, upon our sufferings; we may boldly give expression in these words of our prayer to that never-absent prayer of the heart of all, which cries for help, and longs for perfect rest and peace within and without the soul.

Thus have we in the seven petitions—and *not* beginning with the seventh—prayed ourselves gradually up from the depths of our ruin and misery. We ascended at once to the Father in heaven; we further called upon His name, before we spoke of our own sin and earthly need, for the coming of His kingdom and the accomplishment of His will; then first came we down to earth again, and drew down by our supplications the gifts of the Father's mercy—forgiveness, strength, and deliverance. If the last petition had been placed *first,* the tone of lamentation—from *evil!* would have predominated: but because it is the *last,* the joyful emphasis falls rather upon the equally confident and humble—*deliver* us! as if we should say: yea, thou wilt deliver us! or: deliver *Thou* us in the right time, according to thine own counsel: other deliverance than that we desire not. We acknowledge that evil remains, and that we feel it to be evil, (woe to the man, who is so well with the world and the flesh that he can deride Luther's "Jammerthal," the valley of woe, and dispense with the longing look towards heaven!)—we acknowledge also that we neither would nor could deliver ourselves—but we rest upon the prayer which the *Redeemer* Himself has given us, and are already saved in hope.

And now, can it be that the *thanksgiving and ascription* which sets the crown upon all prayer, is not genuine, that is, that it was not given by the Lord as He gave the petitions! *Euthymius* so early was of this view! But if there is anywhere an internal criticism which may maintain its prerogative over the external testimonies of the manuscripts which we have directly received and historical monuments, it is in this place, as similarly in 1 Jno. v. 7. All the orthodox, who, submitting to the apparent results of all external criticism, concede that the Lord did not Himself append this conclusion, yet give it place in their exposition as if it belonged there, find it most excellently appropriate, and involuntarily confess how aptly and profoundly it connects itself with the petitions of the prayer. For ourselves we rest calmly in hope, that one day, when all that is lost is found again, and the patchwork of history is a completed whole, it will be made clear how it has come to pass that this doxology early fell away, and was omitted from the manuscripts and the fathers, which now certainly confound us. Then will the verbal correctness of the Peschito be confirmed, and the abbreviation in the Const. Apost. be seen to be manifestly an *abbreviation* of the words given by the Lord, just as St Paul, according to 2 Tim. iv. 18, received them, and yet does not quite exactly reproduce them. In St Luke yet more is wanting, and probably not by St Luke's fault; it is at least quite as conceivable that similar causes have been at work in the case of St Matthew's gospel, as it must be in every view *inconceivable* that the Lord actually closed with—deliver us from evil! "Such a conclusion comes naturally to the praying heart;"[1] the church has ever possessed it, and will never more let it go; this is to us an irrefragable argument that the Lord has given it to every heart and to the whole church. If we were disposed to go so far as to say that the Lord had to that end subsequently given it by His Spirit to the church—yet must we pause doubtfully before we hazard such a view. For apart from the question, why should the Lord have left this as an afterthought of His Spirit, we cannot bring our minds to think that He could have given a form of prayer without at least an Amen. (We have previously discovered the Amen of the prayer to have aptly *reckoned in* in the Sermon on the Mount.) But the true Amen, according to the custom of all the Jewish prayers, which found their originals in the Scriptures of the Old Testament, carries with it invariably an *expressed ascription of praise*: similarly,

[1] *Harms*, das Vaterunser in Predigten.

according to the New Testament canon, Phil. iv. 6, no prayer is complete with prayer alone, without giving of thanks. This may be an answer to *Bengel*, who does not think the thanksgiving appropriate to the period at which the Lord gave the prayer. His prayer would have indeed had its introduction without it, but not its fit issue and outgoing; it would not have been, strictly speaking, a complete prayer, and the joyful concluding petition, if it did not issue in such an Amen, would lose its joyousness again, and *would become an unanswered, resultless cry.* Use the Lord's prayer thus for a quarter of a year, *evil* being its last word, it will become intolerable to thee, and its conclusion will victoriously force itself upon thee. Yet once more, if such *internal* criticism may not maintain its prerogative, where is its place and where are its rights? It may be matter for consideration, whether it be only an illusion, that *with* the Doxology the Lord's prayer includes *ten* words; that with it the *Us* and the *Our* flows back again into *Thine*, as first *Thine* flowed from *Our;* that only with it the whole rounds itself off and finds its true close. It may be asked, whether David's prayer (1 Chron. xxx. 11, 12) was not here by the Lord taken up, and for ever sanctified?

This conclusion manifestly unites the two tables of the prayer, but once more presenting the sacred Three-number, which could not be varied from. The *kingdom* embraces the first table by that one word which occurs in the middle of it: the *power* signifies the transition which we found in the gift of bread; the *glory* or honour is the end and goal of the fulfilment of the petitions of the second table, the δόξα or glory of God shining from his redeemed and sanctified creatures. When all is finally fulfilled, evil, temptation, and guilt done away, all desires gratified, the will done, the kingdom come, the name hallowed—then will there remain on earth as in heaven nought but everlasting praise. With this he who prays returns back to the first invocation, which included the Amen of all petition for faith, as in the preparatory trusting confidence which said: *Art thou then* our Father? before the particular petition broke forth: *Be so* to us, show Thyself to us as our Father! Now again, and with the *fullest* confidence of strengthened faith, it is more openly spoken: *Yea, verily, thou art* our Father! "By this little word *for*, we set, as it were, our foot upon one step of the throne, upon which He sits, reminding

Him of *His* matter, for it is His, and not ours alone!" *Thine* is, and can and will be in us, too, the kingdom, the power, and the glory—will be in us, *if* we in harmony, acknowledgment, and obedience give it to thee, and this we have done in this our *prayer*. So, although we yet see it not (Heb. ii. 8), faith cries in defiance of all evil that yet remains, of all wicked devices and contradictory will: Thine *is* the kingdom even now, as it will be for ever! Thus does the Amen of prayer, every time it is uttered, anticipate *the great universal Amen of all creation.*

After all that we have hitherto discovered, there remains much more. The seven petitions, besides the full meaning of each separately, indicate, at the same time, the progress of *human life* in individual man, and the *history of mankind* as a whole. The child cries out to his Father, and learns His name, that it may be sanctified in him; the kingdom begins to come in him, the will begins to be revealed to him in instruction and discipline, that it may be done; then grows up the adult into life, to eat his own bread, who should not forget, in praying for it, his spiritual necessities,—rather should all the more fully discern the gift of God which is infinitely necessary; then follows, commonly, first in the *second* half of life, the thorough seeking for forgiveness, the warfare of temptation; finally in old age the longing, ever-increasing till death, for deliverance from all evil, which is the closing petition of the dying man that merges into the Doxology of Heaven. In the history of mankind at large began similarly the calling upon God's name (Gen. iv. 26); then came the kingdom in the beginnings of its preparation, the will was revealed in the law. In the *midst* of the years the Lord revived His work (Hab. iii. 2) when He who once spoke from Sinai came in the glory of His grace, and descended in Christ as the living bread of heaven for the hungering world. Then came the preaching of the word of reconciliation in all the world, then the hour of the great temptation upon all the world (Rev. iii. 10), specially upon the Church of the saints; finally, in the end of the days will be the universal, closing deliverance, when suffering and pain and lamentation shall cease, all shall have become the kingdom of our God and the dominion of His Christ, and the glory of the glorifying Spirit shall shine from the redeemed.[1]

[1] Compare *v. Meyer's* Blätter für höhere Weisheit v. 388.

Such views may not be despised, for the wisdom of God exhibits strange phases in the word. We should be disposed, further, to investigate to what extent the fundamental principles of all Divine doctrine, especially of New Testament preaching, may be developed from the simple ideas of the Lord's prayer. This would be better apprehended, if we could realize the conception of a people to whom nothing but this prayer had been at first given. Let us be permitted yet once more, and in conclusion, to parallel the *seven petitions* with the *seven benedictions.* The name of the Father is hallowed when the poor and wretched receive as little children the kingdom of heaven as a gift of prevenient grace. The kingdom of the Son, as such, is made now fully known to them, when they as mourners find comfort. The Divine will is done already through the Holy Spirit, when the meek know themselves by the will of God to be the heirs of the earth. The bread is given for the supply of all who hunger and thirst after righteousness. The trespasses are forgiven to those who forgive, for the merciful receive mercy. Temptation is overcome by all those, who have no other will than to see God's face, as pure in heart. Evil, finally, is done away, when the children of peace, as children of God made manifest, dwell for ever in eternal peace with Him in glory.

Vers. 14, 15. The Lord recurs again now to the subject of the fifth petition, because, as we have already said, the prescribed prayer leads through it to the establishment and fulfilment of the Law. Will theologians never come to read in simplicity, and perceive here a key to the *whole* of it? The *centre* of the Lord's prayer regarded in itself is the fourth petition, as we have seen: but it is in the *fifth* that that fundamental truth, which is its root in the Sermon on the Mount, finds first its full expression. That which already in ch. v. 7, 23—26, 44—48, became more and more clearly prominent, and afterwards in ch. vii. 1, 2, is repeated as the head of a new section, stands here, as it were, in the very *middle of the whole discourse*, piercing into and laying hold of the central heart and living source of all true love, disclosing to us that point of union in which " to love as God loves" is seen to be as certainly given to us by His grace as it is demanded of us by His holy righteousness. This saying, which is so perfectly easy in its literal meaning, is at the same time so important and so inexhaustibly to be learned anew, that our Lord in Mark xi. 25, 26, when He is speaking of the gift of faith, inserts it again in similar words. But it is also so deeply engraven on the conscience of man, that the son of Sirach, for instance (Wisd. xxviii. 1—5), could expressly say the same thing.[1] Forgiving on our part is so absolutely an indispensable *condition* of God's forgiveness, that it must not be viewed as the mere fruit which results from it, but rather as indicating the necessary internal disposition and feeling of our heart at the moment in which we actually seek and find His mercy. God forgives us when we, receiving His mercy, are at the same moment disposed and in the frame to forgive others. Although He, on the one hand, knows before the thoughts of the insincere, and the stiff-neckedness of those who will afterwards fall from His grace (Deut. xxxi. 21, 27, 29), yet, on the other, He says in His preventing and anticipating faithfulness—surely they are my people, children who will not lie! (Isa. lxiii. 8). He entrusts, as it were, the gift of His love even to those who will not retain it, in order that He may justify His own goodness against the unthankful and the evil. From those, indeed, who afterwards forgive not as they have been forgiven, that which they received shall be again taken away;—as the parable of Matt. xviii. 23—35 once more inculcates at large.

Vers. 16—18. This has been as a whole already explained and shown in the light of its general connexion; it only remains now to refer somewhat more particularly to the details. The Lord by no means rejects *Fasting* in itself, the humbling of the soul (עַנּוֹת נֶפֶשׁ, Lev. xvi. 29, xxiii. 27; Num. xxix. 7, xxx. 14) by taming and reducing the body, as an aid to repentance and prayer; any more than He rejects almsgiving as the demonstration of love, or uttered words for the exercise and realization of the inner spirit of prayer. Although in ch. ix. 14, 15, He opposed a new and free manner of fasting for His disciples, to the *fasting oft* not only of the hypocrites, but also of the well-meaning disciples of John; yet did He Himself fast forty days

[1] Yet, indeed, when we look more closely, not without one of those errors in the expression which betray the apocryphal:—as if *we* forgive first and *then* should pray.

at the beginning, as certainly many times afterwards, and recommend prayer and *fasting* for such emergencies as required thorough earnestness for the overcoming of evil spirits (ch. xvii 21), just as the Apostle in 1 Cor. vii. 5 presupposes as well known, and confirms, its Christian exercise. The early church laid much stress upon fasting, but should have left it to the freedom of every individual without any ecclesiastical ordinance: we Protestants, alas, have slighted it altogether too much, and have scarcely more than the *name* of our fast-days remaining. The prudence of freedom is necessary, however; hence comes forward the warning again: Not *like the hypocrites!* See it already in the word of prophecy (Isa. lviii. 5). Pharisaism had here also perverted all into a specious external work,[1] forbidding among the rest any greetings during the time of a fast. With such things in His view the Lord here paints the hypocrites from life, and sketches their whole character by one vigorous trait:—They would appear unto men *σκυθρωποὶ*, and therefore disfigure their faces! Such as this in our day is the pietist sour look, downcast head, and penance-wrinkled face, which, while they mar the shining of the true light of piety before men, also betray too much of the Pharisee remaining in those who make such exhibition. The Lord unsparingly condemns all *affectation* in its minutest form, and counsels His disciples, in order that they more securely avoid this sad danger, to adopt as defence against it, where they have only to do with themselves in the sight of their Father in secret, a certain directly opposite *dissimulation of face.* This, however, is no hypocrisy, but the simplest truth; purer, indeed, in its principle of love than its faint type in the social life of the children of the world, the courtly and gracious external demeanour covering a different disposition within. The children of God should ever through faith rejoice in their God; and it should be their systematic *habitus* to exhibit this pleasant aspect to men. Feelest thou within thyself a necessity and constraint to afflict thy flesh by mortification and abstinence of any kind, do it if possible without any interruption of thine external cheerfulness. Yea, rather than detract in the slightest degree from the reality and the efficacy of thy

[1] See Buxtorfii Synagoga Judaica, cap. xxx.

secret humiliation before God, by any such external evidence of it as only too easily glides into ostentation; thou shouldst with more care than ordinarily *anoint* thine head and wash thy face.[1] Before trusted brethren thou mayest, even as before God Him self, exhibit what thou art secretly aiming at; but *men*, as they are found in general, understand it not, and would only mar thy fasting by their censure or their praise.—Finally, let it be well noted, that this rule, in its present connexion, is only laid down for an actual, bodily fasting, in the ordinary sense of the word; such as a man himself, though under the influence of the Spirit, imposes upon his own flesh. Quite otherwise is it, when God appoints to us a day of fasting, for the *weeping* of the soul (Ps. lxix. 11 Hebr.), when the bridegroom's presence is withdrawn: then fast we in the deepest sense of the word (Matt. ix. 15), and it is obvious of itself, that the stranger in our company must perceive that we are *σκυθρωποὶ*. (Lu. xxiv. 17. Gr.). In this there lies no danger of hypocritical seeming before men. But if thou hast already oft experienced, that by it He who was taken from thee is restored again, and if thou wilt be perfect, then hold such weeping of thy soul also, through the power of faith, *in secret places* (Jer. xiii. 17), and let not thy countenance cease to be outwardly anointed, or thy mouth to utter peace and love through the whole of that conflict which thou shouldst gradually learn to regard as joy. Thus shalt thou find consolation in thy secret mourning before God, and experience the fulfilment, even in this respect, of the beautiful and pregnant words of the hymn:—"A stage of blessedness it is—the secret place!"

"And thy Father, who seeth in secret, shall reward thee openly!" This the Lord utters three times, vers. 4, 6, 18, and designedly indicates in this third instance the similar application of His discourse concerning the three works of righteousness, the uniformity of which the interposed prayer only *seemed* to break. This He does before He begins, by a striking interruption of the external connexion, a new line of remark which, however, is internally in strict harmony with it.

---

[1] The Essenes never anointed themselves, which may be mentioned in contradiction of the old folly that would make Jesus an Essene.

Our former general arrangement of the whole has already disclosed to us this internal transition from ver. 18 to ver. 19. The opposition between Christ's disciples and the Pharisees, is closed with that most absolute contrast between the hypocrite who mortifies himself before men and the child of God who humbles his soul in secret—the seeming devotee and the earnestly devout. There now follows (what had been prepared for in the preceding, and was a strict development of it) the second great contrast :—*not like the heathen!* The better kind of Pharisee (or rather the Israelite, inasmuch as Pharisaism took its rise in the true Israelite position), did, indeed, seek at first to establish, like Saul, a righteousness *before God* derived from obedience to the Law: in this there was earnestness and sincerity, and so far this Old Testament preparation led the sincere and upright to the new covenant of grace, even as his almsgiving, fasting, and prayers prepared the proselyte Cornelius for the reception of forgiveness and the Holy Ghost. But *Pharisaism* proper, as it was further developed in the evil hearts of men, performed its works of righteousness only to be seen of men, and *not at all in the sight of God:* thus the Pharisee has inwardly become like the *heathen,* while abhorring him in his pride (Rom. ii. 22); through dependance on earthly good and attachment to earthly pleasure, an idolater as well as he. It will be borne in mind, how often in the Gospels the *covetousness* of the Pharisees is made prominent; and this will help us to understand why it is that with which our Lord begins, when He is about to exhibit His own new Israel as in contrast with the heathen. It is not merely the heathen so called among men, who are to form the second link in this present discourse, but also, as is now sufficiently plain, the heathen in Israel (Ps. ix. 5, 15, 17, x. 16).

The discourse now passes more directly to the *internal disposition of mind,* which is at last shown to be the region of separation and distinction. There is now no more distribution of special commandments and good works, classified according to their principles. Yet it proceeds in a *threefold* order, though in a different manner. This is seen in the three leading ideas :—Distinguish clearly between perishable treasures and possessions *upon earth,* and the incorruptible treasure of *heaven!* ver. 19—20. Seek *this alone,* walk with thine eyes singly fixed upon the true treasure! vers. 21—23. Thus surrender thyself up to God's *undivided* service and trust, seeking first His kingdom, without care for your earthly need! This has the most extended treatment, vers. 24—34. Herein there is exhibited an *inverted* reference to the three fundamental ground-tones of the whole Sermon. The first immediately casts a *warning* glance forward to the test at the end, where all shall be put to shame who have not put their trust in the living God, and all heathens, or *earthly-minded* men (these are in their deepest principle one and the same) shall perish. The second *demands* and urges, a sincere progress towards the goal. The third speaks in language of *promise* and encouragement, presents to faith the internal principle and commencement of a *life not heathen,* and thus most plainly indicates who are the true people of God, who the true heirs of the promised kingdom. But this whole section *carries on* and developes the principle which we have seen in the beginning. For it was absolutely necessary that a firm foundation should be first of all laid, in the right understanding of the Law according to its internal spirit and true meaning; in the full perception that nought would avail but the strict practice of righteousness before God in secret. (Ps. li. 8). Upon this foundation is now built the *devotion of the heart to God alone,* and then have we further (for the development of the principle makes the principle itself more plain, and at the close the rigorous warning becomes strongest) the most urgent dissuasive from the attempt to join another service with His; the turning away of the heart, and the turning away of the eye from all that appertains to earth, in order to our living for the heavenly kingdom.

Vers. 19, 20. A strong contrast is here seized and exhibited in the two words: *earth* and *heaven!* The Lord is standing in the midst of Israel according to the flesh, and his glance, which penetrates through the *type* into its *reality* and *hidden truth,* discloses to us another and a sure distinction: they who live for the earthly and the perishable, they are the heathen; they who live in faith with reference to the Future, heavenly and eternal, are the children of the Father, the subjects and the heirs of the kingdom. In this deep generality, fully set forth at the close in vers. 32, 33, we have the commencement of a new discourse, which unfolds the germ, and includes all the principles of the Apostolical sayings in Col. iii. 1—4. It was to His hearers of that time a clear testimony to the character and nature of the Messiah's kingdom, as the *kingdom of heaven*, spiritual, hidden, and looking for a future manifestation: the kingdom which, then only perfected when the seven petitions are fully fulfilled, begins in the heart with the first look towards heaven, and cry to the Father. Now it is before the Father in secret, then will the Reward be open. The emphatic expression of this general view is to be rightly sought in the plain words which, for every man's conviction, distinguish between the earthly and the heavenly mind, describing him as *laying up for himself treasures*, possessions, goods, and seeking his enjoyments and happiness either *here* or *there*. In *heaven:* that is, by contrast, as the place and region where the true, eternal riches, the deposit against the day of revelation, are laid up, but also as the place and the region, in which the heart that lays up this treasure already lives in heavenly aims and conversation: for where your treasure is, there will your heart be also. The better and enduring substance in heaven, we already have in our own possession and in our own hands. (Heb. x. 34).

Perishableness is the quality of every thing earthly, hence, as *Bengel* critically saw, the little word ὅπου has a distinctive emphasis as *upon the earth, where* nothing either is or can be other than corruptible. "Wer Erde such't, find't Erden last, und geht auf Wind und Staub zu Gast." He who heaps up silver as the dust, and prepares raiment as the clay (Job xxvii. 16) shall find out, that all the earthly and transitory possessions of mortal man pass away like they themselves who dwell in clay, whose foundation is in the dust, which are crushed before the moth. (Job iv. 19). The getting of treasures by a lying tongue is a vanity tossed to and fro of them that seek death. (Prov. xxi. 6). The proverbial and popularly used expressions, *moth* and *rust* and *thieves*, men have been disposed to refer to the three main kinds of layed up goods in the ancient world—clothing, gold, corn. They have been referred, also, respectively (as by *Braune*) to that which is hostile in the inanimate world, in the animal kingdom, and among men: for which, however, a transposition would be necessary. It is only in the former reference that any truth lies;—the moth which consumes *garments* is among the Scriptural figures. (See Job

xiii. 28; Isa. l. 9, li. 6, 8; Jas. v. 2). But, as it regards the next, the question rises, what *βρῶσις* is distinctively and to what it appertains. But since gold and silver receive no specific injury from rust, it has been supposed that the thieves (which *διορύσσουσι*, dig through houses [Job xxiv. 16], breaking through walls) are the enemies of the treasured gold, and consequently that *βρῶσις* must be referred to the granary and full barns (Lu. xii. 17), being the אוֹכֵל of Mal. iii. 11, where the LXX. have *βρῶσις*, weevil or some other enemy of the corn. St James, however, ch. v. 2, 3, evidently quoting the Sermon on the Mount (as we saw above also, on ch. v. 34), attributes the moth to the garments, but the rust *ἰός* to the gold and the silver, having previously used the general expression—*ὁ πλοῦτος σέσηπε*. This gives us the right clue, and teaches us that we must not lay so much stress upon the threefold distinction of worldly goods (save that the breaking through may be especially referred to the underground *ἀποθήκας* of ver. 26) as upon the general idea of perishableness which they together convey. *Βρῶσις* is thus simply the *consuming away*, corruption, mildew, rotting of any kind which takes its rise from within the nature of this world's good, as *σής* on the other hand comes from without. Then rises before us the deeper meaning—all earthly good is subjected to corruption. It is essentially *perishable*, since either the moth comes upon it as upon a garment, (echoing those well known Old Testament passages), or it finds within itself the element of another kind of blight. And what worm and rust consuming from within or without may spare for a while, is still *insecure* in the possession, not guaranteed against the *thieves*, who know how to break through the firmest *defences!* Thus St James appropriately laid down his *σέσηπε* first: then introduces the Lord's words, which he fundamentally explains, while saying in the style of oxymoron and in apparent contradiction with the reality of things, that gold and silver are cankered and rusted, by showing that this *rust* signifies in a wide sense that *corruption* of everything earthly and earthen, which like a *fire* shall eat the flesh of the rich men themselves. If we thus expound it, not overlooking the connexion of the figure with the reality, yet giving its letter a spiritual interpretation, we may extend its range of application further, and think of honour and human glory (whereof the discourse had been speaking) as having its moth, and rust and thieves. All this is obliquely aimed at, although the first glance, which gives character to the expressions, turns towards the *Mammon* which is afterwards especially named, and therefore points to earthly treasures in the narrower sense. And how impressive, in this view, is the contrast which is now first instituted between all these and the *imperishable, and secure* treasures of heaven, which are beyond the reach of corruption and the thief! (1 Pet. 1—4; Lu. xii. 33): *βαλάντια μὴ παλαιούμενα, θησαυρὸν ἀνέκλειπτον.* That first, again, we have *treasures* in the plural, is simply a transition to the next sentence in which it is significantly said, your *treasure* —for in earthly good there is multiplicity, and variety, the heavenly possession alone and especially is a unity, a great whole. (Matt. xix. 21).

Ver. 21. What is then, thus considered, treasure in heaven? The future reward from the Father, for this is the whole of vers. 1—18 collected and condensed into one; thus also it is praise, honour, and glory in God's presence, in opposition to all that vain show before man, in which the hypocrites found their reward. That *giving* which was commanded (ver. 2—4) is itself the true *laying up!* So spake, in old time, Sirach and Tobias concerning the fruits of righteousness and good works. (Sir. xxix. 14; Tob. iv. 10). We may, moreover, regard this verse under two aspects: are your treasures upon earth, then will your heart also rest upon the earth. This lies, however, more in the transition from the last sentence than in this passage itself, which dignifies only the heavenly reward and the heavenly good, with the title of treasure, properly so called. (Lu. xvi. 12, τὸ ὑμέτερον, the true and only property, in distinction from which all other passes away as another's). Alas for those, who become thieves against themselves, to rob themselves of their own eternal and enduring substance! Do not ye so, O men! is the Lord's warning entreaty here. Have ye truly begun to apprehend what and where your true treasure is, then never take away your eyes and your hearts from it again, to turn them upon that which is nought! Ἔσται following ἐστίν here, has the force of a contrast, and contains requirement and promise at once in itself, similarly as ἔσεσθε in ch. v. 48. Your treasure *is*, safely laid up, perfectly ready for you, in heaven: *let* then your heart ever more and more perfectly and undividedly be fixed upon it and absorbed with it there! (See the continuation Lu. xi. 35). Has the kingdom of the eternal inheritance of grace come to you poor, then let your heart, your whole heart, rest *upon it* and upon nothing else with it! That great word *heart* (which in ch. v. 8, 28 was regarded as the seat of holiness or unholiness before God) comes before us now in all the fulness and depth of its scriptural meaning.[1] In the heart dwells the individual guiding principle of a man's life; his perception, feeling, and will in their indivisible unity; the heart determines how, for what, and for whom a man is living. Determine and devote your heart towards the treasure, the inheritance, the reward of heaven! This most impressive requirement, which in the former part of the sentence (ὁ θησαυρὸς ὑμῶν) brings with it its own foundation of promise, is in the two following verses more fully established in its principles; in positive encouragement and promise ver. 22, but then ver. 23, in warning contrast, which forms a transition to the subject which follows.

Vers. 22, 23. In the heart is the life of the whole body, Prov. iv. 23. But the mediating instrument between the central principle and all-regulating direction of life in the heart, and the outward life of the body, is the *eye*, as it immediately follows in Prov. iv. 25, 26:—compare, besides, Prov. xxiii. 26. The body lives and moves according to the guidance of the eye, by its light as a lamp; even as the eye sees according to the desire and impulse of the heart. When Eve beheld the tree, that it was a pleasant tree, the lust after it had already commenced in her heart, and as the result of that, her eye had become a traitor. Hence there might have been interposed between our Lord's former saying and this, the thought—and where your heart is, there does your eye turn also. This is as true with regard to the beginning of every sin, as it is that in its progress, the heart, in return, follows the eye (Job xxxi. 7): the one is tested and known by the other. But such an intervening thought the Lord could scarcely here have more circumstantially expressed: the natural process of His discourse led him, in order to *rivet the awakened attention*, and to excite preparation for His heart-pene-

[1] Which *Beck* lately in his biblischen Seelenlehre has plainly assumed.

trating word, rather to present striking and vivid figures to the mind. First came the very simple saying concerning the treasures in earth and in heaven, the meaning of which would be most obviously apprehended: then followed the equally simple and deeply convincing injunction: if your treasure is in heaven, then let your heart be there also! (which is grounded upon the principle taken for granted, and assented to in every man's breast: that the heart hangs upon that which it reputes its good and happiness). And now follows the unconnected and emphatic: *The light of the body is the eye.* This indeed is obviously true in external things, but the immediate application which the Lord makes of this to the inner man (he spake indeed from *the heart!*), involves in it profound mystery, which does not instantly yield up its fulness of meaning. *Luther* has used "*licht*" for λύχνος, but that does not help the matter, since the Lord presently after interchanges this with φῶς: that translation does no more than carry out the same interweaving of the figure and its meaning which pervades the whole discourse.

The *light* of the world and of each body in it, is, indeed, properly speaking, the sun and its effulgence: but, this shining becomes the light of any individual body, by and in which it may live and move, only through the medium of the eye, formed for the reception of the sun's light. This is its light-organ, not so much here for the purpose of beaming forth light from within (ch. v. 14—16), as for that of *receiving* the light first from above and around, in order that by it the body may be enlightened. Of what avail is the sun to the blind man, the light of day to him who shut his eyes? Every thing, then, depends on the eye, when we speak of light. Even in the bodily eye there lies much mystery, as natural philosophers know full well, to whose researches light is a wonder and an enigma on the confines of the material and the spiritual world; and so also the eye which corresponds to it in the body of the living man, the most perfect mystery of the soul's influence on the mechanical organism.[1] In the eye also there is an actual inner light which corresponds to the outer: hence its not

[1] Hence recently *Hanne* (Vorhöfe zum Glauben u. s. w.) points his rigorously convincing application of the principle of *life* in organism, to the formation of the eye in the fœtus.

fully explained glimmering through the material fabric. It is, at the same time, the outshining manifestation of the soul in the body; we read in the eye what no word utters, the hypocrite can only in the least degree, yea, not at all disguise his look; a right confronting glance looks through him. Hence is not this the natural image of the manner in which the inner man is reflected in the outer? The heathens termed the understanding the *νοῦς*, the light in men,[1] as also Solomon more correctly and truly says: the spirit of man is the candle of the Lord, searching all the secret chambers of the inner man. (Prov. xx. 27). In this general sense the expression of Jesus here may well admit of an *application:* if thy understanding receives rightly the truth of God, it will enlighten thee; if thy understanding is unsound, how foolish and ignorant will thy whole being be! Yet we should much mistake in making this our Lord's meaning in its present *connexion:* He is speaking, indeed, of the mediating instrument between the heart and the body, or the most internal, fundamental direction of the being and the walk, the life and the deed. Thus the *eye* of the inner man is more correctly that which determines the main scope of the whole section (vers. 19—34), the *practical* understanding, so to speak, which regulates the whole conduct, the fundamental *design* which is kept in view in the most proper sense of the word, what a man *seeks* (vers. 32, 33). The *body*, inasmuch as with hands and feet, and other members it stretches forth, moves, acts and exhibits all the energy of life, is consequently the further figurative expression for the whole *action* of the man. (Just as according to missionary reports, the same word in the dialect of the Sandwich Islanders, signifies both *body* and *action*). As thou lookest and towards what object, so will be the act and movement of thy body.

But the Lord, further, with profound discrimination does not say—if thine eye be *open* or *shut:* for this is a point which has nothing to do here with the inner man, and the Lord, as we have already seen, entirely blends together the figure and its meaning in this discourse. The eye may indeed be already, or may be still more, opened in many senses, but here it is not *ἁπλοῦς*, that

[1] *Aristotle:* ὡς ὄψις ἐν ὀφθαλμῷ, νοῦς ἐν ψυχῇ· *Galen:* ὥσπερ ὀφθαλμὸς τῷ σώματι, τοιοῦτος ἐν ψυχῇ νοῦς· *Philo:* ὅπερ γὰρ νοῦς ἐν ψυχῇ τοῦτ' ὀφθαλμὸς ἐν σώματι· See in *Grotius*.

is, not sincere, not true, sound, not rightly measuring or seeing, what is in the light visible to it. Seeing is sound, if both eyes (which is also itself a physical wonder and mystery) see together, precisely as it is, the one object at once which is before them: hence we say, *the eye*—although we have two eyes. The first note of unsoundness in the eye is the seeing double, or looking athwart (ver. 24), and that leads to blindness. "If we see in singleness, the soul is light: if we double see, we lose our sight." Ah! well is it said—"Sacred simplicity, wondrous grace! Not soon is this perfected in us. Alas, much is required to this, and long, long do we sometimes wait before this is reached!" Ver. 22 contains a description of the goal towards which we must struggle, and not merely a condition and requirement insisted on at the outset. In a certain sense and measure, indeed, must our eye singly, from the very beginning, be fixed upon God, His kingdom, and His righteousness, upon the treasures in heaven, but is it not consummate holiness when this is perfectly realized, and there is no oblique or other regard? Yea, by such simplicity of the eye shall the whole body be φωτεινὸν, that is, not merely enlightened, in the true light rightly living and moving, (Jno. xi. 9), but in its inner meaning: illuminated, glorified, all its actions sanctified in the light of God's truth (which is very emphatically expressed in a supplementary manner by St Luke xi. 36). Hence, finally, the otherwise dark mass of the body shall in this glorification become all eye. Thus again the ἔσται is here as in ver. 21. And on the other hand: if thine eye sees altogether falsely, thy whole body *shall be* full of darkness. The Lord sets the extremes in contrast, as they are consummated in perfection, on the one hand, and in entire πώρωσις τῆς καρδίας (Eph. iv. 18; Rom. i. 21) on the other; in order that He may exhort us urgently to seek the one, and warn us against the other: in order to point out to us the way, in which our eye should ever be becoming *more and more single*.

He once more speaks of the eye as the light of the body, in order to indicate the peculiar significance of the image in regard to man's nature generally:—*the light that is in thee*, that which should be thy light, indeed in some degree ever is so, that is, in the ordinary, general condition of mankind, before it has become totally darkened. This is not said to the new-born child of God from the beginning of his state of grace (Acts xxvi. 18), but actually in a certain sense to the natural man. For "the natural light extends just so far as to reveal the natural darkness." Even the unconverted has some degree of sincere respect to everlasting good, and regard for that which avails before God: just as the converted man retains for long some degree of unsoundness and obliquity in his eye. But if thine eye is *entirely* (this must be our Lord's meaning) πονηρὸς, the light in thee become utter *darkness*, then indeed is the whole body dark, as much so as if thou never hadst an eye, as if it were wholly shut; yea, rather worse than that, in case thou thinkest that thou seest, and reckonest thy darkness for light! Then wilt thou by all means and always err, and go astray, confounding far and near, good and evil, life and death, and thus grope thy way into the abyss! Once more we have a mournful oxymoron: the light become darkness, just as in ch. v. 13 the salt becomes saltless, to which saying this seems as it were a supplement. This is the condition of *Heathenism* at the worst, alas also of many apostates, who not advancing in singleness of internal eye, have lapsed through impurity into the opposite ruin. Of this the Lord cries in language of lamentation and terror: τὸ σκότος πόσον, what a total darkness of the whole body, if its light becomes darkness! In this there lies yet another specific thought which *Luther's* "die Finsterniss *selbst*,—the darkness itself" (after the Vulg.), aptly brings out. *Τὸ σκότος* with the article is opposed to τὸ φῶς τὸ ἐν σόι, and the Lord distinguishes two parts of human nature, which he terms light (at least relatively so), and darkness. As the body viewed as a mass dark in itself, has yet its light in the eye, just so is it with the corresponding sensual animal life of man, which eats and drinks, receives pleasure and disgust in close connexion with the lower creation, &c. This dark domain of the life of man sunk into gross matter, into the *flesh*, may itself, through the seeking after righteousness, through spiritual aims, become spiritualized, illumined, sanctified. But if this light is darkness, how great must then the entire darkness of the sensual life become! Compare such passages as 2 Pet. ii. 12; Jude 10, 19.

It remains that we endeavour to lay hold of the point of connexion and transition between this word of warning against total darkness, and what follows in ver. 24. We find it in a partial application of the rigorous word which we have just read, and it is expressed in *Luther's* translation "ein Schalk," which, however, softens the full and proper meaning of πονηρός. We cannot regard the Lord as having designed in His rigid contrast vers. 22—23, to teach, contrary to all experience, that by an unconditional alternative man must live altogether in light or altogether in darkness, that the eye must be either quite sound or quite evil. It is His design rather to excite men by that contrast to the earnest striving after the one, and diligent defence against the other. He proceeds, indeed, to lay down another equally definite and rigid alternative, and testifies: No man *can* serve two masters. But literally true as this must ever be for every individual moment of our internal disposition of mind, and of the action which flows from it and by it is estimated, as well as for the final distinction in the judgment; yet we also know full well that we all are too long tainted with this double-service and doubleness of aim. Thus the expression in ver. 23, standing in manifest connexion with ver. 24, likewise includes in itself such a mournful, twilight middle-state, though it only indicates the frightful end of such a state if it be continued in, or, since that is *impossible*, if the by-service of Mammon, instead of being struggled against and given up, issues in entire apostacy from God. He recommends to us, in this manner, the simplicity of the inner eye, and urges us most impressively to an even more and more decided *decision:* not designing to condemn and frighten us back on account of our shortcoming, but graciously and mercifully to pluck us out of a state of wavering and halting between two sides. Such words must *often* be received, and are ever exerting new influence: all is not ended with the first declaration of the great alternative, though it must be uttered every time as if it were so. That is the nature of the word of exhortation which our necessities require.

Give up yourselves then in pure and undivided surrender, with the devotion and trust of your whole heart, to your Lord and God, to your Father in heaven, who promises *to give* you the kingdom, and its righteousness, as the food and raiment of your new and inner man! As He gives, so also He exacts. Empty yourselves, He will fill you! (Ps. lxxxi. 10, 11). The fundamental promise—I am the Lord thy God! bears with it as the fundamental command—None other shalt thou serve! Neither *can* this be otherwise, whether in respect to God or to man:—the majesty of God, which will not tolerate any rival near Him, demands the whole heart as its due, and again the need and the desire of the human heart can only find satisfaction in the simplicity and purity of dependance upon the highest, perfect, and only Good. This section (vers. 24—34) which as part of the greater one beginning with ver. 19, has in it the emphatic tone of *requirement*, will nevertheless, as we saw above, lead us back to that of promise, and set forth the *first* commandment of the *first* table in the spirit in which it was given to Israel—*Thou shalt not!* but based upon the foundation of that redeeming, condescending, prevenient—*I am He!* (just as we saw in our earlier expositions of the individual commandments of the second table). Again we perceive a threefold division in the discourse which thus leads back towards the promise. First is the commandment itself in the testing, *warning* expression of its exclusiveness: but even here the "Ye *shall* not" assumes the gracious form of "Ye *cannot!*" However dexterously, and with whatever subtilty ye may act on the persuasion which you may reach, that God will tolerate somewhat *beside* Him, on which the heart may hang and which the life may serve,—it must ever remain a thing impossible. *Idolatry*, which pharisaical Israel abhorred in its external forms, is shown to be present in their hearts. The service of *Mammon*, that is, is the most universal note of true and proper heathenism, and that service is nothing else than the devotion to *earthly good* and *earthly enjoyment*.[1] Then follows a transitional paragraph, which enters more into the spirit and detail of this, for the *poor* to whom the Gospel is now especially preached: Take no thought for life and the body!

[1] "The fundamental characteristic of heathenism is the living for the present." *Tholuck* quotes this expression of that great heathen in Christendom, *Göthe*, but without noting how beautifully it illustrates our Lord's sermon at this place.

(vers. 25—30). Thus the language of *requirement* leads on to that of encouraging *promise*, which assumes its full tone in the concluding words (vers. 31—34).

Ver. 24. A fundamental declaration, which is as deeply rooted in the context here, as it is again at Lu. xvi. 13, where the Lord repeats it after a parable concerning the children of the world who live for the earth, and the children of light who care for and live for the eternal, with application to the covetous Pharisees. In this passage we have the basis of all our catechetical instruction on the first commandment. Comp. Col. iii. 5 (there as here it is after the general distinction laid down in vers. 1—4). St Matthew has prudently left מָמוֹן or מָמוֹנָא untranslated; a word of obscure derivation in the later Jewish language, which is not found in the pure Hebrew of the Old Testament, but is used in the Targums for בֶּצַע, הוֹן, שֹׁחַד, כֹּפֶר, equivalent to riches, possessions, money. When our catechists tell our children that the name was derived from a Syrian god of riches, they say what is not historically true indeed, but would have an appropriate sense: for *the Lord* designedly makes the word *the name of an Idol*, giving it a personality in contradistinction to God, in order that His words to the hypocritical Pharisees might have this force: Ye are verily Idolaters, ye serve another besides God,—will ye hear his name? It is *Mammon!* And as the truth and justification of this personification there lies in its back-ground an allusion to the Prince and God of this world, the false god who is concealed in the enticements and deceitfulness of the creature. בְּלִיַּעַל has a similar allusion in the Old Testament. The discourse very strikingly begins with a simple proverb, which is exalted to its most elevated meaning, that the wisdom of the sanctuary may be illustrated and confirmed by the wisdom of the street. Whether men may ever be obliged or be able to serve many masters at once is not the question *here*. That proverb, universally used where the true devotion of the whole service is meant, finds here its highest truth! (The Chinese even have their sayings: Lay not two saddles on one horse! A true subject serves not two sovereigns! A virtuous woman takes not a second husband!) Here that which is taken for granted as an essential truth, admitted in the proverbs of all, is urged in its highest application; viz., that individual actions flow from the *character*, from the inner *disposition of mind* of the entire man, and receive *from that* their value as actions. Hence there is no such thing as an undefined "freedom" of determination by which a man may turn now to the right, now to the left, or *could* depend upon and serve at one time this master and at another time that.[1] An emphasis of deepest meaning is in *Master* and *serve*; but the *two* following sentences of alternative are by no means tautological, nor is the distinction between them properly speaking to be sought in the advancement from loving to holding to, from hating to despising (which is only an explanation of the former, by a deeper disclosure and more convincing enforcement of its meaning in the latter); but in the alternative itself, which indicates, by the transposition of the two expressions, a changing of the persons served. Either at any one time, in one course of conduct and action, in one performance of service to hate God and love Mammon, or at another time again, to hold to God and despise Mammon. This gives us, without affecting the permanent, inmost condition of the heart generally, a *softened* sense of the word to suit the exhortation which follows, to the people, the children of God: Ye are not like the Gentiles! This is the exhortation to those who halt between two opinions. (1 Kings xviii. 21; 2 Cor. vi. 14.) Here have we the deep significance of עַל-פָּנָי in the first commandment, well translated by *Luther's* —*neben mir.* For every thing *out of* God is a "besides Me" which He will not tolerate in His presence—yet finds He much of that idolatry even among those who address Him with Our Father.

Vers 25—30. After such severity the discourse now turns to a most gracious appeal: Act not thus, for your God and Father is essentially enough for you, and will give you all you need! This exhortation, which convinces and puts to shame, stands first (ver. 25). Then follows the proof of the Father's care of His children's earthly need, derived from His providential care, as their Creator, for the lower animals around us; just as in ch. v. 45 His love was proved from His general benefits in nature. This is shown according to the order of the two leading words—

[1] Compare *Jul. Müller*, The Christian Doctrine of Sin (Clark's Foreign Theological Library).

soul and *body*, where the soul in the body signifies, according to the correct language of old times, which did not give it two meanings, the sensitive, earthly *life* in the body.[1] Vers. 26, 27 treat of the *life* and its *nourishment*, (Ps. lxxviii. 18, אֹכֶל לְנַפְשָׁם). Vers. 28, 29 of the *body* and its clothing. Whence we directly gather the only true signification of ver. 27, according to its necessary connexion, in opposition to a false reading which has closely adhered to it.

Thus is this the plainest and most popular part of the Sermon on the Mount, just where it goes into the depth of the heart: there is endless matter of preaching here, but little of exposition. Once more we hear the lawgiver's emphatic—*I say unto you!* of former sections, which seems, as it were, to have its faint echo in ver. 29. It is not found again, not even at ch. vii. 12, where the exposition of the law is closed in one final sentence, still less at ch. vii. 7, where the decisive concluding promise is given—it is reserved in this discourse to mark the requirements of His laws as He teaches them. I say unto *you*—that is, to the disciples of the Lord, the children of the Father, with all, who by His instruction, would become so. *Nourishment*, τροφή (all that is included in eating and drinking together), and *raiment*—the two main necessities for the life and the body, see Gen. xxviii. 20. (So that it almost seems a redundancy, if the Apostle, 1 Tim. vi. 8, includes in His σκεπάσματα, *covering*, the shelter of a dwelling, as well as the defence of raiment). Any one who is disposed to look for its inner meaning, may understand without exposition what the *thought* is, which is forbidden: inasmuch as it *divides* and distracts the soul (as μεριμνᾷν etymologically shows), while thought and prevision without care are not forbidden. The best interpretation of it is found at Lu. xii. 29: μὴ μετεωρίζεσθε, let not yourselves be restless, driven, wavering hither and thither. There it is the antithesis to the soul's rest, here the contrast is with the soul's unity of aim, for only in unity is rest.[2]

1 That is, according to the natural language of the sensualist, which the Lord adopts; as if the soul were not much *more* besides, as if to care for the soul must not necessarily lead to the caring for the higher life, the ζωὴ ψυχῆς.

2 The common interpretation, which *Luther* also adopts, is false: viz., that proud exaltation, presumption is intended, as 2 Macc. v. 17. The

Just as evident and convincing is the sense of the two question-positions: Will He who gave life and the body as the greater gift, keep back the food and clothing which those gifts need?

The birds of heaven, the flowers of the field—how simple, how beautiful this contemplation of nature, as Adam before the Fall beheld it in Paradise! A single eye thus beholds the creature as bearing evidence of its God; the evil eye, on the contrary, perverts all it sees to its own lust. Bird and flower agree together harmoniously, though they are distributed between heaven and earth. The birds of the *heaven*, עוֹף הַשָּׁמַיִם, often referred to as such from Gen. i. 30 downwards, unsubjected and free (like the flowers of the *field)* for whom no man generally cares, in their pure life and song have more affinity with heaven than the flowers, point more directly than they, *above*. Sowing, reaping, gathering into barns: the three main points of *husbandry*, which is to man in a state of nature the immediately appointed *labour* (Ps. civ. 23, עֲבֹדָה, as also Neh. x. 38, 1 Chron. xxvii. 26). The fowl of the air are not *like you*: in which words, to avert all misunderstanding and perversion, labour for man is manifestly enough confirmed as his lot. *Your*—not the father of the fowl: which forms a transition to the question which follows—Are not ye, even as men, as the lords and labourers of the earth, especially as children of the Father, much *better* than they? Toil then according to your human dignity, be not however, contrary to that dignity, subject to care, but know, that without the gift of God all that you can do is in vain. Of what avail would food be without the life? Do ye suppose that man lives of bread, if he have enough of it, and that he will live longer for the forethought that he takes? As God gave you life at the beginning, must not He also, in whose hands your breath is, preserve it to you by His care? Is it in your power, with all your forethought, to *live any moment longer than God wills?* Thus vers. 27 fits well here, and connects itself with vers. 26 concerning the nourishment of the *life;* vers. 28, 29 proceeding with the clothing of the *body*. This decides the meaning of ἡλικία, which certainly

idea of restless tossing is not only found in Wisd. xxvi. 9, ἐν μετεωρισμοῖς ὀφθαλμῶν, but also among profane authors, *e.g.* Thuc. lib. 2. μετέωρος ἦν ἡ ἔλλας, Greece was in troubled state.

here means length of life, as in Jno. ix. 21, 23; Heb. xi. 11;[1] not the body's stature, as only in Lu. xix. 3. (For at Lu. ii. 52; Eph. iv. 13, stature and life are comprised in one). The Lutheran translation introduces something altogether inappropriate, and even monstrous into the plain, well-arranged discourse of our Lord: so that one is tempted to ask in reply to it—Whoever took thought about such a thing as that, to add a cubit to his stature? To change the colour of the hair (ch. v. 36), or to think of growing an inch, would be another matter. The stature of the body is altogether unsuitable to the meaning in Lu. xii., for in the supplementary explanation the addition wished to the ἡλικία is termed ἐλάχιστον, though to add a cubit is so monstrous, in the proportions of human stature, that it is a very rare thing for a fool to lift his wish so high. The Lord must be supposed to signify some *common* matter of care to the children of men, and what is more frequent than the vain wish of the dying to protract their lives, at least a little longer. It is thought that *life* should have come after cubit? our answer is, that it is omitted just as *distance* in Jno. xxi. 8, and in this most natural image πῆχυν ἕνα stands as if we should say—a few paces, a span longer,—and as in Ps. xxxix. 6, a handbreadth.[2]

And *now first*, as the newly commencing *and* indicates, the discourse turns to the *body*, to which the ingenious structure and growth of the flowers correspond, and to which the clothing belongs. Καταμάθετε this second time is stronger than ἐμβλέψατε, look attentively, study diligently! No species of fowl was mentioned (as at Lu. xii. the ravens, and Matt. x. the sparrows), but now the emphasis is more specific—the *lilies*, which name,

[1] *Theophylact* in his time on Lu. xii. has rightly: ζωῆς μέτρα παρὰ μονῷ θεῷ, καὶ οὐκ αὐτός τις ἕκαστος ἑαυτῷ ὁριστὴς τῆς ζωῆς. Many exegetical writers have always been of the same mind, and among our more recent practical expositors, *von Gerlach*, *Richter*, *Braune*, whom *Alford* has not reckoned. Lange is disposed to mediate between the two opinions by ingeniously uniting them both into one: ἡλικία neither age simply, nor stature simply, but "the full unfolding of every individual in *every* respect according to its capacity—the mature manifestation of itself in general." We much doubt if this popular gnomic saying will admit of so deep a meaning.

[2] In *Stobæus* (xcviii. 13) from *Mimnermus*: πήχυιον ἐπί χρόνον: in *Alcæus* (Athen. x. 7): δάκτυλος ἁμέρα.

proverbial already in the Old Testament, embraced many kinds of white and coloured flowers, and was specially connected with the Imperial crown. Lilies *of the field*, not of the garden, growing of themselves, innumerable as the birds of heaven, like the *grass* (to which they belong, ver. 30), little regarded, blooming but a brief space, presently withered away and burned. For that reason overlook them not! See how they grow up without your aid to their slender height! They *toil* not! Agriculture was referred to before, as the fundamental toil of men, now a glance is cast upon that further toil of man in *art*, which provides for itself out of the material of nature.[1] Further, there lies in the words toiling and spinning a reference to men and women respectively[2]: κοπιᾷν is rather every kind of energy put forth in acquisition, and νήθειν naturally has a specific reference to clothing. The lilies have leaves and texture so finely spun, as no human cunning can counterfeit, and yet they spun it not in human fashion, but are clothed therewith by God. In the *growing* spoken of previously, there is hinted a question concerning the body corresponding to that in ver. 27 concerning the age: who among you can by any care or effort of personal will grow a fingerbreadth higher! Not the slightest stalk can man raise up!—But this is passed over unsaid, in order that the words may go on to rebuke the vanity of man, who makes out of his clothing, which is, properly speaking, the mere modest covering of his nakedness, matter of personal ostentation. *Solomon's glory* was in the Israelite proverbial language the ideal of magnificence in apparel; but why is this not like the beauty of the lilies? The Lord leads us by the last λέγω ὑμῖν to a profound thought which we must not fail to discern in it: the flowers *grow* directly with their essentially connate, not merely put on and *invested* clothing (περιεβάλετο is in slight contrast with ἀμφιέννυσιν); this is the beauty of nature and innocence, which in the slightest object shows more beautiful than the most magnificent array, which

[1] By spinning men *supply* what the field may not give—as *Hamann* writes his pithy application to his friend *Herder* about his winter-study: would he but take in the summer, and repair by *spinning* what he may not have been able to get by sowing and reaping.

[2] With far greater propriety may vers. 26, 27 be attributed to the men, who till the field for the sustenance of the household; and vers. 28, 29 to the women, who particularly provide for the clothing.

must be fastened on! "The lily belongs to the paradise of God, Solomon's glory to the hothouse of art" (*Kleuker*). Oh! that men would understand what is signified in this! Oh that they would learn from the flowers, the beauty of growing silently, by the internal law of their nature operating through God's gifts and power, up into a full preparation for that blooming in future glory, which is set before us as the goal of our glorification.

When man is once more elevated by the words πολλῷ μᾶλλον above the grass and flowers of the field, which to-day *are* and to-morrow are cast withered into the oven, we discern in this a sublime appeal to faith, inasmuch as, to all appearance, man's sensitive, earthly life is *just on a level with* the withering grass. The Lord literally refers to Ps. xc. 6. And here He makes the transition to the full *assurance and promise* of eternal life in the kingdom of God, by that henceforward oft-recurring, and graciously admonitory—*O ye of little faith!* קְטַן אֱמוּנָה or אֲמָנָה was also an expression of the Rabbies,[1] but what power and significance it assumes in the mouth of our Lord, requiring only *Faith* and yet again *Faith*, great Faith, large and wide as the grace and goodness of God Himself! Here this once in the Sermon on the Mount does the Lord *touch lightly* that great word, and that in the right place and with deep earnestness.

The end leads us back to the beginning, in order to embody in most clear and simple expression the whole of what has been meant from ver. 24, nay from ver. 19. The commandment is once more repeated, but now most plainly: Seek ye obediently, undistractedly and *trustfully* the kingdom of God! Trustful for what? The general, and inviting *promise* is given of the supply of all earthly need, as being necessarily included in and added to the promise of the free gift of the kingdom of heaven. The contrast with the Heathen or Gentiles, which has been contained in this whole part of the discourse, is now fully expressed: but we find it at the conclusion, not as in the contrast with the *Pharisees* (ch. v. 20), where *their* description came first. For the Pharisees, so terming themselves, were visibly before his hearers; but the internal heathenism of the heart must first be detected

[1] *E.g.* Rabbi Elieser the great: He who has a morsel of bread in his basket, and asks—what shall I eat to-morrow? is one of the men of little faith.

and disclosed. Here again, as always, we have *three* positions. The first reiterating at the conclusion: Therefore *take no thought*, for thus do the Gentiles! The second: For ye are God's children, His people, the chosen heirs of His kingdom! The third, once more: *Take therefore no thought!* Yet with a weighty qualifying reference, appended to the promise, to the indispensable and wholesome necessities of everyday life even in the case of the children of God.

Vers. 31—32. The *οὖν* is not simply such a *therefore* as we had in ver. 25, *διὰ τοῦτο*, but it is a very emphatic *deduction*. Else this is a repetition of ver. 25, with a strengthening addition of *saying* to taking thought;[1] and this is connected with the saying —for after all those things do the Gentiles seek; which has a very comprehensive reference. For it means first, that in God's presence there is such a distinction: Ye are not as the Gentiles! Then, with reproachful test, reversing the words—Who seek after these things are Gentiles: Therefore, should ye not be like them! Will ye then retain heathenism in your hearts? Finally, it is a gracious exhortation, which becomes a permission: Leave all such care to the Gentiles, who have no Father in heaven, who know not, that they have a Father! *For your heavenly Father knoweth that ye have need of all these things:* an intenser repetition of what had been preparatorily uttered in ver. 8, following ver. 7. The stress of emphasis falls upon the *knoweth:* ye have *a living* God, *who knoweth!* But in addition to His knowing, His willingness is already secured in the name of Father; so that we may say that every single word in the whole sentence utters a ground of assurance and strong consolation.

Ver. 33. This is the middle one of the three great fundamental laws of the Sermon on the Mount. The first ch. v. 48 pointed up to the *Father* of love in heaven. This second bears witness to, and assures us of the descent of heaven to earth in that *kingdom*, which is already come, and is open to violent entrance. But it adjoins the condition of *seeking* in order to the laying hold of the

[1] The Lord forbids two things: Taking thought—and then saying, giving open utterance to the same; because the taking thought weighs down and dispirits the heart of one only, but the saying infects others also with despondency. (*Zeller*, Monatsblatt.) Or is *saying* here only a Hebraism for *thinking*?

treasure held forth (Phil. iii. 13, 14), namely, through the *righteousness* of God which alone avails in His kingdom, the actual having and performing of which remains ever the straight gate of entrance to it. This paves the way for the *third* great law, (ch. vii. 12). Let us observe and weigh well the retrospective view, comprehensive and concentrated, which is taken from this vantage point of the discourse! The *kingdom and righteousness* together remind us of the petitions, ver. 10. The *kingdom* of God embraces the entire introductory ch. v. 3—20, where at first the kingdom of heaven came down to the poor and remained at last only righteousness. God's *righteousness*—comprehends all from ch. v. 21 to ch. vi. 18, with especial reference to ch. v. 48 and ch. vi. 1. For ch. v. 48 closed the first part (not like the Pharisees) by way of anticipation just at the point where the induction of the commandments ceased; and found in the following chapter only its further development: before the Father in secret!

It has been made matter of wonder that the Lord only says "*first*" and not "*alone*"—exclusively. He says, indeed, elsewhere —One thing is needful; and in its profoundest principle this πρῶτον is also a μόνον. But here we discern a certain softening of His gracious utterance at the outset; experience will bring out its rigorous strictness afterwards. Only begin to seek the kingdom of God *first;* and ever let it be first! If thou hast ever thought in thy heart that when thou art fully furnished with this, every thing else will be superadded, it will become evident to thee in due course that thou canst never be thus fully furnished. This one great concern will so fill up the heart, that no room will be left for aught else. The righteousness of *God* is to be understood here strictly according to its subsequent Pauline use, as indicating both that which He requires and which alone avails before Him; and also that which He *imparts*, since He Himself feeds us with the establishment of His will in us, as with the true bread. (Ver. 11; Rom. xiv. 17).[1] In St Luke's repetition of the discourse (ch. xii.), the express promise is connected therewith: fear not,

[1] Thus much, at least, as *Roos* remarks, is already clear, that man must not make for himself a righteousness, but by hunger and thirst *seek* it: and that such a righteousness as will cause him to be reputed, not only by the council-chamber of his city, but by his God, a righteous man.

little flock; for it is your Father's good pleasure *to give you* the kingdom—with the righteousness which appertains thereto. Which promise is here included in the sense, and probably, as St Matthew does not record absolutely every particular, might have been uttered by our Lord on this first occasion also. Is not this heavenly *feeding* more than the earthly, even as much so as the true, eternal life of the soul is more than that of sense? Is not this *clothing* of the inner man more than the covering of the mere body? Consequently, further, in the highest application of the former conclusion: Will he who gives you the eternal good, suffer you to lack that which is temporal? Faith answers this—προστεθήσεται.[1] It is only the wantonly presumptuous who, in mockery of God, would reap without sowing; and seeking first the perishable riches of earth, fondly imagines that the eternal good will be added to him over and above.

Ver. 34. This closes once more with the original word (ver. 25). All undue care goes over the immediate present into the future: but we can only be said to be assured of *this day* (ver. 11) in this uncertain life, and for *to-morrow* have so little to care, that it is not included in our prayers. That applies even to the spiritual life; be only every day faithful, obedient, and righteous, no more is wanting! How much more for the earthly life, as the daily manna in the wilderness daily sent foreshowed. You might lose the very last day of your time of grace, taking anxious thought about a morrow that is not to be yours. If the morrow comes, it will provide for its own. Are we to understand that God, who sends the day and all that it bears with it, arranges all things rightly and forgets not one of its necessities? This is in part the meaning, but the words go further and are still stronger: let *the morrow* care! Further, does not the Lord refer to a *care* of every day as it passes, and with the same expression (μεριμνήσει) which has hitherto denoted the forbidden

[1] What *Braune* advances is superficially correct, but goes not to the depth: "How is that? Quite naturally. For they who seek the kingdom and the righteousness of God, are not careless, thriftless, idle, spendthrift people, &c." Certainly, but the meaning goes far beyond that labour, and thrift, and economy which save God's people from want. An apocryphal saying of our Lord extracts its meaning more fully: Αἰτεῖτε τὰ μεγάλα, καὶ τὰ μικρὰ ὑμῖν προστεθήσεται, καὶ αἰτεῖτε τὰ ἐπουράνια, καὶ τὰ ἐπίγεια προστεθήσετα ὑμῖν.

anxiety? Assuredly, and that forms the transition to the final saying, containing allusion to that necessity of human life which, for sin's sake, even the heirs of the kingdom will not shake off till the days have reached their end. The word is thrown out, as it were, enigmatically, as we here find it; probably the Lord added some further elucidation and development of it. We catch its meaning in all its depth, with the progress of the inner life. *Κακία* is in general just what τὸ πονήρον is in the seventh petition, and serves for its interpretation: the evil and the trials of life upon earth, the ills and infirmities of the body in the flesh, all troubles external and from within. So that this evil must be taken into the account with the daily bread of the body and the soul, and is equally with that your *need*, better known as such to your heavenly Father than to you, and may in no case be put away by taking thought! Be not so foolish as to double and multiply your plague and disquietude: every day's evil is *enough* for itself, will you add to it that of to-morrow, and the third day, and yet further? But the more fully we learn to cast away that μεριμνᾷν for earthly things which is conceded to the weakness of *to-day*, and give up all disquietude about all that pertains to eating and drinking and clothing, health and sickness, and all things bodily and of earth—so much the more does it become impressed upon us that there is a deeper, unexplored meaning yet in the Lord's utterance. That very seeking God's kingdom and righteousness, that ever-new devotion and sacrifice of the will to an entire obedience, must be to the children of God, while they live in the flesh and in the world, the trial of every day, the daily cross of self-denial. (Lu. ix. 23). With this we are *content*; we would not presumptuously burden ourselves beyond the will of our Father in heaven, nor throw off any of His load. This is the perfect spirit that should be aimed at by all who are pilgrims to the kingdom, till they finally enter it. (Acts xiv. 22).

Ch. vi. 19 showed an apparent break in the discourse without any expressed connexion, and this is much more the case with the beginning of the seventh chapter. It appears, indeed, as if down to the fourteenth verse, it was composed of successive, unconnected, fragments; and hence many, who are incapable of tracing the mind of the Spirit and of supplying what is left to be understood, are rash enough to say that all connexion is here entirely lost, and that the Evangelist has undoubtedly only strung together the sayings of various times. Yet as the connexion has not hitherto eluded us, we shall find it still even to the end. Let our preliminary view be brought to mind, which laid it down that after the two contrasts—not like the Pharisees! not like the Heathen! were exhibited, there followed a third, viz., not like those of *my disciples*, and those of God's children, impure and imperfect, who instead of carrying on in their own inner life the pursuit of God's kingdom and righteousness, and regulating their outer life in accordance with that pursuit, fall back into that Pharisaism again, the roots of which were not eradicated, and thus either unrighteously judge or improperly proselyte others! Is not this the last and most stiff-necked Pharisee remaining yet in the Christian man? Yet, let it be observed whether the statement (vers. 1—6) concerning censoriousness and desecration of that which is holy, does not perfectly adapt itself to the natural progress according to which the delineation of the perfect righteousness of a disciple of Christ is now to be completed. Are they not half-disciples (we know not how better to term them) who act thus in a manner against which the Lord warns, and who thus are in danger of relapsing into mere hypocrites, mere *Pharisee-Christians?* And does not the law of Christ for His own people rise into its most rigorous and *restricting* expression, in these *warnings* which follow, in harmony with the internal progression of the Sermon on the Mount in its dealing with the needs of man's life?

We must look closer that our observation may be both developed and confirmed. The *goal of discipleship* which, as we advance towards it, rises ever higher before us, is after all that has been said, no other than the perfect righteousness of *pure and unselfish love*, as it will be announced in ver. 12. This goal of *pure* love is now indicated by means of two warning opposites: it is love as *humble* as it is *wise* (vers. 1—6). These together form the first part of the section. And as to the *way*, or rather the ever-repeated beginning, by which this goal is to be reached—what is it, as we have already seen, but *prayer* to God for His grace to that end? This is, therefore, rightly the *second* part (vers. 7—11). And what may and must be the *third* (for everywhere we find triplicity) but the condensed compendium of the whole great middle portion of the Sermon, containing all that is made obligatory for fulfilling the law, as we find it in the last all-comprehensive *requirement: therefore walk in this way to reach that goal!* which is the actual and literal meaning of vers. 12—14. Let this be pondered well, and it will be found that it is not an imposition of ours upon the text, but an exposition of it.[1]

That the Lord's requirements should now be indicated by *warning contrasts* we have more and more prepared for since ver. 19, and indeed it naturally corresponds with the character of the close as containing the rigorous exclusion of all the impure and imperfect. Thus through the opposite error that *pure love* is discriminated first, in virtue of which *every* disciple of Christ is according to his capacity to become a peacemaker, a witness of the truth and ambassador of the kingdom (ch. v. 9, 13). This is first exhibited as an altogether *humble* love for the salvation of others, *after and in connexion with a thorough judgment of self.* We should assuredly judge, but only for others' benefit, from a principle of love, not in the spirit of condemnation, and never forgetting ourselves in the same regard. Whether we can do this in general is first of all and most rigorously to be tested and proved *within the circle of discipleship:* hence the mirror is here held up for the relation of *brothers* to one another in a more restricted sense. First, the fundamental principle itself, expressed almost as an absolute *prohibition,* yet with some slight recognition of the opposite and not excluded duty of the disciples:—judge not! (ver. 1.) Then follows the ground and confirmation of this warning, which at the same time encourages us to mete with the right measure, that of mercy (ch. v. 7), and thus to the judgment of charity, which tends to amendment, like that of God's mercy. Ver. 2. This prohibition or command is yet more clearly placed upon its true foundation, in the intui-

[1] That holds good for New Testament criticism also, which the departed *Drechsler* so keenly and clearly laid down against "unscientific treatment:"—the great problem is to perceive the object of what is transmitted and testified! But here the authenticity and *unity* of the Sermon on the Mount is the before-attested object which we have to discern.

tively *convincing explanation* of ver. 3—5, which presses home with Thou instead of Ye. Here again we have *warning* first, then *requirement.* The warning (against judging without humble charity) puts two keen *questions:* Is not the principle of such censoriousness, that thou forgettest to judge thyself? ver. 3. Comes not hence the *utterance* of it, thy proud and presumptuous *saying:*—Let me pull out? ver. 4. (May we not then point out and correct a brother's fault? Certainly, but only after and with a searching judgment of ourselves! Thus there now follows:) the *requirement* of a true exercise of our brotherly obligation, the *pulling out the mote* (Jno. xiii. 14) not merely the seeing it; with the necessary *title* to do so added: first judge thyself—*after that* with *wisdom*—look well, how thou *pullest it out!* ver. 5. Here we may narrowly observe the transition which is interwoven in these words, to the following remarks concerning the *wisdom* of charity.

The Lord's discourse suddenly turns from the *most internal principle* of the sincerely seeking, faithfully devoted heart, the clear and single eye, to the *external deportment;* and, inasmuch as we have only to do with God or with men, to our deportment when we are constrained to see around in our fellow-men and our own brethren, imperfection and sinfulness. Did the Lord orally interpose, at such points of transition, any words of connexion? we have a right to presume generally, and a comparison with St Luke, whose report of so important a discourse the Spirit could never have left open to falsification, drives us to the conclusion, that our Lord uttered more than is recorded here. But it may very well be doubted whether any additional words would take the form of *our* modern way of discoursing, which takes care to show the process of the thought, and aims to lay it bare in its internal arrangement. This is opposed to Orientalism generally, and to the genius of the Hebrew in particular, which, as it exhibits but little conjunction of individual sentences, so also it has but little expressed logical connexion of its discourses as a whole. It is opposed, also, to the necessary, and more highly natural character of prophetical utterance, that language of the Spirit, as it meets us everywhere in the Old Testament, even where the discourses were written by the Prophets themselves. This manner of speaking, indeed, as it came down from Solomon's original use of it, to the Rabbinical style of teaching and laying down their sayings as the Lord found it, is essentially the natural and universally human method. The thoughts of the teacher who speaks from the fulness of his heart, when art (or artifice) has not yet learned to adjust them to the limitations of words, flow forth livingly in their own simplicity, and are bound by no obligation to give a strict account of their sequence and order. And, finally, *such* discourse is more likely to be understood by the right kind of hearer, for it makes a rigorous claim on his attention, it excites his own thought and keeps it on the stretch. As a book exacts something from its reader, and leaves something for him to supply, so also does a discourse require something from the hearer. Our Lord's Sermon on the Mount presents in this respect a reproving example to our occidental and modern style of sermons.

In consistency with this our Lord at ch. vi. 19 assuredly did not say: "The Pharisees, as it has been shewn, are in their hearts before God no better than Gentiles: therefore I say unto you further—Live ye not after the manner of heathens an earthly life, but deposit it before all things in your hearts, as a fundamental principle, and in order that your righteousness may exceed theirs, that ye must depend upon God supremely, according to the first commandment, and seek only the treasure and reward of His kingdom." We feel how untrue and human such explanations and deductions would be in our Lord's lips. Consequently He does not say here: "And if ye are now decided and entirely devoted, determined for yourselves to seek first the kingdom of God and His righteousness; see to it that ye do not blunt the keen edge of your self-judgment and self-renunciation, and finally altogether lose it, by hasty and unholy, that is uncharitable judgment of those without you, by censure and correction of others, seeing that not only in the world but among your own brethren, sin and shortcoming enough will obtrude itself upon your notice and be your temptation. The more clearly you see this, the more earnestly guard yourselves against sacrificing your charity: for if ye would be my *perfect disciples*, then must your righteousness, as perfect love, be ever humble in bearing and forgiving, wise and thoughtful to heal and take away the sin that it sees." That we rightly seize the connexion in this place, we are additionally assured by an explanatory saying of our Lord recorded in St Luke (ch. vi. 40) similar to this but more detailed. But we may be assured that the Lord did thus unconnectedly set out with sudden appeal—Judge not! just as St Matthew has abruptly recorded it. He spoke indeed not for His disciples and that people, then on the mountain, but for the church of all ages, which should afterwards investigate His words. But even a hearer of that time, who should recall to mind those words, which from their proverbial form would cling tenaciously to the memory, would well understand how they were intended.

Vers. 1—2. This is the evil-eye of the natural man, that he ever prefers to apply the rule of right of which he is perfectly conscious, to that which is without rather than to that which is within, himself; that he seeks out and bemoans the sins of his neighbour instead of thinking upon his own; and thus losing his charity towards his brother, loses also his humility and sincerity before God. Every one knows, and vindicates for himself, *what men should do to him:* and so far this beginning is internally connected with the concluding word at ver. 12. Further, to judge others and not ourselves, is the spirit of *Pharisaism* as developed from this natural principle of evil, the spirit of that misapprehension and misuse of God's law which the Lord had before disclosed, and against which His whole discourse, even in the second and third contrasts which only more fully removed the mask from what was the *Pharisee* still, had from the beginning been directed.[1] Read Rom. ii. 1—3, 17—23. The Pharisee, himself at heart a heathen, would yet condemn all the world: himself no better than a publican would yet uncharitably censure and cast from him the poor people around him. And this Pharisaism pursues the disciple of Christ, adheres to him long, even as worldly care and the worship of Mammon do.

[1] Generally speaking, as *Braune* says, the judging others is the foul stain of social life! Hence the otherwise innocent expression "jemanden *bereden*" has come to mean "to speak ill of him." For the *falseness* of all men (Rom. iii. 4) reveals itself, at the same time being uncharitableness, in their intercourse with one another.

Therefore:—would ye be perfect, then put this utterly away! The very perception and experience which the new man has of the evils of his old heart brings with it a revived temptation and tendency to such an evil: hence censorious judging, as the usual transition-weakness of the new converted, breaks out now though it may not have been manifested before.

In vers. 1, 2, then, as a maxim expressed in general terms, the object of this censorious judgment is the whole evil world without us, from whom we feel ourselves to be separated as the children of the kingdom: but in ver. 3 there is a manifest restriction of the reference to our *brethren* in a narrower sense (to whom in ver. 6 those who are without stand opposed). For otherwise we should not hear of *motes* in the eye, but of a more entire blindness and wickedness.

That the Lord in this prohibition of *judging* refers to a disposition and posture of the heart, and not the utterance of it as such (as already in ch. v. 22), is obvious of itself, especially since—He has (in ch. vi.) penetrated so deeply into the heart's sentiments. For we are, as the witnesses and ambassadors of His kingdom, to preach His truth, which condemns the sin of the world,—His Gospel, according to which unbelievers stand condemned before God. But it is one thing to testify as His humble ministers the Lord's word in Mar. xvi. 16, and altogether another thing to say presumptuously, yea even to think in our hearts:—This or that man is condemned, or to address to him the direct appeal—Thou art condemned! This is ever forbidden to us on the simple ground that we can never say, as searchers of the heart: Thou believest not, thou wilt never believe, though the love of God by us or by others may continue to strive with thee. Sin itself we should term such, when we perceive it and where it concerns, as well for our own sake as for the sake of others: for the Lord also requires of us, that we judge righteous judgment (Jno. vii. 24), and the Apostle says: He that is spiritual judgeth all things (1 Cor. ii. 15). But this ἀνακρίνειν is very different from that κατακρίνειν, which belongs only to God (Rom. xiv. 4). We, who are sinners and expect ourselves the judgment of God, may not judge *before the time*, until the Lord come, who will bring to light the hidden things of darkness in us and all the world (1 Cor. iv. 5). Let us only be ourselves doers of the law, the lawgiver Himself will be the judge, according to His own supreme authority and righteous distribution (Jas. iv. 11, 12), (which is again an inwardly and spiritually apprehended general citation from the Sermon on the Mount). What is then in itself, as the prohibition stands in its literal severity, the judging which is forbidden? The Lord presupposes the cognizance in our own minds of the sin which is to be condemned, but it is His will that in all the judgments which we pass upon it, we should not *condemn* the individual for the individual's sake and as such, that is, that we should not regard and deal with our fellowmen and brethren *independently of the forgiving love of God*, which is free for them as well as for ourselves, as long as that goal is not reached when He will say—Depart from me! (ver. 23). Beware of men, beware of false prophets, yea, of dogs and swine (ver. 6): that is judgment severe enough, and yet it involves no judgment unto condemnation, out of our own assumed authority, no rejection on our part, as if we already were assessors with Him upon His judgment seat, and the final separation were already come. *This* sense of His words our Lord himself has more fully explained in Lu. vi., since there He adds as an epexegesis—μὴ καταδικάζετε[1]—and then lays down the opposite—*forgive* rather (ἀπολύετε) and *give*, that is, out of the treasure of grace which is in yourselves: and St Luke in his epitome wisely puts this in close connexion with the preceding—be ye therefore *merciful*, as your Father also is merciful! For does not the Lord here actually point back, though according to St Matthew He had said much else in the interval, to ch. vi. 14, 15 and ch. v. 42—48? Is it not His purpose to teach just here in all its fulness that *perfection* of pure *love* which He had there enjoined upon His disciples?

That ye be not judged! as in ch. vi. 15. The fundamental principle of this is here presupposed:—as ye have not been judged, as ye have been forgiven, and as ye are ever being forgiven. But in addition to this there is the threatening of the withdrawal of the mercy which had been received, as had been

[1] Not, indeed, as a climax, according to *Alford's* still more subtle distinction, who concludes that κρινειν in St Matthew is by no means fully equivalent (according to generally-received opinion) to κατακρίνειν, but that it is forbidden, in general, to form *authoritative* judgments of others.

already gently intimated at ch. v. 7, in the opposite case. (Jas. ii. 13). Consequently the requital here referred to signifies of course requital *from God;* although its type and beginning, the *measuring again on the part of man,* is by no means excluded, nay, rather, is used for the sake of founding upon it a convincing warning. That sinful man should requite upon his fellow man the evil that he has done to him, is in itself *sin* (ch. v. 38, 39); and yet this right of retaliation thus wickedly arrogated, is but the utterance and reflexion of that eternally valid principle of justice which the Lord God has given to those who are judges in His name, and which He Himself observes. So that he who unrighteously judges another in his own name must, when he is thus judged in return, reflect in his conscience :—this injustice of man is only my due in the sight of God, and one day He who has the right to do so, will thus deal with me! The maxim which the Lord lays down in ver. 2, is a *fundamental law,* so universally recognized, so fully exhibited in the perverted estate of the world, so well known in man's natural conscience, that all the heathen express it in the same way, that it is found variously laid down in the Old Testament, and that even the Jewish Talmud, in other respects the very perfection of perversion, has retained it as an indelible proverb.[1] But when our Lord takes it up, and says: ἐν ᾧ κρίματι, ἐν ᾧ μετρῳ, rightly translated in the German—with Welcherlei, what kind of judgment and measure—He gives us, in transition, to understand that we should indeed judge with right judgment, and measure again with the righteous measure of truth in the spirit of love. For the κρίνετε which is admitted in ver. 2, has manifestly another and a wider meaning than that which is forbidden in ver. 1. Forgive, and ye shall be forgiven: give, and it shall be given unto you.

Vers. 3—5. This more specific figure of the *mote* and *beam* the Lord found also ready prepared, as we see it in the Talmud in the form of a Rabbinical מָשָׁל. He whose Word of truth gathered to itself all the anticipatory, preparatory truth in the world and especially among Israel—He, who in all things came not to destroy but to fulfil, disdains not, in His holy love and wisdom,

[1] Countless times we have, במדה שאדם מודד בה מודדין לו or the like.

to speak sometimes as a Rabbi what other rabbies had spoken. He after their fashion constructs His own parables and figures—*new*, intelligible to the people, and taking fast hold of their minds. This He could always have done, but he rather condescends sometimes to use their unsavory similitudes of beams in the eye, and camels through the needle, in order that His word may enter their minds, and direct the fools to the yet extant remains of their own wisdom. How does the great Teacher put to shame us the under-teachers, who must fain speak in original, and elegant and characteristic words of our own!—Yet the old becomes new in the lips of our Lord, and the extant words of man are replenished with a higher spirit. Thus here the beholding a *brother's eye* derives a profound meaning from its reference to what had been said concerning the eye in ch. vi. 22, 23. An entirely single eye has no mote, no beam in it; in the eye are to be sought the peculiar faults both of the judged and of the judging brother. The Lord reproves such *beholding* another as is proved to be wicked and severe, by the very fact that it does *not* see what should first have been seen, personal evil in self. (See Lu. vi.) *Βλέπειν* and *κατανοεῖν* are used together with their distinction. One *sees* without himself the mote in the brother's eys, but *marks* not the beam in himself, which lies nearer to him, and is even to be felt. (*Κατανοεῖν* is to be cognizant of, to observe accurately, rightly to take account of). A keen and critical eye for the veriest mote, the slightest trifle, in the brother's eye, where (which the Lord leaves unmentioned) there may be no mote present: but the same eye so keen in looking without itself, is obtuse and insensible for self-scrutiny! The gnat is strained at, the camel swallowed. Is it not so? *Is it not made manifest* that it is so too often among brethren? This is the meaning of the convicting *or*, by which the discourse passes from the principle to its exhibition; comp. the subsequent ver. 9. If it were not so, how *couldst*, how *wouldst thou*, whom I now signify, and with whom it is thus, proudly and imperiously and dictatorially say: *Stand*, and *let me* pull out the mote out of thine eye? I will do it, and I can, I demand that thou submit obediently *to me!* Why else is the appearance and language of such assumption? *Luther* has well resolved ἐρεῖς by *dürfen*, for in Lu. vi. it stands: πῶς δύνασαι λέγειν. Yea, the *beholding* was already a blameable, unjustifiable thing:

thou shouldst first have cast thine eye inwards, and *beheld* what thou in thy blindness hast overlooked, *the* beam is in thine own eye! The definite article is used in each case in connexion with mote and beam: the existence of *the* mote is not denied—but what is *the* beam? Just that thou now so actest; thine incompetent, hasty, uncharitable, assuming judgment is this beam. Let this be well noted in opposition to that superficial exposition which supposes that in order to lie under the sentence of this saying, one must have a great failing in himself, and know himself to be guilty, in a higher degree, of the sin which he condemns. Rather the supposing that I am in this matter better than thou, and therefore may bear myself reprovingly towards you—is just what is here termed a beam. The figure goes enormously beyond actuality, but the Lord retains it, for it suits excellently well the idea of *proportion* which He designs to give.[1] In Lu. vi. 39, *blindness* is spoken of, and certainly a beam in the eye makes blind. But if the blind man will yet lead others, and will keenly think to search out motes, then is he more than blind. (Jno. ix. 41.) Hence, *thou hypocrite!* This is cast into the face of the disciples, much more severely than in ch. vi., where it only stood—be ye not *as* the hypocrites! The disciple of Christ, as far as he is in this sad state, again becomes a true Pharisee. The πρῶτον in part reminds us of that great πρῶτον in ch. vi. 33. First become thyself righteous before God, stand *thyself* sincere and lowly before the judgment-seat of God. (Sir. xviii. 19; Gal. vi. 3, 4.) Art thou so well able to pull out little motes, use thy skill upon thine own greater ones! But it may be said, in what sense can our Lord ascribe to us the puri-

[1] *Braune:* "Mote and beam, are of one matter and of one kind; the one is not a precious metal: the only distinction lies in the greatness." That is, not that the censor has the same fault *greater* in himself, but, first of all, he has only such acuteness in detecting the failing of another, because he knows it well from the monition and sting of his own conscience, and then again, it becomes in him a greater fault, a beam, *inasmuch* as he "would appease his own conscience by censorious judgment, and repel the Word of God, which comes to his own heart, as the cold rock gives back the echo." *Alford* further observes upon men's false estimate who would discover in others beams only, in themselves only motes! *Daub*, again, differently: "The perception of a mote is rendered more acute by the feeling of a beam." (Judas. Isch. ii. 349).

fying our own eye? We answer, that he is not here speaking to the merely natural man, but to His disciple, who, as such, has the requisite grace, though he will not use and seek its increase. It is no other than if He should say: Let me pull out, first, the beam out of thine own eye!

Καὶ τότε—and then comes the time to discharge the brotherly duty of rebuke for amendment. That duty is imposed by love, but that it may be effected by charity, with spiritual authority, but in the spirit of meekness, that he who has been overtaken in a fault, may truly be restored. (Gal. vi. 1). Now comes out first the deep and hidden significance of the figure that has been used. As the beam in the eye is found in the internal sight and direction of the heart, not in this or the other manifest vice; so also we should there seek out and find the motes and beams of our brethren. *Seneca* (de vit. beat. c. 27) addresses the censorious thus: *papulas observatis alienas, obsiti ulceribus.* This is directed to the outward appearance, though well intended: but the disciple of Christ must not, in his neighbour's case, and especially in his brother's, look at the external countenance, mien, and appearance, at the movement of hand or foot, and applying the standard of his own deportment, pass judgment upon his brother for differing from himself—dictatorially saying: this man *acts* thus, and consequently his *heart* must be evil, acts differently from me, he must be wrong; for the outward appearance deceives, and there is much variety of manner, and there is much variety of circumstance, to be considered in judging of the actions of men. Look with a single eye *into thy brother's eye*, that is in a brotherly spirit, and if thou canst not but see a mote there, help him from it! Here is our Lord's commandment (Matt. xviii. 15) out of the Law of Moses (Lev. xix. 17), placed in its true light. *Τότε*—all before this is also *before the time*, before the Lord's coming in judgment to thyself. But τότε διαβλέψεις, not properly speaking, as a command (according to *Luther's* translation), but as a *permission*, as is sufficiently obvious; a permission, however, further accompanied by *promise;* so wilt thou, with purified eye, see clearly and rightly how the matter is. (*Διά* is intensitive, but not in the sense of an artificial carrying out of the figure, such as *Bengel's: transspicies, trabe e medio sublatâ).* But see what? Merely the mote? But the true discernment and wisdom lie not in that, though many seem to think so, and consequently lay more stress upon the *saying*—Let me pull out! than upon the actual pulling out itself. And yet this latter is the main concern! *Luther's* interpretation, seizing the spirit in the letter has it: look, *how* thou pullest it out! For the εκβαλεῖν, the thing successfully, tenderly, and prudently accomplished, is now the real accusative to the διαβλέπειν, as previously τὸ κάρφος was simply to the βλέπειν. He who lives by the grace of God in the continual exercise of self-judgment, he who has retired from the footstool of mercy, delivered from the old and evil beam, knows well how tender an operation such purification of the inner eye is; and that it must be attempted by man with such exquisite delicacy that the diseased brother, marking the hand of God, may submit without any command of thine; and that thus the evil may not be increased by unskilfulness on thy part and opposition on his, for the one, alas, provokes the other. Begin not at once with that *saying*, the surgeon only does this when he is obliged: help thy brother rather, if possible, from his mote in such a manner that he may not discern *thy* hand and will: *say* to him afterwards what thou hast to say, or not at all. But if without thy bidding him, he will not submit, take good heed, that in thy bidding no little mote of pride may glance upon him from thine eye, but the pure light of love beaming upon him from a brother humble before God. Is not this certainly the highest and severest test of the spirit of a disciple, only to be demanded within the narrow circle of brotherly fellowship? If the children of God thus acted always in relation to one another, the motes and beams would finally be all for ever done away.

With this the transition is made to the other main property of that charity which would compassionately save the world and the brethren from their sin: to that *wisdom*, which accompanies humility. But *on that account* the mirror is held up to the disciples in their relation to those who are without. (Eph. v. 15; Matt. x. 16). Within the circle of the disciples themselves friendly correction takes place according to and in connexion with a thorough judgment of ourselves; in our intercourse with the wicked world, however, the opposite test is brought in as to whether we can also keep silence, or can speak, exhort and rebuke under proper restraints, according to and in connexion with a *true perception of susceptibility in others and calling in ourselves.* Then follows, again, a severe prohibition of the contrary, exhibited in most mischievous and striking examples.

Ver 6. *Bengel* says quite correctly: *Hic occurritur alteri extremo*—but this observation must be more strictly defined. The Lord here turns from the brethren, in exhorting whom, the more lovingly it is done the more effectual it is, to the dogs and swine, who only repel the mild words of love. These are to be first rebuked and disciplined to repentance, by those who are called and qualified from above so to do; and the Gospel is not to be directly thrust upon their acceptance. To do this by misapplied and inappropriate preaching of it is the general error of the new converted, inclined as they are to a too easy and unwise proclamation of it to all the world. It is by no means contrary to humility, but only righteous judgment, when we discern how *evil* the state of mind of the wicked is, and regulate our deportment towards them accordingly. There are to be found *dogs* and *swine* among men; this is the Lord's own assurance even in the midst of His gracious preaching: and he gives us His injunction to mark them and distinguish them, between the warning against censorious judgment and the encouragement to prayer. Dogs in the East are not esteemed as they are among us, they belong with swine to the unclean, and contemned animals (2 Pet. ii. 22). It was a proverbial way of speaking among the Israelites (and is now among the Turks), that those who are without are dogs: and this is referred to its right meaning in the New Testament, (Matt. xv. 26; Phil. iii. 2; and, finally, Rev. xxii. 15). Thus the sense is: such as in their present condition are unsusceptible of good influence, grossly sensual, proudly contradicting sinners. What then is meant by *that which is holy*, and which is not to be *given*, nay, not to be *offered* to such people, remaining in such a state? It is essentially explained by the opposite: Give that which is holy to the holy, or at least to those who acknowledge its holiness, and accept it as such. But this apparently abstract expression must also have here a sensible foundation, which will make it appropriate to the *figure:* just as the holy flesh of the offering (Hag. ii. 12; Jer. xi. 15), was not to be cast to the dogs, and to them was to be thrown that which was carrion, or torn of wild beasts (Ex. xxii. 31).[1] The saying blends profoundly the figure and its signification: hence *pearls* are introduced, with a latent allusion—these are not acorns for the touch of swine. The *holy thing* is God's, and that it may not be desecrated, preserve it from the profane! But it has become also *our* treasure and property, hence it is added in the second place, *your* pearls, partly in the same sense as ch. xiii. 45, 46, partly with a specific design in the plural form. So act for the sake of God's honour that the holy things may not be despised: take care that your treasure and the good that is in you be not evil spoken of (Rom. xiv. 16), for your own sakes: exhibit your special experiences, the precious things of your inner life, before God, and not before such people as understand no more about them than swine do about pearls. This warning of our Lord thus condemns many things in one word, with an advancing meaning and heightening application. It forbids, first of all, the imprudent, unprofitable, yea, injurious preaching of *the Gospel*, where the law and its discipline are first required: it further goes on to condemn all reckless pouring out of the secrets of the life of grace before the world, without discriminating reference to time and place, with all unseasonable relations of conversion, and confessions, and experiences, and colloquies of the devout. The latter, however, is *less* referred to since it is the practice of the *hypocrites*, with whom the preceding—*thou hypocrite!* already connected them. This vilest mockery of devotion our Lord leaves unmentioned, just as before the seeing of motes not existing: He pre-supposed, there, the presence of the mote, and here that they are *our own pearls* which are in our hands.[2] But He warns against that thoughtlessness, which is rebuked by its consequences; the evil which is done crying out—Fool, thou shouldst have thought that this was not appropriate here! He tells us this, in His wisdom, to anticipate and prevent the evil.

[1] *Alford* reminds us of the primitive Christian use of the expression τὰ ἅγια to denote the elements of the Eucharist.

[2] *Lange's* interpretation of the hypocrites, who thus desecrated the good things of the church in their dealing with them (iii. 85), is a more widely extended application, true enough in itself. The Lord, however, speaks to His own actual disciples, when He says: *Ye* shall not do in like manner, as the Pharisees! ye with *your* pearls!

A wise man's heart discerneth both time and judgment (Eccles. viii. 5), and doth not instruct a fool, when his incorrigible folly refuses instruction (Ecclus. xxii. 5—7; Prov. ix. 7, 8). Many of the children of the world remain altogether thus till their hour comes, many at least are such at times. Who would preach the Gospel to a drunken man, or make the gentle appeal to a man raging with the frenzy of wrath, and *ask* him to be reconciled to God? There is much that is analogous to this, though in cases not equally monstrous, and the spirit of wisdom must decide them as they occur. The mournful results show us that there are more dogs and swine than we had supposed, and this should teach us ever the lesson of prudence. The figure has been further interpreted as if the swine more particularly trod thoughtlessly the precious things under their feet: the dogs, on the contrary, turn again and rend us. In this case the former would be the worse; but the latter would indicate, as all opposition does, that there was some understanding of the thing rejected. But in 2 Pet. ii. 22, the dogs are regarded as unclean inwardly, the swine rather as outwardly unclean: that distinction the Lord does not make.[1] In the concluding sentence He adheres only to the swine and the pearls, as the *αὐτούς* referring to *μαργαρίτας* shows, and His twofold saying concerning trampling under foot, and rending (for the swine may be as ferocious as a dog) contains something much more important for the meaning of the whole:—they despise and destroy both the precious *gift* and the well-intentioned imprudent *giver*. Ye have then needlessly handed over the holy thing to prostitution, and exposed yourselves to mockery and persecution! Finally in the *στραφέντες*, which is certainly not the mere finish of the figure, lies the inmost point of the discourse. They would have remained at rest, had you left them alone: but you have *provoked them* to sin against God and man, ye have through imprudence multiplied offences, whereas they ought to have either been silently tolerated, or more wisely attacked.

This word of our Lord therefore puts, as it were, a limiting *restraint* upon the universal zeal of our charity, which would

[1] That the dogs (according to *Lange*) signified the "untrustworthily-servile," is quite opposed to the *fidelity* universally imputed to them.

without further condition be disposed to let the sun of grace and truth shine upon all the evil: so that it is also a limitation of the law given in ch. v. 48. It is not for us, indeed, to do as men, what God in Christ has done. Luther, in answer to the warning—Give not that which is holy unto the dogs! cries out *Atque, O Domine, jam habent!* And Zinzendorf thinks that the Father in heaven has Himself given that which is holy to the dogs, and cast His pearls before swine, in surrendering His beloved Son into the hands of sinners. That is true, but thence came the world's redemption, and the sanctification of the Father's name through the determinate counsel of the highest wisdom. Therefore says also the Lord,—who exposed His own silent meekness to the contempt of the soldiers and His bitter cry to the scorn of the bands of the wicked,—*Ye* shall not do thus, for ye are not saviours of the world. But though in a certain sense the children of the world are dogs and swine, yet no man is to be given up by us, and cast out as reprobate: and it is, indeed, clear that they who sometimes fall under the application of this prohibition, yet may have the holy things offered them through the grace of God, and that we may be required to offer it to them, we who are never directed, in unconditional rejection of any fellow sinner, to retain *our* pearls merely for ourselves. Thus this prohibition touches rather the time and manner, than the testimony of the truth itself, which we are ever bound by obligation to all men to utter: the emphasis lies upon the inconsiderate, indiscriminate *giving* and *casting about* of these treasures, in such manner as itself to hinder their being accepted. But wherever we find susceptibility, our duty is to utter the "Peace be to this house!" (Matt. x.; Lu. x.). And at all times should we speak God's word, as sinners are able to hear it (Mark iv. 33), yea, our enforced silence bears in it a concealed love and mercy, of which in due time they may become sensible. That Pharisaical perversion of this word, which makes hypocrites keep the holy things so entirely holy and hidden, that there is no place in the wicked world, as they term it, and no time found for offering them to any, was at the utmost distance from our Lord's thoughts.

Have we been cast down by this paragraph (vers. 1—6), and driven almost to the anxious question: How shall we poor

Christians attain to such perfect humility and such prudent love, as to hit the precise and narrow way between the evil judging on the right and the squandering of blessings on the left, among our fellow-disciples and in the evil world; how may we, without exalting ourselves over our brethren, yet put them right, and while not provoking the dogs and the swine, yet take all stumbling blocks out of their way? The Lord answers the question with His never failing grace, and calls upon His disciples once more to *pray!* to petition! This is the open way to the goal of perfection, unbelief and lethargy in prayer the one only secret of our unperfectness. This gives a supplementary illustration of the sense and meaning of the prayer (ch. vi. 9—13); this gives the beginning of the discourse (ch. v. 3—6) its full explanation, and brings out in its clearest expression what was intimated there. *Persevering prayer* will assuredly conduct every one who has begun in sincerity, through this way of earnestness, to perfect righteousness and wisdom.[1] First, there is a general promise, which follows in strong contrast with the rigorous law, vers. 7, 8, (and, indeed, ver. 7 is *requirement* with promise, ver. 8 conversely is *promise* under the condition of the asking which is enjoined). Upon this we have, once more, just as vers. 3—5 followed upon vers. 1, 2, a *convincing analogy*, which, pointing to *our own love even while evil*, by the highest possible elevation of the argument forbids us to doubt the all-perfect Father's willingness to give, ver. 9—11. Who among you repels his asking child? How much more will the Father in heaven *hear prayer!* There is much that might be preached to the heart from this word of our Lord, so transparently clear in its overflowing grace and condescension, but there is little room for exposition to the understanding. We might, indeed, have said no more upon it, but that there is much misunderstanding which needs to be rectified, and the profound meaning of every one of the plainest sayings of the eternal word in this so entirely human discourse requires to be pointed out.

Ver. 7. Most sublime is the simplicity of this repeated—*Ask*,

[1] This is the profound *connexion* here, and it is the only one. *Alford* exhibits in a very strange way: that we should not be terrified as if God would keep back from us in our impurity and unworthiness His holy things, but should *ask* in full assurance.

(not like Jas. i. 8). *Whom* we are to ask is self-understood—Him, who knoweth all that we have need of (ch. vi. 32. 8). The Father in heaven is first mentioned at ver. 11. Neither do we hear at once *for what* we are to ask: that being obvious in itself—for the grace needful for righteousness, for the good gifts of the Holy Spirit (Lu. xi. 13), that we may attain to this humble, and prudent and sincere love. This great utterance was not given in the foregoing chapter, where the discourse was of *earthly* need, but was reserved for this place. It is understood, moreover, that having now received it, we may apply it in all its full universality (as Mar. xi. 24) with every other reference besides that which it has especially here: as for instance, in the case which we have before us, when we pray for those wicked men (ver. 6), to whom we are not able to give more than our prayer. The Lord gives a *threefold* encouragement and promise: there is the one general strong assurance first, and in the subsequent *seeking* and *knocking* there is no heterogeneous element introduced (as seeking in the Scriptures, &c.), for the similitude that follows unites them all in *asking* simply. The three expressions refer less to three distinct apprehensions of our general need (although that has its truth[1]), than to an *advancing*, *persevering* asking, which makes it a *labour*, to the process of the internal wrestling, comp. Ps. xxvii. 4, שָׁאַלְתִּי and אֲבַקֵּשׁ. The *seeking* points back to the ζητεῖν of ch. vi. 33, and reminds us of that fundamental promise to Israel: then shall ye find me, when ye seek me with all your hearts (Deut. iv. 29). The discourse has all its significance in the *seeking*, generally, in the seeking again of the highest good which was lost (as *Lange* says): as to the *opening* to those who knock, who seeking already have come *nigh*, we have it fully disclosed afterwards at ver. 14; and it is the appointed gate of life, the entrance into the kingdom of heaven, the strait gate that is referred to. Our Lord's teaching knows

[1] *Menken:* Ask, what ye need and have not: seek, that which is lost and hidden: knock, ye that are without. This last is scarcely expressed aright, for so viewed it should have been placed first. Somewhat better is that of the *Beuggener* Monatsblatt: He who has not, should ask: he who has had, but has lost again, should seek; he to whom the way out or in is shut up, should knock. But the *seeking* (ch. vi. 33) does not signify just what has been lost *again*.

nothing of that Quietest abandonment and stillness which finds rest in God before the time, without asking and seeking, as having already entered and no more needing to knock: the injunction to *ask* goes forth over all the way of life, unrelaxed and unceasing prayer is itself alone the way to that high end. The promise stands fast: Ask, and it *shall be given* you—though it be first but the impulse and power to inward *seeking!* Seek and ye shall *find*—first, it may be, only the strait gate to knock at!

Ver. 8. seems to be a repetition, but adds much to the strength. The πᾶς is designed to encounter the specific unbelief, by which men may except themselves and their own present prayer. It leads further to the following similitude, inasmuch as that is made to concern all men, even the wicked. Hence in St Luke ch. xi., it is placed between two parables, showing how importunate petition, and the prayer of children, avail *with men.* It is very needful that men should be exhorted to give to those who ask (ch. v. 42), they do not always do this: but in most cases the defect lies rather in the lack of persevering urgency in the *asking.* "Asking wins" is in things generally a proverb of encouragement to persist even among the children of men.

Vers. 9—11. *Or* is it not so? Is not that true? The same turn to the discourse as in ver. 4. Alas, proud men are not disposed to *ask* and ask much, in the full sense of what we mean by asking; but children, at least, feel not thus, the τέκνα of ver. 11, *they* ask. *What man* is there among you, who would not give to his son (or daughter) who asks him? that is, if there be such, he is not to be called man. With special graciousness does the Lord work out the moving similitude, but there is not a touch or a word, which is merely pictorial and without its spiritual meaning. *Bread* and *fish* are taken from the Galilean manner of life (Mar. viii. 6, 7; John xxi. 9). The bread is unconditionally necessary for their hunger, the fish is the additional good which the children's confidence asks. (In St Luke's repetition of this, Lu. xi., the children venture to go further, and would have an egg, as it were for gratification). Will the father, instead of bread, *reach out* (ἐπιδώσει, give away) a *useless* stone, similar in appearance but uneatable, or the *serpent,* resembling the fish, but hurtful? (Yet stronger in St Luke—instead of an egg, a scorpion!)

What man would thus bitterly and unfeelingly mock his asking children? Thus ye *know* how to give good gifts unto your children: οἴδατε, equivalent to—you have learned it from the instinct and impulse of nature, implanted in you by *God;* ye are *able* thus to treat them, comp. Phil. iv. 12. (Hence *Luther* has rightly translated here, as there, and also in Luke, simply: könnet). The ostrich, which is hardened against her young ones, as though they were not hers, is also without the wisdom of animal instinct (Job xxxix. 16, 17). There is more, however, in this, inasmuch as it contains the *transition* of the reference to God: Ye know how to distinguish good and evil for your children, so that you freely give, and indeed only *good* gifts, which only are truly *gifts*—how much more your Father in heaven! This has a deeper significance than might first appear. The not hearing, and not giving, might at first have seemed to be analogous to the offering stones and serpents: but now the *wisdom of God's love* does not always give that which is *asked*, for His foolish children often ask, in matters pertaining to the soul, what would be only the stone and the serpent—and should the Father answer such prayers? He no more does this than a father upon earth would in such a case, which is lightly hinted. He gives us always ἀγαθά, the true bread of the soul, the only wholesome food to accompany it; and were it to assume a form of scantiness, this must be steadfastly believed. He gives to *them that ask Him!* it does not stand in the words which would have corresponded —*to His children*, or *to you;* for His Father-love extends so far, that every one who prays to him is by that circumstance as a child in His regard. Consequently, from this there arises the great conclusion, the strong argument and assurance: He who thus gives, is *your* Father, and if *ye* ask Him, shall it be in vain?

But the inconceivably important ὑμεῖς πονηροὶ ὄντες comes into strong contrast with this address to the disciples as distinguished from others. The praying children of God are, as to their nature, placed among the ἄνθρωποι generally, and, in the midst of His most affectionate tenderness, He testifies to them, that they are in themselves *evil* and *niggardly* (for *good is communicative*), and thus that all natural goodness and love is only the contradiction which an equivocal instinct makes to the corruption of our ruined nature—and not geniune and pure love! Thus, as it was before said, our own *evil* love (which in children loves only our own flesh and blood), is merely a *figure*, which through the *antithesis* of *πόσῳ μᾶλλον* points to the pure love of God. Was it possible to bind together the testimony to God's mercy and the essential testimony to our own utter *corruption*, more expressly and emphatically than is here done? Thus does the Most Blessed, with all His grace, yet speak concerning *us men!* concerning our human father-and-mother love! This word cuts deep and inexorably into all the beautiful soft sentimentality which talks about "good men;" yea, this word appears to me the most rigorous *dictum probans* in all the Scripture,[1] for original sin; and, at the same time, one of the strongest testimonies to the superhuman dignity of our Lord, who, excepting himself from the whole race, can say to all mankind: *Ye* being evil! (Jno. viii. 23, 24).

From this point let a general view be taken of the manner in which the Person of the "Preacher on the Mount" exhibits itself and bears its own witness, in ever increasing majesty throughout the whole discourse, so that all that the Lord afterwards uttered concerning Himself (Matt. xi. 27, 28), and all that St John has recorded from His lips, seems already involved and asserted in this sermon. Its first words distribute blessedness, impart the kingdom of heaven. Who is He, that hath such authority? He says in ch. v. 11, *for my sake*, as quite one with—*for righteousness' sake.* He calls His disciples the light of the world, the salt of the earth,—what must He be, their Lord and Master! He begins in ver. 16 the oft-recurring: *your* Father in heaven but He avoids, here as well as throughout all His discourses in the Gospels, placing Himself by any Our in conjunction with them, before the Father. It is only—Pray *ye*—*Our* Father! He remains the only One who can, by His own high authority, give them this command. He is come, to *fulfil* all things:—

[1] And, indeed, as a matter of presupposition, and not now to be first asserted and maintained! (Comp. 1 Kings viii. 46). The same who were before directed to say *Our Father*, are in themselves evil children, though themselves fathers. *Chrysostom* in vain denies, that the Lord speaks this as *διαβάλλων τὴν ἀνθρωπίνην φύσιν, κακίζων τὸ γένος*, and in vain would merely understand it of the *ἀντιδιαστολὴ τῆς ἀγαθότητος* between us and God: for *πονηροί* admits of no *ἀγαθότης* at all.

He utters his testimony as no prophet had ever done before—*Verily, I say unto you:*—He knows what will take place till heaven and earth pass away, who shall enter the kingdom and who shall not, who shall be called great or small therein:—He opposes His own *But I say unto you*, to every other saying:—He knows the entrances to hell, and the laws of the everlasting prison house:—He lays down requirements which enter the heart, and go far beyond man's ability whether to do or to bear, while He gives corresponding promises of grace from His Father in heaven, which embrace the whole heart and the whole life, all time and all eternity. He gives (ch. vii. 7) full assurance of the answer of every prayer;—remains, while among men in most gracious condescension, alone, above, and apart from the whole of humanity, being evil;—testifies, as if He saw at one glance the whole of mankind as viewed by God, how *many* are in the way of perdition, how *few* are in the way of salvation;—He arrogates, finally, to Himself the right to receive the name of *Lord* from men, and presents Himself as the *judge of all the world* at last; who will *at that day* utter the words of final decision for eternity, even as He now utters His present words that, hearing and doing them, men may not fall into fearful, irreparable ruin! O ye Rationalists, who take so much complacency in the morality of the Sermon on the Mount, *hear* and appreciate its Dogmatic teaching too!

Or will ye have nothing but its pure *ethics*? Then here you have it at once *in nuce* (ver. 12.) It appears a very simple saying, and yet the Lord cries: *This is the Law and the Prophets!* But the same Lord requires also hearing *and doing* for this His so ethical, so intelligible saying. Be it so—*do* ye it in very deed? Oh beware, ye false prophets, of the false prophet in your own evil hearts, of the arch-liar, who beguiles you into the deluding supposition that you do this, that you can do it—without *Christ*, without the righteousness of God, which comes through faith in Jesus Christ, as it was before testified by the Law and the Prophets. The Lord places this great requirement, so well understood by all, yet only through Him by any to be fulfilled, between that one word—*Ye men being evil*, and that other—Here is the *strait* gate, the *narrow* way; for this all asking, seeking, knocking avails!

This is, as we may see, the distinctive and comprehensive final expression of the *law of Christ,* which perfect love imposes upon us, who even in our love are evil (in our love as parents, ver. 11, as brothers, and as enemies, ch. v. 46, 47); but only through the life-giving grace which is both promised and imparted. This is the concluding requirement at the close of the whole great section of the *requirements: Walk in this way towards this end,* the only way, narrow but sure! The goal (ver. 12), the way thereto (ver. 13, 14). The Lord here lays down in the simplest manner the *substance*[1] of the law of perfectness in regard to our neighbour: for it is only another expression of the Mosaic command—to love thy neighbour *as thyself*—passing from the *love* itself to the confirmation and approval of it in *deed.* It embraces in one the whole second table of the Decalogue (as that from which all the rest proceeded, ch. v. 21); in the same manner ch. vi. 33 embraces the first table; and ch. v. 48, both in their central unity. It is uttered with respect to the outer and the inner life (for, as we saw in ch vi. 1, the Lord accounts no doing of the law as genuine but that which is internal), for the greatest and the slightest cases in which the general law becomes a specific commandment. It refers to our *own self-loving sense of duty,* in which that which is most difficult to do is yet easily seen to be right. It is the expression of the *third fundamental law,* which points us, and urges us to that *self-denial* which can only be attained through the grace of God, to the deliverance from that internal, deep-rooted *self-contradiction of evil human nature* which would desire from others what to others we deny. (See Lev. xix. 18, in its connexion with this). And it is just at this point that the great—Enter ye in! (ver. 13), is attached, embracing the promise of the opening of the gate, nay, the assurance that it is already opened. And immediately upon this, as the ground of that solemn and simple sentence which had just been uttered: *for* there is no other gate, no other way, all beside this is the broad way which leadeth to the wide gate of *destruction!* (vers. 13, 14) which immediately paves the way to the remaining *third main division*

[1] The particle οὖν, on which much exposition has been expended, is just the indication of the result of all, summing up all that had gone before. In this sense it does not merely connect the sentence which it begins with the immediately preceding, but takes a sweeping retrospect of the whole.

of the Sermon, which draws the final limits between the good and bad, setting forth the great tests and separation at the end of all.

Ver. 12. Is this any thing *new*, to *teach* which as a higher and more perfect morality, the Lord must come down from heaven? By no means, rather is it the primitive commandment, extant among all nations, by which every man who sincerely looks within his own soul, must utter his own condemnation. It is found in the Talmud: for example Rabbi *Hillel* thus speaks to one who would become a proselyte: "Whatsoever is hateful to thyself, that do not to thy neighbour: in this is the whole law, all else only comes out of this. Go and be perfect." We find it in Sirach: *Νόει τὰ τοῦ πλησίον ἐκ σεαυτοῦ, καὶ ἐπὶ παντὶ πράγματι διανοοῦ* (Ecclus. xxxi. 15), and in Tobit: *ὃ μισεῖς μηδενὶ ποίησῃς* (ch. iv. 15). In *Isocrates* we find: *ἃ πάσχοντες ὑφ' ἑτέρων ὀργίζεσθε, ταῦτα τοῖς ἄλλοις μὴ ποιεῖτε.* But the tendency of our *selfishness* to extract the keen severity from the testimony which it is constrained to bear against itself, is betrayed in this, that in nearly all cases the negative only is seized: what thou wouldst *not* have thyself, do not thou to thy neighbour! The Lord on the contrary fetches it up from the depths of conscience as an inexorably *positive* demand: "*Whatsoever* ye would that men should do to you, *do* ye also to them"—as unlimited a requirement, therefore, as the will and the desire of self-love itself. We said rightly: our own self-loving feeling of duty—although this is just as much a *contradictio in adjecto*, as our own love, being evil, in ver. 11 was. It is, as it were, the theoretical and practical side of that self-contradiction, which is our natural condition. With strict propriety has *Luther* said: "Here Christ lays the Bible upon thine own bosom, and so clearly, moreover, that thou needest no gloss." But to how many limiting, *apologetic* glosses and imaginations has natural conscience resorted, to silence, in unrighteousness and self-delusion, the great *accusing* gloss: I am not thus! I cannot do this! Selfishness perverts the relation between me and my neighbour, so that, notwithstanding all, the most-loved *I* comes before and comes after my neighbour, and remains above him. Why am I to do good to my neighbour? That he may do me good in return—this clings to the evil heart. So runs the common proverb: First comes myself, then my neighbour, then myself again—which is being interpreted—by my neighbour I mean only myself. The Lord refers not to this perversion, but to the great truth that lies at its foundation. He goes back to the Mosaic כָּמוֹךָ, *as thyself*, in unconditional equality without any before and after: confirmed as it was by an אֲנִי יְהוָה, for in the sight of God no *self* of the creature can have place.

The Lord's meaning is not that which a superficial misapprehension of His keenly penetrating rule would make it—as if He only spake "of the external, material, obvious actions of life," and consequently "had not in His purpose to set up a principle of morality." *(Neander)*. The Lord, in all that he lays down, will be understood according to the internal principle, and never gives "external tests, merely, of character and life." He neither acknowledges nor alludes to any other act than that which is truly such, springing from the heart. It is His aim, that the consciousness of equality and of mutual need (as *Braune* better says, though without fully reaching its depth of meaning) should exhort and urge us to the practical love of our neighbour.

In this *πάντα ὅσα ἂν* is included and summed up with most significant definiteness every individual case that could prompt the question: What is here my duty to my neighbour? It is this—let the relative position be changed, conceive thyself in his place, and he in thine! That fellow-feeling and sympathy which naturally is excited by the sight of another's sorrow, which may be almost called the conscience of our physical nature, will show me the way, as it makes me feel as if I were in his place. Then do to him, what thou wouldest desire him to do to you, were you in his case? But who is there who does not stand mid-way, instead of going the whole way and entering through the door —*who doeth this?* Who doeth it *before God*, as the genuine and true acting of love, which would do no ill to his neighbour, nay, not by the omission of any good that he might and ought to render him? He who *thus loves*, has fulfilled *the Law*, the whole Law, for the fulfilment of the second table is only possible through the fulfilment of the first—who can love independently of the love of God? The commandment requires *love* out of a pure heart, a pure heart comes only through a good conscience, and a good conscience only through a faith unfeigned—in the fulfilling grace of the great fulfiller in us (1 Tim. i. 5). Hence the Lord does not merely say: This is *the Law* (of both tables)—but in addition: *and the Prophets!* In the same sense, that is, as ch. xxii. 40. For he means to tell us that all the preparatory, prophetic Scripture which pointed to *Him* who was to come, took its rise from the requirement of the Law, and is one with it: He refers back to ch. v. 17, and all which that word disclosed to us; His design is that we should now at the close connect with it the beginning and understand: this is the Law and the Prophets, *to fulfil which* in your righteousness, *I am come.*

Vers. 13, 14. By a false disposition these verses are generally placed at the beginning of the subsequent paragraph; whereas they only form a transition to it, and are in themselves most distinctively a *conclusion*, which plainly enough refers to the parallel conclusion of the first division (ch. v. 20). Now is that righteousness, which must be better than the Pharisees', exhibited; now it is said, receive it, that is, seek for it in prayer with full earnestness of spirit, and *thus enter into* the kingdom of heaven! Through the *strait gate?* Yes verily, for your *knowing* all that is in ver. 12 will avail nothing; that *I point it out* to you and *teach* you will avail nothing; but your own prayer and your own laying hold must proceed from self-denial to self-denial, until the whole of perfect righteousness is established within you.

How then are the *way* and the *gate* related to each other in the following discourse? The late von Meyer thought this an idle question, inasmuch as the figures are here not connected with each other, but *parallel:* I cannot, however, agree with him. It is an error all but universal to understand the Lord, because the strait gate emphatically stands first, as having placed a *strait gate* of conversion, or however else it may be expressed, to be pressed through *before* the way is entered on. Thus do most preachers apply the spirit of the text. But this entirely contradicts the simple character of the figure, the connexion of the whole sermon, and much other illustration of the Lord's own meaning. *Doors* lead not to *ways,*[1] but a way leads to the gate of the town or the house whither I would go: when I reach the

[1] As we see it figured, unnaturally enough, in old books of devotion.

gate I am at the end of the way.[1] If I have entered through the gate, my point is gained definitively, I am either in security, peace, and joy, or—in the prison of eternal ruin. The narrow way is that which the whole sermon has pointed out, the *gate*, or the door (for πύλη is a general expression, which includes, as here, the widest gate and the straitest postern) is no other than the entrance into the kingdom of heaven, which as the close and crown of all their struggles and endeavours, is thrown open to those who knock; see vers. 7, 21 ; ch. v. 20. Thus does the Lord explain Himself. (Lu. xiii. 24, 25.) So also He speaks again of the needle's eye (Matt. xix. 24). In the preliminary εἰσέλθετε the Redeemer has certainly *brought near* to us the gate, as if it were directly before us, but only in the same sense as the future kingdom of heaven is come nigh to us, in the same sense as we now continually stand knocking at the gate of heaven, as we are now already *saved* through the asking and receiving of prayer, which brings heaven into the heart. The Lord, to be more particular, includes in His invitations the way and the gate in one; since the way is already the gate to those who, walking in that way, are sure to reach that gate. When He would summon us to walk in the right way, He prefers at once to take His language from the decisive goal to which it leads: *Enter ye in!* For all our walking in the way is but the beginning of our final entrance. And in this lies the truth, and the justification of our customary way of speaking about the strait gate. It would be even exegetically right, if it were simply derived from the first part of the verse, and confined to it: but if the remainder is thus read, and the gate is placed *before* the way, it is at least exegetically incorrect, and would be inapplicable in speaking and preaching about the inner life. This exegetical error, alas! may become the occasion of much misapprehension of the plan of salvation, both in theory and in practice. The Lord acknowledges those who are entering, who are struggling to enter, but none as having entered till the end comes. And what then would become of

[1] Thus quite appropriately in the passage of *Cebes* (quoted also by *Olshausen)* : θύραν τινὰ μικρὰν καὶ ὁδόν τινὰ πρὸ τῆς θύρας. *Lange's* reason for placing the gate first, that the fundamental idea is that of a *departure* from a city, of decision in the choice of the right way, is quite opposed to the letter of the text, which rather speaks of an *entrance*, and of a way leading to *this*.

the *wide gate*, through which the children of the world would have *already* entered: since *in their case* there is no distinctive beginning or passing through a gate, no passing out from any state whatever into the broad way, in which by nature and by their birth they walk. Rather is the wide gate the gaping pit of hell, opening her mouth without measure (Isa. v. 14; Hab. ii. 5; Prov. xxx. 15, 16)—into which men walk, and dance and stagger and fall by crowds.

The Lord lays down the eternally decisive alternative and contrast—damnation or rather *destruction* and *life*: this great antithesis, and the others connected with it—wide and broad, strait and narrow, many and few;—He further strengthens the whole, however, by the words which we must not overlook: many there be which *go in thereat*, few there be that *find it*. Εἰσερχόμενοι δι' αὐτῆς—it may be asked, whether ὁδοῦ or πύλης be signified. Obviously and primarily we are to understand as the word itself and the previous εἰσέλθετε show—who go through the wide gate into hell: yet *Luther* has understood it of the way thither, and rightly so far as the Lord includes this likewise. The ambiguous δι' αὐτῆς most significantly confirms the view we have given above. The Lord's glance beholds the way and its termination as inseparable, and the many who walk in the broad way, He warningly and lamentingly describes as *entering in* to destruction! This "going in thereat" is sorrowfully, catachrestically spoken: as if they were entering into their own eternal house, instead of entering into life! (which is lost in *Luther's* text). To this is opposed in solemn tone of exhortation the εὑρίσκοντες, for to this *seeking* is first of all needful. The broad way to the wide gate no man needs to seek; it is broad as the world (εὐρύχωρος marks rather a great country than a way); thou standest and walkest upon it already, thou canst not fail, swim only with the current, live only according to thy inherited custom and after the impulse of thine own nature, the gate of hell will then receive thee, to which all ways converge as if one single broad way by the side of the one only narrow way. But this narrow way and this strait gate must be perseveringly sought, till it is *found throughout and to the end*. It is "a mountain-path, narrow, insignificant, and not obvious to the eye." (*Tholuck*). Few there be that attain to its end, for even to those who are seeking to pursue it there are by-ways issuing from it to the right and to the left (Isa. xxx. 21; Deut. v. 32), and many who have come near to the gate, fail of it at last! (Lu. xiii. 24). What the Lord here says of the many and the few, is similar to Matt. xx. 16; xxii. 14. Only the *doing* of the Divine will leadeth unto *life* (afterwards ver. 21); for the word of Moses (Lev. xviii. 5) still holds good, and the grace of our Lord establishes and fulfils it in us. *Life* and *destruction* are set before us. Who regards the way, its agreeableness or its difficulty, when his eye is on the goal? Who would be guided by the *number* of those who walk in any way, instead of thinking *whither* they tend, and whither himself? The foolish world, indeed, "loves the wide, and the broad, and the numbers"—delights in the majorities! But who ordinarily investigates the door, its width or its straitness, instead of the place *to which* the door conducts him who enters? Look only at the goal and the end! This is the emphasis of the twice-repeated ἡ ὁδὸς ἡ ἀπάγουσα, instead of which *Luther* has constructed another antithesis which is not in the words: the one *leading away* to destruction, the other *leading* to life. Could the Lord then have meant to speak of a *leading away* into life, (conversely as entering *into* destruction), and how might that be taken? It would be hard to find a meaning: we should have to understand it as leading away from all need, from all evil and danger and temptation into perfect security: as in the other case from all pleasure and security into everlasting torment. But then the emphasis is alike in both, and it simply denotes the *eternal decision*, the sure result. *Bengel* seizes the meaning exactly in his pregnant—*ἀπάγουσα, ex hac brevi vitâ!* Then there is no middle-path, thus there is an irrevocable and fixed alternative! *Tholuck* seeks in one of his sermons over-critically to soften this: as if the Lord says nothing of the eternal fall of these many, but speaks now only of their *present walking* in the wicked way that leads to it—many of them might yet turn aside from it. Assuredly they *might*, but the ἀπάγειν signifies the completed result, the εἰσερχέσθαι is not their present *walking*, according to the weakening translation of the German Bible.

We have now to give our view of the remarkable reading: *Τί στενή, how strait* is the gate! for which certainly the external evidence of manuscripts is favourable, whence even *von Gerlach* declares it the true reading. We cannot, however, agree with this : and if *Tholuck* with a delicate and true perception says that "wherefore so strait ?" would be a human, sentimental pathos which does not accord with the whole discourse ; we also say the same of the wondering appeal—O how strait ! The Lord is here speaking in a tone of simple assertion and keen testimony ; the τί by no means suits that tone, and must have originated from the transcribers, who understood not the point of the second striking ὅτι. This is justified by internal criticism, but what is the meaning of the expression as here used ? We should expect a simple "and" of contrast, as *Luther* has translated it ; at furthest a "but" or "on the other hand." Yet ὅτι can be made to mean none of these, by any art. We understand it that the Lord has the former injunction—Enter ye in through the strait gate ! still in His thought, and connects with that the two sentences which follow, as if it had been in each case repeated—"*Enter ye in ! for* wide is the gate— ! (once again : *Enter ye in !* being understood), *For* strait is the gate— !

And yet it is and must ever be a *gate*, which is not shut, but stands open and wide enough for ever for those who would enter it by the right way. "The narrow way to life is broad enough, for men who carefully, gently, evenly walk in it." That is the *consolation*, which even this rigorous saying contains. What more is wanting than a way wherein I may have room, and a gate that will let me through ? To this end the Lord stands in fulness of truth and grace, calling and inviting us with all earnestness : *Enter ye in !* meets us, as it were, with "enter in" before we knock,—prays us that we ask,—commands us to seek, encourages us Himself that we may knock ! Connect with this His other great word : I am the way ! I am the door ! and thou shalt in thy experience learn to unite Matt. vii. 13, 14, with ch. xi. 28—30, and find that both are truth, that both sayings are essentially one in His meaning.

The *requirements* which are enjoined upon us, on the foundation of a promised grace, are now ended, being condensed into that one appeal : *Enter ye in !* This speaks as encouragingly and graciously of a free admission, as its appended statement speaks severely of all that belongs to the *successful prosecution of the way till the final entrance.* It is through the *strait* gate, the straitness of which is previously proclaimed in the narrowness of the way that leads thereto. Its meaning is just what a later explanation of it says: ἀγωνίζεσθε εἰσελθεῖν (Lu. xiii.)—addressed to those *especially* who already walk in this way, to the disciples, who would be and who may be perfect. Whether they shall *find* the way directly to the gate, the "few there be" makes matter of solemn thought. This of itself is a warning appeal: Beware! and thus the discourse passes over to its conclusion, showing the dangers of the way external to ourselves, and lifting the curtain from before the final judgment-seat.

The *third division* of the Sermon, as it was defined in the distribution which we made at the outset, may not appear to correspond immediately with our preconceived expectations of what it would be; yet will it exhibit itself to a closer observation as quite consonant with the nature of things, and the whole course of thought throughout. Its beginning seems to fly off abruptly from the subject which had been treated, the way, namely, of a progressive advancement towards the goal: but it is not so. For just because at the close of the whole of the *Requirements*, the "Enter ye in!" had been so closely connected with a strait gate, and the bye-ways to right and left of inward unholiness which leave the narrow way, had been so fully and clearly disclosed: on that account the section of *warning* was not required to make any distinctive and express reference *to the internal state*. But this did not render unnecessary a glance at the dangers of the way which rise from without, through the false teaching and guidance of a specious deceit. Thus the *introductory* warning against *false prophets*, is first introduced strictly in its right place (vers. 15—20); with which, nothing now being withheld that is requisite for distinguishing the right way, the discourse has free scope to pass on to the remaining fundamental *warning* (vers. 21—23) of the final judgment, in which no evil doer will be able to stand. We are wont to preach about the false prophets in ourselves, and that application is indeed permitted, yet it wrenches the passage from its place in this connexion. The Lord simply means such *prophets* as are the opposites of those mentioned in the beginning, ch. v. 12, (and again v. 17, vii. 12), so that the beginning and the end agree in one. According to St Luke He had previously cast a side-glance upon the *false* prophets. The reference in the discourse *to ourselves* is to be sought not in this, but in something else, namely, in the specification of the *fruits* as marks, not merely of the office of prophet, but as the judgment-day presently shows, of *discipleship* generally. It is a perversion of the sense to regard these fruits, as is commonly done, as the proofs by which true guides must legitimate their claims: the *fruits* are, as the reference to the Baptist's words in ver. 19 shows, no other than what the common usage of the Old and New Testament understands by them. In the whole section vers. 17—20 those fruits, by which the Lord will distinguish His own, are *at the same time* demanded of all his disciples, and, as befits the tone of this concluding division, with all severity; though the first tone of *promise* is once more gently heard in the reference to the good tree which bears those fruits—a tree planted in us by the grace of God. Whereupon, secondly, in ver. 21, *the doing of the will of God* is *required* of us in the final utterance of law: and finally at the minatory conclusion the *warning* against not doing it is heard in the last stern tones of all. Thus we find that the fundamental principle of trichotomy as we laid it down at the beginning is preserved and justified down to the end.

We subdivide vers. 15—20 thus: 1. The simple appeal—Beware of false prophets! 2. The detecting reference to the contradiction between appearance and reality: Wolves in sheep's clothing! 3. The laying down of a *mark* to distinguish them, which, however, is and can be no other than the *same* which will avail *us* now and ever before the Lord:—the fruits of righteousness, the fulfilling of all the commandments from that new nature which grace creates in us. Let it be observed how that which is here said was foreshadowed in ch. v. 19. This further resolves itself into, *(a)*, The general position: the tree is known by its fruit, put in ver. 16 in a convincing manner in a double-similitude of natural and Scriptural symbolism. *(b)*, An emphatic *repetition* of this, which however in its generality now includes the disciples generally, and the key-note of *promise* is heard in the "good tree." The good and the corrupt tree are contrasted: twice positively (ver. 17), twice negatively (ver. 18). Conclusion of both: the corrupt tree is cast into the fire! (ver 19), which directly leads over to the *judgment* which follows—yet to complete the organization of the discourse, first *(c)* we have *once more the truth repeated*: Wherefore by their fruits ye shall know them? (ver. 20). That is, at the same time, according to the intimation that lies in the words (in accordance with the πᾶν of vers. 17 and 19): By their fruits will *ye* be known, even as ye know others. This is the *verification* of discipleship before *men* in the time of *the present life* (the shining before men, ch. v. 14, 16); and with it the transition is strikingly made to the impressive sequel.

Vers. 21, 23. The approval of their discipleship in the presence of God in eternity now follows, or rather *on that day*, which divides time from eternity, and the days of grace in the way from the goal of eternal decision and doom—*the judgment.* And now we find not —before God, but before *Me*, the Lord, the Judge! Not—your Father will know you and receive you—but: I! The same who at ver. 11 excepted Himself alone from the whole evil race, now in language, simple and sublime, presents Himself as *the Judge* at the end of the way, even as He now exhibits Himself as the *Lawgiver* in the way. Presumption, if He also belonged to the men who are evil and to the corrupt trees: quite natural and necessary, however, to this testimony of truth, from Him who may speak to us from the Judgment-seat and say (as it now *for the first time* breaks forth in majesty)—*My* Father—as the eternal Son, the *Lord*. All this is but the consummation of what had been prepared for in ch. v. 22, 25, and still earlier in ver. 20. He determines now, for the first time, who shall enter into the kingdom of heaven, and who be cast into the prison. The end goes back to the beginning: the whole Sermon is a building, of which every stone, from the first to the last, is laid in its place according to a pre-arranged and wonderful order. It says already, as the beginning of sermons, what every other discourse proclaimed—*I am He!* for the conviction and assurance of every one who hath ears to hear, though without specifically and in so many words proclaiming it.

His words are now more closely compressed, as their force becomes more solemn. They lay down *three* positions. The *first* (ver. 21), begins gently with the mere "not every one," and mentions, affirmatively and with a tone of promise pervading this *last* requirement, the "doing of the will" as the sure and certain way into the kingdom of heaven. In this is embraced, as in the *most simple possible* compendium, the whole middle division of the Sermon, from its preface (ch. v. 20) down to its close (ch. vii. 14): particularly the three critical precepts (ch. v. 48, vi. 33, vii. 12) as they are condensed in that central *petition* of ch. vi. 10. The *second* sentence (ver. 22) strengthens the negative "not every one" by a threatening "many": the third (ver. 23), is the inexorable conclusion: *Depart from me!* although the "then" leaves us a period of grace for the doing of those sayings, which we now *hear* from the lips of the Lawgiver who came to fulfil them, and will come again to be our Judge. Thus—He who hath ears to hear, let him hear! Let him who is a hearer, be also a doer of the work! (John vii. 16, 17).

Then ends the mighty Sermon with a cry of *most direct and urgent warning,* with ἐξουσία seizing the heart and conscience before the judgment-seat of God: *whosoever* heareth *these sayings of mine* and doeth them not, is a *foolish man,* has his own destruction to impute to himself, because he has not received and applied my gracious—enter ye in! my faithful—beware! It is in gracious condescension from its highest dignity, a *winning* tone being mingled with the *threatening,* that even such a conclusion as this takes the form once more of a popular *similitude,* the balanced and contrasted members of which bring directly home to us the great alternative of everlasting decision, exhibiting the final judgment in warning preparatory judgments, and the test of the last day in manifold tests, which are applied upon earth, and within the day of grace. For *this* alone is the true meaning of the figure (vers. 24—27), which generally and indefinitely comprehends in one the approval of the house (before exhibited) *in time and in eternity*: in strict conformity with the Apostle's meaning—*the day* shall declare it, time present and future (1 Cor. iii. 13). In many cases the morrow, but in every case the last day! The reference to the *wise* man who built securely, comes graciously first: although no longer (for every turn of the word and thought is significantly adjusted) in the form of an express appeal and injunction, but with a decisive—*Whosoever* thus heareth and doeth! The last appeal to the warned occurred at vers. 15 and 20, but in ver. 21 the warning and threatening remains only in the third person, just as the discourse, in its great promise, had commenced (ch. v. 2—20). The fearful fall (ver. 27), preaches *condemnation* at the close, as blessedness had been announced in the beginning.

Let the process of our Saviour's preaching and teaching according to the Evangelists be compared with the process of the Sermon on the Mount: and the procedure which is marked out here, will as a whole be found reproduced throughout. We refrain from referring this to the details, and will only exhibit the analogy, as it is strikingly shown with respect to the conclusion. The warning against *false prophets* recurs at the end of His ministry for His disciples and the people, in Matt. xxiii. (comp. Lu. xx. 46), for His disciples particularly in Matt. xxiv., as also at the close of the New Testament, in the epistles of Peter, Jude, and John. The *fruits* are demanded at last (an evidence this, also, of the soundness of our exposition here) in Matt. xxi. 34 ; Jno. xv. The *judgment*, the rejection and casting out, is threatened in all the final parables to the disciples which we know of, in the last discourse to the people (Matt. xxv.), as in the Apocalypse we find it closing the whole New Testament. The reference to the word of the future Judge, *heard in order to be done*, is found also in Jno. xii. 47—50; compare for the disciples particularly Jno. xiii. 17, and the final *conclusion of the whole Bible*, Rev. xxii. 6—21.

Ver. 15. The Lord here bears witness to *Himself* as the true *Prophet*, who should come into the world (Jno. vi. 14 ; 1 Macc. xiv. 41, προφήτης πιστός) : the whole series of heralds and witnesses of God from the first prophecy of Moses downwards, converging into the one, last, perfect utterance of God's will, through Him whose prerogative it is to say "My Father," and concerning whom the Father responds—*Him shall ye hear!* even as Moses in the beginning had testified (Deut. xviii. 15). *Hear*, and bear well in mind, what I now say unto you : after me will *many other voices* speak to you, beware of them all. In this lofty generality His warning is to be understood ; and what the Lord declares for the hearing of all ages, must not be shrivelled into a narrower application to this or that emergency, to any present or following time. It is altogether the same as if he had now also said—All who come besides me, not genuinely in my name, all who shall teach anything other than *I say to you*—are thieves and robbers, whom the sheep may not hear! (Jno. x. 8). As comprehensive as was the word in ch. v. 12, concerning the true prophets of former ages, is the contrast to them in this passage—as universal as that contrast had been already exhibited by the Lord Himself in Lu. vi. 26—with this let Matt. x. 41, xxiii : 34 be also compared. For the sake of the people and the disciples, who then heard him, the scribes of ch. v. 19, 20; Lu. xx. 46, are first of all intended; but then all are included, against whom Matt. xxiv. lifts up a warning voice, from the last days of Israel to the end of time. It may be taken in connexion with the words which had just preceded; and they are then false *guides*. This must not, however, be restricted by a one-sided limitation to those who would make the narrow way *broader* to you: for there are false guides who would make the narrow way, apparently at least, narrower than the Lord has made it.[1] They *come* to you—there is a slight contrast hinted in this: they come though they are not *sent*, by their own authority; thus pointing to such ancient warnings as Jer. xiv. 14, xxiii; Ezek. xxxiv. God sends them not, but He permits them to come, for the trial and confirmation of his people (1 Cor. xi. 19; Deut. xiii. 1—4).

What then is the *sheep's clothing;* does the genitive προβάτων mean—with ἐνδύμασι: clothed *like sheep*, as if they were sheep,—or—with sheep skins? Men contend about this with idle pains, for both are one and the same: and the word is chosen for its twofold reference. It is at once, assuredly, clear from the simple tone of the words (especially with reference to the Old Testament warnings against false pastors and prophets which is connected with the discourse), that it should mean :—they demean themselves as guides and shepherds, going before you as if themselves belonging to the flock, but it is only a counterfeit and mask, for they are not sheep as ye are, to whom they come. In this we have a prelude to what is more strongly expressed soon after in ch x. 16 : it is an early note of our Lord's manner of describing His own as His sheep, as it appears in St John : a usage which is rooted also in St Matthew, as we see in

[1] Indeed only *apparently*—for the heaviest yoke of human imposition is always lighter to us and more agreeable, than the true and narrow way.

such sayings, derived from prophetic style of language, as ix. 36, x. 6—and in the shepherd-similitudes (ch. xviii. 12, xxv. 32, 33). But this alone does not exhaust the expression as used *here:* for these first hearers were not sufficiently prepared for this view, and there was yet needed some intermediate point of connexion. This lies certainly in the ἐνδύμασι, which to Israelitish ears would immediately carry a reference to the *prophet-costume*, known to all of them, in their proverbial language, and of late brought before their very eyes by John the Baptist. That this included also sheepskins, μηλωτάς, we are taught by Heb. xi. 37; comp. 1 Kings xix. 13—19 Sept. If it is asked, whether the sheepskins and goatskins, the rough leathern garments (שֵׂעָר 2 Kings i. 8) of the prophets, were the symbol of innocence and the natural character of sheep, we answer by again asking—may not the Lord give the figure this application, and extend it from its historical use so far? His word is certainly directed to this point that the prophet's garment is made a pledge and pretence of an honest design, and thus their lie is cloked under the appearance of truth and sincerity: just as the prophet has it (Zech. xiii. 4). We thus see that the Lord comprehends in their inner unity the symbolism of nature and the Bible, combines the Old Testament phraseology (even the Rabbinical which sprung from it) with the well-understood usage of the Gentiles, so that His words are equally intelligible to the Scribes in Israel and to all people who dwell upon the earth even to the distant אִיֵּי הַגּוֹיִם. The Æsopic wolf in sheep's clothing, and the Jewish perverter in the garb of a prophet, are united in one similitude which comprehends the idea of both, and combines what had been true as a historical fact with the common truth of nature. The ἅρπαγες added to λύκοι does not merely strengthen the figure, but makes emphatically prominent the destruction and ruin of the poor, deluded ones; as subsequently in Jno. x. 10—12, and again by the Apostle (not without reference to our Lord's word) Acts xx. 29. How, then, shall we strictly define the *sheep's clothing?* A *fair show* generally, as far as it is a mere ἔνδυμα striking the eye of those who are said ἔσωθεν εἶναι: then, further, it includes on the one hand the specious *discourses* (πιθανολογία, Col. ii. 4; κενοὶ λόγοι, Eph. v. 6; χρηστολογία καὶ εὐλογία, Rom.

xvi. 18) of an attractive doctrine and counterfeit orthodoxy, and, on the other, the simulated *walk* of a righteous and devout spirit, μόρφωσις εὐσεβείας (2 Tim. iii. 5). Although in the latter case the deficiency of the δύναμις is perceived by those who look searchingly, and it is scarcely possible (as Nitzsch preaches) to counterfeit the stamp of godliness to the eye of those who are well-grounded in the experiences of Christian self-denial. As manifold as is the form which their hypocrisy assumes, so comprehensive is the Lord's meaning with regard to them. It must be observed, however, that what it is attempted to impose as pure and true doctrine, must bring with it also false doctrine and error, else how were they *false prophets?* And further, that what appears to be a righteous and blameless life, can be no genuine fruit of righteousness, else how could the Lord have specified fruits as the tokens by which they should be known? With the most perfect propriety of truth, He places *fruits* in opposition both to the word and the work of these hypocrites.

Vers. 16, 17. Once more a universally appreciable natural emblem, which at the same time finds its deep significance in the symbolism of Scripture: for the Bible explains to us from its rudiments the book of creation. (St James cites once more the Sermon on the Mount in ch. iii. 12). The fig tree and the vine, the noble productions of the holy land, the vine, indeed, the noblest of all lands generally, are in the language of the prophets, the emblem of Israel: thorns and thistles indicate (rather under a theological than a physical presentation) the weeds of sin which have sprung from the curse, as may be seen particularly in 2 Sam. xxiii. 6; Mic. vii. 4. What, then, are the figs and grapes, the good fruits? As far as the reference is here especially to the prophets, certainly *not* pure doctrine simply as such, as an exposition would maintain which springs, however unconsciously, from an evil principle: for that would contradict the whole consistent usage of the Scripture when speaking of fruits, and especially the words of the Baptist, to which the Lord here refers, and which must have occurred to the minds of all His hearers upon the Mount. If appeal is made to the context and connexion of Matt. xii. 33, 34, with equal appropriateness at least may we refer to the disavowal of the mere *saying*, Lord, Lord, afterwards in this same discourse (ver. 22). *Confession* alone, *doctrine* however pure, is by no means a decisive mark, may be no more than a hypocritical pretension, which itself must be brought to the test. Still less may we, further, limit the words, as has been done, to the fruit which the false teachers may produce *in their disciples:* look well, what kind of people they create out of their adherents! Although this view is not altogether excluded, as in Jno. xv., among the much fruit of the disciples, their so-called ministerial fruit must be included with the rest. But still this refers to the teachers and guides themselves: they cannot make their disciples what they are not themselves. Thus is it the *life* of these prophets, by which we are to take knowledge of them? Certainly mainly this: for while they for the most part speak fairly, their error is manifest enough in their life; their sheep's-clothing is mostly woven of *words*. Yet there are, again, though not in such numbers, deceivers of an opposite kind, who come the more boldly, the more they appear to be authenticated by the well-ordered, decorous, resplendent character of their deportment. Hence the Lord's words must be rightly understood, as fastening upon these likewise: we are not to look only at the *superficial* cast of their words and works, their walk and their teaching, which is far from a sufficient test, but *we are to learn by it to distinguish*, what are *genuine* grapes and figs, from the thorn sloes and thistle-heads which might, whether nigh at hand or far off, be mistaken for them. This is the inmost point in the meaning of the Lord's words, this is the only true sense of the καρποί, in which He by no means lays down a merely preparatory, external test, while St John afterwards goes deeper into the matter (1 Jno. iv. 1—3);[1] for though St John refers there to a fundamentally sound doctrine, yet this note itself requires, in order to its not deceiving, the complement to it which is here given: *Fruits* and *work* decide alone at last unerringly.[2] But

[1] So *Olshausen* in his frequent overbold manner!

[2] In which we are not misled by the strange assertions of *Löhe* (von der Kirche S. 93) who, relying on Lu. vi. 45, would actually have all otherwise illusory holiness of life tested by doctrine and confession alone. A sad misunderstanding, exposed to yet sadder abuse! If possible stranger yet is the well-intentioned explanation of the Beuggener Monatsblatt—that the fruits are the aim and tendency of their actions, since we have regard to the fruit in the planting of a tree. Who can discern *that*, and use it as a test?

let this be rightly understood! The question might be put in reply: But, O Lord, thou who speakest of fruits, how should we then distinguish the fruits, the true and the genuine, such as Thou callest such, and as will avail before Thee? For there is many a vine of Sodom, which produces its grapes and wine, but gall and poison are therein (Deut. xxxii. 32, 33). And this quèstion he has already answered in the whole Sermon, in which He has defined the fruits of righteousness so clearly, that we cannot err therein. He who lives and acts before us after this standard, can be no false prophet, can be no corrupt tree. The *criterion* is an *objective*, absolute moral law: not as if, in entire *perversion* of the order and relation, "the peculiarity of the individual" should be the measure and standard of appreciation, according to the crafty *Wallenstein:* "Let me first search out the nature of the man, and I will tell his will and his deed." Who can search into that, but from without inwardly? although it must not be forgotten that a sound eye is requisite for rightly seeing what is visible before it. If we ourselves stand in the living apprehension and inward experience of the Sermon on the Mount, *then*, but only then, *can* we be on our guard, and discern all the counterfeit of hypocrisy. The ἐπιγνώσεσθε repeated in ver. 20 is less imperative than a *promise:* ye *shall* know them, that is, ye who are my disciples, who live and abide in my words. For, as we saw above in our general glance, the *fruits* which are wanting even to external observation in the false teachers, as certainly as they are inwardly evil, are the same which the grace of our Lord produces in all His disciples, and which therefore the judgment of our Lord will exact finally from all His disciples, sheep and shepherds alike. Such a general meaning is rendered incontrovertible by the sequel.

Vers. 18—20. That which in ver. 17 was expressed with *πᾶν* as a natural law exhibiting itself in things generally: that the inwardly good man bringeth forth truly good fruits, the evil man on the contrary, evil fruits (in which the *ποιεῖν καρπούς*, עֲשׂוֹת פְּרִי of the original brings out the doing of the work more fully than we can express it, see for example Ps. i. 1, 3);—is now once confirmed by a negative *οὐ δύναται*. He who is born of God cannot *commit sin*, according to St John's meaning (1 John iii. 9), although he hath sin and weakness arising from within him and from without. But the natural, sinful man (above ver. 11), cannot do anything good, in the sense in which grace only is effectual however much he may simulate it: they who are living in a state of grace can well distinguish it. It is indeed possible for a while that the wild tree should be graffed into grace through faith (Rom. xi.), but there follows a judgment which finds the tree as it then is. And this is said here equally for the good of the disciples themselves. We have this same expression of the Lord in St Luke (ch. vi. 43—45), independently of any connexion with the warning against the false prophets, but in the closest connexion with the reference to the perfection of the disciple (vers. 40—42), as also with the judgment upon all who call Him Lord without obeying Him, and hear Him without doing His words (vers. 46—49). In this St Luke, though in a briefer extract, has rightly seized and preserved the leading idea of the discourse. But whether the Lord actually then upon the Mount uttered what St Luke appends in ver. 45, or whether it was transposed from the repetition of the Lord's discourse in Matt. xii. 33, 37, where regard is rather had (after the precedent of Ecclus. xxvii. 6), to the *words* as springing from the heart, we venture not to determine. But as this particular reference to words can scarcely be made to suit the Sermon according to St Matthew, either as a mark to distinguish the prophets, or as to the *doing of the will* (ver. 21), we might be led to suppose that in this instance St Luke, standing at one remove from the event, has slightly departed from the original text and its meaning, which would, in that case, be the only instance of the kind in his exhibition of it.

The being "hewn down and cast into the fire" is literally according to the words of the Preacher of Repentance in ch. iii. 10. From which we may perceive that the fruits demanded by the Lord are no other than the *fruits meet for repentance* required there in ver. 8, καρπὸς ἄξιος τῆς μετανοίας. But what μετάνοια in its full and ever-deepening sense is, the Sermon on the Mount, as the development of that compendious announcement of ch. iv. 17, fully expounds to us; and in such a manner that that first requirement must always recur, whether it be at the close of the Sermon or the close of life,—or to speak more definitely, whether it be at the close of the gospel, or of the life of grace. That which as a legal threatening and before the consolatory message of grace, impelled, to a first repentance, afterwards impels with all the might of the gospel to the perfecting of holiness. It is a fixed decree—the Lord utters it as strongly as it could be uttered—God wills inexorably the *doing* of His will: I am not come to relax the Law, but to fulfil and establish it. In the judgment there is no respect of persons: the *tree* must bear its *fruit*, *each one*, be he whom he may. If he produces *not good* fruits, then must he assuredly produce evil fruit: this follows as a necessary conclusion from vers. 17, 18. But that only the lack of good fruit is expressly mentioned (just as ch. xxv. 42—45), has its severe meaning for the wilful blindness which asks: What evil can I do, that deserves damnation?—Finally, in these sentences we have a criterion indicated for the two most obvious classes of false prophets: the one speaking of fruits without planting the tree, the other speaking of the tree without its fruits. As for that most dangerous middle-class between these two extremes, including those who teach faithfully the fruits of the tree which the Lord plants, and also seem to possess such fruits, not merely in saying Lord, Lord, but in mighty works and deeds; for them the Lord's word, with ἄραγε emphatically repeated, has its keen force: by their fruits ye shall know them, namely, by those same fruits by which the Lord knows you yourselves to be His own, when you walk sincerely before Him, and for the lack of which He will judge you in common with all who persist in wanton self-blinding.

Vers. 21. Let it be carefully observed, for this alone gives the conclusion of the whole discourse its true meaning, that the Lord designedly interweaves together the judgment upon the deceivers and the judgment upon all generally who cannot then stand before Him. He continues to speak in vers. 21—23 of false prophets (yet not now as known hypocrites and wolves, but by a transition as self-deceived); but generally also of all who know, proclaim, and call upon His name. Κύριος is here, as it mightily announces itself to be, infinitely more than the usual title of reverend men (Jno. xii. 21; Acts xvi. 30); He who now in the highest and only sense arrogates as befitting *Himself* the name of "Lord," never from sacred propriety bestowed that title on any one in the inferior sense, even in His lowest subjection.[1] To call *Me* Lord in life, to call *Me* Lord in the day of judgment—

[1] Ipse neminen, ne Pilatum quidem, Dominum vocavit. *Bengel.*

is the claim of Him, who now at the close of His sermon, every word of which (even in St Matthew) is strictly measured, pronounces that great and all-comprehensive "My Father." That perversion of the Lord's words in the mouth of the Rationalists, which represents Him as laying no stress upon the calling of Him *Lord*, on the honour of His own name, provided only the doing of God's will is secured[1]—is the most wilful perversion that can possibly be imagined. Does the Lord, then, lay such emphasis upon the contrast between the saying Lord, and the doing the will of the Father? Assuredly not, He only says: not *every one* that *saith* unto me Lord, Lord (however earnestly and repeatedly he may say it, to hide his deficiency, as the repetition of the word indicates), *if* it be no more than *saying*, if the evidence of the sincerity of this profession in holy life is wanting. Moreover, He expressly exacts in Jno. xiii. 13, at the moment of His deepest humiliation, not merely the slighter Rabbi, but the full and unlimited "Lord." When He prophecies in Matt. xxv. of such among the nations of the earth as shall stand before His great tribunal, on the evidence of their works of mercy, without having lived in the conscious knowledge of His person, He yet represents them as addressing Him at the last with nothing less than "Lord." His Spirit testifies afterwards in the Apostle, that every tongue shall confess that he is Lord (Phil. ii. 9—11)—as also that to call Him Lord is precisely the same as to belong to Him, and possess His Spirit (1 Cor. xii. 3). Only, however, when this profession is a reality of the heart and of the whole life, the serving, depending upon, and obeying Him as the Lord, in the absolute and most distinctive sense of the word, as it was found above in ch. vi. 24. Hence the perfectly appropriate *question* (Lu. vi. 46), which was probably added by our Lord (between ver. 23 and ver. 24 of St Matthew). With such generality is the saying of Lord, Lord, laid down with reference to the *semblance of discipleship*, which may deceive many, even as many deceive themselves; and now comes in for the sake of the reality of that profession the simple—*he that doth the will* of my Father which is in heaven. Which indeed does not merely mean—he who keeps the Ten Commandments—but the commandment

[1] *Fichte* led the way by maintaining that "if Jesus only should find obedience and fruit, He would ask very little about the connexion which His name or His person had therewith!"

of faith, the revealed will and council of the Father in the sermon (Jno. vi. 39, 40; 1 Jno. iii. 23) is essentially included in it. Not otherwise does the Lord speak elsewhere, when He is defining the limits of His own, as for example in ch. xii. 50: and His Spirit in the Apostles similarly promises eternal assurance and salvation, the final possession of the promised kingdom, only to such doing of God's will. (1 Jno. ii. 17; Heb. x. 36.)

Vers. 22, 23. The concrete individuality of the preceding *οὐ πᾶς ἀλλ' ὁ ποιῶν*, (the plural translation of which in the German does not so markedly designate every one), is now followed by *Many!* which introduces in its sad and warning severity, a more convincing application of His words, and lifts, as it were, already the curtain of the judgment-seat. *Many* again, as in ver. 13, but still more definite and strict: not merely the many who run with a wicked world in the road to hell, but many even among those who appeared to honour Me, to walk as mine in words and works, who thought themselves to be such! *In that day:* according to the exact language of Prophetic Scripture, the so frequent בַּיּוֹם הַהוּא. The worst development of *hypocrisy*, the result and judicial self-punishment of deception, is at last seen in the deluded belief of its own lie, *self-deception* become hardened into reprobation. Hence the Lord represents as the extreme contrast to those who stand before Him accepted in judgment, those who at that day will *vainly imagine* that they also shall find acceptance.[1] For *that* is indeed all that is meant by their saying to Him: and of course not any actual so speaking. There is a self-deception which holds out to the end: a frightful truth, which the Lord once again reminds us of, in the discourse Lu. xiii. 25—27—a discourse closely related to this. We ask in our curiosity—is there then a self-deception *which continues through Hades*, even to the last day? The Lord's word answers Yes, but we dare not ask further how that may be. The word of Revelation does not lift the curtain from this intermediate state. We may forecast and anticipate, but nothing certain is told. Theo-

[1] They are as thoroughly assured of their righteousness and salvation, as the Pharisee, Rabbi Simeon, in the Talmud, who says: If there are only two righteous men in the world, my son and myself are the two: if there is only one, it is I myself!

sophy alone teaches and understands (although with no small danger of being over-wise) the continuance in the empire of the dead of the errors carried thither.

The threefold progressive exhibition of their word and deed, upon which the evil-doers relied, advances, according to their conception, from the less to the greater: but in reality and in the Lord's estimation, the progression is downwards, and the order must be reversed. *Δυνάμεις*, wonderful works or miracles, are the least of all attestations according to the general doctrine of Scripture: there are many signs and wonders ascribed to the false Christ, and the false prophets (ch. xxiv. 24). More plausible are *profitable* miracles, by which the *Devils are really cast out*, as we find the Lord Himself evidencing by them, in ch. xii. 25—28, the divinity of His miracles. Yet it is requisite, in order that this token may not deceive, that the accordant, confirming evidence of all the works which spring from an inner life, *good fruits*, should be added: the spirits are subject to the name of Jesus, even when pronounced by such as have not their names written in heaven, though it be by Judas found among the twelve. It is indeed a kind of *faith*, by which they are produced, but not the faith which saves and sanctifies the soul. (1 Cor. xiii. 2). Finally, the most specious is the first mentioned *προφητεύειν*, not merely the revealing futurity (which belongs rather to the *δυνάμεις*), but according to the use of the expression in the Old and New Testament, the speaking and teaching from inspiration. But there is even an *inspiration*, which consists in the being transitorily *possessed* by the Spirit of truth, without penetrating to the regeneration of the heart and will. Alas, how many a powerful preacher of Christendom falls into this condemnation, that of preaching thus to others, himself remaining or becoming reprobate!

There *is* such a self-deception which continues to the end, but it is *detected* at the last: and the detection is as righteous as it is fearful, for this self-deception is only hypocrisy made perfect in its own guilt. If then—for this is the conclusion which the Lord designs to produce in the minds of His hearers—such as can point to the evidence of prophecy and miracle are *rejected*; how much less will the unfruitful trees of a commoner kind be saved from the burning! If even their thrice-protested—Lord, Lord, *in thy name!* is insufficient for *their* salvation, how much less will the saying Lord, Lord, with their lips only, avail for the multitudes of the utterly idle and unprofitable, in the day of His wrath! Let it be observed how significantly the Lord maintains the honour of His name, by thus declaring that it is not a mere empty external honour that it requires. Let our hearts *feel*, without many words, the inexpressible *ἐξουσία* of the judicial *τότε ὁμολογήσω*, which scattering to the winds the delusion of lies, pronounces the *truth* against all imaginations and self-delusion! There is no 'Ἐγώ prefixed, and yet in these most simple words it is most solemnly implied:—I, the Judge, will say unto you; I the searcher of the hearts, will reveal to you your long-hidden heart and conscience, will only confirm to you what you should have known, and must now know. If all the world, if all God's children have held you for my people, I *never knew you*, that is, as truly and effectually mine; the word says nothing more, that is enough. It is remarkable that in fore-announcing his final judicial sentence, the Lord appropriates a word of His great ancestor and type, King David; and not any such royal utterance as is found in Ps. ci. 3, 4, 7, but that which occurs in Ps. vi. 8: which was given to David after he had cried in deep, personal, most lowly penitence—Rebuke me not in thine anger! This is intended to intimate (for it cannot have been chosen without signification) that *whoso hath not learned thus to speak with David*, will be constrained to hear it from another mouth. From the mouth of Him whose Depart from me! (ch. xxv. 41) is cause enough for condemnation: of Him, who needed to have said nothing more, yet in His righteousness makes the explanatory addition: ye *that work iniquity!* This is, further, a solemn expression taken from the Old Testament, פֹּעֲלֵי אָוֶן, as for example, in Ps. v. 6, xiv. 4, xxviii. 3, xxxvi. 13, xcii. 8—10, xciv. 4—16, ci. 8, cxxv. 5; Job xxxiv. 8—22; Prov. x. 29, xxi. 15, (1 Macc. iii. 6, comp. Lu. xiii. 27). Ye have named my name, but ye have not departed from iniquity! (according to 2 Tim. ii. 19, where there is manifestly an echo of the Sermon on the Mount, whether by the conscious design of the Apostle, or by the inspiration of the Spirit). In *τὴν ἀνομίαν* of the Greek expression we may detect the great truth—with all your other appearances, your life and work, judged by its internal principle, was one great *ἀνομία*, nothing but unrighteousness, lawlessness, and transgression in my sight![1] Whether the Lord did thus keenly express His meaning is questionable, on account of the Old Testament פֹּעֲלֵי אָוֶן.

Vers. 24—27. From His utterance at the day of judgment the Lord suddenly turns to what His lips, *the same* lips now utter, in the day of grace, and with the judgment yet in the future. *These sayings of mine:*—these words, utterances, testimonies, as I have now given them in one entire and perfect harmony of connexion. This requires us to regard *τούτους* as implying a fundamental sermon of peculiar solemnity: and it forms its sublime conclusion as such, its direct and authoritative *Dixi*, by which the whole discourse makes its appeal to the conscience as the word of the future Judge even before its λόγοι have ceased to be spoken.[2] It is with the *hearing* of these sayings as with the saying Lord, Lord: it avails not of itself, but must not be omitted. The *hearing*, indeed, is the first necessary condition: for faith and supplication, asking, receiving, obeying, and doing, come all from the previously received and accepted word of grace and truth, Heb. ii. 1, xii. 25. Yet see with this Rom. ii. 13; Jas. i. 22—25. Again there is the concrete antithesis: a wise *man*, a foolish *man*; as in vers. 17—19, tree set against tree. The very popularly conceived and condescending similitude which follows, is found in similar terms, though more superficially, in Sirach (Ecclus. xxii. 16, 17), who points, as the Lord does here, to passages in the prophetic Scripture. To Isa. xxviii. 15—18, namely, where the great foundation is more especially referred to, and Ezek. xiii. 10—15, where the falling of the untempered wall as well as of the whole building is threatened in similar figures. Ezekiel may rather refer to temporal judgment (comp. Ecclus. xlix. 11), Isaiah to the final fall into death and hell. Our Lord's word here embraces both, as we showed above. The *house* which a man builds for himself as a secure abode,

[1] Hence *Lange* would translate boldly—ye who pursue lawlessness as your calling.

[2] Τοὺς λόγους τούτους seems to bind together the Sermon, and preclude, as indeed does the whole structure of the Sermon, the supposition that these chapters are merely a collection of sayings uttered at different times.—*Alford.*

as a defence and protection against wind and weather, signifies the abiding and standing before the judgment of God both in time and eternity, the salvation of the soul into perfect security; in this sense Solomon also says—The wicked are overthrown and are not; but the house of the righteous shall stand (Prov. xii. 7). If the house falls, which thou hast built for thyself, then wilt thou thyself be overwhelmed and buried in its ruins. The Lord speaks not directly concerning those who think nothing about all this; who have no concern where or how they shall stand; *who build not at all;*—their fate is understood without being mentioned. They also who, having laid the right foundation at first, yet have neglected to build fast and firm upon that foundation, will find their condemnation in the simple word which afterwards makes prominent the extremest contrast of folly, with those, namely, who seem to think mere *hearing* without doing to be foundation and superstructure enough. (As before in ver. 22, the uttermost extreme was contrasted, designedly to embrace all else). If, however, we look narrowly and hear attentively, we shall find that all are actually included who fail in the persistent doing of the will of God: for *these sayings* speak directly *of this*, and require of all, who hear and do them, perseverance and consummation of their holiness; and we might add, taking this similitude generally to ourselves, that a foundation is not itself a dwelling, there must be something built upon it. This, however, is contrary to the close connexion of the figure with *all these sayings*. Rather the Lord regards the entire and full performance of His whole will as itself the *foundation of rock*, on which all depends: the superstructure thereupon is understood without any specific mention, in both cases alike.

A house must be built with direct reference to protection against wind and weather, for *the* rain, *the* floods, *the* winds will not fail or cease:—this is the significant meaning of the article here designedly used. Specially does this apply to Eastern countries, with regard to the physical character of which this figure is chosen, where these commotions are more sudden and more violent than ordinarily in our own land. The rain descends from *above* (κατέβη), the floods come side-long, washing their way to the very foundation *beneath;* when in addition to all this the winds blow and violently *beat upon* the building, none but a foundation of rock can sustain the whole. This has been pursued into more exact detail, as referring to the sorrows and afflictions which God sends from heaven like heavy rain; to the current of the spirit of the age, of temptation or persecution, which presses around and shakes the foundation; to the additional storms or marked judgments of God, in which He blows with His breath, to separate and make manifest what is only flesh.[1] We leave this to the judicious application which every word of Holy Writ will easily admit; but the generality of the final tone of the whole discourse will not permit us to deduce such specific views from the text. In St Luke, where the whole reads somewhat differently in the freedom of the variable letter, the winds and the rain are wanting, a simple πλημμύρα is all that is spoken of. On the other hand he brings into more prominence the *fundamental idea* of the parable, which is the firm foundation:—he *digged deep*, till he could lay his foundation upon a rock. There, further, our Lord's first ὁμοιώσω is made strongly emphatic, in entire harmony with St Matthew's meaning: ὑποδείξω ὑμῖν τίνι ἐστὶν ὅμοιος. For the sovereign authority of the Master employs here, as emphatically as condescendingly, a customary mode of speaking among the Rabbies, comp. Mark iv. 30. In the second member of the sentence, it is merely ὁμοιωθήσεται or ὅμοιός ἐστιν. The conclusion, with its solemn tone of threatening, is the same in both, though expressed in different words: a manifest token that we have in St Matthew and St Luke one and the same discourse of our Lord, pursuing its course of instruction from the same beginning to the same end.

St Matthew conclusively and irresistibly confirms this by the postscript (vers. 28, 29), which points back to the superscription in ch. v. 1, 2, and we, for our part, can never accede to the

[1] *Braune's* interpretation is just like this, as far as concerns the first reference; but when the *winds* are made only human temptations attacking us sideways, and the floods of the ocean, "the ebb and flow of the despairing and then froward heart," this seems to us to be more subtle than skilful. Father *Zeller* of Beuggen speaks again of the heavy rains and floods of revolutions, the wind of false doctrine, *storms* of the "judgments of God," agreeing in this last point with what we have given above, which is the best exposition, after all, if we must make these distinctions.

position that this is a collection of sayings uttered at various times. How mischievously a hypothesis may beguile is shown by Olshausen, who finds clear evidence of St Matthew's having formed such a collection in his expression τοὺς λόγους τούτους, since a connected discourse could only be spoken of as λόγος in the singular; while the συνετέλεσεν, which contradicts this supposition, is altogether passed over. As if St Matthew had not received this very expression, which he designedly repeats with great emphasis, from the Lord's own mouth in vers. 24. and 26! Ὁι λόγοι οὗτοι cannot there be "extracts from several discourses," but have the same meaning as τὰ ῥήματα ἃ ἐγὼ λελάληκα ὑμῖν in Jno. vi. 63, and ὁι λόγοι μου in Matt. xxiv. 35.

What the Apostle remarks of the impression of the discourse upon the ὄχλοι, *appears* to be one of those unfrequent reflexions of his own which he inserts in he simple narrative; but it is evidently, when closely examined, itself only *narrative*, a record once made in the most appropriate place, just as St Luke afterwards says the same thing, (ch. iv. 32). Indeed, what St Matthew says in ver. 29 may be almost received as the actual expression of the people's feeling, as an epitome of all their sayings concerning it: just as in a similar manner he gives in ch. x. 36, a word probably spoken by the Redeemer himself.[1] That was, in any case, most naturally the necessary impression upon the minds of the multitude, whether they thus uttered it or not; that was the inward ground of that outward ἐκπλήσσεσθαι, of which they were thoroughly conscious in themselves. *It was so:* the Apostle himself remembers it well, for his own emotion at the first hearing was living yet in his soul. *Not as the scribes!* In this is summed up yet once more the great contrast which pervaded the Sermon from ch. v. 20. But alas the mere ἐξεπλήσσοντο in which the whole terminated with regard to most (Lu. ii. 18, 19), transmits to us a melancholy example of that *hearing* and not doing, with warning against which the Sermon closed.

[1] *Roos:* ὡς ἐξουσίαν ἔχων as one who was though incognito the *King* in His kingdom! *Chrysostom* earlier: πανταχοῦ ἑαυτὸν ἐνδεικνύμενος εἶναι τὸν τὸ κῦρος ἔχοντα—on account of the "I say unto you," and the assertion of the judgment at the close.

ST LUKE'S EXTRACT FROM THE SERMON ON THE MOUNT.

(Luke vi. 20—49).

We have already shown in passing that *St Luke's* report of the Sermon on the Mount perfectly agrees with St Matthew in everything essential, that there is not only no contradiction between their several statements and view of it, but that the comparison tends to their mutual confirmation and elucidation. St Luke gives an *epitome* of the Sermon, like St Matthew: hence it is natural that each gives something which is wanting in the other, even in the case of St Luke, who gives a much more *concise* presentation of it. That which we read as given by the apostles and ear-witnesses, was brought to their remembrance, selected for them, and set in order by the promised Spirit (Jno. xiv. 26, xvi. 14); the historical writer St Luke, who derived his information from the original witnesses, and whose testimony (in relation to Jno. xv. 26, 27) is human-mediate, although he is not without the Spirit of truth, yet may naturally be supposed not to have caught so central a view, and to have spread out the whole amplitude of a long discourse, which was poured forth at once in such depth and fulness. For we must allow in the New Testament as the synagogue admitted in the Old degrees of inspiration, a difference even between St Matthew and St John, and how much more between both these and the two other Evangelists. All proceeds *naturally* with each, in the miracle which yet approves itself as nature; how otherwise would the higher and lower nature come together as a true and living reality?

Here we are constrained in a second edition most decidedly to oppose a view propounded in *Lange's* Leben Jesu. That excellent man having thoroughly entrenched himself (his work is pervaded with it) in the notion at first broached by *Augustin*, and since his time sometimes emerging into notice, of two discourses delivered at a short interval, endeavours to convince us that there was a sermon on the mountain-level in addition to the Sermon on the Mount, a platform sermon besides the hill sermon, a sermon for the people after the sermon for the church:[1] but few we think will concur with him. The reasons which are adduced, more confidently maintained than well-grounded against the long-prevailing view, are indeed actually very weak, and provoke our instant opposition. Apart from the ingenious turns of thought and forced interpretations which *Lange* in this as in all his hypotheses has abundantly at command, the arguments for this view are reduced to these two positions: that the Evangelists themselves indicate separate localities and circumstances, and that St Matthew's discourse could not from its intrinsic nature have been openly and publicly delivered.

We are to understand (Matt. v. 1) that the Lord at the sight of the great multitude of people, retired into the narrower circle of His own disciples! But what man in his senses and not already pledged to a hypothesis, can fail to see that the connexion with ch. iv. 25 will not allow of a retreating from the crowd, but rather requires that that crowd is itself taught? (Comp. ix. 36, xv. 29, 30, xix. 2). Thus the disciples are either those who in a narrower circle more immediately surrounded Him; or more generally and in a wider sense, all who were disposed to hear Him and followed Him for that purpose. This is rendered more certain by St Matthew's own declaration (vii. 28) that the ὄχλοι were hearers of this discourse! Further, the ἔστη of Lu. vi. 17 is not to be pressed (as *Braune* takes it) to mean, that Jesus delivered *this discourse standing* upon the plain, but it simply signifies, as coming after the καταβάς, that then he *stood still, halted* at the place which He would choose for His Sermon. The τόπος πεδινός, the "high or mountain-level," a platform of the ὄρος, was naturally selected as adapted for the gathering together of the people.

But the very doubtful exegesis in favour of distinct locality is

[1] Since the Lord, in contrast with the second, and more bare redaction of the law by Moses (!) reduces the first form of the Sermon on the Mount which only His *devoted* disciples could apprehend; and in tender consideration of the people's weakness, gives a second, more concrete, and easily apprehended. Against all such distinction see the testimony of Jno. xviii. 20.

supported by an internal criticism, which comes to its aid with the bold affirmation that Christ could not have delivered the Sermon on the Mount to all the people indiscriminately! It cannot receive a view which would indiscreetly put to the utmost peril its whole design, for this discourse has altogether an esoteric and confidential type![1] The common people were not yet ripe to receive such an illuminating criticism upon the precepts of the Pharisees! We appeal against this to our whole exposition, which has seized and exhibited the spirit of the whole discourse as a public programme of doctrine for the whole people. We think we can decisively overturn this whole position by three brief questions. First: did not the discourse which the Lord might utter before his formed circle of disciples (which, however, could not possibly be a closed circle, since whosoever would might go up to them) instantly and necessarily and always become *public*—especially a discourse so strikingly delivered as this? As to its being confidential, a mountain in the very sight of the following crowds would not have been chosen for a discourse which was to be withheld from the people. *Can* we suppose the Lord to have commanded them to remain below, until He should come down and speak also to them? Secondly: where do we find in all the Gospels the slightest trace of any such delicacy and consideration, of any such disposition to spare the Pharisees, in the first period of His ministry? Finally: was John the Baptist's public and unsparing and severe opposition to the Pharisees in the presence of all the people an imprudence, which the Lord can be supposed to have desired to repair, or to have been in a condition to do so?

Enough, no further detailed refutation is necessary. *We*, at least, observe not in St Luke any such "dim and exhausted representation of the discourse" as the supposition of its identity is thought to involve: he gives another extract of it, and indeed each Evangelist can be supposed to have given the longer discourses of our Lord only in such extracts. But we hold it a far worse evil than even a dim presentation at a second remove by a collator, *if* such language may be used; yea, we reckon it the

[1] It is even said that in the midst of a gathering of thousands of people Jesus could not have preached *sitting*, "tarrying so patiently and composedly."

worst possible evil, and one that decisively condemns and overthrows the whole hypothesis of Lange, that *untruthfulness* is thus necessarily imputed to an *Apostle* and eye-witness. Is it said that by his "inexact concluding words" concerning the astonishment of the *people*, he has in some degree weakened his own first "more exact statement" in ch. v. 1? Assuredly not, he tells us only at the close himself, how his words at the beginning are to be understood. It is said that "he has allowed the sermon to the people to mix with the sermon to the church;" nay that "minute transpositions from the one sermon to the other may have taken place through evangelical tradition." We have a quite different opinion of St Matthew's Gospel, and of his narration, so simple in its truth, and exhibiting so entirely as it does the marks of an eye-witness. He is said, finally, to have taken the popular and lucid similitude at the conclusion of the exoteric discourse, and attached it to the esoteric:—but what assertions, what imputations are these! and *how* did, then, the Lord close His confidential sermon? Was it not also with the rejection of the workers of iniquity, ch. vii. 23? And how did the fit and appropriate conclusion pass into oblivion, the other taking its place? Then must the wisdom of the Great Teacher, which led Him to deliver two sermons, and which *could* not have spoken the Sermon on the Mount to the multitude, have remained hidden from the Apostle Matthew as well as from all "evangelical tradition," so that they mixed together in early times what it was left to *our* later skill to discriminate. Against all these absurdities we have our consolation, reading the Sermon to the people even in St Matthew's account; and regarding it as returning to us again abbreviated in the derived Gospel of *tradition.* "Devoted" disciples—how came these such so early? were they not rather made so by this Sermon, which was designed to call out and to separate those disciples from the mass of the people?

St Luke hands down what his sources gave him,[1] and arranges more after the manner of human skill and wisdom the words which his reporters had seized and preserved as then spoken by our Lord. Thus *in his case* there may be something of that which is improperly imputed to St Matthew, a working up, if we

[1] Not, however, just a "Postscript"—as *Schleiermacher* once said, as if talking about *his* Berlin sermons!

may so call it, of his materials. He constructs out of the details a whole of his own, and in doing so we must suppose that the original letter may have been departed from in some cases by his vouchers, as well as that he may in some cases have departed from it himself, just in order to give it more closely. He gives his own spontaneous expression sometimes so as to make his narrative move more harmoniously; generalizes the concrete, for instance, in order that it might lose any fragmentariness or indistinctness, being conscious in himself that in some cases he had not received the *ipsissima verba* of the Lord. We concede all this, for it lies before our eyes; and *yet* we, on our side, maintain with equal confidence, that St Luke could not in this manner incorporate any thing of his own, or any thing that by others before him had been falsely attributed to our Lord. For that the Spirit of Truth miraculously guided him also, preserving him from all essential error in the matter of his Gospel, is most evident, however more or less conscious his Procemium shows himself to have been of this. It is manifestly stamped upon the very character of His whole Gospel, and is proved by the many discourses of our Lord which he alone gives in all their self-evidencing truth. Consequently we have in the Sermon on the Mount even of St Luke nothing but the *Lord's word* actually spoken by Himself: even there where *for once* he may be thought to have transgressed the bounds of his own faculty by introducing a saying from another place (ver. 45); yet even this is a saying of our Lord, actually spoken on another occasion.

The more closely genuine criticism examines the contents of the two Evangelists, laying them side by side and subjecting them to a comparative exposition, the more incontestably does St Matthew's evince itself to be the original, according to which St Luke's is to be understood. For what the latter gives us bears the natural character of having been transmitted and derived from hearers at a second remove.[1] To make this the proper original, and St Matthew's a deviating and expanded collection and compilation, is not criticism but folly, which heedlessly and superficially talks about what has never been thoroughly investigated.

[1] Not, however, in the sense in which *Schleiermacher* says, "that the reporter had a more unfavourable place for hearing."

This is our avowal and testimony; the detailed grounds of which appertain not to this book, though we hold them in readiness.

Let the entire arrangement, closely compacted as it is in St Matthew down to its slightest details, be now surveyed; and let the elements of the discourse as given by St Luke be assigned to their place in it. The commencement and the conclusion fit well together, although the great bulk of the expansive middle-part is wanting. Of the *first main division* we have the *Benedictions*, apprehended in their starting-point and in their essence, and illustrated by distinctive contrasts.[1] Of the *second* part we find little, yet that little is well-ordered and correct. Of the first contrast as opposed to the righteousness of the Pharisees, we have the *commandment of the love of enemies* which disannuls their wicked gloss upon the falsely interpreted law; as well as the accompanying reference to the perfect merciful benevolence of God. (The express polemic against their apprehension of the law in individual precepts is wanting at the beginning, as also that against their specious conformity to the law in alms-giving, prayer, and fasting). The whole of the second contrast as against heathenish care is pretermitted, *probably* with the Evangelist's knowledge and design, certainly under the Spirit's direction, since this gospel (ch. xii. 1) contains a record of it afterwards as having been spoken by our Lord. The third contrast, on the contrary, as against *judging* and *mote-seeing*, comes forward with tolerable fulness, even enlarged upon the main idea. (On the other hand the profound observation directed against the imprudence of charity in exhorting and preaching, is wanting: and so, indeed, is the whole close of this division, viz., the injunction to *prayer* and to enter through the *strait gate*, but only for the reason given above, that both are to occur in a later repetition (xi. and xiii. chs., as well as the preceding Lord's prayer.) Finally, in the *third part* of the discourse, only the warning against false prophets is passed over, as before the general controversy with Pharisaism. Instead of this the requirement of the *fruits*, the exhortation to *doing*, and the warn-

[1] Not as if (according to *Schleiermacher*) the reporter *had appended the woes*, in order to fill up a gap which he felt, but knew not how to complete! But in the sense in which we shall afterwards explain ourselves.

ing against *not doing*, follow immediately next, in strict harmony with the fundamental course of thought. And now we ask any man whether in St Luke's extract also, the *characteristic* element of every section is not preserved : the heart of the *promise* at the commencement; the point of the *requirements* in the middle, piercing the heart of every hearer who keeps them not (in ver. 40 these requirements merge into that of a *perfect discipleship*); and finally the conclusion with its no less emphatic and solemn *warning*. We have fresh evidence in this, that we have rightly seized the course and order of the discourse in St Matthew, since it is not contradicted here but confirmed. We find a reason and justification of St Luke's omission of the reference to the Law and the Prophets (Matt. v. 17—19), as well as of the subsequent controversy with Pharisaism upon its interpretation of individual commandments, in the relation which his Gospel bears to the first: he has less directly than St Matthew a Jewish interest and aim, but the Spirit uses him as a witness for the Greeks and the Gentiles.[1] Thus in the marvellous domain of inspiration, where human consciousness and divine direction most wonderfully unite in concert, even deficiencies approve themselves as parts of a well-ordered arrangement.

Vers. 20—23. In the benedictions as here given according to the conception of a less immediate report, we do not find recognized St Matthew's internal progression through the number seven into its close and confirmation in the eighth, and the complete systematic view of the inner and outer life of discipleship which he has stamped upon them. Hence not only is the second part (Matt. v. 7—9) quite wanting, but also the previous benediction of the *meek*, as it stands at the turning-point of the development. But so much more sharply comes out in striking paradox the *contrast* between the promised blessedness and the present external circumstances of the disciples, as St Luke's main point of view: blessed are ye who are now miserable, needy and persecuted! In *this* view the transposition which places those

[1] *Von Gerlach* simultaneously concurred with me in this reason for regarding St Luke's discourse as "without doubt the selfsame" which St Matthew gives more in detail.

who hunger before those who weep, is fully justified: and thus viewed the benediction of the persecuted and separated ones, (vers. 22, 23) was all the more indispensable. It is in harmony with this point of view, further, that the discourse just here assumes the direct address of *Ye*, (which in St Matthew first begins at ver. 11); and the preceding observation that the Lord thereby signified *His disciples*, is so entirely correct, that we cannot but suppose in connexion with St Matthew's form of expression such a direct turning of the Lord's eye upon His immediate and near disciples. To give this idea, as a human illustration which, however, is faithful to the true reference of the discourse, *νῦν* is now appended: for if a present internal satisfaction and consolation are promised to those who hunger and those who weep, yet does the full *contrast* as here viewed stretch its *futurum* onwards to that time of which such a passage as Rev. vii. 16, 17, speaks. Then will the *consolation* which now begins be consummated in *laughing* in its highest sense (Ps. cxxvi. 2).

But here a false criticism and exposition—even that of *Neander*,[1] to our great regret—will have it that the Lord's word is misunderstood, as if He had spoken of the physically and externally hungry and poor. Assuredly it is not! Let it be observed narrowly and it will be seen that as in St Matthew the אֶבְיוֹנִים are by transition included, so also in St Luke internal poverty, hunger and sorrow are not excluded but implied. He had already (ch. iv. 18) quoted Isaiah's *εὐαγγελίσασθαι πτωχοῖς*, and now indicates the true meaning of that expression, the only one which it will bear in the prophetic Scripture: viz., that which includes both senses in the indeterminate language of the Spirit. Are mendicants, as such, inheritors of the kingdom of God? Only as far as their external poverty becomes true poverty of spirit; as on the other hand the externally rich may be truly poor before God. The *τῷ πνεύματι* is wanting to *πτωχόι* and *τὴν δικαιοσύνην* to *πεινῶντες*, but that they are to be understood in the Lord's word follows necessarily from its being His word.[2]

[1] Who sees here only narrow-minded misunderstanding combined with rhetorical painting.

[2] *Alford* remarks very truly that a comparison of other passages in St Luke without reference to St Matthew, would render a spiritual sense necessary.

In the sequel we have as a mere change of expression, instead of *persecute*, its principle sharply defined in μισεῖν, and with this, its manifestation in ἀφορίζειν; the Lord may have uttered both; let His corresponding concluding discourse *to the disciples* be compared with this, and let the probable allusion in Jno. xvi. 2 to Isa. lxvi. 5 be duly noted.[1] The ἐκβάλλειν τὸ ὄνομα ὡς πονηρόν is probably the same as הוֹצִיא שֵׁם רַע· (Deut. xxii. 19). Yet is ἐκφέρειν ὄνομα πονηρόν as the Sept. translates there somewhat different from the stronger ἐκβάλλειν of our text (which rather includes the idea of excommunicating or putting under ban), and from the just as much stronger τὸ ὄνομα ὑμῶν ὡς πονηρόν. This ὡς and this τὸ point rather to *the Name* which they preach and glory in; which they thus make *their own* and bear; see, again, the Epistle of St James, which is pervaded with the spirit of the Sermon on the Mount (ch. ii. 7), where we the rather find allusion to our text, as the *poor* and the rich, ver. 5, 6, had just been spoken of. In the intense σκιρτᾷν St Luke only remains true to his fundamental aim, to make prominent the contrast between the future and the *now*: but inasmuch as not a future but an imperative stands connected with "*in that day*" (comp. Matt. vii. 22, a prelude of which we may have here), it must be taken with ἀγαλλιᾶσθε: Leap up joyfully in faith and hope, in anticipation of your future joy.

Vers. 24—26. Just in these words the Lord assuredly spoke, though they may be reported with more or less literal exactness. It is not conceivable that any reporter could have falsely appended such contrasted *woes* to the distinctly marked benedictions; even leaving out of view the Spirit's guidance of St Luke. St Matthew, who makes prominent the *progress of development* as the main idea of the Sermon, has omitted these as well as much else that is similar, here however they take their place with the full force of perfect *contrast*. Here, still less than before, the externally rich, and full, and laughing, are intended as such: and we have new confirmation of the spiritual interpretation of the preceding. These sayings of our Lord find their type in the Prophetic Scripture, Isa. lxv. 13, 14. St James, in whom,

[1] Though there לְמַעַן שְׁמִי is to be construed differently from *Luther* as my commentary on Isaiah shows.

we discern so many elements of the Sermon on the Mount (as found whether in St Matthew or St Luke), to which he immediately went back through the medium of living tradition, manifestly refers to it not only in ch. iv. 9, but also in ch. v. 1; with which he also in vers. 2, 3 combines (as we saw before) an allusion to what is found in Matt. vi. 19, 20. Both in the former and the latter passage he designates the externally rich, but as they are at the same time rich and self-satisfied in the sense of Lu. xviii. 24, 25; Rev. iii. 17; Hos. xii. 9. Ye have received your consolation—once more an anticipatory note of Matt. vi. 2, comp. Lu. xvi. 25. Very significant also is ἐμπεπλησμένοι, *full* indeed, but not properly satisfied. (Lu. xv. 16; Ps. xvii. 14). They are the rich and the full, who, because they have the good things of this world and earthly consolation, think themselves also contented in soul: such are immediately spoken of, but they are taken only as a most striking type and example of those who are spiritually satisfied and at ease, of whom there are many, indeed, who have no external abundance of earthly goods and earthly joy. But he whom earthly good does *not* content, belongs to the hungry ones who were before blessed, even though he may abound in provision for his earthly life. The *four* woes correspond, as they are here arranged, to the four benedictions: hence the laughing has no bye-meaning of mad earthly exuberance of joy (as in Eccles. ii. 2, vii. 3, 6); it is only the exact converse of ver. 21. In reality it includes not only that wicked laughter, properly so called, which being a mere convulsive excitement of the animal nature is exhibited as unworthy of man, but also and more than that, the malevolent laughter of those who hate righteousness and triumph over the righteous, which is referred to again in Jno. xvi. 20, but not in the same terms. Thus it forms a good transition to the mention of hatred and persecution, which follows presently afterwards in contrast. How apt is the proleptic allusion to the *false prophets* in the Lord's discourse, which in the first part already shadows out its whole course, we have noticed already upon St Matthew. What St James says in ch. iv. 4 may refer to this expression as directly as to Matt. vi. 24, probably to both together: his main idea, at least, is certainly an echo of the Sermon on the Mount.

The whole of our Lord's discourse, from Matt. v. 21 to ver.

48, this account compresses into that one pointed and prominent saying: *Love your enemies!* which here commences as it there closes all, with condensed and emphatic brevity. Here we find it again in ver. 35, and thus at the beginning and at the end it is the boundary of the whole discourse upon this subject. Hence the transposition of vers. 29, 30, which according to St Matthew were spoken before, and formed the appropriate transition to this topic. Similarly ver. 31 was probably placed here instead of later, as in Matt. vii. 12, since to an inexact remembrance this seemed its point of connexion. According to their sense and meaning the two sayings are strictly connected, for the one explains the other. Instead of the many contrasts in which the Lord so emphatically spake His *But I say unto you!* we have only now the ὑμῖν λέγω remaining, which does not so much indicate a contrast of His words with other sayings and teachings of the scribes (the false prophets of ver. 26, with which the ἀλλά in ver. 27 may be a slight link), as the absolute *authority*, which, even thus abridged, they emphatically announce, of Him who now speaks. We observe here also how thoroughly St Luke's account brings the earlier portion of the discourse into connexion with the fundamental idea of its conclusion, the ὑμῖν λέγω with vers. 46, 47 afterwards. It is partly to express *this* that τοῖς ἀκόυουσιν is added; and partly as equivalent to πᾶσι τοῖς ἀκούουσιν—in contrast with the αὐτοῖς of ver. 39, which specially points to the μαθητάς of ver. 20. Precisely in conformity with the Lord's meaning, who, beginning with his disciples in particular, then included all people universally in His address. Finally, again, returning especially to those who were His own disciples and stood in His presence.

In vers. 27, 28 there is a transposition which disregards (as in the benedictions) the inner sequence of blessing, doing good, praying for, as St Matthew preserves it, the *contrasts* merely being aimed at. In ver. 29, the concrete going to law for coat or cloke is generalized as a mere αἴρειν, taking away; hence, naturally, as we saw before, the cloke comes first. The essential power and truth of our Lord's words, do not lie in these specialities: and this the Holy Spirit designs to teach us by the more exact or inexact expressions found in parallel places of the Evangelists. The αἴρειν is even not necessarily now robbery by force, but, generally speaking, a *taking away* without asking, which should, however, be regarded as equivalent to asking it: and so we find ver. 30 carrying on the idea, in conformity to its peculiar fundamental design as we discovered it in St Matthew. *Ποία ὑμῖν χάρις ἐστί*—another form of St Matthew's *τίνα μισθὸν ἔχετε*. We might almost say that it embraces in its generality the *τί περισσὸν ποιεῖτε* which is there found hard by. For *sinners* also do—a general idea instead of the concrete Publicans and Gentiles. St Matthew says nothing of the *lending*, but the Lord probably, as we there saw, added that, since it most strikingly represents the *ὑπόνοια* of all Scriptural teaching: unselfish love, without regard to its return, or to previous love in its object, a readiness to *lend* without interest, even at the peril of not receiving again even the principal, at least from *men*. Let Moses' prohibition (Lev. xxv. 35—37) of usury and increase be reflected on, and the commandment to lend to a poor brother, without hope of the principal, even though the year of release was nigh. (Deut. xv. 7—10.) *Τὰ ἴσα*, in effect, refers rather to principal than to interest, as the antithesis *μηδὲν ἀπελπίζοντες* afterwards more directly declares.[1] Ver. 35 corresponds in its threefold expression clearly enough to the three sentences vers. 32—34. The form *υἱοὶ ὑψίστου* here used, is after the Old Testament (see Ecclus. iv. 11, *καὶ ἔσῃ ὡς υἱὸς ὑψίστου*) and might have been used by the Lord, as well as the other, in a more detailed and copious discourse. The *χρηστός ἐστι* once more *generalizes* the sense, if we compare St Matthew, and *ἀχαρίστους* is a human illustration at the close, corresponding with the context. "Ingratitude is the world's recompense"—this also experiences the Most High God, the Merciful One to all: let it not overmuch grieve you to bear the like. In this we have, and must not overlook, a keen *exposition* of the word which St Matthew uses. God maketh His sun to shine and sends His rain upon the *evil*, that is, not

[1] This ἀπελπίζειν which is only found here in the N.T. is explained by its context: hoping for nothing *of* it, *for* it, again. *Nullo modo desperantes* (a signification which is found in *Diodorus* and *Polybius* as also in a var. reading of Eph. iv. 19) would be altogether inappropriate; but the transitive sense which the Syriac gives it, is quite contrary to the language.

merely upon those who were before evil and therefore deserve it not, but who remain so afterwards also, and thank Him not.

Although so much that is intermediate is omitted, how spiritually correct and true to the whole harmony of the discourse is the condensation which attaches ver. 37 immediately to ver. 36. St Matthew commenced a new subject with these words, but the thought was closely connected with what had just been said concerning a God-resembling, forgiving, blessing love of our enemies: and the fundamental idea of the whole section (Matt. vii. 1—6, 12 is pure, *unselfish* love. St Matthew sets down the simple and impressive μὴ κρίνετε, but here we have a more detailed commentary upon his word, one which cannot be thought to have been added by any one *ex propriis*, for it is too definite, and striking, and appropriate. The Lord assuredly uttered these words, nor could *that* conception of the discourse, which has found "love ye!" to be the centre and heart of the whole second part of it, willingly dispense with them. We have, further, in St Luke a gradation, a threefold progression in the thought: judge not, even *forgive*, and finally (as practical evidence of the same) *give*, impart, do good, that is, as the preceding verses require, to all alike without distinction, enemies as well as friends. (*Luther's* explanation of the *fifth* petition). The *having it measured again*, is, as in St Matthew, an undefined promise, which in part finds its fulfilment from man, assuredly in full from God. This latter we hear in the μέτρον καλόν. The threefold detail of the figure (*Bengel: in aridis, mollibus, liquidis*) is so familiar and acceptable to all, and clings so fast to our hearts, that we strongly suspect, though we cannot positively affirm it, that the Lord actually added these very words,[1] and all the more as εἰς τὸν κόλπον, with a changed application, however, from threatening to promise, comes from the same chapter of the Prophet (Isa. lxv. 6, 7), to which vers. 21, 25 referred us, as ver. 22, to Isa. lxvi. 5.

Vers. 39, 40 are peculiar to St Luke, but suit very aptly the connexion of St Matthew. The signification of the subsequent *beam* is before indicated by the idea of *blindness*: the

[1] If others think, rejecting *Bengel's* interpretation, that the same measure is designated only with the climax of full rising into overfull; we accept this as a subordinate sense, yet must cling to the threefold application of the figure.

ground-thought of Matt. vii. 1—6, as we showed before, is then emphatically made prominent: be *perfect* as disciples! Even if it were an expository addition, we should think it to have penetrated the depth of the Lord's meaning.[1] But the Holy Ghost has expressly provided against this, by inspiring the Evangelist to insert εἶπε δὲ παραβολὴν αὐτοῖς—which remark certainly cannot signify that here a parable spoken elsewhere is interpolated:[2] for the αὐτοῖς is only to be interpreted by ver. 20, and was used here to show (in contrast with ver. 27) that the disciples were particularly addressed. St Luke also (ch. vii. 1) asserts beyond all doubt that it was a connected discourse which he had given. The Lord consequently uttered this at this place, and by a significant parable more decisively taught what in St Matthew we find Him teaching without it: that a censorious disciple is still, or has become no better than a *Pharisee*. For he has repeated the same words, afterwards, concerning the Pharisees, Matt. xv. 14, (xxiii. 16). Let it be noted that in this one word St Luke also has given some intimation of the general tendency of the discourse to oppose the Pharisees.

When expositors and preachers refer ver. 40 to ver. 39 in such a manner as to interpret the words *only* that a blind teacher makes also blind disciples[3]—they entirely pervert the text. That would be too keenly-expressed irony,[4] and κατηρτισμένος then would be an altogether unsuitable word. No, the discourse passes into a severe contrast, and opposes to these false and yet-blinded teachers and censors, the one true *Master*, that perfect διδάσκαλος who now speaks to His disciples. That

[1] As *G. K. Rieger's* Herzenspostille on Lu. vi. 36—42 (the Gospel for iv. Sund. after Trin.) takes from this verse the comprehensive theme, ein *ganzer* Christ—a *whole* Christian.

[2] In Lu. v. 36 the Evangelist inserts the same before a strictly connected discourse; similarly also ch. xii. 16, xxi. 19, xiii. 6, xix. 11, xx. 9.

[3] *Hilgenfeld* thus drivels: the Pauline Lucas-Evangelium could have only intended in this distorted saying thus patched in,—according to the *connexion* (in the Expositor's brain!)—to have condemned the Jewish-Christian teachers.

[4] According to *Von Gerlach:* even in the best case the disciple is only as his Master.

meaning which has been incorrectly imported from Matt. x. 24, 25; John xiii. 16 (where the Lord places the significant Maschal in an unusual, and altogether new application of His words), as if he meant that the disciples must suffer like their *Master*, is foreign to the discourse, where the παραβολή occurs in a general, and well-understood sense. The *Irony*, which indeed adheres to the *first* sentence (οὐκ ἔστι ὑπὲρ) though not to the second, lies deep, and the Lord intends to say: take care that ye do not in your rash and unmeasured condemnation of your brethren, exercise a *severer* judgment than I, in my love and forbearance, have exercised upon you! For does not the censorious judge place himself, as it were, above His forgiving, graciously correcting, long-suffering Master? *Πᾶς* in its position here is not "every," but *totus quantus est*—when he is perfect, has learnt all as μαθητής, will he be altogether whole and perfect, as His Master. The ἔσται is a hortatory promise just like ἔσεσθε (ver. 35).

We have already seen that, in conformity with the spirit of the section, vers. 43, 44 omit the false prophets, and require from the disciples themselves the good fruits of the good trees: we only now observe, that nothing may be unmentioned, the change of expression ἐκ βάτου τρυγῶσι and the transposition of σῦκα and σταφυλήν, as well as the *generalization* here suiting the thought: ἕκαστον δένδρον γινώσκεται, instead of St Matthew's ἐπιγνώσεσθε αὐτούς. That the Lord *signified*, though he may have only said this.

Of ver. 45, we have spoken again and again: we may point out that we are unjustly charged with maintaining a stiff mechanical theory of inspiration, since we here (though with the proper reservation, that it is only till we obtain a deeper insight) are willing to allow that this passage has been transposed from another place, and that it does *not* harmonize with the connexion (not even with ver. 46). We may have frankly to concede the same in the case of *St Luke*. We regard this, however, as possible only in his case and in St Mark's: not in that of the Apostles. But with equal confidence do we discern and assert the wisdom, correctness, harmoniousness of the whole residue of St Luke's report of the Sermon on the Mount, down to this one word: would that all criticism penetrated into the depths of the whole context, before making assertions of the same nature so abundantly and hastily as it does.

Ver. 46 gives in few words what we find in Matt. vii. 21—23, condensing the Lord's teaching after the manner of the shorter extract. As the original concrete presentation has been given up throughout, we have it here in *a general position*, which corresponds most perfectly with our Lord's meaning, as we find it later explained by Himself in a parable (Matt. xxi. 28—31) which St Luke has *not*. Finally, we have the same generalization in the πᾶς ὁ ἐρχόμενος πρός με, which, though probably not thus spoken by our Lord, yet indicates at the close and fitly illustrates, the universal and all-comprehensive character of this first Sermon on the Mount, in which all other sayings were already bound up. Is there nothing but "dim and weakened exhibition" in an extract like this, so wisely selected, so skilfully knit together, according to its own independent point of *view* and aim?

THE LEPER.

(Matt. viii 3, 4 · Mark i. 41—44; Luke v. 13, 14).

The first miracle of healing which St Matthew records in detail, after the general statement of ch. iv. 23, 24, belongs assuredly, as far as regards its time and place, to the position which the "behold" of an eye-witness here assigns it. That the Lord's Sermon on the Mount had only resulted in a vague, unimportant, and uninfluential impression—That was a mighty discourse! the Evangelist has just informed us. Nor is there more significance in the *following* of the multitudes, when the Lord had ended speaking. What inwardly passed in individual souls at the time, or afterwards recurred, to the conviction and salvation of the inner man, the sacred narrative does not reveal;—this belongs to the κρυπτὰ τῶν ἀνθρώπων (Rom. ii. 16). There was a poor leper, having ventured to approach or actually to mingle (probably, at least), with the ὄχλοις πολλοῖς as they listened at first and afterwards as they followed, whom the final close of the discourse, stern and severe as it was, had not discouraged from laying hold upon the loving-kindness of its first promises to all the poor and wretched; nay, rather by the very ἐξουσία of its severity had given ground to his *confidence*. A wonderful type for us all in this respect, the truth and applicability of which are manifest in the narrative as given by the Spirit, even though the leper's prayer had no immediate connexion with the influence of the sermon. This leper tells us parabolically what the true and entire result of that sermon is to be in our minds :—*Lord, if thou wilt, thou canst make us clean!* This is the right "Lord, Lord," which will not be cried in vain. As God sends the leprosy, so God only can heal it—said the Jewish proverb : and Moses cried to the Lord concerning Miriam—Heal her now, O God! Above in ch .iv 24 lepers are not as yet expressly mentioned: but in any case, even if such had been already healed by Jesus, and it had come to this man's ears, and still more so on the likelier supposition of the contrary, it is a strong faith which his words utter—Thou *canst* make me clean! (Unlike Mark ix. 22). This faith it is which urges him further, even to the fearless approach and falling down before the Lord: even as to His *willingness* he does not really doubt, but his "*if*" is the becoming expression of an humble supplication,[1] which by this word seems to tarry afar off, as it was prescribed to the leper bending under the plague of God.

Ver. 3. The Lord is now, as ever, ready to help. No sooner is the request uttered, than it is heard. The hand anticipates the word (St Mark adds, σπλαγχνισθείς), He stretches it forth down towards the leper, who scarcely knelt quite close to Him, He *touches him*, as Elijah and Elisha touched the dead without defilement,[2] the word and deed are one, an immediate moment of most immediate *answer*. Alas, the majestic utterance may not be fully rendered into our own tongue, as the three Evangelists unanimously preserve it in those two only words so full of grace and authority :—Θέλω, καθαρίσθητι. The first is not merely an instant echo of His mercy to this present single request :—I will

[1] But not unbelieving, for, as *Von Gerlach* has well put it : "*Faith* always says, if thou wilt! not, if thou canst! The opposite of Mark ix. 22."

[2] The contagion of pestilence is overcome and kept off from the Lord, and can as little attach itself to Him as sin—*Braune*.

do it. No, the Lord, who ever contemplates and perceives in His spirit the whole in each, inclines Himself to this man, as to that entire unclean humanity which He only can cleanse, with an avowal and testimony which comprehends everything:—*I will!* The appealing If awakened the whole full tone of love in the depth of his heart:—If I *will* heal and help? Yes, verily, it is for that that I am come! It is the same great *I will* with which He came into the world, and with which He leaves the world, which is consummated in that *I will* uttered to His Father on behalf of His sanctified ones, in Jno. xvii. 24.

And now is added that word of authoritative command which was essentially contained in the former, but is now expressly uttered as a testimony to man:—*Become clean! Be thou clean!* (Comp. Luke xiii. 12; xviii. 42). Because *I will!* Therefore *I can!* I say not, I *can*—faith, awakened by my discourse will confide in me for *that.* My power is necessarily included in my willingness. In this manner never prophet before Him healed, and He thus speaks only in the power of God who speaketh and it is done. An imperative this, which human language had never known before. The leprosy of the body must visibly and instantly obey Him. The leprosy of the soul, indeed, not equally so: yet is there in the word of our Lord's authority, which *speaks clean*, at once both the power and the *will* on His part, to *make clean* also.

Ver. 4. It was for the sake both of an internal and an external propriety, that the wisdom and consummate prudence of the Lord adds to His first utterance, which had sprung from the mighty impulse of His authority as well as of His love, something more, viz., a *prohibition* and a *command,* both wholesome and expedient. The prohibition, to tell no man of it, is not simply to be taken in connexion with what follows—delay not by so doing, but hasten to the priest! It is certainly to be understood in the same sense as many other similarly recurring prohibitions, in connexion with one of which (when it was imposed upon all the healed together), St Matthew (xii. 16) gives its most immediate signification and cause in the prophetic word,—He shall not strive nor cry; neither shall any man hear his voice in the streets. The Lord's design is—not indeed to suppress all that we may call rumour or noise in connexion with His works, for He knew that

His prohibitions were in most cases to no purpose ; but to testify most expressly that it was not desired or demanded by Himself. A deeper cause which is in Mark viii. 26 for example and elsewhere, more distinctly intimated, was the wise aim of His love to direct the healed ones themselves into the seclusion of thankfulness before God, to a profounder penetration of the matter where injurious talk about it might not dissipate their thoughts, in order that, if possible, what had taken place in their bodies, might lead to their inner healing. This, however, our Lord seldom attained, but He continues in every new case to impose it with unwearying patience. On the present occasion He spoke the prohibition all the more emphatically, because of the publicity which already had attended His healing word of authority. (St Mark—*ἐμβριμησάμενος—εὐθέως ἐξέβαλεν αὐτόν*—thus as it were, strengthening the *μηδενὶ μηδὲν εἴπῃς*).

With this is connected the recognition of the levitical regulation, the reference to the priest's authority and prerogative, upon which the true High-Priest meekly falls back, even at the moment when He has exhibited most impressively His own supreme authority, in order that we should not offend against it (ch. xvii. 27). Go thy way instantly, that if possible the fame of what has taken place may not outstrip thee, and give occasion to the evil-disposed to interpret My act of power into an invasion of their office. What lowliness of the Mighty One! What condescension of the Righteous One on account of unrighteousness! *This* healed one, forsooth, might have been justified in thinking himself released from the offering; but just because He might so think, the Lord reminds him of it, and will not have that which He has done, otherwise regarded than as what God does when a leper is healed of his plague. (Mar. v. 19). The article in *τῷ ἱερεῖ* and *τὸ δῶρον* points plainly to what was written in Moses: which St Mark and St Luke, having said indefinitely *ἃ προσέταξε, καθὼς προσέταξε Μωϋσῆς*, supplement and complete by the addition of *περὶ τοῦ καθαρισμοῦ σου*. We may not regard *τὸ δῶρον* as being the offering especially prescribed by Moses for the first day in Lev. xiv. which was followed on the eighth by another, but it comprises the whole obligatory duty in one word.

In the conclusion *εἰς μαρτύριον αὐτοῖς* which all the three

Evangelists have in common, there lies a comprehensive meaning: that *they*, these priests so especially malevolent against me (this is signified in the transition from the singular to the plural, in the emphatic αὐτοῖς), may learn *at once* both the miracles which I accomplish and that I do not invade their office by them (comp. further on Lu. xvii. 14). The former, however, is the special sense of that solemn expression, which recurs again in ch. x. 18, xxiv. 14, where the general rejection of His testimony is presupposed. We must further guard against the error of many well-meaning persons (who are here unconsciously following Roman Catholic precedent), in interpreting this commandment to show themselves to the priests, as referring to our present spiritual guides, who must inspect and sit in judgment upon souls.

THE CENTURION.

(Matt. viii. 7, 10—13; Lu. vii. 9).

A second, equally prompt *I will!* A believing proselyte of the Jews from among the heathen placed in opposition to that unbelief of Israel, which the last word of the Lord had just indicated. Did the reader suppose that the stretched out *hand* and the *touching* were necessary in connexion with the mighty "θέλω καθαρίσθητι:" it takes place now through a simple Γενηθήτω spoken at a distance. But He who *can* do this, yet graciously and condescendingly complies in every case with man's request. That request, as St Luke expresses it more definitely, was ὅπως ἐλθὼν διασώσῃ τὸν δοῦλον—and the Lord does not instantly utter His Γενηθήτω, but Ἐγὼ ἐλθὼν θεραπεύσω αὐτόν. Whether the Centurion came himself and spoke, or only by those whom he sent, can scarcely be determined with certainty, and affects the question but little. Without St Luke's account we should unhesitatingly understand the former from the *letter* of St Matthew, but the exceedingly definite account of St Luke must have as much weight as the prerogative of St Matthew's eye-witness. Both have been united in the supposition that the man, in the unrest of his great desire, had sent once and again, and at last had come himself. This might be possible, but appears to be contradicted by St Luke (ver. 7). If according to St Luke the first request was not urged in person, yet must vers. 5, 6 of St Matthew be understood in connexion with this, and St Luke ver. 10 admits most assuredly of no other coming and going than that of those who were sent. Therefore we, for our part, would concur with *Bengel*, who holds St Matthew's account to have been written *sublimiore divinæ quam historiae humanæ lege.* That is, not that it is indeed immaterial whether any man speaks by himself or by messengers (for there would be no justification of untruthfulness in this); but *it is no untruthfulness* to place one instead of the other, as the authoritative language of Scripture elsewhere teaches. How often in the Old Testament does speaking by the medium of others assume all the living reality of speaking in person! Compare in the New Testament Mar. x. 35 with Matt. xx. 20. Thus St Matthew's προσῆλθεν with its sequel may well be regarded as a living representation of St Luke's ἀπέστειλε; the λέγων (continued afterwards as ἀποκριθέις) equivalent to the Old Testament לֵאמֹר in countless instances. So also is the εἶπεν of Matt. xi. 3, and in this very place St Luke uses ἐρωτῶν in ver. 3, of the sending and saying by others, and in ver. 6 uses λέγων also. Let what we have elsewhere said be remembered, concerning the just distinction between the represented and the acted narrative, the historical writing which gives us the very life of the events, and the mere recital of the events themselves. In accordance with this let the higher grade of *freedom of spirit* in St Matthew be here observed as it is contrasted in this external circumstance with the more human exactitude of St Luke.

This freedom, however, proceeds not so far as to place a word in the mouth of our Lord, which He might not in such a sense have spoken. Thus when St Luke (ver. 6) only intimates that Jesus *went* with them, but St Matthew announces a word of willingness and promise as spoken by Him, they mutually supplement each other So he who reads St Luke, thinks almost necessarily of such an utterance in answer. Here also the word and the action are immediately united.

The humbly believing words of the Centurion which follow, and which St Luke records as having met the Lord when He had approached near to the house, appear in St Matthew's living presentation of the whole circumstance as the answer of the man himself; so on the other hand even St Luke in his external particularity has represented a similar approach of the man as if in person, who yet was not present. He writes in ver. 9 ἐθαύμαζον αὐτόν, and then gives the *commendation of his faith*, just as St Matthew does. (Only without Ἀμήν, which, as it was so often spoken by the Lord, is not by all the Evangelists, and by St Luke especially, mentioned with uniformity.) He also more definitely states (with στραφείς) what St Matthew does not neglect to record, that the Lord spoke this praise τοῖς ἀκολουθοῦσιν, τῷ ἀκολουθοῦντι αὐτῷ ὄχλῳ, that is, not so much to the Centurion in commendation,[1] as to the Israelites for their shame, and as a testimony against them.

It has been said that this is the first time that *we* find the word "Faith" in the New Testament: but the Lord had not only given utterance to it in the Sermon, ch. vi. 30, but on many occasions from Mark i. 15 downwards: compare Jno. i. 50; iii. 12, 15, &c., iv. 48; Mar. vi. 6. He everywhere *seeks* and demands faith, not only as a susceptibility which his miracles and wonders must meet, but as that without which He cannot confer that blessing which He is so willing to bestow. Much else was to be praised in this eminent man, his amiable care of his servants, the humility so unwonted in a Roman, the profound recognition of God's revelations manifested in his retreating behind the despised people of God—but the Lord only makes prominent his *faith*. He even *marvelled* at his strong faith, as it is only once elsewhere (Mark vi. 6) said that He marvelled,—but in that case it was at *unbelief*. He must have in some way given express utterance to this, else how could the Evangelists have ventured to record it? But let not this be hastily read and passed over; let us thoughtfully penetrate the depths which that *wonder* at faith or unbelief in the Spirit of the Son of Man discloses to us.[2] *So great* faith—He says: so strong,

[1] *Bengel's* remark that the Lord would not thus have praised the man if present—appears to us a refinement, almost in direct contradiction to St Matthew, who felt nothing of the kind. The word would assuredly be very soon reported to him, and thus was just the same as if spoken to him and in his presence.

[2] *Julius Müller* seems to us to pass over this deep meaning in a loose and inconsequential manner, thinking that goodness can only

so great (Matt. xv. 28), by which this man, a *man* under authority, absolutely and nakedly trusts in Me, confiding that I have power to command sickness[1] by a *Word* without coming or laying on of hands in the name of *God*, just as he himself can command his servant in the name of Cæsar! I have not *found* it in Israel, I who came to seek it, and to seek it there first of all, where it should have been to be found. For is not *Israel,*—the Lord while He puts them to shame in His language of reproof, yet uses the glorious and honourable title of their calling—beyond every other people the people of faith, called by God from the time of Abraham, and prepared, and through long ages trained unto *Faith?* The Lord thus, as manifestly as expressively, indicates the great leading idea of the Divine dealing with His people, the essential aim of all the institutions which had preceded His own coming.

Vers. 11, 12. St Luke, who elsewhere makes prominent the calling of the Gentiles, and for this reason records in detail the history of the Centurion directly after the Sermon on the Mount, yet contents himself here with the Lord's first saying, which indeed involved all the rest. The extended development of it into that clear and ample prediction which now follows as taken from the Prophets, he introduces in another place, (ch. xiii. 29,) where the Lord uttered it a second time. (Just as we found in the Sermon on the Mount). Ample occasion, however, was given by the retiring humility of the Gentile, and yet more by the self-complacent obtrusion of "our nation" (Lu. ver. 5) in the saying of the elders, for such an utterance of our Lord,—probably the first such testimony that fell from His lips, as probably this was the first heathen who ever came to be admitted into the kingdom of

astonish *us*, because we have participation in sin. The ground of Christ's marvelling at the Centurion's faith lies only, as His own words show, in its *contrast* with what the Lord was accustomed to find.—Not also generally in its contrast with the "evil unbelief" of mankind, since the Lord knows its *sin* without participation therein?

[1] Certainly his meaning was simply—command the *sickness* that it depart, (comp. Lu. iv. 39), somewhat as the modern fashion of aiming to speak to, and drive away, bodily evil. What *Lange* says of "Genii of recovery and health, powers of life, a genius of healing sent as a servant," sounds very beautiful and delicate, but is an importation from another quarter altogether.

God. It was nothing new that he spake, for it was only the blindness of Israel which failed to read it in the Prophets, and to find in the Promise to Abraham. Yea, it was only the remains of this blindness which rendered it necessary to the Apostles of the Circumcision with Peter at their head, even after all that the Lord had said down to Matt. xxviii. 19, and after the uncomprehended testimony of the Holy Ghost in Acts ii. 39, to receive another and distinctive revelation of this mystery (Eph. iii. 5). The Lord expresses Himself, as it were, euphemistically; avoiding the word "heathen," as also in Lu. iv. 24—27. But He uses the prophetical expressions, *probably* alluding to the Apocryphal passage (Bar. iv. 37; v. 5, 6)[1]—or directly to that fundamental promise (Gen. xxviii. 14) which the book of Baruch seems also to have in view, and the echoes of which are heard in such prophetic passages as Isa. xlix. 6, 12; lx. 4, &c. In contrast with Israel, and comprehending those gathered from all the nations of the earth, they are regarded as *many* who come into the kingdom of heaven. The *sitting down at table*, ἀνακλίνεσθαι, is not to be specially referred to the last futurity, although it points as far as that: it is obviously and first of all, the general Scriptural metaphor, firmly established in the phraseology of Israel (Lu. xiv. 15), for the enjoyment of all the blessings and benefits of the kingdom of God. It has the same signification as in Isa. xxv. 6, and as it has in all the parables of our Lord concerning marriage feasts and suppers. The Israelites would not *eat* with heathens: the Lord puts them to shame by the express contradiction of this. We also see that the *coming* of these many signifies their first entrance into the fellowship of the kingdom of heaven set up on earth, by the contrasted simultaneous rejection of Israel in ver. 12. The *children of the kingdom*—that is not ironically spoken, as if meaning those who vainly thought themselves such (comp. ch. xiii. 38, where we find the expression in its most distinctive sense): but those who are already the authenticated heirs, the guests already called, those who were *born* in the typical kingdom of God in order to the inheritance of the

[1] Where, indeed, the discourse is only of the children of Jerusalem returning, yet the Vulg. reading Sicut *filios regni* remarkably suits our passage. That the Lord elsewhere has apocryphal places in His mind, is undeniable.

Messianic, promised kingdom; they who as the children of Abraham stand already in some sense in its possession and enjoyment. With this sense only does the expression used in the later parallel accord: the kingdom of heaven *shall be taken from you.* (ch. xxi. 43.)

Let it be observed, further, how the Lord proclaims faith n His person, confidence in His Divine power and authority, as the distinctive condition of entrance into the kingdom of heaven. Throughout and entirely this and no other. For the whole discourse proceeds from this point, beholding in this *one* heathen the type and earnest of *many*, who in point of faith shall be like him. I have not found such faith in Israel, that is, at the same time—I have not been hailed and received with faith: a general and indefinite faith in God (Jno. xiv. 1) is no more the question since He makes His appearance, and when He proposes His claims, the evidence of such faith is to be sought and found as faith *in Him.* But just as little are we to seek the Lord's meaning in a more far-reaching, free development of faith as to its object; as if the insight into the person of Christ, as the Lord of spirits, from the *heathen* standing-point, is placed in advantageous contrast with the limited and straitened *Messianic* ideas of the Jews! (as *Neander* imposes his meaning, contrary to all Scripture). When Christ and the Apostles speak of the measure, the greatness, the strength of πίστις, they never refer directly to its extent of perception and acknowledgment.

Let it be observed, further, that the Lord gives those who are to be cast out their full rights at first as "Israel," and "the children of the kingdom," as also that He describes even the entrance of the strangers from the east and the west as only an opening to them of fellowship *with Abraham, Isaac, and Jacob* (quite in harmony with the Prophets);—but that yet the *casting out* of the unbelieving on account of their unbelief is, on the other hand, most definitely and decidedly fore-announced. For the *outer darkness* which is opposed to the feast of light and joy, although it seems in part to have its accomplishment in the blindness and obduracy of Israel upon earth, yet stretches its warning and threatening meaning to nothing less than what the Lord afterwards by similar expressions indicates (ch. xxii. 13; xxiv. 51, xxv. 30; xiii. 42). For as all the Lord's legislation does no more than fulfil and unfold what had before been written and spoken, so in all His prophecies He only illustrates, and perfects what the preceding prophets had included in their field of vision and range of utterance. *Darkness* in the Old Testament is equivalent to the prison. (Ps. cvii. 10—14; Isa. xlii. 7; Eccles. xviii. 4). But finally to the *kingdom of heaven* stands only opposed the kingdom of him, who keeps bound in the everlasting bonds of death. The article before κλαυθμὸς and βρυγμὸς τῶν ὀδόντων does not simply oppose emphatically the future torture to all pains of time,[1] but points obviously to the prophetic word, in order to connect the whole discourse with that in its conclusion. Isa. lxv. 14 is indicated (as elsewhere ch. lxvi. 24 is brought forward), and placed in connexion with such passages as Ps. cxii. 10, with which, again, Judith xvi. 21 may be compared. Whether in the significant contrast, weeping and gnashing of teeth (not chattering as with cold), a farther antithesis between the softer bewailing, and the mad fury of anguish is intimated,[2] we leave undecided: we prefer taking the description as a simple Scriptural emblem of self-engendered, useless sorrow of every kind.

But let it be noted, finally, that the Lord, with wise discrimination, does not proceed as we might have expected—the children of *Abraham* shall be cast out. For in the back-ground of this saying He designs to leave room for the *second* historical fulfilment of the great relative change between the far off and the near, those who are there within and those who are without, —as it is perspectively announced by the Prophets. Twice must the children recede that those who were before strangers and afar off may enter into their place: the second great change is when the Gentile-Christians have become ripe for rejection, and the seed of Abraham dispersed through all lands return back again from the east and the west, from the north and the south. (Isa. xliii. 5. 6). The Lord does not say or signify this immediately, but He leaves room in the prophetic perspective, for this second and inverted fulfilment of His word.

Ver. 13. St Matthew's representation, which from ver. 5 has

[1] Articulus insignis: in hac vitâ dolor nondum est dolor. *Bengel.*

[2] According to Von Gerlach: "probably the former represents the grief of the softer natures, the latter that of the more rugged." He also observes the more obvious contrast with the songs of the blessed.

more and more clearly set the nobleman before us as if present, now passes from a spiritual intercourse between him and Christ, to what would seem to have all the vividness of a bodily intercourse. He who may think that the ὕπαγε, spoken as if to a person present, departs too far from the reality of the occasion, may suppose, with many, that the Centurion himself came afterwards: whereby, however, the greater inaccuracy of St Luke, nay the only irreconcilable inconsistency in the whole narrative is immediately involved. The *signification* of the word, whether we regard it as thus immediately spoken or not, lies in two critical points, which now recur in their relation, and which the Evangelist now points out and makes emphatic for the analogy of similar cases. *Faith*, with the praise of which the discourse began, is ever the ground of help, as the Lord now testifies, with joy that He has found faith and therefore may help, but keeping back in His lowliness the mention of His own power which is ever spontaneous and ready to help. Be it done *unto thee*, as thou hast believed, namely to thee in thy servant, for whom thy affectionate faith may avail. This expression is a universal word of mercy and of power, which the Lord had for every one who came, and may have spoken to many unmentioned ones, *with the same meaning in various expression.* It is the design of the Evangelist to record *this*, and in this lies the truth of his narrative *according to the mind* of the Spirit. As to the external historical letter of our Lord's words, we may safely resign that up, while the Spirit continues from age to age to illustrate its living meaning in the world through the holy Gospels. Moreover we know not in any case, at least know not in the most important discourses, nor is it necessary for us to know, in what language they were uttered by the Lord.

THE TWO DIVERSE FOLLOWERS.

(Matt. viii. 20, 22; Lu. ix. 58, 60.)

The chronological connexion, which has been preserved hitherto, begins now to fail us. It *seems*, indeed, as if St Matthew placed this transaction expressly between ver. 18 and ver. 23, yet St Luke's account from ver. 51 has certainly the appearance of having adhered very strictly to the order of time. Who shall decide this? Thus much in general we may regard as certain, that, as St Luke often collects into one homogeneous whole, events occurring on various days of our Lord's eventful history, so also St Matthew by no means makes it his design to relate everywhere every thing *acoluthistically*, or in the strictest order (to quote the recent eminent critic *Ebrard*). It must remain undecided, also, whether *the two* incidents occurred in succession as it appears in the narrative.[1] The sayings of our Lord are the marrow of the Gospels. Much stress is laid upon the connection of the more connected and longer discourses, but little or none upon the date and sequence of single incidents and shorter sayings, the beginning and the end of our Lord's history being excepted. A comparative harmony may be very serviceable as it regards these. Here St Matthew, who gives us in his eighth and ninth chapters a selection of the earliest and most remarkable miracles arranged on the whole in strict order, but while doing so is preparing the way for the mission of the Twelve in ch. x. (hence ch. ix. 9), gives us in connexion two solemn sayings of our Lord concerning the following of Himself, which contain a most highly significant *contrast*.[2] This is exhibited in the different treatment of the different cases, as the Lord's wisdom, in the most impressive manner, speaks to each what His all-seeing eye discerned to be necessary. For to this we may refer Jno. ii. 24, 25. The enthusiastic one, who offers himself at once and with so much alacrity, is repelled almost abruptly: the considerate, reflecting, lingering one is quickened to his duty by a word of power which in his case dispenses with every other permitted and bounden duty.

[1] It is our unbiassed judgment that according to the express words of both Evangelists the former of these examples occurred twice.

[2] See, generally, the contrasts in St Matthew, as they are shewn in *Lange's* biblischen Dichtungen, second part. We cannot, however, discover with him any dispositions or preparations for the Apostolic office; or find Judas Iscariot, Thomas, and Matthew, in the three candidates for following, though *Rothe* too (Ethik iii. 419) appears to take such a view. It was not thus in the selection of the Apostles: and the Lord had, moreover, other close *followers* besides the Twelve.

Scribes do not offer themselves in great numbers, and this St Matthew seems to intimate in the unusual εἷς. But nothing was less aimed at by our Lord than to have *followers,* unless they were genuine and sound: He is as far from desiring this, as it would have been easy to attain it. He tests the Scribe severely, whether this was a matter of solemn earnestness to him. That he did not offer himself as *tempting* Christ is manifest: for in such instances it is generally either stated in the account, or detected immediately and exposed by the Lord. The man's speech sounds honest and decided, like Ithai's word to King David (2 Sam. xv. 21),[1] yea, as if he was prepared to reap the reward promised in Rev. xiv. 4. But it springs, probably, from a momentary paroxysm of feeling not uncommon at that time, and is not without a certain affectation of promising much: he by no means understood (like Thomas afterwards, Jno. xi. 16), whither matters would tend with the Lord and his followers. Therefore the Lord tells him the rugged and naked truth which he little expected, that with Him it would be otherwise than might have been usual in the case of a Teacher so honoured. This presses upon him the unexpressed question—Wilt thou still go with me? Hast thou understood and pondered all this? Probably the consequence was as in ch. xix. 22.[2]

The Lord's accompanying word has all the terseness and strength of a proverbial saying, and is in the highest degree vivid. Every thing living upon earth, even among its wild beasts, has its home, its secret place of rest and protection: not thus provided for am I! Places of abode are generally *upon* the earth; but the Lord designedly makes the variation:

[1] With which we may compare Ruth to Naomi (Ruth i. 16, 17). Thus the expression "Whithersoever thou goest" assuredly does not refer to the various roads the Lord may journey in! (according to the great *Schleiermacher's* very small interpretation.)

[2] "The book-learned are generally fastidious and love warm housing: Thus on this account as well as on account of their burrowing in dialectical subtilties and the dust of books, they are least useful for the practical work of life, and for labouring in the Lord's vineyard—hence is the first immediately rejected as unfit!" So *Sepp* after his manner, rather too express in his anachronism about book-dust, yet with some ground of truth. As to the general sentiment *Braune* says excellently, "Many would be pious, but would keep their nests—houses, riches, honour, and respectability."

even *under* the earth and *above* it the animals are cared for. The foxes are set against the more familiarly and proverbially used birds of the air, with this distinction, that while the former are among those beasts of the earth which are most secret and native under it; the latter are, on the contrary, free, unrestricted, and apparently homeless and unsettled. Nevertheless, just as the foxes have their cunningly prepared and secure holes, so *have* (and on this word the emphasis lies) even the birds their *κατασκηνώσεις* at least, and this contains the general idea which was appropriate to the occasion: nests are not meant, as such, but some little branch on which they may sit, or some tree or shrub under the shade of which they may find refuge. See ch. xiii. 32; Mar. iv. 32; and Ps. civ. 12; Dan. iv. 18 Sept. But the *Son of Man*—and here first occurs in St Matthew that name of deep meaning by which the Lord is wont to designate Himself, and which has already been found in Jno. i. 51. That it is a name which indicates and avows the Messiah, is certain from Daniel's prophecy: but it is equally manifest that it is most immediately a name of humiliation, of humble self-renunciation, (a lowly *Son of Man)*: which meaning holds also in Daniel, where it is used (as in Jno. i. 51) in contradistinction to the angelic nature (ch. vii. 10): as the invocation "O Son of Man," Dan. viii. 17 shows, and the repeated use of it in Ezekiel. Other significations are not excluded, as further, the Universal Man, the Second Man, the Son of God who yet has become man, and for man's sake will ever be such. Now the one meaning and now the other is prominent, according to the ever-varying connexion. Here we have the identity of the Messiah-name with the name of a lowly neglected son of man, and the second meaning holds good—*men* usually are better and more commodiously sheltered than beasts, but I am one of them of whom even this cannot be said! Again in strong and proverbial expression—not a place where He may lay his head, no pillow for his weary sleep. Is there here allusion to Jacob's stone for a pillow, as in Jno. i., Bethel had been referred to? Certainly the Lord does not merely say—I know not even for the coming night where I shall lay myself down. *(Herder.)* He speaks of His entire homeless and needy life, and lodgment, and wanderings since he entered upon His ministry: and if in His abode at Capernaum, or any where else for a short time, this expression might appear too strong, it was a great truth on the whole, and was even more and more literally working out its full accomplishment, till He bowed His head on the cross. This has the Lord most distinctively in view when he gives the answer to the avowal, I will follow thee *whithersoever* thou goest—*Thither go I*, that is my way and my goal! Wilt thou still go with me? If we take St Luke's chronology, this would have a yet deeper significance, see vers. 51—53. But the Lord could well have said the same at an earlier period, fore-conscious of the whole course of His career: and would do so, doubtless, when necessary in order fundamentally to repel all Jewish expectation. Not improbably the Scribe or others who heard these words would say: Is this language for one who assumes to be Messiah! Is this Daniel's Son of Man?

The second belonged already to the *disciples*, as St Matthew expressly remarks; that is, in the more comprehensive sense to those who, coming and going, attached themselves to the Lord; with this St Luke's account that the Lord uttered to him a special "ἀκολούθει μοι" perfectly agrees, for this summons might in its higher and additional meaning be repeated a second time, as we find in the case of the Apostles. The hitherto disciple is required to attach himself yet more entirely and inseparably to his Lord, and probably it was His intention to include him among the seventy. (Lu. x. i). Even in St Matthew's account a second summons of our Lord is evidently presupposed, since the words of ver. 21 can only be understood as an answer to such a summons: *suffer* me *first*—! The Lord, however, qualifies not His ἀκολούθει μοι, and speaks to this wavering lingerer who was in a danger that he knew not of failing to return, with such keenness and urgency as He would not have been likely to use in the case of an entirely new disciple. For the rest, it is entirely inconceivable that the meaning of the request was simply —let me first go and await my aged father's death and burial. This is contradicted less by the letter of the petition,[1] than by

[1] Yet as *Alford* well remarks (against *Theophylact*): πρῶτον ἀπελθεῖν καὶ θάψαι must refer to a specific *act* to be previously performed.

the spirit of our Lord's refusing answer, which lays the stress of the emphasis upon the *burying*. The entire meaning of the expression, as we shall unfold it, would be then entirely displaced: and an incomprehensible severity unnecessarily infused into it, by refusing the attentions of an affectionate son to a yet living father. The man could not have thus come to Jesus from a house of death, the affliction and legal uncleanness would have forbidden this:[1] but having recently come to him, he received the intelligence of the death which summoned him home, while the Lord required him to remain. By *this* obvious supposition alone the whole is disengaged of difficulty, especially the command of Jesus—Therefore *go not*, but follow me! The man thought indeed that he might with propriety ask to perform the duties which nature and religion exacted, especially as in Jewish law the obligation of burying released from most other engagements. Hence it is with modest submission that he says—*suffer* me first! Or should we rather say, with a *wavering* tendency? Certainly the position of this man's conscience, vibrating at that critical moment between return to his old relations and a persevering, yet closer adhesion to the Lord, manifestly betrays itself here: if he did not suspect danger in returning, would he have put the question—*May* I go?—1 Kings xix. 20 is generally compared, but this still more closely applies to Lu. ix. 61. And in connection with that, the difference between the Old and New Testament is referred to, between the relaxation of requirement and its strong enforcement: but that does not apply here, since our Saviour also can in fit cases relax His demand, even as Elias did to Elisha. His expression has primary reference to the individual instance before Him, and only applies in all its rigour to those who shall be found in the same precise position of mind. That is, He makes available in its literal significance a truth and a principle which, though in themselves perfectly general, are not always applied in a manner so directly interfering with human life.[2]

[1] Such left not the house of mourning before the entombment.

[2] Very true and discriminating is *Goschel's* observation, that Lu. ix. 61, 62, explains the foregoing, and that the Lord in both cases condemns the *looking back*. (Zur Lehre von den letzten Dingen S. 70. Onthe other hand what follows in pp. 61, 62 concerning reference

There is at first sight a tone of rigour and of harshness in this word of the Son of Man, who ordinarily is very far from breaking in upon any human ordinance, and certainly is at the utmost distance from a condemnation or violation of the most natural exhibitions of human love. The dead must be *buried*, according to the very ordinance of God, (Gen. iii. 19). If it be said that burial is a matter which affects not the dead, and therefore that it is immaterial who performs it, whether a son or any one else; such a cold thought, which our Lord has not in his view, is contradicted by the recognized and universal right feeling of man. Is it not a *duty of love* which a son might be supposed to have permission to discharge without asking for it at all? And yet He who directed the cleansed lepers to the priests, refuses to concede to a son the duty and the right of burying his own father! Assuredly it is because He had said Follow me! and to the same extent goes that other word—Whosoever loveth father or mother more than me, is not worthy of me. We may be tempted to regard this requirement as being too high and strained for humanity, we may find it difficult to reconcile this saying of our Lord with His ordinary manner of speaking. But this should lead us all the more diligently to seek that hidden meaning which is concealed under the intentional paradox: and if we seek it we shall find it.

We set out with the proper burial of the properly dead, for the request referred to this, and the refusal must, first of all, have referred to it likewise. But that the *dead* who are to be buried must be figuratively understood, admits of no doubt, and needs no proof, for it can occur to no man to impute so meaningless a saying to the Lord as that the burying must be deferred, till one dead man shall bury another—let the already dead care for the companions who join them! Who then are the *dead?* Not those who are, being only mortals and soon to die, reckoned as being dead, for then the contrast here would be lost. The disciple to whom it is forbidden, is himself one of such. No, the Lord speaks here as in Jno. v. 24, 25, of spiritual death, according to

here to the mutual care of the dead in the church beyond—to the performance of obsequies in the name of Jesus—may be set down as ingenious wanderings beyond the letter of the text).

the Spirit's usage throughout the whole New Testament. Thus the "burying," as an external work belonging to the things of this world, should, in regard to persons and circumstances where the doing of something more important is involved, be left to the children of the world, who can perform such matters, are good enough for them, and are in their generation better adapted for their performance. Thus far we have light arising in this dark word, and observe by this increasing light that the Lord goes still further, and *taking the present circumstance as a similitude*, designs that we should also understand the *burying* itself, and even the *dead* to be buried in their figurative meaning. Here we discern Himself and His manner of teaching once more. How often do we find in studying His words, that His penetrating glance beholds the most internal and general significance of individual occasions and circumstances: and then, elevating the particular circumstance into an example and emblem, connects with it sayings of sublimest, and most far-reaching application. It is not otherwise here. When one called to be His follower has mentioned a "burial" which he must first take charge of, which, however, may very probably lead to the withdrawal from Him of this called disciple, the profoundly wise Master gives him as an answer, not fore-thought on, but issuing at once from the depths of His Spirit,—an answer which at the same time opens up a wide field of thought.

But to perceive this, we must think of the still more harsh and mysterious saying: *Let* those who are dead in sin, perform their burial-work one for another! This may appear to sound like what many loveless ones in their pride say in their thoughts or with their lips—let the evil world perish, let it remain in its ruin! For a moment it may so sound, till we reflect *Who* thus speaks. Did He then leave the dead in their death and burial? Did He not come for the very purpose, that whosoever believeth on Him, should not remain in death? and is it not for this very object, that the great *work of revivification* should proceed upon earth, that He called His disciples, and sent them forth among the dead as His witnesses, with the word and spirit of life? and here we remark that His words to the disciple whom He called, contain a very impressive contrast between the work to be *left* to others, and the work which he himself must with his utmost diligence engage in. We should find this antithesis in the occasion and in the person, even if it was not expressed in word, but it is so. In St Matthew we have the *Follow thou me*, that is, hear the words of eternal life which will give life to thy soul: and again in St Luke—But go thou and *preach the kingdom of God*, that is, arouse those who are dead, being called to this, leave burying to others, who alas do it naturally enough, as long as they themselves are as dead as *their* dead (Διάγγελλε, cry aloud everywhere, far and wide, as in Rom. ix. 17). The dead, indeed, are *not* to be thus left, but to them the true word of life is to be preached. The very reverse holds here. The Lord's stern saying is one which springs from the consuming zeal of his love for the world's salvation. He will have the one thing pursued without distraction and intermission. He holds fast His messenger of life, that the life-giving work may take no harm through his attention to the "burying." As in a great hospital, where many are hourly dying, the physicians' sole concern is healing and saving; others may charge themselves with burial, *they* have no time for that. So is it with the followers of the Lord in this world! When separation to this great calling is concerned, everything else must give way. The proper burial of a father, even, is not excepted: although generally it is fit and right that a mourner should bury *his own* dead out of his sight (Gen. xxiii. 4, as here—*their* dead), and the Lord Himself, Matt. xxvi. 12, gives us proof, in what estimation he held such a service rendered by love to its object. Much more must all that give place which the Lord likens to such *burying*. *Luther* says very appropriately on this place: "some there be who alledge good works, for their not following and believing, but Christ regards them as only dead and lost works." Oh how much of such lost and valueless work is there under all kinds of forms and names, and with very specious pretension, but which bring no service to the kingdom of God, bring no dead to life, and from which the Lord not simply by permission but by express commandment gives His people dispensation — *leave* these things to others! Much of such mere burial-work passes under the title of political or generally human obligations, yea is to be found in the holy ceremonies of an ecclesiastic death. These things not only make no dead soul live, but bury the dead yet more deeply in their death, (Rom. vi. 4). Thus do the dead bury each other! For all things in men's mutual commerce have the effect and influence either of *burying* or of *raising from death.* But this difference does not so much lie in any external act as such, as in the manner and spirit of its performance. The burying may be so ordered, as to conduce to awakening from death: men may so "preach the kingdom of God," as that the people who hear be preached into death.

This is the far-reaching, universally applicable meaning of the word, in which it has its truth and force for all His disciples everywhere: *Ye* are called, as the living, to diffuse life, *leave* everything else as burying-work to the dead![1] "Take with you who is fit to go: but miss not a step of your own way," *(Zinzendorf).* But *when* does this general principle lay hold of the soul in its full severity, and cut off from us by an unconditional prohibition, things otherwise permitted, and even demanded by the very instinct of life, such as the burying of a father in the present case? In *cases of collision* and *critical times of decision,* known to be such by the Lord's inward monition in the conscience. This man was in actual danger of burying himself again, while burying his father; and the third example in Lu. ix. 61, 62, is an explanatory parallel of the second. He who felt in himself while he put the question the waverings of his spirit, perceived in his spirit more clearly than many expositors have done, the true meaning of the Lord's stern answer. Suppose it thine own case, should any the holiest obligation of life, even that of showing thy filial affection at the dying bed or the grave of thy father, call thee away at the critical moment when thy Lord's service most imperatively claims thee, tell it to Him in the sincerity of thine heart: Lord, suffer me *first* to go and discharge this obligation! and if this *first* should *not* be approved of by Him, as involving danger to thyself: then art thou released from all, hold thyself bound, *to follow Him!* What thou thoughtest thyself bound to do will be done by others, and no more will harm result from thine omission, than the dead will fail to bury their dead.

[1] As typically the consecrated Nazarite might not defile himself even at the death of his father, mother, &c., though the High Priest was not forbidden to do so. (Num. vi. 7; Lev. xxi. 1—4.)

THE STILLING OF THE SEA.

(Matt. viii. 26; Mark iv. 35—39, 40; Luke viii. 22—25).

The significance of this history belongs not simply to the place where we find and expound the words. The whole human life of the Son of God is in all its circumstances and details altogether symbolical, because He who is the image of the invisible God in the flesh appears in commerce with the world, with nature, and with men: and this symbolical, typical, prophetical character meets us with special significance on some most striking occasions. The passage over the sea is human life generally, disciple-life in particular: the ship in which He protectingly and savingly voyages with them, as it is the heart of His disciple, so it is also His Church, the antitype of the Ark. The three Evangelists note *three* sayings of our Lord in connexion with this event: St Matthew only records the central and most important word, to the right understanding of which belongs the right understanding of the whole narrative, inasmuch as in that word the Lord regards the occurrence prophetically and symbolically. He stills the storm, in order to teach by signs, how He could and He will still all storms: He rebuked the little faith of His disciples, in order to speak in doing so a permanent word for all similar conjunctures and circumstances in all time to come. The Spirit secretly teaches this in the concise and measured words of vers. 23, 24, in St Matthew. The disciples *followed* Him, when He, evening being come (according to St Mark), summoned them to the voyage by entering the ship, and announcing His will. *And behold*, where He voyages with His disciples, there arises the storm!

The *first* word (in St Mark and St Luke) is the Lord's purely human—let us pass over unto the other side! On which we have only to remark that the Lord who so often is under the necessity of opposing His majestic I to all other men, all the more condescendingly on that account speaks of the We and the Us in the external things of ordinary life:[1] yet as the whole tenor of the

[1] Compare 2 Kings iv. 13 (especially in the original) with ver. 9. Just so do the Apostles speak, in the same spirit mingling themselves

Gospels evinces, *the Lord* in His own pre-eminent dignity *only* thus speaks in such relations. All the more impressively does the *third* word follow, with which He, the only one, and concerning whom the question is for ever rising anew—*Ποταπός ἐστιν οὗτος*—rebukes the winds and the sea!

The word of main importance, however, is that central word to the terrified disciples, which the Evangelists remarkably enough give us in variety of literal expression, but with the same meaning. The power and force of *such* words must ever leave the mere letter behind, and fasten upon the heart as the immediate speech of spirit to spirit. "He rebuked us that our faith was little, that we were not ready with our faith, that we had no faith"—this was the never-erased impression of words which in the perturbation of the moment were not distinctly heard, but profoundly understood. One thing was beyond all else plain; that he pointed to *faith* as the principle through which fear is overcome. There was, indeed, great peril according to human appearance, in a ship already filling with water: St Luke *καὶ ἐκινδύνευον*. Four fishermen familiar with the sea were there. But the Lord, whose office and work was not to row the ship, knowing no care as to the passage (critical from the beginning), *slept*, laying his weary head upon the wooden railing of the ship.[1] Slept so sound and tranquil, that the storm and uproar around did not awake him, but only the hands and cry of the disciples. (All three Evangelists mention distinctively the *awaking* Him, before they spoke to Him). And how does the awakened wake up? In the same majestic tranquillity with which he had sunk to sleep, in the most perfect self-possession and power of His spirit. Let any man reflect how one suddenly roused with outcries of distress and danger of death around him, would in the weakness of humanity comport himself: and it will help him to perceive and estimate the unapproachable dignity of this Being, even while one with us He is paying His tribute to

and their attendants, ministers and servants together, even in spiritual things—though not with so much condescension as Elisha showed when he spoke of *respect* shown towards him and *Gehazi*.

[1] For even though *προσκεφάλαιον* may signify ordinarily a second pillow or cushion, yet the *article* in Mark iv. 38 seems to indicate something belonging to the ship, which might serve *as* a cushion or *support*.

the infirmity of our flesh. Yea, verily, *this* Son of Man sinks into sleep, and wakes again even like ourselves, and yet not like ourselves. This gives His word, spoken at this critical moment, its foundation of majesty, and must be considered in its exposition. That the Lord thus speaks and thus can speak, is at least as wonderful as that He in Adam's primeval authority and dominion controls the element: rather this latter is to be understood by the former. The Son of Man slept, the Son of God in Man awakes and speaks. For Himself exhausted, for others almighty.

St Matthew gives the words of the disciples in their simplest expression, St Luke indicates more strongly the urgency of their feeling by the twice uttered "Master! Master!"—St Mark adds their reproachful appeal, "Carest thou not that we perish?" Canst thou sleep tranquilly, while we are in anguish and straits? He utters no reproach for the violent awakening, but perceiving instantly the whole significance of the occasion, He penetrates to the very heart of the matter, by speaking, as the great Master a great word of instruction for all who are so terrified. *Why are ye so fearful?* So fearful? This St Mark also places first. He never entertains fear of any creature; there is no trace of any such feeling in Him throughout the Gospels. When anxiety, fear, or grief falls upon Him, it springs from quite another principle. To fear is human, belongs to fallen human nature in its sin and fear of death: but *faith* in God should again expel this fear. This is the great thought in the mind of our Lord: it is only He who can speak to the terrified, in perfect fearless composure, concerning *fearing* and *believing*, as opposite one to the other. The Holy Ghost revives in the Apostle the remembrance of the word, as if it had been: *O ye of little faith!* as in ch. vi. 30. The disciples were also in unbelief, which cried out—we perish! Yet were they at the same time sufficiently *believing* to awake and call upon him—*Lord help us!* Even weak faith is faith still, the trembling hand yet holds fast the Deliverer. If others among the people had called upon the Lord in such a storm to help them, in them it would have been a stronger faith. Thus the idea of little faith is relative: the disciples, more intimately familiar with the power of their Master, should not have allowed themselves so lightly to be whelmed in distress and deadly fear by the mere appearance of danger: to Peter already walking on the sea, the rebuke is yet stronger—O thou of little faith, wherefore didst thou doubt! St Mark and St Luke give us another form of expression: *how is it that ye have no faith,* just now, when ye should have been able to trust? Hence equivalent to *where is your faith?* for there is in truth no difference of meaning. More depends upon another difference: viz., that the Evangelists, not Apostles, relate first the rebuking of the storm, and then the word of the disciples; while St Matthew, on the other hand, tells us, and with a literal and express Τότε, that the Lord spoke *first* the word of admonition to the disciples and stilled their disquieted souls, *before* He turned to the winds and the waves. In this lies the sublimest trait of the whole: He looks not round on the uproar of the elements, before He has discharged to His disciples in severity and love His accustomed function of Master.[1] Further it is τότε ἐγερθείς,—still sitting, the awakened one in the midst of all the tempest remaining unperturbed.

But then follows the act which sets its seal to the word. And just as this, so also does that carry its own meaning with it. And yet this *empire over nature* is a new thing which St Matthew has to record concerning Jesus. His narrative of selected miracles in chs. viii. and ix., rises through a gradation of importance: cleansing of the leper (a great thing even to begin with)—healing at a distance by His word, Be it done!—commanding the wind and the sea—saying to the devils, go!—*forgiving the sins* of the paralytic (more indeed than saying arise! or go hence! more than ruling the sea)—and finally giving life to the dead! St Matthew and St Luke both give us to understand that the Lord *addressed* the excited elements, as we speak to living and conscious beings; St Mark gives us the *two words* of His invocation: *Σιώπα! Πεφίμωσο!* If we are to seek in the repetition any thing more than mere emphasis, that additional meaning is not to be found by referring (as *Bengel* does) the former to the *sonus,* and the latter to the *impetus,* but by regarding the previous words of St Mark: He rebuked the *wind* and spoke to the *sea.* This is so significantly echoed in the subsequent exclamation of the astonished men, as recorded by all the three Evangelists, that we may even

[1] "If they had awaked Him, to restore their disorder and presence of mind scared away by danger, He would have entered on His function without rebuking them." *Braune.*

on that account readily believe that the Lord literally spoke, as St Mark records it:—that he uttered one word of authority to the storm raging above, and another to the waves below. It surprises us to read in *Lange* that as the wind and the billows were no "spiritual power" opposed to Him, the invocation was not "properly such," but a "*prophetic* announcement with a mysteriously *symbolical* design," and to find that with a diluted rationalism he traces the "*immediate* causes of the stilling of the air and of the sea to the *atmosphere*." Oh no, there is an authoritative word of God's Spirit's power, which can speak into the atmosphere more than was before latent in it according to the *harmonia præstabilita.* This word of authority was not a manner of speaking which meant only a knowledge that it would become still! It is, moreover, generally true, as *von Gerlach* understands the passage, that "the destructive powers of creation are for the sin of man in the service of evil spirits." That profound thinker *Daub*, for example (Jud. Ischar. II. 353), has referred to this history in connection with his views of the demon-element in the terrors of nature and the war of the elements, and of the authority of God which can alone command them to be still. Whether the Gergesene devils, whose history presently follows, were the spirits who raised this tempest against Jesus (according to an old opinion), and thus their ordnance is spoken to instead of the beings who directed it, is very much to be questioned: and the invocation will certainly admit of no application to the intermediate agency in nature of *angels*, according to the opinion of many. We, for our own part, are not at all disposed to rest the simple truth of this history upon any such inappropriate and needless conceits: it is quite in harmony with the whole exhibition of the character of God's power, thus to exert authority over nature. Job. xxxviii. 11; (Ps. lxv. 8, lxxxix. 10). What that mysterious question in Prov. xxx. 4 attributed to the "Son" of whom the Old Testament prophesied, now receives its manifest realization. Here is something much beyond Elijah's dividing the waters of the Jordan. We have no need too elaborately to work out the picture, and refer (with *Pfenninger*) to the imperative form of the Lord seen reflected in the instantly still water (it was, indeed, evening or night): we have ample foundation already for the amazed exclamation of the *men* (of the disciples themselves also according to St Mark and St Luke) concerning this Son of Man: *What manner of man is this!* But He remains Himself in His high dignity amid such an outcry of astonishment, the same as when He heard it later from the lips of Pilate—*Behold, what a man is this!* (Ἴδε ὁ ανθρωπος, Ecce homo! Eng. Behold the man! Ger. Welch ein mensch!—Tr.)

THE DEVILS IN THE SWINE.

(Matt. viii. 32; Mark v. 8, 9, 19; Luke viii. 30, 39).

One single word of the Lord does St Matthew set within the margin of a wonderful narrative,[1] which, amid all the wonders to which we have been accustomed, stands alone and distinct in its kind. Thus much is by it clearly designed to be taught, that this Jesus who commanded the wind and the sea to be still, rules also in His unapproachable dignity over the devils, to whom His ὑπάγετε, mighty in its tranquillity, points the way of departure, and permits them to go: just as in ver. 16 it had been already said in general that He cast out spirits with His word. There is a simple grandeur in the account of St Matthew, who brings forward no part of the circumstance which is not absolutely necessary for its right understanding. To the other three Evangelists there remain the individual and more exact details, and three other words of our Lord in connexion with them.[2] The records agree perfectly in all essential points, and particularly

[1] The geographical investigations about Gadara, Gerasa, Gergesa, we gladly hand over to the learned.

[2] But it is no part of this greater exactitude, that they speak only of one possessed. We cannot agree, either with *Olshausen* who says, generally, that Matthew has confounded the accounts; or with *Ebrard*, who regards the second as taken from Mark i. 23—27, and connected with the first. We adhere to the simple conclusion, that according to St Matthew there were two, while St Mark and St Luke, without denying that, speak more especially of one. We have only to add that the one might very naturally be prominent throughout the whole proceeding. He who would investigate further, forgets in subordinate and useless questions, the main point. *Schleiermacher* repudiates the second as false, because madmen never affect such close friendship and fellowship, but there are answers enough to that observation.

concur in placing the incident immediately after the stilling of the sea.

That truth, which had only been testified in St Matthew's Gospel by the Father from heaven (ch. iii. 17), and which Satan had in vain endeavoured to assail, viz., that this *Jesus*, the Virgin's son, Emmanuel, is truly *the Son of God*—the devils have since understood, earlier and better than men. But while they know it they tremble before Him! St Mark, ch. i., has already announced similar testimonies of the spirits in the possessed. We understand, with all our science, so little of the natural history of hell, and of that interference of its spiritual powers with the affairs of human life which is ever being exerted, but was specially intense in our Saviour's time, that it might well be accounted the most infatuated of all imaginable folly to hazard the rash assertions of our ignorance against the plain declarations of Holy Writ, which have their thousandfold confirmation in our consciences, in history, and in religious science. These Gadarenes or Gergesenes disclose to us a dark and awful province of humanity, as lying under the ravages of the devil, the counterpart of which, at least in moral life, if not in such horrible manifestations of bodily possession, may be found in Christendom to the present day—to say nothing of its full analogies in Heathenism. But over this region also *Jesus* rules, *the Son of God!* To believe and to understand this is the main concern, and we would not bury or obscure this fundamental truth by any irrelevant discussions!

St Matthew's expression, ver. 29, gives us at first to understand that the possessed called out upon Jesus, but it is afterwards made plain that the devils, ver. 31, spake through their mouth, especially that of the one. The incident is made more vivid by the additional information of the two other Evangelists, that the men, in their frenzy, rushed towards the Lord, as they did towards all who were in the way, but that in His near presence there came a change upon them suddenly. The one devil who united together many in them, marks the great Ruler and Judge; hence the falling down before Him, the cry of horror against Him who is come to torment them, who has power to bid them go away into their abyss. And how came this? *For* (thus both Evangelists add in explanation) He had commanded the unclean spirit to come out of the man, had uttered a word which arrested the mad attack upon Him: *Come out of the man, thou unclean spirit!* I am He who can utter this command, who am come first of all to deliver *men* from the power of Satan. *Unclean* spirit—this was the ordinary phrase, used by the Lord because it has in His use a profoundly true significance. Did He address in these words the ruler of the host "Legion?" He was in His humiliation by no means omniscient, but, unless in cases when the Father gave Him special and instant revelation, subjected to the successive perceptions of observation, like humanity in general. He appears here to have seen in effect at the beginning only an ordinary instance of demoniacal possession. But His first—*come out of the man!*[1] not indeed impotent, rather efficient to bring down the spirits to entreaty, was not instantly obeyed, as we often read, *e.g.* in Mar. i. 26, ix. 26. Then does the Lord discern a possession of an aggravated kind (Matt. xvii. 21), and maintaining the sublimest composure in the midst of the raging fury of the demons, condescends as his king and judge to the being thus brought, as it were, before his tribunal; and enters into a most marvellous and mysterious colloquy with the unclean spirit.

What is thy name? (St Mark τί σοι ὄνομα, St Lu. τί σόι ἐστι ὄνομα). It is marvellous and quite peculiar (the only instance recorded) that the Lord should ask the unclean spirit concerning His distinctive *name.* For that this spirit is intended, and not the man of whom he had taken possession, is most decidedly shown in the context, according to the two other Evangelists. It has been well urged, that a question which would have been otherwise quite inappropriate and unmeaning, might in this case be regarded as quite useful, inasmuch as it would help to bring the confused madman to sober recollection. But the frenzy of

[1] By no means, as *Neander* thinks, a mere remark of a subsequent compiler, in order to find a motive for the words of the demons. Worse still, we find *Schleiermacher* deeming it incomprehensible "that the spirits are so considerate and thoughtful for themselves, and like children who have no inclination to obey, make their proposals and subterfuges"—and therefore that the παρήγγειλε γάρ is an incorrect addition. That the devils, indeed, have no wish instantly to obey, is their very nature—and in that they are actually worse than mere headstrong and obstinate children, who are full of cunning reasonings.

possession is not to be treated thus, and we perceive at once that the conversation is not opened up between the man and Jesus, but between the devil who usurps the man's mouth,[1] and His Lord and Judge who commands him to stand and render account. That the devils as *spirits* are individual persons, and that gradations and kinds obtain among them, we already know: and can understand the object of our Lord's real question: what devil art thou? The *name* which he may have uttered, was indeed only intelligible to Jesus: for what we find in the Talmud or in any other books of ancient or modern times concerning the names of fiends, may be regarded as containing a little truth mingled with much fable. But expositors should be content to stand apart while the Son of God speaks to a being out of hell; well assured, however, that they perfectly understood each other. The malicious spirit, we further mark, made bold by the unlooked for condescension, evades the proper meaning of the question, and gives an answer which is in the genuine devilish manner, by a name which is only a disguise, and says proudly, impudently, and half-mockingly, as though a prisoner on defence—my name is *Legion*, for we are many. All this St Matthew passes over, and hastens on to the request of the devils founded upon it, for permission to *enter into the swine*. This is the turning point of the whole narrative. The Lord who has *not* hitherto exhibited to us *merely* "a kind disposition to enter into the disordered fantasies of a maniac" *(Weiss), nor* His wisdom in the gentle, gradual, accommodating treatment of a sick man, (as, alas, most of even orthodox expositors, down to *Lange* and *Braune*, would have us believe), but who has shown us, in this *the first direct and violent incursion of hell upon Him*, the sublime tranquillity of the Son of God in the Son of Man—at this critical moment

[1] Not however as if the notions and manner of speech of the possessed man were mingled with those of the possessing subject. This has been discovered in St Mark's "adjuring *by God*," but incorrectly. For Dr *Bauer's* question: When was the devil so devout as to take the name of God into his mouth? is answered most pointedly and well by *Ebrard*, when he writes "die Posaune des jüngsten Gerichts gegen Hegel!" *Von Gerlach* observes generally that the "manifold abuse of the name of God among wicked men, shows how false the ideas of former times were, which conceived that the devil could not utter it."

knows, through the full revelation of the Father shining through His spirit, what the whole occasion is, and what it becomes Him in this conjuncture to do. The trial and hearing are broken off abruptly, the request even of the devils is granted, and soundness is imparted to the men through the majestic and decisive decree—go! Here the whole narrative finds its consummation, and just at the point where Jesus is revealed as their absolute Ruler and Lord, our curiosity concerning the mysteries of the devil's kingdom and subjects is left ungratified, and for ever silenced. Whether there lay in the request merely the appetency for the unclean,[1] with a superadded disposition to destroy, or whether it was a malicious scheme to bring the Lord into evil repute through the death of the swine—sublime over all rises His calm, sovereign word of permission—*Go!* What calm supremacy, what mysterious depth is there in this one word! Latent within it is an answer to the question before put, ver. 29. *It is not yet time* for your final judgment. How much is there intimated yet not spoken, and which we dare not trust ourselves to penetrate, concerning the influence of unclean spirits even upon animal life, the only example[2] of which in Biblical history here meets us.[3] We do not read that the man or the men rushed upon the two thousand swine, to drive them into the sea: it is only said, that the devils went out, and entered into the swine. Even *Neander* here recognizes the improbability and inappropriateness of the demoniac's being let loose upon the swine—although

[1] "The ancient affinity between the serpent and swine, the union of which is exhibited in the dragon, the affinity of the demon nature for swine," as *Lange* labours to express his idea. The *mere* "inclination to the external, towards flesh, or towards a bodily dwelling" (*von Gerlach*), does not seem precisely to explain the desire to enter the swine in particular.

[2] The inhabitants of the destroyed Babylon in the prophetic description might have been made to illustrate this, where animals and devils are in mysterious fellowship: Isa. xiii. 21, 22, xxxiv. 11—15; Bar. iv. 35; Rev. xviii. 2.

[3] Even the English *Trench* (Notes on the Miracles) refers us to the *Tellurismus* of our *Kieser*, and *Passavant's* Unterss. über das Hellsehen, for the susceptibility of animals, to demoniac influence. *Alford's* subtle observation goes to shew that the same animal soul, which man has in common with animals, and through which the demon exerts influence upon him, may undergo the same influence in them.

he then ventures to suppose, in explanation of this "obscure point" of the narrative, that the entering of the spirits into the swine has been inferred from their rushing down into the sea, and that the permission of Christ as it is recorded here has been fabricated in consequence. We altogether protest against such dealing with the Scripture. *Braune* ventures his doubtful remark, that the swine were seized with this madness from some "altogether undefined, and unknown cause," but we must read it as we find:—it was the simple result of the devils entering into them. Not indeed, only to possess them, but to *destroy* them, that going out of the men they may yet accomplish some work of destruction. The whole record shows that *this* was the sole object of their request. Nor were they in any special sense "stupid devils"—as Dr *Paulus* ironically solves the mystery of their so soon forfeiting the transitional bodily homes which they had just obtained: —they were more cunning than *this* Paulus!

But now come forward the silly expositors, orthodox and heterodox of every shade, and think they have a right to ask, whether the Lord Jesus could have spoken this—Go! Many fly from this narrative, as if the spirits had entered into *them*, and driven them into the sea of unbelief; they enter upon all kinds of uncalled for apologies for the swine and their owners, forgetting, or seeming to forget, what the apologies of ages have testified on behalf of Jesus. Others, with better views, adduce many ingenious reasons for the act: as that the Lord would hereby give the most convincing evidence of the entire dependence of all spirits upon His word; and with this to give palpable assurance to all Sadducees of the existence of such spirits; so also to punish the probably Jewish owners of these swine (which we cannot think of); further, to test the Gadarenes, how they would receive the destruction of their property; finally, to teach the value of the spirit of man, his healing being well worth some two thousand swine; or what else has ever been suggested. We have no need whatever of any of these remarks, true or otherwise, concerning this sublime transaction, the σκάνδαλον of

[1] *Sepp* (ii. 393 seq.) gives us some interesting and learned notices of the Jewish greediness of gain which was shown in the breeding of swine, and the employment of Gentile labourers therein, for traffic among the Gentiles.

which all three Evangelists have ruthlessly placed right in the centre of their several accounts: for we fix our eyes upon the plain fact, that *the deed itself is its own justification.* They did not then sue our Lord for any loss they suffered in the destruction of the swine; no more will we—we will not indeed dare to speak boldly concerning it. The question, why our Lord permitted the devils to enter the swine, is already answered by another question—Why had the Lord *permitted* them to enter the men?

But far more fearful than the hearing of this devilish request, is the Lord's granting to the Gergesenes *their* supplication. (They dare not, however, cast any reproach on him concerning the swine). He who does not desire Him, as He is and as He acts, the Ruler of hell, the Lord of nature, the Physician and Healer of men, may beseech Him to depart, whether courteously or ungraciously, and have his request granted. Yet is his departure softened by the word which, according to both St Mark and St Luke, He uttered to the men who were healed. It is not now, as sometimes, when it was forbidden to make it known: here upon the very outskirts of the Jewish land there was no danger to be obviated. The poor people of Δεκάπολις shall have, though against their will, a testimony and living monument of His power—one who had lived among themselves. Not indeed to publish abroad everywhere (as he actually did) is the healed man, with his brother not mentioned, sent back: but the command is,—Go home to thine house, ὑπόστρεφε, *to thy people*, from whom thou hast been so long estranged! Not indeed with a prudent care against relapse, and in order to his full recovery, which would be prevented by his being alone: for he wished to go with Jesus, and the devils were clean gone from him.[1] But this springs from the gentle graciousness of our Lord, which desires the return home of this man, thus restored to his family. It is in accordance with this universal ordinance that the ἀναγγέλλειν and the διηγεῖσθαι should take its beginning from the social circle, and sound out from the home. It evinces also His constant humility, for He here speaks of His great miracle as

[1] As it regards the "inner and moral healing," the remaining with Jesus would have been the most effectual guarantee, as *von Gerlach* remarks, in defence of the immediate *bodily* healing.

what the *Lord*[1] hath done for thee. St Mark adds, "and *hath had compassion on thee.*" The miracles of Jesus are ever God's acts of compassion towards men. This is one such instance, standing alone in its kind, and takes its place among the rest, with a word at its close which contains an exhortation which applies to this day to all who have received God's compassion in Christ.

THE PARALYTIC AND THE SCRIBES.

(Matt. ix. 2, 4—6; Mark ii. 5, 8, 8—11; Luke v. 20, 22—24)

The chronological order of this occurrence is not to be obtained with full certainty from the separate accounts: St Mark's *δι' ἡμερῶν*, and St Luke's *ἐν μιᾷ τῶν ἡμερῶν*, however, allow latitude enough to permit our following St Matthew—as is always the most obvious and natural—and to view his *καὶ ἰδοῦ* as immediately hanging upon his preceding narrative. The three Evangelists entirely agree in the matter itself, although the accounts of the two others are more detailed and vivid. The words of the Lord Jesus are repeated by them all in nearly the same terms. We read, first of all, in all three, that Jesus saw *their* faith, *ἰδών*. It is generally, but very improperly, supposed to be that of the bearers, and of *him who is borne*—as it were "the *united* believing efforts of the sick man and his friends." For not only is the latter *distinguished from* the former in the passage itself, but it was obviously the faith of those who brought him to the healing power of the Lord that made itself so *manifest* in the painstaking and zealous means which they adopted;[2] and finally, the Lord's word to the sick man, so unlooked for and

[1] This, and ch. xiii. 20, both in St Mark, are the only places in which Jesus speaks of God, His Father, as *κύριος*;—supposing that he is literally exact. (For Matt. xi. 25 has not *κύριε*, absolutely). The demoniac was not "probably a heathen" (as *Braune* thinks), in which case *κύριος* would have been to him just Jehovah, the God of Israel. The sayings are altogether Jewish in their structure.

[2] *Schleiermacher* would explain "the uncommon and almost tumultuous excitement about a home-born (?) sick man, whose case would have been no worse for delay," by a festival near at hand. But how much else is to be thought and said about that!

striking as it was, finds its explanation in this, that He saw in *him* a state of mind and feeling *different* from theirs, aiming at an object distinct from that of the bearers who only sought for his bodily healing. It may be understood, therefore, as a paradox and by way of *opposition*—although He perceived their believing desire, He did not immediately gratify it, but spoke first a word quite different from what they had desired:—or, it may be regarded as giving a profoundly significant reason :—when He perceived that their strong faith would well bear the test of delay. In any case the key-note of the narrative is this, that he acted in a manner *unexpected :* but the secret reason of our Lord's dealing is left concealed in the narrative, even as it first revealed itself in the transaction in the concluding reference. The Lord perceived in the soul of the paralytic a sentiment more akin to despair than faith, rather a doubt whether his healing would correspond with his friends' confidence: for he was greatly troubled on account of his sins, which probably had a particular connexion with his sickness. This penitent state of mind, on the one hand, was more than the confidence of the others which had reference to bodily healing, and the Lord, rejoicing more over his *penitence* than their *faith,* does not fail first of all and immediately to invigorate the troubled spirit with the best consolation. On the other hand, although *their* faith might have availed for the healing of the man, the Lord prefers to excite within his own heart the spirit of faith, that so he might come to experience a greater healing than that which would have been imparted through the faith of others. When preachers on the eighteenth Sund. after Trinity lay down faith as a presupposed condition for the forgiveness of sins, they forget, in their dogmatising, that the encouraging word must be uttered first, which then faith lays hold of and appropriates.

A gracious and most affectionate word of consolation to the dejected man precedes the utterance of the great and express word of absolution. St Luke has only retained the ἄνθρωπε, which marks an address to the person himself: and that only in general terms, while the other two Evangelists mention more exactly and literally τέκνον, which is more affectionate even than θύγατερ (Matt., ver. 22), and the same word which our Lord afterwards used in addressing His disciples. St Matthew only adds θάρσει, and we feel it to be quite natural that the Lord should utter just such a word: while the other two Evangelists, presupposing that, give only in full prominence the assurance of the *forgiveness of sins.*

We might now go on to exhibit and expound the testimony given in this narrative, so as to bring out its reference to that which is of the highest moment, of infinitely greater importance than bodily help. We might make some remarks upon the interval, however short, which the Lord permits in this case between the taking away of the guilt of sin, and the removal of its punishment; and show how that in the counsels and plans of the Most High many must be contented with hearing the first essential word of grace, Thy sins be forgiven thee! while they must still continue to lie on the beds on which those sins have laid them. This, however, must be guarded, by bearing in mind, that when forgiveness is received, the punishment is in reality taken away; what remains of suffering is no more punishment. All this instruction, however, lies in the matter of the narrative itself: it was scarcely the Lord's conscious design to express all this Himself, or to give any testimony directly on these subjects. It was so natural to Him to greet a penitent sinner with His immediate θάρσει, it was so great and so rare a joy to His own heart, that in the sublime simplicity of His full authority, He uttered the words which we find, without any oblique or subordinate reference in them whatever.

But since no prophet, no son of man had ever, with power and confidence like this, spoken to men this word of absolute consolation, astonishment and prejudice are excited against the Divine voice of His authority, and this its authoritative utterance. Not among those who brought the sick man, but among the Scribes and Pharisees, who, though they were not now gathered together as a "first inquisitorial assembly," (according to *Sepp's* fancy), yet occupy there their seats of pre-eminence, and now take occasion to vent upon the Lord the enmity of which their hearts were already full. They might have used opposite language, and said:—such a word of spiritual consolation is very *easily uttered*, He only feeds thus the sick man's confidence, but He can do no more! But they give it a far more malicious turn, and say that He blasphemeth. Christ has not said:—I forgive thee thy sins; but His simple word contained this latent within it, and their spirit of opposition did not engender in them an incorrect suspicion; they rightly understood His meaning. They do not *say* it, but they think it, every one regarding his neighbour with looks which said, as St Matthew tells us,—ὅυτος βλασφημεῖ. The others filled up what they intended, by adding the obvious position—who can forgive sins but God only? a perfectly true proposition in itself, and the inference from it, that "he who assumes this power, being no more than man, *blasphemes*," was more correctly deduced by these Scribes in the *reasoning of their hearts*, than by the rationalists of our time who leave the Son of Man all His full honours as Son of Man, but are not so scrupulous about His claims of Divine power and authority.—The Lord *saw* the reasonings of the Scribes,[1] just as He had seen the faith of the bearers, and the penitence of him whom they bore: for in relation to His spirit, the penetration through the conduct or countenance to the internal heart of man was one and the same with His knowledge of that which was in man, as man's great Archetype and Head. It was not with the omniscience of God that He pierced the thoughts of all men's hearts, though nothing could remain concealed from Him, and nothing could deceive Him, when His spirit in the Spirit of God entered into relation with man. And thus He here exhibits Himself, first as the Possessor of all grace for the penitent sinner, and then immediately as the Searcher of hearts and Judge, for the proud and reprobate and self-blinded.

He most impressively lays bare the secret language and murmuring of their hearts, by a piercing question which referred the origin of their *thinking* to their evil *heart*.[2] St Mark has only ταῦτα expressed, St Luke still briefer, only τί, but St Matthew is here as before more precise: as is seen in the conscience-stirring ἱνατί, as well as in the addition of πονηρά. This latter would probably refer the Scribes to Zech. viii. 17 (although the Sept. does not

1 Whether we read this second time εἰδώς or ἰδών in St Matthew, does not affect the case, for compare ch. xii. 25. St Luke has ἐπιγνούς, and St Mark in the most express and pregnant words has ἐπιγνούς τῷ πνεύματι ἀυτοῦ.

2 "A proof, how far unenlightened reason may lead us, when child-like simplicity of heart is wanting!" (*Von Gerlach*). In this sense the emphasis in St Luke has been laid, with ironical meaning: "and they began to *reason*."

accord). Their application of these remarks to the Person of our Lord was as *wicked* as their conclusion *in thesi* was sound; so that we may regard *them* rather as having blasphemed in charging Him with blasphemy. For first of all, they exhibit no sense and feeling for His gracious consolation of a dejected sinner, which every right-minded person would in its first impression have sympathised with and understood. Then there is the malicious, unprincipled, wilful, presupposition that Jesus is no more than any other man, which stands in direct contradiction to the emphatic and distinctive words of *His* consolation, and which those very words, addressed in supreme dignity to the paralytic, were quite sufficient to have confuted. Yet the Lord does not leave them to their folly, as they had deserved. He would, in any case, have effected the healing, but it is *for their sakes* also that He utters the other word of authority which all are waiting for and desiring. To put their perverted reasonings, however, to shame, and profit them, He puts an enigmatical question concerning the relation of the *two words* which He has *spoken*. It is a light thing to Him to cast down all the folly and wickedness which exalts itself against His acts: but He condescends to their weakness, in that Divine wisdom which knows how to accommodate its teaching to the folly of men. He enters more deeply into those thoughts *of theirs*, which He has just condemned in their wickedness. Are ye not now thinking, that it is easier *to say* (with baseless assumption, without authority and without effect), thy sins be forgiven thee! than to say (what would immediately convict itself of impotence), Rise up and walk? This is manifestly the immediate connecting meaning, with which the Lord condescends to their imaginings. He does not directly express Himself thus, but leaving the question indefinite and in suspense, intimates that the answer should be very different from what he presupposes in them. In effect, the converse is to be understood in his question:—Many have performed miracles of healing, prophets and apostles, as well as false wonder-workers, but to forgive sins with the authority of God is greater, nay the greatest of all. Or to apprehend it in another way:—To God in Heaven, and His Representative on earth who is now speaking and acting, both are one and the same: the forgiveness of sins is not consummated without the certain, though subsequent, removal of all their punishment; and the bestowment of health is not truly making whole without its accompanying and essentially blended communication of forgiving grace. However we take it, there is much to be pondered in the question of our Lord, and a very different answer to be found than that which was presupposed in the general thoughts of men. He intimates this Himself in this enigmatical and sacredly ironical manner, before He proceeds, in accommodation to their foolish thoughts, to give the evidence they need.

We have here, consequently, in a particular example, a general explanation of the significance of the external miracles of Jesus. The immediate self-evidencing clearness and truth of His word, spoken in the power of His spirit, should have, in strict propriety, required no further evidence. When a soul like Nathanael's heard from His own holy lips,—I came forth from the Father! or a sinner truly poor in spirit heard His great invitation, Come unto me all who are heavy laden! such souls needed no further evidence, before they would believe and follow Him. The paralytic, who embraced with a ready heart the first word of comfort, did not put the doubtful question—By what authority does thou thus assure me? Heal my frame, that I may believe in thee! and so all Israel would have needed no more than to hear, —I am come to bring you grace! if all Israel had been found in true repentance. But the less must become evidence for the greater, to their hardness and folly of heart: although by an inferential reasoning which has not always and to all, absolute validity; for the word of the Holy One which testifies the forgiveness of sins is just as much a proof of the divinity of His miracles, as these again are the authentication of the truth of His word. By this we may understand the only sense in which the Lord might say—*But that ye may know* or perceive, that not without power and authority to do so, I forgive sins! To the sick man, on the present occasion, such evidence was not necessary: he was already comforted, and thought less than before of the healing of his body. Let preachers upon this text beware, also, of a perilous ὕστερον πρότερον into which a false spirit of allegorising has led many: as if the words, *rise up and walk!* were spoken first to the soul, (renewing unto holiness), and an *evidence* to it of justification. That would be to reverse the evangelic order of grace, since in a spiritual sense the rising up and walking can only result from an appropriated forgiveness. It is not so much for the paralytic as for the others that the act of healing follows: this is as evidently declared in the whole narrative, as it is that forgiveness of sins is essentially the greater thing, and sufficient for itself. Let it be further observed, how meekly the Lord veils His Divine majesty, even while He must testify and assert it. The fully developed answer to their evil thoughts might have been :—That ye may know that I do not as man invade the prerogative of God, but as the Son, one with the Father, forgive sins in My own Divine right and dignity. He says not this, that He may not cast a stumbling-block in their way: just as throughout His whole testimony He ever kept back the simple declaration —I am God! in order to avoid the provocation of unbelief. (Let Jno. v. 17, &c., x. 33—36 be noted, for example). He calls Himself, also, here the *Son of Man*, while he appropriates a prerogative of God, and the son of man *upon earth*, which was equivalent to saying, the fully authorized representative of God *in heaven*.[1] Quite correctly *Bengel* remarks: *cœlestem ortum hic sermo sapit.* It is not admissible to construe *here* ἐπὶ τῆς γῆς with the following ἀφιέναι ἁμαρτίας (as at Matt. xviii. 18 in a lower degree); although certainly (as *Richter* says) the earth is essentially the proper place where He does forgive sins. And now He turns in the concluding sentence from the Scribes to the paralytic, lets the immediate word of His power speak in act, and utters, without further preface, the command which He had prepared them for—Stand up and walk! In this *change of His word without drawing the conclusion*, there is a sublime breviloquence: the Lord does not first say: I will then speak what ye require—but He *speaks it!* This is proved by the Σοὶ λέγω of St Mark and St Luke, in which (as *Alford* fails not to observe) the emphasis lies on the σοί. To connect with this the λέγει in St Mark, as being part of the Lord's own words, is an unskilful forcing of His language and meaning ("That ye

[1] *Neander:* "God forgives the sins in heaven, but Christ, as man, announces to the sinners the divine forgiveness. *Son of Man* and *on earth* are correlative ideas." This is at the same time directed against the Pharisaic-catholic doctrine, that there must ever remain uncertainty among men concerning God's forgiveness in heaven.

may know, that the *Son of Man* hath power, He saith now in your presence to this paralytic, *I say unto thee!*") Besides which, this construction is not admitted by εἶπε in St Luke, nor by τότε λέγει in St Matthew, which is an insertion of the Evangelist, as we infer by the use of the same narrative λέγει afterwards in ver. 9.

It is immediately obvious in this as in all similar instances, that the taking up of the bed, and going to the house, was designed as convincing evidence of perfect soundness instantaneously imparted. What the Lord bestows, he bestows with full hand and in unrestricted measure: when He condescends to attest His power in the sight of man He will have it worthily esteemed and magnified. And more worthily by us who believingly read than by the astonished people of that time, who in all probability when they glorified ἐξουσίαν τοιαύτην in His hands, rested upon the lesser instead of the greater manifestation of power. But the Lord restored soundness to the paralytic man, in order that we might apprehend Him as One who could also say to us—Thy sins be forgiven! *This word* may neither be criticised nor wondered at, but *experienced.*

THE PHYSICIAN FOR THE SICK.

(Matt. ix. 9, 12, 13; Mar. ii. 14—17; Luke v. 27, 31, 32).

This is another example how various is the meaning which we should attribute to our Lord's *Follow thou me!* according to the development of circumstances. In Lu. vi. we find that St Matthew had been, suddenly to himself, chosen into the number of the Twelve before the Sermon on the Mount. It does not follow because he himself relates his final call from his public office two chapters after the Sermon, that therefore that final call must have occurred later: but a comparison of the Evangelists indisputably proves it, since otherwise the parables of ch. xiii. must also have occurred before the Sermon on the Mount, which is not to be supposed. St Matthew appears to have returned more or less to the business of his office, just as Peter had returned to his nets; and the Lord who in His wisdom regulated all things according to their respective conditions, allowed this to be so; until the critical moment came when He saw fit to repeat that first call, strengthening it into an unqualified command to follow Himself permanently. The very artless manner in which St Matthew records *this* final summons, omitting the former choice of him altogether (in which the two other Evangelists follow him, according to the established tradition), proceeded on the one hand from a most amiable modesty, on the other from a deep consciousness in his own memory that it was the last "Follow me!" which came *to him* at the critical moment of release from all. This, however, we deny, that his conversion had been, as *Sepp* says, the work of a moment. We hold against *Ebrard* with the profound *Bengel*, whose harmony is not to be lightly and superficially rejected. (See his § 55. "Peter and Andrew, James and John, had been *followers* before they became *Apostles:* Matthew is called to be an Apostle, before he has become a daily follower of Christ.")

But, without any argument, such an apparently sudden summons from office and function presupposes some previous acquaintance and connexion. It is nowhere written that no one of the Twelve left the person of our Lord after having been first called: but the remarkable, and, in its kind, singular procedure in the case of St Matthew, affords us much subject of thought, which however here we may not speak of more particularly. His "rising and following Him" is not to be understood as if he left everything as it then was, according to the mere letter of the narrative. It is to be understood that he set everything in order pertaining to his house and office, and the text itself allows us to think that he even made a parting feast for his former companions, at which he might introduce to them his new master and his other fellow-disciples. He only intimates that this occurred in *his own* house, because that must be mentioned in order to explain the following sayings of the Lord, so memorable to himself. We may doubt whether, as *Menken* has it, "before long, some Pharisees added themselves to the company," for the Pharisees were not wont thus to mingle, at least unbidden, with the Publicans. We only understand by the ἰδόντες of St Matthew (even in connexion with St Mark's ἐσθίοντα) that they saw it, or became acquainted with it, it may be, as they departed again, or sometime afterwards. (St Luke designates by *οἱ γραμματεῖς αὐτῶν* the Scribes belonging to the place, where Jesus, always watched closely by this kind of people, participated in such a meal). They do not venture to address themselves directly to the Lord, just as we saw in the foregoing history. In ch. xii. 2, xv. 2, they do indeed address the Master, but only alleging as against the disciples, what their Master did or approved: here they mockingly attack the disciples on their Master's account. At furthest they only proceed once to utter their murmurings in the third person, as in Lu. xv. 2.

The Lord is immediately ready with His answer, to deliver His disciples from their embarrassment, and to inflict salutary shame upon the questioners. His answer and vindication consists, according to St Matthew, in *three* propositions, which indeed are one in their fundamental meaning, but advance in a three-fold progression of conviction in their expression. He begins in a popular and gracious style with a well-known proverb, figuratively to set forth a principle, applicable in this case, which they, in their perversion, utterly forgot. He then attaches to this a word of Scripture for the scripturally learned Scribes, which neither the wisdom of the market place, nor the wisdom of the sanctuary, had yet understood and learned. His conclusion gives a most penetrating and direct *answer, in an utterance of the Lord himself*, concerning Himself and the design of His coming, which at once explains the proverb and expounds the Scripture which He had quoted, as *fulfilled* in Himself. St Matthew alone gives us the passage of the prophet which mediates between the figurative and direct expression, partly because of its immediate interest as occurring at his repast, and partly because he especially has preserved the reference to the Old Testament Scriptures.

The proverb concerning the physician for the sick, and not for the sound, which occurs as well in the Talmud[1] as in profane authors, and is of universal use, is given by St Luke in the most simple form, with the anthesis of *ὑγιαίνοντες* and *κακῶς ἔχοντες*. The other two Evangelists have the more exact *ἰσχύοντες*, which probably made the contrast still more emphatic, as we should say, the robust, who are of radically and permanently

[1] Thalm. Babyl. tit. Bava Kama fol. 46. col. 2, as Antisthenes in Laertius, Diogenes in Stobæus, Pausanias in Plutarch, Ovid de Ponto.

sound constitution. (Although, indeed, to be strong and grow strong is a scriptural expression for recovery and healing after sickness, as in Isa. xxxix. 1; Ezek. xxxiv. 16.) Apart from the confirmation of the common practice to send the sick to the physician, which lies already in the use of the proverb, its application here has a further two-fold reference. First of all, being spoken to the teachers and spiritual guides of Israel, it puts *them* to shame as bad physicians, who, although called to strengthen the diseased, and heal the sick (Ezek. xxxiv. 4), yet in their loveless selfishness acted perversely as the physician would act, who should avoid the sick man *who needs his help*, in order to escape the danger of infection! But then *the Lord* announces Himself as the true Physician for the sickness of the soul, using thus an expression wide and deep in its meaning, which contains at the same time an *interpretation* of the miracles which He performed on the bodily sick. The Lord speaks here in the sense in which the Evangelist had already given that interpretation by a prophetic passage (ch. viii. 17), and it is for the sake of this that St Matthew appends these sayings of our Lord, with their occasion (and its continuation in vers. 14—17) to the record which He had given in the eighth and ninth chapters of bodily healing of all kinds. It may indeed be said, with some propriety as far as regards the first of His expressions, that the Lord uses the language of humility, and appears to place Himself only in the ranks of physicians in general; yet we cannot but perceive immediately afterwards an intenser and peculiar meaning in the sing. ἰατροῦ as spoken by our Lord in the person of *Him who has come* (ver. 13). It is no other than if He had said: I am *the* Physician, the one and only Physician for the souls of men; just as He had said, I am *the* good shepherd, and as He presently afterwards in ver. 15 distinguishes Himself as *the* bridegroom. These are nothing but names of God and His Christ through the whole prophetic Scripture. Even in Ex. xv. 26 more than merely bodily sickness is intended.

How wonderful is the union of gracious tenderness and supreme dignity in this as in every other word of the Great Physician who is come into the world: assuring every one, who will receive it, of forgiveness of sins in God's authority, and of the healing of all his iniquities by the Divine power! In uncharitable perversion they criticise and condemn the peculiar exercise of His function: He only and simply answers that this is, nevertheless, His office and work. It is the voice of that compassionate love which brought him from the bosom of the Father, that is heard in the χρέιαν ἔχουσιν. It is the gracious view which Divine compassion takes, to pass by the idea of *guilt* and to regard our sin as *sickness*, which, though it does not deserve yet *needs*, to be healed:—it is thus often represented in the Old Testament; *e.g.* Jer. iii. 22, and more particularly, Isa. liii. How deep and grievous our injury is, we learn indeed from this, that God only can repair it, and that only by the wounds of His dear Son. But who are the *whole*, who *need no* physician? We shall hear in this, with *Calvin*, an *ironica concessio*, if we rightly consider the subsequent explanation of our Lord, which goes beyond the mere literal meaning of the proverb, and tells us plainly that the Lord never recognizes upon earth any "righteous" and "sound" but such as think themselves to be so. This is opened up to us by the quotation from Scripture, to which the Lord refers the Scribes with a keenly penetrating hint:—*Go ye and learn*, what that often read, but never yet understood Scripture meaneth. (In the Talmud the Rabbins frequently say to their disciples: צא ולמד.)

Let us also go and read the words in their connexion in Hosea, in order that we may read and expound them aright. Not reading and expounding them, however, as the modern Scribes of our day do, who allow the Prophets to say no more than what dim-sighted investigation of the present age thinks reconcilable with the history, and the views, and the range of thought in the times of the Prophets themselves; and who thus remain at the utmost distance from that one, only exegesis, according to which the Spirit of Christ Himself who spake by the Prophets, expounds and opens to us by the mouth of Jesus and His apostles, His own fore-written word; and bears witness to it as now first fulfilled, and now first accessible *in its full and consummate meaning*, to our understanding. We cannot penetrate too deeply into the words of the Holy Ghost, specially cannot we hold too firmly by the principle that the quotations and expositions of the Old Testament in the New, give to us the right key for their interpretation.

Misapprehending this, even orthodox expositors have missed

the inmost and fundamental meaning of the impressive ἔλεον θέλω, which the Lord has appropriated out of Jehovah's word to Hosea, at the same time carrying it on to its development, in the person of Him who was to come. It is almost universally understood, as *von Meyer's* note upon St Matthew expresses it: "as a gracious condescension to teach sinners, and not a rigid, external separation of Himself from them," thus referring to that mercy and love which man should exercise towards man, according to God's good pleasure. Though this seems at the first glance to suit the connexion, yet might we, penetrating deeper, already mark that the Lord who has proclaimed Himself the Physician of sick humanity in the power of the grace of God, in the following words refers rather to God in heaven, and must mean the *mercy, which God exercises towards sinners for their healing and salvation;* and in effect, this is the first and only true meaning of the word in the prophecy quoted.

The great theme of the fourteen chapters of Hosea from the beginning to the end, is generally, as in all the Prophets, an annunciation of punishment in order to subsequent mercy, a prediction of the dispersion and return of Israel. His whole discourse passes from threatening to promise, and is arranged in four sections, ever strengthening its hold, and widening its view, as it goes on. The second of these sections embraces ch. iv. to ch. vi. After long rebuke and threatening there is a sudden transition in ch. v. 15 to that *healing mercy*, which will survive the judgments, be prepared for by them, and even effectually work in and through them. That God only, as His people's physician, can heal them and will, is a fundamental idea which runs through the whole of Hosea's prophecy: and our Lord's citation therefore seizes the central idea of the Prophet. The Assyrian could not *heal* them, nor *cure* them of their wound, ch. v. 13. When I would have *healed* Israel, then the iniquity of Ephraim was discovered (ch. vii. 1)—finally I will *heal* all their backslidings, ch. xiv. 5. But how is this to be effected? They must acknowledge their offence, and seek my face: this they will do, they will in their penitent affliction say—Come, and let us return unto the Lord; for he hath torn and he will *heal* us; he hath smitten and he will bind us up, (ch. v. 15, vi. 1). The Spirit of Christ in the Prophet here glances forward into the *new covenant*, the covenant of *grace;* and in the reference ver. 2, to *the third day*, after two days, as in its most obvious meaning, the critical time of God's speedy turning from judgment to mercy, we discover a latent typical under-meaning, such as, despite of all modern exegesis, the Old Testament abounds in, by which the resurrection of the Redeemer on the third day is foreshadowed.[1] Then is the future, New Testament grace further commended and set forth in vers. 3, 4; where, assuredly, חַסְדְּכֶם (comp. Jon. ii. 9 חַסְדָּם) can mean no other than, the *mercy, which I will manifest to you*, entirely as מִשְׁפָּטֶיךָ in ver. 3, signify my judgments against and upon thee. That other interpretation which is generally preferred, and which *von Meyer's* note also approves as "the most immediate and obvious," is altogether to our thinking inapplicable here: for the passage from the first to sixth verse has no tone of rebuke, but is full of promise and encouragement. The coming of the Merciful One to heal and make alive is foretold in ver. 3, as the full preparation of the morning dawn, and as a fructifying rain: and presently afterwards it is testified in ver. 5, that through judgments and after them *light* should *break forth.* How then could we suitably interpose a rebuke that "*your goodness* is as a morning cloud, and as the early dew that goeth away, that is, *fleeting* and *transitory*." We must not, therefore, be misled by the passage in ch. xiii. 3, which designedly applies the expression in another meaning, but take the decisive conclusion of ch. xiv. 6 as a strict parallel: I will be as *the dew* unto Israel! Comp. Mic. v. 6. The only true exposition of ch. vi. 4 is that of *Burk*, Gnomon in xii. prophetas minores, who says: "Iram comminantem, in quam nonnuli (omnes fere hodie) interpretes hæc verba vertere conati sunt, totus tenor textus et connexio cum antecedentibus et consequentibus plane excludit. Sicut *nubes mane*, quæ *auroræ* correspondet, et in quâ radii auroræ eo magis conspicui sunt. מַשְׁכִּים הֹלֵךְ—cito, tempore matutino, summo mane *ros* venit. Mox ubi efficaciam et virtutem suam terræ communicavit reliquitque, iterum

[1] According to *the Scripture*—says St Paul 1 Cor. xv. 4. But where shall we find it, save here and in the typical history of Jonah? This latter does not seem to us enough of itself to sustain the emphatically asserted "on the third day."

abit videturque evanuisse; revera vero prodesse non posset, nisi abiret, et dum evanuisse videtur, *quam maxime adest* et in effectibus lætissimis, in pratis virentibus, in herbis celeriter succrescentibus, novo habito indutus, splendide prodit."[1]

We have been constrained to discuss all this beforehand, in order to found upon it our protest against the ancient and modern misapprehension of our Lord's citation of the sixth verse. The fifth verse forms the transition from the gracious promises, ver. 1—4, to this all-comprising conclusion of the whole discourse; and indicates the aim and object of the prophetic threatenings, of the word which rebukes and kills, and of the chastising and purifying judgments, to be that light should break forth upon the people thus humbled and prepared. *For*, saith the Lord, *I desired mercy*, to show mercy, and not sacrifice. This does not *immediately* mean—I am well pleased, when *ye* shew mercy one toward another,[2] but there is a *twofold* contrast between God and men. Israel would *give to God* in sacrifice and *offering*: this is the leading mistake of the Old Testament, and it is here once more protested against: I will *take nothing* from you. (See Hosea v. 6). I will rather *give to you*, it is for you before and above all things, first and last, to seek and to find my compassion and my love! This is the true knowledge of the Lord, דַּעַת אֱלֹהִים which ver. 3 had spoken of, and which ch. ii. 19, 20 confirms. Taking this sentence, which forms, as it were, the central point of our Lord's discourses out of Hosea, let us look backwards and forwards through the prophecy, and see how the *mercy* and *compassion* of the Lord is testified to be the only source of healing from the beginning to the end. Ch. i. 7, אֲרַחֵם—ch. ii. 4, רֻחָמָה—ch. ii. 21 (19) וּבְחֶסֶד וּבְרַחֲמִים—ch. xi. 9, נִחוּמָי—especially the sublime conclusion, ch. xiv. 3—5, which shows that that is the true sacrifice, when sinners confessing their sin

[1] *Reichel* also, from whom I extracted in my commentary on Isaiah, was very vehement for *Luther's* translation and interpretation. In an unprinted manuscript upon the twelve minor Prophets, which I have looked through, he complains much of the damaging and disfiguring perversion of this passage into a threatening sense.

[2] As the Chal. בְּעָבְדֵי חִסְדָּא—and the Rabbins who indeed think directly of their עֲשׂוֹת מִשְׁפָּט וּצְדָקָה.

seek forgiveness, when the fatherless find *mercy* of God, and He *heals* their backsliding.

This then is the first and most essential meaning of the word which the Lord bids the Pharisees study, in order that they might discern the healing mercy of God as now having appeared unto sinners :—your God had ever in the Old Testament testified, as the end and aim of all His revelations to His people and dealings with them, that He alone is the true Physician for the healing of His sick people. He will *impart mercy, not take sacrifice.*[1] We do not deny, for it is perfectly obvious, that on the foundation of this meaning, a further hortatory application is intended :—he who has found mercy, should be merciful, affectionate, and full of kindness towards sinners. Hosea himself speaks, ch. iv. i. and xii. 7, of חֶסֶד among men, just as Mic. vi. 8, and Zec. vii. 9. But in this fundamental passage he discloses the foundation of the Divine compassion, which must and will itself prepare the sacrifice which is well pleasing to Him, that is, the living sacrifice. Unless we err, the Apostle in Rom. xii. 1 makes allusion to this same passage of the prophet, as would appear from the conjunction of his three fundamental ideas : the *mercies* of God, the *sacrifice offered*, and *acceptable* to God.

And now observe, further, how profoundly and sublimely the Lord, continuing His words with γάρ, connects them with the words of God in Hosea! I have had pleasure in showing mercy, saith God—I am come to call sinners, saith the Son of God, in whom the God of Israel comes and manifests Himself as the promised morning dawn of righteousness and grace. As Jesus had, in the previous healing of the paralytic, called Himself the Son of Man, while assuming to Himself a prerogative of God; so now He directly speaks in the person and name of God, when His human action, which is also Divine, is measured by a false standard and judged by man. He now gives full utterance, having prepared the way by the quotation from Scripture, to His interpretation of the previous proverb : but His interpretation and application of it must go beyond its ordinary meaning.

1 *Lange*, whose opposition cannot lead us astray, says himself "that God only rejects sacrifice, when it is offered to him in contradistinction *to mercy*, and quite correctly, *scilicet* the mercy *of God*, that alone is the true and deep *contrast* here.

The proverb presupposes some who are whole, who need no physician, but now the great Physician who is come, the revealed God of Israel, who will heal all sin and backsliding, finds none but the sick or *sinners*, none who are whole or *righteous*. Therefore *the article is now omitted* which had been prefixed to ἰσχύοντες and κακῶς ἔχοντες, and this has a critical significance. The Lord knows no class of men, whom He might term τοὺς δικαίους, whom He is not come to call. That great "I am come!" which He so often repeats, thereby indeed *testifying* Himself to be the Messiah, has its application for all. His *calling*, which sounds forth to *all*, regards all as *sinners*, not as righteous. If they had not needed such a Physican, He would not have come at all! This is the final and full answer to the question of ver. 11, in words which correspond to it—It is for *sinners* that I am here!

Yet does this simple expression, which knows nothing of the righteous, assume, when connected with the preceding proverb, a severe tone of irony against the proud, who think themselves sound, just as in Luke xv. 7, there are righteous referred to, who think they need no repentance, but there is no joy, but sorrow rather in heaven over them. That He speaks of a righteousness of the Pharisees, which availed before Him, no rational person will admit. But because they perceive not and feel not themselves to be sinners, in this particular sense not needing the physician, not κακῶς ἔχοντες, the gracious Physician can only say to them, in His angry sorrow—For you, such as you are it is as if I had not come at all, for ye receive me not, although I call you too as sinners—ye are not such, ye are the strong and the righteous! And in the very fact of uttering this in their presence, He does nevertheless call them, and they might have known it. It is as much as if He had said—ἦλθον καλέσαι πάντας (εἰς ἔλεον, εἰς μετάνοιαν), οὐχ ὡς δικάιους ἀλλ' ὡς ἁμαρτωλούς.

The question whether εἰς μετάνοιαν is the right reading in St Matthew and St Mark, as well as in St Luke, does not affect the case: for on any supposition St Luke has rightly completed what must be included in the full meaning of the καλέσαι. To what does the Lord *call* sinners but *to mercy*, and how can this be obtained but in the way of conversion from sin to God, that is, of *repentance?* We should regard it as more probable that the Lord's words were uttered as we find them in St Luke. He thus manifestly referred to the preaching of John the Baptist, continued as it was by Himself, whose cry Repent ye! went forth to *all* without exception.

Jesus does not merely eat with publicans and sinners, He sanctifies this eating and commerce, as He sanctifies His whole life and work, by the testimony and *call* which pervades it. And not only so: His graciously condescending, never-repelling fellowship with them, is itself a call, and an invitation and an attraction most powerful.

ANSWER CONCERNING FASTING.

(Matt. ix. 15—17; Mar. ii. 19—22; Lu. v. 35—39.)

St Matthew's *τότε προσέρχονται*, which will not admit of a relation of anything past, indicates a close connection between this and the preceding discourse. The conversation with the disciples of John must certainly be conceived of as having first taken place after the answer given to the Pharisees; and, consequently, the chronology indicated in Mar. v. 21, must not be so far pressed, as to leave no room for all that St Matthew relates as having transpired before the request of Jairus. St Mark, who has related these circumstances earlier, places the discourse concerning fasting immediately after that concerning eating and drinking, though with but slight bond of connexion: St Luke, however, connects the one directly with the other, as if the subsequent objection had been urged by the same circle surrounding the Lord, from which the previous one had sprung. (*Οἱ δὲ εἶπον πρὸς αὐτόν*). It seems nearly certain from the whole, that the two conversations, closely related in their matter, should be placed, according to St Matthew's *τότε*, not merely in relation as facts, but in strict chronological conjunction: with which it will well accord, if we perceive in the second discourse a reference to the former, which was still in our Saviour's thoughts.

The *disciples of John*, too, who now came, according to St Matthew, to our Lord, (that is, *certain* of them, as *Luther* expresses it in

St Mark, whom the article indicates as representatives of their kind), present themselves to our Lord and His disciples, with their objections and scruples, just as the Pharisees had already done. For even they stand *in part*, if not for the most part, on that footing of the old, which will not comprehend the new as revealed in Christ. This is the general fundamental idea, which our Lord's discourse makes prominent. They themselves, with great simplicity, indicate this their position :—*we and the Pharisees*.[1] Whether they were incited to bring forward their objection by the Pharisees, may be left to conjecture: we may very well suppose the impulse to have sprung from within themselves, without any such external stimulant. We are very far from saying, with *Schleiermacher*, that "such a question from John's disciples themselves would have savoured of simplicity"—many as wise as he, might in their case, have shown only the same wisdom. We *fast so oft* (St Matt. *πολλά*, St Lu. *πυκνά, καὶ δεήσεις ποιοῦνται*), does not mean that they thought it too much, and would rather have it lightened like the disciples of Jesus : it is rather the proud zeal of their righteousness which expresses itself thus, upon which they value themselves. Thy disciples *fast not :* a slightly ironical, euphemistic expression for *eating* and *drinking* as St Luke has it, which is now made objectionable in itself, as before it had been objected to for being in company with *publicans* and *sinners*—almost in the spirit of sympathy with the invidious meaning of Matt. xi. 19.[2]

We have then here to do with the contrast between that dis-

[1] In St Mark, they speak of the practice of the two discipleships in the third person, just as (according to *Ebrard*) a Lutheran might say to a Roman Catholic:—the Lutherans and the Reformed do not keep Corpus-Christi-day. We may very well conceive, (with *Von Gerlach*,) that after the imprisonment of the Baptist many of his disciples would rather attach themselves to the *better kind* of Pharisees than to Jesus. The opinion, on the other hand, that the Pharisees proposed this question to Jesus, only referring to John's disciples; and that St Matthew's Gospel derived the account from a misunderstanding and transposing tradition, is one more of the petty shifts of Scripture-dishonouring modern theology.

[2] They speak, however, as *Roos* says, with simple hearts, and hold probably the *disciples* of Jesus only in suspicion, as being an undisciplined people, who would not so readily acquiese in their Master's enforcement of prayer and fasting, as they had acquiesced in John's.

tinctively and entirely new thing which the Lord brings in, exhibited in Himself and His disciples, and both the entirely old, to which Pharisaic Judaism adhered, and that intermediate position of John's disciples, which, vibrating between the old and the new, had rather a preponderance of the old element. We have it clearly recorded, how the Lord openly and decidedly opposed himself to *both.* If this collision is confined to the special point of *fasting*, all who were susceptible of faith might have perceived in His words a token that the *Messiah* was come: for it was the Jewish teaching, as we find in Maimonides, that "all fasting should cease in the days of the Messiah, and that there should be then only holidays and festivals, as it is written in Zech. viii. 19." Resting on this our Lord utters in His first response the great contrast, openly and decisively expressed; thus proclaiming Himself as the giver of joy now come, and present among his disciples, and designating the period of His presence among them as the marriage time. He had already declared Himself to be *the Physician*, and this gives additional emphasis to a second title: I am also *the bridegroom!* But the weighty significance of this Messiah-name, pointing as it does by the definite article to the prophecy and its fulfilment, would be altogether weakened if we should limit that article to its mere use in the figure, instead of deriving the figure itself from the prophetic name; and interpret it as only meaning—so long as the bridegroom is with them—that is he who is, as it were, a bridegroom to them, *as being the source of their joy.* It is incontrovertibly obvious that the Lord here refers the disciples of John to the testimony of their own master, as we find in Jno. iii. 28, 29.[2] In that passage ὁ χριστός and νυμφίος are strictly parallel. There the Baptist named himself the friend of the Bridegroom, παράνυμφος or παρανυμφίος, νυμφαγωγός, Talm. שׁוֹשְׁבִינָא, he who

[1] Which we find here "in a marvellous union which is perfectly natural, but on that account full of instruction and warning." It is thus *Seyler* preaches: see his Mittheillungen über die zehnte Versamm-lung in Gnadau.

[2] Subordinately a not unimportant example, how the contents of the fourth Gospel are presupposed by the Synoptical Gospels, and are confirmed by them.

demands and leads the bride to the bridegroom. He does not indeed there say ὁ νυμφίος, but the Messianic reference in the preceding τὴν νύμφην is even yet stronger than that would have been, when we consider the whole meaning of John's demonstrative discourse. (All men come to Him, *the* bride, the church the people of God turn towards Him : and this is as it should be, for, as this proves, He is indeed *the* bridegroom of *this bride:* I have no other function than to lead her to Him). But the Lord's words here have a more extended reference : all His disciples generally appear as υἱοὶ τοῦ νυμφῶνος, friends of the Bridegroom : and with this we may compare ch. xi. 11. This expression, indeed, indicates something much more intimate than *marriage-company* or wedding guests generally, since νυμφών signifies the bridal-chamber, and not merely the hall of the wedding-feast. It refers already to the calling of the Apostles to be the bringers of the bride, in the same sense as the Baptist had intimated : for in such indefinite parables as these, which hint more than they say, the narrower and the wider meaning pass one into the other.

It remains, however, clear and important, that the Lord here, by a general-citation of the Old Testament, terms Himself *the Bridegroom.* That was according to a general Orientalism, which thus exhibited the relation between ruler and people, and with a much deeper meaning it was applied to the sacred relation of Jehovah, the God of Israel. But the Prophets testified clearly that the true betrothal, the true marriage (which Ps. xlv. and the Canticles predict) would take place when God, the King, the Husband of Israel, should come as his Messiah. Thus are given first of all the great promises in Isa. lii. 6, 7, 12 :—I myself, who now speak, will be He ! Thy God reigneth ! The Lord will go before you ; and the God of Israel will be your rereward ! Then is interposed the marvellous prophecy concerning the Servant of the Lord : but immediately after follows again in ch. liv. the prediction of the fruitful marriage, ver. 5 : For thy Maker is thine Husband, the Lord of Hosts is His name; and thy Redeemer the Holy One of Israel; the God of the whole earth shall he be called. Hence are to be understood the subsequent marriage parables of our Lord, which are already prepared for in this discourse to the disciples of John. It is, finally, a very striking circumstance that the same Hosea to whom the Lord had referred the Pharisees, as he testifies of *the Physician*, so also testifies of *the Bridegroom*. For in Hos. ii. 19, 20 (which is to be regarded as an interpretation of the typical conduct of the Prophet, with an allusion, at the same time, to a meaning of the idol-name בַּעַל) we find it said: I will betroth thee unto me for ever: yea, I will betroth thee unto me in righteousness, and in judgment, and in loving-kindness, and in mercies. I will even betroth thee unto me in faithfulness; and *thou shalt know the Lord*. Now this is the true explanation of חֶסֶד and דַּעַת אֱלֹהִים (Hos. vi. 6), which the Lord Himself supplementarily brings, while he blends in His answer a reference to that testimony of the Baptist with the thoughts of His own mind, which still linger in Hosea's prophecy. Thus by means of both the Prophet's predictions, that of the Physician and that of the Bridegroom, uniting in strict harmony and concert, the Lord declares with ample clearness for all who have ears to hear, who Himself is.

Where I thus am present, the Bridegroom, there can be nothing but joy for my chosen disciples especially, who are elected to be Paranymphs, Friends of the Bridegroom. To fast now would be a plain self-contradiction, for fasting pertains to *sorrow* and not to joy. But these are glad, and rightly so, because the long-expected is come at last, and are conscious of nothing but this. The Bridegroom is come, the marriage must and will now go on! The presence of the Bridegroom is already to them the beginning of the marriage. Interrupt them not, they will soon enough discover that an interval must take place: yea, these and my future disciples shall, during many a dreary season, find cause to fast—for the actual marriage is yet far in the distance. Such generally is the meaning of this prophetic discourse, though, alas, most Bible readers accept it with difficulty, for *Luther's* word, without explanation derived from oriental biblical customs, misleads them to think of the actual marriage at once.

The Bridegroom is taken from them, just as the king first takes his journey, in order to receive his kingdom (Lu. xix. 12; Matt. xxv. 14). The very generally announced prediction which the Lord gives[1] concerning this, refers immediately and first of all to the days of His sufferings and death: for the disciples of John, whose Master according to every correct harmony was now in prison, the words would contain a latent analogy, which the Lord more fully utters in Matt. xvii. 12, "*Your* Master, for whose imprisonment ye would mourn and fast, is not, however, the true Bridegroom, who will similarly, yet quite otherwise, be taken away!" The first presence of Jesus among His disciples, however full of joy it might make them, was nevertheless quite transitory; there stood the cross before Him, by which the Bridegroom would become the Physician, and lead the truly healed through deep affliction to perfect joy. (Jno. xvi. 20—22). All this the Lord knew from the beginning, and in the midst of His gracious acknowledgment and approval of the joy which surrounded Him in His own disciples' hearts, He alone looks beyond into the days which were coming. (*Wizenmann* may well cry: "What man ever looked down so tranquilly, so cheerfully, from so great a height into so profound a depth?") Indeed the ἐλεύσονται δὲ ἡμέραι andthe τότε (which St Luke still strengthens by ἐν ἐκείναις ταῖς ἡμέραις, which is more exact than St Mark's singular) stretches the prospect far into the times of the Church, in which, as well for the whole as for individuals, there will be a manifold and perpetual recurrence of the departure of the Bridegroom, and the pressing through the sorrow of the cross to the joy of the resurrection.

Nevertheless, the Lord will not permit any to disturb the present joy of His own, however transitory it may be, in Himself and His personal presence (ἐφ' ὅσον, St Mark, and St Luke, ἐν ᾧ μετ' αὐτῶν ἐστιν—St Mark again ὅσον χρόνον μεθ' ἑαυτῶν ἔχουσι τὸν νυμφίον)! Although the most fearful suffering was at hand, although the greatest of the prophets awaited in the prison his death, yet even these things may not suppress the joy of the disciples, and make them fast, so gladdening is the presence of the Bridegroom. It is *in this* that we are to seek the peculiar contrast between the Old and the New, which is now intimated, and afterwards expanded more fully: not, indeed, merely through

[1] Where the grammatically unusual ἀπαρθῇ, the same in all three Evangelists, stands alone in the New Testament.

the presence of the Bridegroom (for this is limited by an ἐφ' ὅσον, and fasting even in the new time is plainly contemplated), but rather in the distinction between fasting as genuine and corresponding to the occasion, and fasting as enforced and legally imposed as an external obligation. This specific point of the Lord's saying becomes obvious to us in St Matthew (who has here the exact word in preference to the other two), for He speaks first of all of *mourning* instead of fasting, and with a frank μὴ δύνανται asks if it be befitting and right to enforce fasting in a time of joy? (St Mark strengthens it with a repeated οὐ δύναν-ται; St Luke expresses this fundamental idea through a less direct tradition, but in a vigorous manner and quite consistent with circumstances: μὴ δύνασθε ποιῆσαι νηστεύειν). What gives truth and reality to external fasting is the internal mourning: all such exercise as outwardly imposed and enforced belongs to the old and legal position, which in the circle of our Lord's discipleship is utterly removed. And further, what was all the עַנּוֹת נֶפֶשׁ, even as imposed in the Old Testament by God Himself, but a preparation for coming joy? It was never an end in itself, only the transitional means. And when now He that is come inspires the joy, where is the occasion for fasting?

It will return, but never again in the legal, Old Testament, pharisaic spirit and manner, but in the truth and reality of the fulfilment of its design. *Then shall they fast*, that is now conversely, they shall mourn of themselves, naturally and truly and necessarily fast. This is no commandment, but a prophecy of those Fast-days which God Himself will appoint to souls, and not they themselves impose voluntarily upon themselves. That which in the time of the first fulfilment happened symbolically to the disciples, who in their affliction forgot to eat and drink, though it never occurred to them to say, "we must appoint ourselves a fast," will have a perpetual realization in the Church. It might indeed in a certain sense be said that the whole time of the Church during her Lord's absence, the whole interval between the Ascension and the Second Coming, is a time of solemn earnestness, of sorrow, and of fasting. Yet there is a qualification of this, since for the Church, as well as for its individual members, times of the Lord's presence alternate with times of His absence, the one profoundly preparing the way for the other. There freedom and truth must be uninterfered with in all their conduct. If a soul has found its Saviour, let no one disturb it when rejoicing as the disciples rejoiced in the beginning: the hard ways of the cross will come afterwards, let them be prophecied that they may be provided for, but nothing more. The final end and consummation, which already appears to our first apprehension, and with truth, to be so near, is the marriage of the Bridegroom with His own, a time of joy and delight, in which all fast-days are lost.

Ver. 16. We shall now be better able to understand what the Lord goes on to say concerning the *old* and the *new*, and indeed in marriage similitudes still, for garments and wine may well occur to our thoughts when preparation for the marriage is spoken of. What is the altogether new? That freedom and sincerity of deportment which ever corresponds with the reality of the inward state, and which should henceforward alone avail: not, assuredly, a mere vain joy, as before a mere vain sorrow, but the eating and drinking when man is glad, the fasting when he is sorrowful; that is, as we are wont to say, the government of the *evangelical* spirit, rule of life, and guidance. What, on the other hand, is the *old* which the Lord thus by the very word emphatically announces already as done away, even as His apostle afterwards (Heb. viii. 13) must do again? All that pertains to the legal, Old Testament, imperfect, preparatory, typical relation, as it opposes itself, in the Pharisees and John's disciples, to the spirit of the New. What then is the mixing and mending which would put a new patch upon an old garment? It would have taken place, if the Lord in His instruction of the disciples whom He was now training for the entirely New, had still retained the pharisaical, Old Testament spirit as His foundation: for then nothing fundamentally and permanently new would have resulted, *they would not have agreed together*. No one acts thus, who will provide a durable garment, that is, no practised workmen, for of this unintelligent, wretched, and indeed holding to the external figure, necessitated *patching*, there is abundance. It is very plain that here as elsewhere, our Lord's word, which in its dignity condescends to the meanest details of the earthly, and common realities of life, enters into the history of a mended garment, elevating in His wisdom the most trivial thing into a glorious similitude. If the garment itself is *old*, worn out, and holds not together (and the whole rests upon this supposition), no new patch inserted will do it any service. The ἐπίβλημα, which was intended to be a πλήρωμα αὐτοῦ ("put in to fill it up"), can accomplish that purpose only for a short time and very badly: it αἴρει ἀπὸ τοῦ ἱματίου, that is, although it rends not itself, it does not hold to the seam of the old, the new piece taketh away something from the old,[1] the consequence is, as St Luke expresses it, καὶ τὸ καινὸν σχίζει, in the end the new is thrown away, inserted in vain, no better than rent, like the old itself. The new is not entire, the old is not firm. (Comp. the parallel, ver. 17). St Luke gives the fundamental idea quite correctly, whether the Lord now uttered it or not, οὐ συμφωνεῖ, the old and the new, fit not, agree not together: but St Matthew and St Mark say most distinctively and decisively χεῖρον σχίσμα γίνεται, such improvement only makes the evil worse. See here in the history of an unskilfully and vainly patched old garment the prophecy of many injuries and schisms made worse, in souls, in congregations, and in whole Churches! Oh that wicked piecing of evangelical patches upon the old ground! Oh that it were in the thing signified as it is said to be in the figure —no man doeth this![2] Poverty constrains us not to do this, now that He is come to provide us the new wedding garment: *that* we should put on *whole* and *new*, in the new nature of the spirit and of liberty, the old nature of the letter and of bondage being entirely cast off. Let it be once more observed, with what far-reaching wisdom our Lord, passing beyond the present occasion which gives birth to His words, makes them universal; and with what irresistible conviction the thought thus clothed in parable teaches us to hold fast His doctrine.

Ver. 17. Are we to suppose that the Lord is saying *the same thing* in a second figure? Many are of this opinion, though it runs entirely opposite to our Lord's manner of teaching. It is

[1] St Mark, according to the correct reading, αἴρει τὸ πλήρωμα τὸ καινὸν τοῦ παλαιοῦ, see *Bengel*, and on the construction of αἴρειν with a genitive, *Winer's* Grammatik § 30. 6.

[2] "Christians should never call God's work upon them through Christ, a *mending*, but a *new creation*" (*von Gerlach*). But there have been sad times, when men have talked about "moral mending and perfecting of our nature."

not sufficient to say that He views the subject of His discourse under two distinct relations: as if He first condescends, as it were, to figure the new "only as a subordinate element, repairing the deficiencies of the old," and then in the second similitude speaks more definitely and strongly of the new spirit and nature, for which an altogether new external form is necessary. For if the former were true, the Lord could not have blamed the coming to the aid of the old garment with a new patch: whereas He already in the first figure requires a totally new garment. The difference between the two ideas is certainly not to be sought in this, for the full contrast is the same in both. What then is it? We must not take the old and new *bottles* as corresponding directly to the old and new *garment:* he who retains this notion, must misunderstand the whole discourse. Rather that which the Lord has compared to a *garment*, He now in the second instance compares to a *wine.* As, in the first instance, starting from the *old* garment the opposite entirely new one is intimated only by the new patch, which is not, however, the new garment itself; so, in the second instance, the contemplation sets out from the new wine (for so should it be translated), with an understood contrast with the old wine, which as we shall see in St Luke, is actually mentioned. Thus much is here plain: a garment is put on from without, but wine is received from skins or vessels inwardly: and what was first viewed rather as external manner of life or even doctrine, appears now as a spiritual principle, as the spirit that moulds the habits, the life within which shapes the life without.[1] The new garment is the New Testament *freedom and truth of external life*, in which man lives and moves, the new wine is the *internal spirit* of such freedom and truth itself. And what are the *bottles* which contain and hold this spirit? They must necessarily correspond to *the men* who wear the garment; consequently that is true which might now be raised as an objection, that neither "the ancient Jewish nor the new *forms*" are alluded to, but the *persons* who may or may not be capable of being used. The

[1] When *Seyler* suggests that "garment and bottle are the external forms of life: the garment, to wit, the inner life exhibited in outward things, the *bottle*, as enclosing and containing that life on account of its self-preservation and refinement," is there not an inharmonious confusion between the bottle and its *contents?*

figure is, moreover, scriptural (see Job. xxxii. 19): where the "new bottles" are either, as is probable, equivalent to bottles with new wine, or Elihu, in his inflated discourse represents the spirit which urges him as so mighty, that even new bottles would be burst by it.

The expression of our Lord, which is now shown in its completeness, has a twofold aim: that the new must not be mixed with, or inserted into, the old; and that *rightly disposed people* must be chosen for the freedom of the new which He inculcates. But in the nature of things, the similitude will not absolutely suit in every respect, inasmuch as men and nations in themselves are no other than *old* men and nations; it suits, nevertheless, relatively at least for the relations of the time then present, and for all similar relations; inasmuch as while many are too firmly rooted and fixed in the old, and cannot, like old bottles, receive and retain the new wine and the new spirit, many, on the other hand, are found susceptible, unprejudiced, prepared, and, *as it were*, already corresponding to the new. Men put not new wine into old bottles;—the Lord by this *justifies* at the same time the conduct of *John*, who treated quite rightly his disciples who were not yet ripe for the evangelical freedom and joy, and *His own* conduct, in seeking for Himself new bottles;—or rather He justifies the wisdom of God, which sent to the men of that generation in near connexion and succession, both the severe Elias and the benignant Son of Man. (Ch. xi. 17—19). The Lord, indeed, received His disciples in part from John the Baptist, but not those of them who were pharisaically narrow-minded and rigid, such as now put the question to Him; his accepted new bottles were publicans and sinners, whom He immediately called to Himself. John indeed predicts the new wine, but not many receive it, as is proved by the very fact that there are yet fasting disciples of John, even long after their master had pointed them to the Bridegroom. To such the Lord meekly replies:—Remain ye in the old, and leave to my disciples the new! Thus it is meet, and thus will we for a while be separate.

Finally, wherefore and what means the *breaking* of the old bottles, so that the good old wine is spilled, and the bottles perish, and thus a twofold injury arises from the false conjunction of things that agree not together? The new wine *ferments*, in order that thus it may out of must become true *wine:* Thus the wine *bursts* the skins;—*will*, as it might be foreseen, *burst them*, as we read in St Mark and St Luke. As St Matthew and St Mark condense and break off the Lord's expression, it seems just to hint at this explanatory fundamental idea; but St Luke in vers. 39 gives it plain and significant utterance. Yet how have short-sighted expositors on all sides perverted this undoubtedly genuine and important addition, because they cannot deal rightly with its meaning: and yet how simple and clear, how entirely appropriate to what precedes, when that is rightly understood, is the thought which it expresses! The emphasis lies in the εὐθέως, for the *genuine new*, of which the passage speaks (not an externally new form or mode as such, which people readily enough seize, as they do new garments, but a new and free and living Spirit), does not easily and immediately take possession of people who are accustomed to the Old. Not, by any means, as if the old wine were actually better: but he who has hitherto drunk it (being accustomed, that is, not merely to "old habitudes," but to the life and principle stamped upon them, the *Spirit* of legal exercise and righteousness), feels that to him it *tastes* better; he *says*, the old is more agreeable and pleasant. The Lord in His gracious wisdom says this, partly in blame (for men cannot and should not always tarry in the old, the years as they roll on bring their new growth), partly, also, in gentle apology for them.[1] Thus it must be, it lies in the nature of the case. I know well that your much fasting is to you, with all its severity, preferable to the freedom of my disciples. Length of time makes the old habitual pleasant to us; the yoke, otherwise intolerable, bearable and even easy. Here at the conclusion our Lord is also answering the *first* part of the question: *Why* do *we* with the Pharisees fast? He teaches, finally, that a time will come, when the new, which so few now relish, will better commend itself. When the new wine is old, thou shalt drink it with pleasure, said Sirach anciently, Ecclus. ix. 10. *This* is the meaning! Not merely, as *Schleiermacher* says, that "he would not find fault with them for not liking the new wine,

[1] *Seyler* calls it emphatically a "word of excuse, inexpressibly mild, and almost in '*scherzender*' form," but where the Lord seems to speak *almost* in this style, He is only giving utterance to the deepest earnestness of truth in the most *affectionate* manner. Compare Lu. x. 42.

but holding the old wine, as usual, for better: the *value* of the *new wine* would *come out* in the taste, but this would be the case with them only *by degrees*." It is not our taste merely which is concerned here, but the actual fermentation and clarification of the new life and the new spirit, which, after the manner of new wine, is unready and imperfect within as at the first. The figures proceed with each new turn in the discourse more fully and deeply, into the reality, and its whole process. The *bottles* which *contain* the new wine, but should not, indeed, retain it for themselves, are the constantly chosen bearers and instruments of the new spirit: the *people*, who should drink it, are all others to whom then and thus are communicated the new power, doctrine, and discipline. This distinction must be well seized; typified in the relation of the Apostles and the first disciples, it finds its ever-recurring application to all times. Hast thou, for thy part, received the new wine of grace into a sincere and humble heart, into a mind which lays aside all that is past, as into a new bottle; then take good heed, that thou do not impetuously pour it out before all people to drink, and complain if they relish it not. Thus does the circumspection of our Lord's word fill up its meaning:—Rejoice in thyself, no man shall constrain thee to fast, but cry not out too soon, Rejoice all with me as I rejoice! The Divine spirit in the spirit of man, when it at first approves itself a fermenting new wine, must itself become ripened and mild.[1] But when it is so, there is nothing more lovely, more heart-rejoicing, that goeth down more sweetly (Cant. vii. 9) to every unperverted taste and conscience, than the thoughtful, powerful, affectionate testimony and exhortation of such disciples as have prepared themselves in wisdom and patience for the Bridegroom's will, from their first joy through all succeeding mourning, until His new thing in them is fully ready to be offered to the world. The more fully this testimony of the whole apostolical church since Pentecost has been published to Israel, with so much less sincerity of excuse can they allege of their old wine, that it is better.

[1] A Jewish saying (quoted by *Sepp*) has it: he who seeks instruction from the young and inexperienced, is like one who eats unripe grapes, or drinks new wine out of the winepress: to learn from the old, is to taste ripe grapes, and old wine.

THE ISSUE OF BLOOD.

(Matt. ix. 22; Mar. v. 30—34; Lu. viii. 45, 46—48).

St Matthew records in the most concise manner in three verses, the incident which was interposed on our Lord's way to Jairus. As his recollections rise to him in more and more rich profusion, the Apostle and eye-witness employs in His Gospel a more pregnant brevity of style (that the book may not become too great, Jno. xxi. 25); and suffers himself not to be diverted to the right or left from the prescribed design of His plan. In addition, we must regard as coming to the aid of this as foreseen and provided by God for the *first* Gospel, the Apostle's own individuality, which is less adapted for sharply defining the small, characteristic traits of an incident, and on that account more fitted to arrange and combine events and discourses under great leading aspects: though never, however, contrary to the strictest truth of fact. St Mark and St Luke then fill up many things left in outline by St Matthew; in perfect consistency with their characteristic, that of more searching, reflective, accurate, and most exactly faithful reporters. Yet this filling up must also be regarded as strictly faithful to truth. If any man, for example, would regard the narrative of the Ruler's daughter and the woman with the bloody flux, so self-evidencing in their incomparably artless originality and living freshness, as invented, or either with or without design elaborated and adorned, we must lament his critical failing and account him fundamentally perverted.

But in these narratives the *words* of our Lord are so interwoven with the circumstances occurring, that without understanding these, those cannot be understood: yet must we be on our guard against entering into the history too much. In this view, we must rather reckon upon too much than too little in the reader himself: that so our book also may not grow too large.

Who touched me? or, more properly: Who is it, *who was it*, that touched me? This question the Lord asks in the midst of the press of the crowd: the disciples marvel, and instead of answering they use that liberty to which they had been encouraged by His lowly intercourse with them; and by Peter's ever ready mouth throw out a kind of demur as to His putting such a question at all. According to St Mark, who may here be the more exact, it was, Who touched *my clothes?* or more properly, *Me by my clothes?* A well-meaning but incorrect dogmatic prudently remarks here that the Lord had well known all from the beginning, but that for the sake of men, and because He would not have His wonderful power thus experienced in secret and kept hidden, He procured its disclosure by such question as this: but this springs from a purely human mistake as to the essentially human in the Son of Man, and plainly opposes the most distinct words of the Evangelists. First of all, the indefinite masc. *ὁ ἀψάμενος* does not favour this view: but St Mark further reports that the Lord turned round to find him who had done, or, as he speaks in relation to the known fact, her[1] who had done this thing, yea, that the woman came and *told him all the truth.* Consequently He did not yet fully know her from the beginning, rather nothing more than that which his genuine question expresses, that *some one* had *touched* Him with such longing of faith as had drawn from Him His healing virtue. St Mark selects the words very carefully and with exact propriety: the woman ἔγνω τῷ σώματι, marked or felt *in her body,* that the fountain of her blood was suddenly dried up; but Jesus puts his question ἐπιγνοὺς ἐν ἑαυτῷ τὴν ἐξ αὐτοῦ δύναμιν ἐξελθοῦσαν; as He not merely felt in His body, but at the same time knew in Himself (τῷ πνεύματι αὐτοῦ), what had taken place.

According to St Luke the Lord Himself testifies this by a second word, which we should have been required to supply in St Mark, even independently of this, as the Lord's explanatory answer to His disciples' demur. *Somebody hath touched me,* and, as I think, in a different way from the thronging crowd: hath touched *Me,* and not merely, like them, my clothes: thus does the Lord defend His unintelligently blamed question, and explains its reason by the same word which St Mark has woven into his narration: *for I perceive that virtue hath gone out of me.*

[1] Which expression narrating *post eventum* (τὴν τοῦτο ποιήσασαν) should not be urged (as *e.g.* by Alford) as a proof that Jesus, when He put the question, already knew.

Ἐγώ first and emphatically: if no one else, I at least must well know. *Ἔγνων* in the same proper sense as St Mark has explained it: the bodily feeling with an inward consciousness of the internal and essential import and reality of what was taking place. The *ἐξελθοῦσα* connected with the *δύναμις*, especially with the emphatic *τήν* in St Mark, teaches us that it signifies more than an ordinary *miracle*, as many would sophisticate it. And consequently it remains undeniable after the distinct evidence of this narrative, that that *power to heal* (Lu. v. 17, vi. 19), which was there inherent in Him, and went forth from Him, bears some analogy with that in human nature of which we know some little under the name of magnetism, as exerted through the medium of a special bodily relation: and this is confirmed by further analogies, such as that of the Apostle's handkerchiefs in Ephesus. But then the whole narrative, with the words that pertain to it, is especially recorded in such a manner as to show us the *difference* between the higher and the lower, between the healing and living power of the Godman, and the influence exerted by magnetising physicists and physicians. The immediate discussion of this, however, belongs not to this place. But thus much, the Lord's word which we are expounding testifies, that to the *efficacious influence* going forth from Him which heals the body, there must correspond a bodily *virtue* in Himself, which might be imparted through the hem of His garment: but that this did not occur in a physical way without or against the intervention of His conscious will. And it is just to refute this very error of the woman which would otherwise have been confirmed and propagated, that He speaks and will not keep silence; and that He is constrained in all kindness to abash still more the ashamed woman, by bringing her into prominence. The physical virtue which passes over does not go from Him without His *will:* that will is *always disposed*, stands, as it were, always open and prepared for approaching faith, and *this* is the reason why that which occurred could take place. Further, not without His *knowledge*, as is immediately shown; the touch which derived the virtue from Him, was assuredly unexpected, but He *marks it* immediately, knowing it within Himself, rejoicing over the *faith*, by which he is well pleased to allow Himself even to be thus *touched*. We can only apprehend this spiritual-physical virtue through taking into account this *spiritual relation:* the people generally throng and press Him, without *that relation*, but the timid touch which scarcely laid hold of His garment brings healing to the sick woman, because she has faith to be healed. A striking figure for the preacher, often used to distinguish the crowds from the little few around Jesus![1]

It is this *Faith* which touched His person, that the Lord makes prominent in His last word, discerning what was directly needful in this unexpected occurrence. We find it only in St Matthew, who thus in his brief narrative retains the essential point of the whole, namely, the *contrast* of our Lord's word with the woman's thought as given in ver. 21. That there was a certain admixture of an improper, and in the gentlest sense, *superstitious* notion in this thought, is proved by the circumstance that she thought she might steal away unobserved and unknown with the healing she had secured. There was something in her, as *Grotius* on this occasion profoundly remarks, of that idea of the Philosophers, *Deum agere omnia* φύσει οὐ βουλήσει, and this our Lord could not allow to pass current, lest wide-spreading error should arise from it. *Thy faith*, thy touch in faith hath saved thee (σέσωκέ σε—as she had said, σωθήσομαι and St Matt. adds ἐσώθη), not merely thy touch or My garment![2] It was indeed, with all its lack of perception or acknowledgment, which does not affect the matter,[3] a strong faith which trusted that the hem of His garment could do more to heal her than the instrumentality of all physicians of whom she had for twelve years suffered many things, and was nothing bettered, but rather grew worse. The Lord now as ever *praises* such faith, and compensates her for all the pain and shame which His testimony for

1 *Augustine*: Sic etiam nunc, est corpus ejus, id est, Ecclesia ejus. Tangit eam fides paucorum, *premit* turba multorum.

2 St Matthew does not most assuredly design to report, in contradiction to St Luke, that *now first at this word* the woman was made whole. This is that reading of a modern exegesis which beforehand expected *its* contradiction.

3 *Alford* refers very beautifully to this as being a miracle full of the highest encouragement to all who might be "disposed to think despondingly of the ignorance or superstition of much of the Christian world—that He who accepted this woman for her faith even in error and weakness, may also accept them."

truth had required that He should not spare her, by His gracious θάρσει, θύγατερ (St Matthew retains only the paternally affectionate θύγατερ), which was immediately uttered in anticipation of the word which praised instead of blamed her act. Oh how His love rejoices over such faith, in whatsoever form He finds it: that love which delights to *give* to all, rather than to *receive!* It is his continual manner to ascribe all that His virtue effects to faith, since notwithstanding His δύναμις always ready in Himself, πίστις is yet the *conditio sine quâ non* of its ἐξελθεῖν: comp. Matt. ix. 29, viii. 13; Lu. vii. 50, xvii. 19, xviii. 42. Thus does He speak in every new instance, to encourage others that they also believe, as well as to confirm those who have already believed. St Mark and St Luke add here His usual *Go in peace;* St Mark besides this gives the assurance, so welcome to this poor woman, that the instantaneous cure of this twelve years' disease should retain its permanence:—thou hast believed, go in the peace which this faith brings, which hath healed thee; and *be* for ever *healed of thy* sad and long-suffered *plague!*

JAIRUS' DAUGHTER.

(Matt. ix. 24; Mar. v. 36, 39, 41 [43]; Lu. viii. 50, 52, 54 [55, 56]).

Be not afraid, only believe! once more the same gracious invitation and excitement to faith, and the same contrast between faith and fear, which we have already seen in Matt. viii. 26. All that is to be held as true in the doctrine of "faith *alone*" is represented to us by this μόνον in the region of external things, which the Lord Himself everywhere regards and exhibits as similitudes of things internal. In St Luke we have the promise connected with the πιστέυειν of Jairus for his daughter: καὶ σωθήσεται. This does not indicate that our Lord doubted the correctness of the subsequent intelligence that the daughter was now actually *dead,* as the ordinary language of man terms dead, for the mother especially would not send the sad intelligence prematurely to the father on the way. If Jesus had hoped or certainly knew, as His word afterwards, even before He saw the particulars, might seem to say, that the maid was not dead, He must, to preserve the truth, have contradicted the intelligence at once before the people, and could not have allowed it to pass current, as He nevertheless did. His promise does not fully and openly announce, for so it seemed good to His humility, that He would, because He could, make her live again: but under this veil of generality it contained such an intimation. Fear not—be not disconcerted by even this message of death: let what may take place or have taken place, thou hast summoned me to be thy Helper, and I will assuredly help. *Only believe—tu contra audentior ito.*

That the man had from the beginning been aware of his daughter's death, and had attributed to Jesus the power even to awake the dead, is inconceivable in itself, would be unexampled in the whole evangelical history, and is opposed by the resignation to the event of even Martha and Mary when their brother had actually died. The rapid condensing brevity of St Matthew at the commencement of his narrative might lead the unwary reader to think so, but to prevent such inconsiderate reading we find the contrary expressed both in this and the other Evangelists. St Matthew passes over the intermediate message, which was certainly not unknown to him, and in his brief and comprehensive reference to it *throws back upon the former part of the transaction the impression and feeling of the latter.* This is his manner: his first Gospel delivers its narrative in this unstudied style, because he can presuppose a living tradition of the more minute details of important occurrences, before the subsequent Evangelists had rendered them permanent. But with all this he ever writes the truth: for strictly considered, the ἄρτι ἐτελεύτησεν[1] means no more in the father's mouth than St Mark's ἐσχάτως ἔχει,—she lies now in the article of death, there is the most critical danger, all haste is needful, probably she may be, while I am calling Thee, already dead. Nothing else is obviously meant—and this is decisive—by St Luke's ἀπέθνησκεν, (as ἀποθνήσκειν is elsewhere the beginning of dying, the danger and anguish of death, *e.g.* 2 Cor. vi. 9), from which he himself in ver. 49 distinguishes the τέθνηκεν. Consequently ζήσεται is not

[1] Which is no false supposition of the reporter, as *Schleiermacher* thinks.

directly,—she shall again return to life, but, she shall continue to live, *survive* the immediate peril of death. St Mark quite correctly: *ὅπως σωθῇ, καὶ ζήσεται.*

And now between the hope and fear of struggling faith, the Ruler's mind is agitated by a new thought. He who at first pleaded for the healing of his only daughter suspended between life and death, has now to ask:—if she should be now dead, can the Master's helping power help me then? The people, whose excitement had been increased by the incident on the way, were now intent upon something marvellous which would take place in the Ruler's house: for the circumstance which had at first vibrated in uncertainty between life and death, has now reached its highest interest in consequence of our Lord's word of encouraging promise in reply to the message of death. Common curiosity now rules all, even to the extent of irreverent pressing and thronging. Our Lord submitted to this as to the customary pressure of His great work, yet no longer than to the door of the house. Entering, He beholds the scene which Jewish custom exhibited in bewailing the dead; even there where He has determined in the power of the Father to bestow life. What is more natural than the first cry with which He arrests their lamentation: *give place!* Ye weepers are not wanted yet! Thus we have it in St Matthew: St Luke, on the other hand, expresses it, *weep not;* and St Mark, *why make ye this ado and weep?* The sense in all is the same: it is the indication of absolute assurance that He was bringing help,[1] as well as the deprecation of all that tumult which too commonly mingled itself with lamentation for the dead, as unbefitting the dignity of His own person and of the present solemn occasion. And then He adds—let it be remembered, before He had entered in and seen the child—that word of wonder which all the three Evangelists have retained alike;—for *the maid is not dead, but sleepeth!*

This is so definite and precise that one might at first understand it in the letter, and yet with but few exceptions the whole church has understood it otherwise: rightly indeed, for the whole connexion constrains us to do so. It is well known that it was the caprice of the late *Olshausen* to maintain the

[1] *Bengel:* certus ad miraculum accedit.

literal interpretation, from which many of his friends in vain endeavoured to dissuade him.[1] To what St Matthew and St Mark briefly intimate:—and they laughed him to scorn, St Luke adds decisively, εἰδότες ὅτι ἀπέθανεν, and in the clearest manner records afterwards, καὶ ἐπέστρεψε τὸ πνεῦμα αὐτῆς, just as it is written in 1 Kings xvii. 22. She was thus certainly dead, though the Lord speaks concerning her as concerning Lazarus, (Jno. xi. 11—15). This is His *first* raising from the dead, the *only one* which St Matthew records, which could not have been wanting in his Gospel because of his testimony to the Lord's saying in ch. xi. 5.[2] *Three* awakenings from death the Spirit has caused to be recorded for us, although others may well have taken place; and these indeed in a remarkable and significant progression, which is in itself a corroborative testimony for this first:—the maiden is here dead upon her bed, the young man at Nain was carried forth upon his bier, Lazarus had lain four days in his grave.

But why did the Lord speak thus? His word has a sublime universal meaning as it regards all who are by us termed "the dead" generally, and specifically with a twofold design as it regards His then present hearers. To the tumultuous people without, it is veiled and repulsive, the opposite of that lofty language which would not have suited His lowliness, such as—even if they were dead, I nevertheless can, and will raise her up! But to the desponding, wrestling father it would be no other than a repetition of—*Be not afraid, only believe!* Therefore He rejects the

1 *Hase* indeed in his Leben Jesu calls the maid "the sleeper!" *Braune* also, unhappily, will unconditionally contend that the Lord literally said and meant:—she is *not* dead. Even *Neander*, although "all the circumstances make it probable to him that it was but the condition of a trance," yet concludes that the Lord (who does not know or observe that?) spoke with reference to the *result* of the awakening rather than to death. *Lange*, on the contrary, rightly maintains that the decisive account of St Luke that she was dead, is the only supposition on which the conduct of Jesus can be understood —quite truly! If it must be taken literally, it would be *sleep* merely, and not trance. Even *von Gerlach* acknowledges that St Luke gives it as his view that she was dead—but such a view of the Evangelist *we* hold for undoubted testimony.

2 Which we find in St Luke had been just preceded by the resurrection of the young man at Nain.

word of fear and dismay—she is *dead!* and substitutes another which promises to faith a re-awakening—she *sleepeth!* One whom it is His will to awake immediately as in this instance, sleeps indeed only in a short sleep of death. Even we have no other way of speaking of it than to call it a *re-awakening,* and consequently thereby confirm the right of Him who re-awakens, to speak of it as a sleep. But the Lord does not speak now with reference only to the present occasion. At this first Resurrection which the Father gave Him, there rises to His soul, in one great comprehensive view, the death and resurrection of all the children of men, and He speaks in language of sublime and majestic superiority over the narrow thoughts and limited lamentations of mortal mind. He speaks with the deep meaning of His subsequent word, in which he says concerning the God of the living that all live to Him. (Lu. xx. 38). *Bodily* death is not essentially *death:* we know how the Lord elsewhere speaks of *death* and destruction, and may appropriately call to mind His words concerning the dead to be buried, in Matt. viii. 22. This the poor people understand not now, and they show how unsympathizing their lamentation had in reality been, how untouched their hearts by passing at a bound from weeping to *laughter*, only seizing the manifest contradiction between His assurance and what they knew to be true. But the father, prepared beforehand for faith, may well in a certain sense have felt the meaning of the disguised words, as if the Lord had openly said:—I will raise her up, as one that sleeps, so that she, notwithstanding all, is *not* dead!

The curious and the laughers must all be put out. The three alone, whom the Lord now for the first time makes prominent among the Twelve, with the father and mother who will receive from His grace their daughter again, may be witnesses of the deed which was not to be performed for idle wonder. Not as Elijah and Elisha in old time enforced his prey from death with effort of body and spirit, does the Lord awaken this dead one: He utters the same simple word, in His immediate personal authority, with which He heals the sick; and takes her by the hand (Matt. viii. 15) to wake her up, as one would take a sleeping child. He addresses the dead as already living, so that they must hear the voice of the Son of Man (Jno. v. 25, 28); and utters, with perfect confidence in the Father who hath given Him this power, that incomparably sublime cry, which veils the loftiest dignity in the most tender affection, *Talitha cumi!* St Mark, probably from St Peter's communication, preserves to us this most distinctive utterance of the resurrection-word from the all-holy lips, which recurs once more with the same simplicity—*Young man, I say unto thee, arise!* (Lu. vii. 14): and finally in the last, *Lazarus, come forth!* (Jno. xi. 43). St Mark thus also teaches us, as by the "Ephphatha," ch. vii. 34, that in the ordinary intercourse of life our Lord spoke the language of the country: although this does not decide the question as to the language of the many longer discourses which were uttered before companies composed of learned and unlearned, Jews mixed with Gentiles. But the Evangelist does not translate it in its bare literality, but adds, in order to indicate the emphasis of the invocation and its authority *σὸι λέγω:* whence we learn further, how the translation of our Lord's words in the Spirit of their letter, was intended by the Holy Ghost.

The two other Evangelists report two further expressions; yet only in *indirect* citation, as if with the exquisite feeling that no other and lesser word should follow upon the great ἔγειρε. The command *to give meat* to the awakened one, is not so much a confirming assurance that she now truly lived and was quite restored (although that might be necessary for the astonished people who were unable to realize it at all), as, if we mistake not, an indication of an affectionate care, which, even in the midst of the greatest things forgets not the least, and which would provide for the necessities of the exhausted child on her return to life. This word springs from the same amiable regard to this child which dictated the affectionate *Talitha.* He has given back life and health, and thus imparted help beyond the father's prayer or thought. But at this period He restrains that miracle-working power; it had restored a life physically healthy, of which the surest mark was the ordinary ability to eat and drink; and He now points them to the restored functions and ordinances of nature. He might, indeed, have awakened her as already nourished; but that would have gone, as we feel, beyond that fitness and propriety with which the miraculous energy of Jesus ever adjusted itself to the circle of earthly life.—The second expression is that well-known prohibition with which He interdicts the publication of what had taken place, and thus would prevent, as far as in Him lay, all mere vain-glorious rumour; yet the fame thereof went abroad through all that land:—He has made even the dead to rise! Had this, indeed, not been the fact, He would not only have repeated his former *οὐκ ἀπέθανεν* more distinctly to prevent error, but instead of the mere prohibition to tell *τοῦτο, τὸ γεγονός*, He would have given a full explanation of what *had* been done, and what had *not*.

She who touched in secret was constrained to avow it openly: he who publicly asked his request, is led into secret and exhorted to stillness. Let this be pondered well, that we may understand our Lord's meaning in all His wise and symbolical discourses and deeds.

THE TWO BLIND MEN.

(Matt. ix. 28—30.)

Through all the manifold variety of the *ten* miracles of healing which St Matthew, placing among them the raising of the dead and the stilling of the sea, relates in these two chapters,—as examples of what is generally stated in ver. 35, recurring to ch. iv. 23,—there runs one idea, which our Lord three times distincly announces, and the Evangelist (ch. ix. 2) once more testifies; viz., that *Faith* is the great essential, and that the Lord, in the exhibition of His power, causes it to be done to his petitioners "according to their faith." The word to the two blind men is the same as that to the centurion; it was His chosen and loved expression—how often afterwards uttered by Him! We observe, however, here already in this extract of the history of the first period of our Lord's public life, the point of transition, by which He passes from instantaneous fulfilment of the desire, to the keeping of his petitioners waiting, in order to the trial and exercise of their faith. The foundation of this is, in general, that the Lord cared not so much for the acts themselves, as for the faith, which should afterwards seek and find spiritual help. In this particular case it must be added, that our Lord is fully aware of the increasing enmity of the embittered Pharisees (ver.

34), which keeps pace with the progress of His miracles, and therefore does not instantly respond to the cry of "Son of David" with which these two blind most movingly address Him, as if He would at once hasten to acknowledge such a title. He kept them waiting, till they came to the house. And now the question does not run, *Believe ye*, then, that I am the Son of David? but, *that I am able to do this*, that is, what you signify by your ἐλέησον ἡμᾶς, *open your eyes?* Believe ye this firmly and faithfully, is it in this faith that you have persevered in following and in crying? Oh how his heart is rejoiced by the firm *Yea, Lord*, which they reply! *According to your faith* be it unto you! It is not co-operation that the Lord requires, so much as an acknowledgment and acceptance in accordance with His power. Everywhere beholding in the external its internal significance, our Lord can never too often, or too decisively bear witness for posterity that *this* is what is distinctively necessary.

The prohibition finally—*see that no man know it* (as in ch. viii. 4, at the beginning)—has on this occasion, for the reason above mentioned, a yet deeper emphasis than before. St Matthew designedly says here first ἐνεβριμήσατο αὐτοῖς (as before in Mar. i. 43 in the case of the leper—with another meaning, Mar. xiv. 5; Jno. xi. 33) which certainly indicates human emotion. *Suidas* explains ἐμβριμᾶσθαι by μετὰ ἀπειλῆς ἐντέλλεσθαι, μετ' ἀυστηρότητος ἐπιτιμᾶν. Here there is mixed with the affectionate kindness which can never deny itself to faith, the vibration of that feeling still, which had made the crying in the street (Matt. xii. 19) so displeasing to Him: but this again had its prudent reason in that wise penetration of all relations, which constrained Him thus to throw a guard around His actions. If the Lord had never again thus forbidden and threatened, how would the perpetual concourse of all the sick have overburdened Him, so that neither time nor strength would have been left to Him for preaching the Gospel (Lu. iv. 43), and the contradiction of the crucifiers to the people's hosannas would have broken out before the time.

THE MISERABLE SHEEP AND THE GREAT HARVEST.

(Matt. ix. 36, 38; [Mark vi. 34; Luke x. 2]).

A new scene is now in preparation—the first mission of the chosen heralds of the kingdom; now in the first place to the lost sheep of the house of Israel, but foreshadowing in this beginning the future ambassage to the whole world. St Matthew introduces it by our Lord's discourse concerning the labourers for the great harvest, spoken actually at this time and afterwards repeated by St Luke on the sending forth of the Seventy. But he previously mentions (ver. 36) the Lord's compassion for the people, and gives us in connexion with it what we can scarcely consider his own reflexion, but (as in ch. vii. 29) an indirect citation of the words in which that compassion may have been uttered. The ἰδὼν δὲ τοὺς ὄχλους is immediately dependent on ver. 35, so that Hess seizes it rightly, "wherever He saw a crowd of Israelites" He manifested His pity over and over again, in these or similar words. (Hence in St Mark vi. 34, we have the same on another occasion). See Matt. x. 6 presently after, and again somewhat later xv. 24. Yet may it well be, that just at this time and to be inserted immediately before ver. 37, the Lord uttered these very words.

For the rest, the expression is evidently taken from the prophetic Scripture; for from the prayer of Moses before the Lord in Numb. xxvii. 17 downwards, we find this very natural image (by which in heathen antiquity also, the people are called flocks and kings their shepherds) occurring in proverbial use through the entire Old Testament. As, for instance, in this its more obvious sense the Prophet Michaiah uses it, when prophesying the death of the king (1 Kin. xxii. 17). Then do the Prophets use it with a deeper meaning in reference to the spiritual shepherds; and, condemning and mourning over these shepherds, describe in the same terms the poor neglected people: as in Jer. l. 6; Ezek. xxxiv. 5, 6; Zech. x. 2, 3 But its inmost significance is seen most clearly in that leading text Isa. liii. 6, where wandering sheep are used as a type of the state of sinners generally: not without intimation of their own fault (compare ch. lvi. 11), but with the compassionating reference to their misery predominant, as it is here. The two expressions in St Matthew view the pitiable condition of this shepherdless flock under two aspects: in themselves and as individuals the sheep *faint*, but regarded as a flock that should be united in one, they are *scattered abroad*. The true reading is ἐσκυλμένοι from σκύλλω originally to rend, lacerate, thence to harass, exhaust, and (especially in long journeying) to tire out, as it recurs in a milder sense Mar. v. 35; Luke viii. 49, vii. 6. Here it is stronger—sunk on the road, driven about without pasture; compare Zech. x. 2 יַעֲנוּ, xi. 9—16 נִכְחֶדֶת and נִשְׁבֶּרֶת, Joel i. 18, אֵין מִרְעֶה. On the other hand ἐῤῥιμμένοι is not merely cast away (as if a mere gradation upon the former) but scattered one from the other here and there, wandering sheep, a flock no more: compare נָסְעוּ Zech. x. 2, תָּעִינוּ Isa. liii. 6. וַתְּפוּצֶינָה Ezek. xxxiv. 5, נְפוֹצִים 1 Kings xxii. 17. Without unity and connection, like the then Israel split into sects, their fellowship in the way of God dissolved. One by one overdriven, as a whole scattered abroad!

For they have *no shepherds!* With such compassion does He behold them who Himself is come, their true and rightful shepherd, to revive them again, and bring them back to the fold: thus deeply is He afflicted for the "poor, misled people" whose guilt He merges in their misery, imputing that guilt all the more severely to those who had been instead of their shepherds their deceivers. Oh how His heart yearns to heal and to help! But how? It were a light thing for Him who gave back health to the sick and even life to the dead, to bestow upon His people all needful earthly good, and defend them from all external evil; but all this would have been unavailing, and have rather aggravated than lessened their wretchedness! Quite different is the view which His word discloses to the disciples. The healing of their hurt must be a long process of labour upon their souls, and to be effected again by the instrumentality of man. But the discourse glides into another figure:—the invigoration and gathering together of the poor sheep into the one fold of God, reappears under the notion of a seed-time and harvest. The Lord indeed mentions, definitively, only the *harvest;* hence many, comparing Jno. iv. 35—38, apprehend here an antithesis of the Old and New Testament economies, according to which they are related as seed-time and harvest. In that passage, however, when narrowly investigated, there is no such meaning to be found, for in vers. 37, 38 the Lord places Himself, the only and pre-eminent sower, in opposition to His Apostles who should only labour upon the produce of His previous sowing. Such a notion is especially unsuitable to our context, inasmuch as the allusion of these words is not to any preparation already found, but, on the contrary, to a condition of absolute neglect. We have only, then, to understand the expression according to the analogy of the subsequent parables. Assuredly must the seed of the word of the kingdom be first scattered by the Son of Man and His succeeding sowers: but this entire divine husbandry upon and among the men whom He will prepare and gather to Himself, is here embraced under this one name of harvest, as regarded from its final consummation. This is at once a consolatory and a mournful view, inasmuch as it is thus emphatically suggested, how much *labour* will be needed before so wide and desert a field can be transformed into the *harvest* of God: and yet that waste as it is, it is the Lord's and decreed to be His harvest-field, even as the wandering sheep are still His flock! The labourers are thus regarded not as at once reapers, who would only have to bind up the sheaves (which misunderstanding can only derange the general sense of the allusion); but their office and work embraces generally the preparation of the future harvest from the very beginning.

The harvest is *great* or *plentiful!* The Lord's *immediate* reference is only to the people and land of Israel, whose numerous and crowded towns the apostles, as is intimated ch. x. 23, would not very soon have gone over. He thought of many among the mass of the people who, susceptible of faith, should be called and made meet, even as He afterwards saw beforehand His much people in Corinth, (Acts xviii. 10). *The* labourers—genuine, and worthily so called, are few, however many bear the name! But although the Lord had Israel especially in view, it is nevertheless impossible to admit that the thoughts of His heart in such a discourse did not stretch further, and that there did not mingle with them anticipations of that great harvest of God which should extend over all the earth; and this is our warranty for taking this word of His mouth, which brings before the contemplation of every age the times then extant, as the text, also, of our own world-embracing missions. Is then the labour needed in order to the harvest, in one people, the neglected people of God, so great, how *great* will it be when extended over all the nations of the earth! Who is *the Lord of this harvest?* Jesus, in His meekness, speaks of the Father as such: but we also understood it also of Himself, the Son, to whom already the Forerunner had assigned the thrashing-floor and the wheat as *His*. Even as He Himself then forthwith *sends forth* the labourers, those who were called to be fishers of men.

A special emphasis has been traced in ἐκβάλῃ: that He would send them forth with vehement impulse of His spirit, as zealous labourers; just as according to Mark i. 12, the spirit ἐκβάλλει the Lord into the wilderness. But this word, which we find presently in Matt. x. 1, and often afterwards down to Jno. xii. 32, applied to the casting out of devils, and then in other places of other forcible sending out (as Matt. ix. 25; Luke iv. 29), has yet in all other passages quite lost this accessory meaning.[1] Consult Matt. xii. 35, and more especially Jno. x. 4, concerning the leading out of the sheep. We must regard it here as nearly equivalent to ἀποστέλλειν, ch. x. 5, only that *here* there may be a superadded meaning in the ἐκ, in harmony with the connexion of the whole train of thought, such as—send *out*, from rest and comfort into the heat and toil of labour, for the performance of which none but the *Lord* of the harvest can give commission and power.[2] They labour not, in effect, whom He sends not.

But the weightiest element in our Lord's saying, the solemn key-note, the clear tone of which we would hear ringing at the

[1] Its use in the Sept. for שָׁלַח in the Old Test. is at least doubtful:—*e. g.* it may have, as in Ex. xii. 33, the sense of "release and let go," or that of actual driving out as in Ps. xliv. 3.

[2] Not, however, on that account to emphasize βάλλειν:—to urge, to *drive* out—as recently Father *Zeller* (Beugg. Monatsbl. 1851, Nr. 3) has explained it.

close, is the challenge to the disciples—*Pray ye* the Lord! all the more emphatic, as this very Lord Himself it is who announces that He will be prayed unto, and that He waits for their prayer in order that He may send. By such words of the Scripture is our weak thought ever anew confounded, while it is constrained to submit to the thousand-fold attested, but inscrutably marvellous mystery of the power of human prayer as a condition. That the saving of the lost sheep, the preparation of the great harvest, should be effected by the instrumentality of mortal men, we have before understood: but that the sending of such labourers, again, should be suspended on man's prayer; consequently, that the all-merciful God should permit the salvation of the world, and the gradual furtherance of His kingdom, to be dependent upon that compassion in men which having been by Him first excited, urges them to pray and long for His own compassion;—must ever remain a wonderful and impenetrable mystery. It is so,—Scripture and experience attest it: What remains for us, then, but to comply with His command, and *pray* for ourselves and the whole world around us?

Certainly the disciples would not, nor could they, at that time, understand the Lord as saying—ask of *Me*, that I may raise up for the wretched people true pastors and preachers, who may gather out of them a people for God! He directed their thoughts by δεήθητε, which is obviously an expression of the highest prayer, to the fountain of love on high, to the God of Israel whose will it is not that His poor people should be left in their lost estate, who regards the scattered sheep as still His flock, and the field now waste as yet hereafter to be His harvest-field. Do *ye* not also take compassion upon the people? Pray then the Father, with me, that He send forth labourers! Whence it is necessarily inferred, that whosoever thus prays offers himself, if it is possible, to labour too. So that it is—Will *ye*, my disciples, not lend your aid, when so much is to be done? Thus He reminds them of their calling to the Apostleship, which had been certified to them already before the Sermon on the Mount. And thus He prepares them for the mission which immediately after followed, when He suddenly, and in a way which even this preparation had not led them to expect, declared Himself to be the

Hearer by anticipation of the prayer which He had just prescribed, and in the Father's name the Lord also of the harvest, whose prerogative and whose will it is to send. He now first begins their mission, certainly, according to the common acceptation, as a discipline, preparation, and trial for themselves and their future Apostleship: but that there was blended with this an earnest zeal for the miserable people, yea, that regard for them was the main impulse of this mission, the Lord's own preface to it clearly assures us.

END OF VOL. I.

www.ingramcontent.com/pod-product-compliance
Lightning Source LLC
LaVergne TN
LVHW021150110826
845150LV00005B/1176